The Many Faces of Wisdom

Great Philosophers' Visions of Philosophy

Edited by

PHIL WASHBURN

D0721144

Prentice Hall

Upper Saddle River, New Jersey 07458

Library of Congress Cataloging-in-Publication Data

Washburn, Phil.
    The many faces of wisdom : great philosophers' visions of philosophy /
Phil Washburn.
        p.   cm.
    Includes bibliographical references and index.
    ISBN 0-13-094120-4
    1. Philosophy—Introductions.   I. Title.

BD21.W355 2002
190—dc21   2001059817

VP, Editorial Director: Charlyce Jones Owen
Acquisition Editor: Ross Miller
Assistant Editor: Wendy Yurash
Editorial Assistant: Carla Worner
Senior Managing Editor: Jan Stephan
Production Liaison: Fran Russello
Project Manager: P. M. Gordon Associates, Inc.
Prepress and Manufacturing Buyer: Brian Mackey
Art Director: Jane Conte
Cover Design: Bruce Kenselaar
Director, Image Resource Center: Melinda Lee Reo
Marketing Manager: Chris Ruel

This book was set in 10/12 Sabon by DM Cradle Associates, Inc.
and was printed and bound by RR Donnelley and Sons.
The cover was printed by Phoenix Color Printer.

© 2003 by Pearson Education
Upper Saddle River, New Jersey 07458

Printed in the United States of America
10   9   8   7   6   5   4   3   2   1

ISBN   0-13-094120-4

PEARSON EDUCATION LTD., *London*
PEARSON EDUCATION AUSTRALIA PTY, LIMITED, *Sydney*
PEARSON EDUCATION SINGAPORE, PTE. LTD
PEARSON EDUCATION NORTH ASIA LTD, *Hong Kong*
PEARSON EDUCATION CANADA, LTD., *Toronto*
PEARSON EDUCACIÓN DE MEXICO, S.A. DE C.V.
PEARSON EDUCATION—JAPAN, *Tokyo*
PEARSON EDUCATION MALAYSIA, PTE. LTD
PEARSON EDUCATION, *Upper Saddle River, New Jersey*

*This book is dedicated
to our students.*

Contents

Preface

My colleagues and I had several goals in mind as we wrote this book. We wanted to give people an answer to the question: "What is philosophy?" We wanted to make our book as broad and wide-ranging as possible and avoid a narrow perspective. We wanted it to be interesting and readable. But we also wanted it to be serious and accurate so that teachers could use it as a reliable introduction to the discipline.

Many books that introduce people to philosophy have similar goals, but our book is a little different from the others. All the great philosophers have different ideas about God and human nature and right and wrong, and most introductions to philosophy try to explain those ideas. Some emphasize the ideas themselves; others emphasize the great thinkers and their historical context.

But the philosophers not only disagree about morality and knowledge and the big questions, they also disagree about the nature of philosophy itself. The sixteen philosophers we discuss in this book all have different views about what it means to be a philosopher. And these differences have profound consequences. They result in different priorities, a different focus, and different methods of inquiry. We have emphasized the different answers to this particular question, "What is philosophy?", rather than the other questions. Of course, to explain the philosophers' visions of philosophy, we have to discuss their ideas about God, knowledge, society, and other well-known issues. But we look at those theories through the lens of the philosophers' distinctive conceptions of philosophy itself. In fact, we think that beginning with a philosopher's sense of what it means to be a philosopher makes his or her other ideas easier to understand. This emphasis makes our book different from other introductions.

We wrote the book for anyone who is curious about philosophy or the great philosophers. We didn't assume any prior knowledge of philosophy or history. We tried to avoid technical terms, and if we couldn't avoid them, we explained what they mean. When we talked about people, we explained who they were. But we also kept an old saying in mind: "Never overestimate your audience's knowledge; never underestimate their intelligence." The ideas in the book are challenging; some are profound and subtle. We haven't tried to oversimplify the philosophers' theories, although in a brief space we could not explain them in much detail. This book is a beginning. We hope that these essays lead readers to take up the philosophers' own works, where they can add to their understanding of each point of view. (Each chapter ends with a list of suggested readings. Appendix 1 lists web sites where one can find the great philosophers' own works online.)

We intended this book primarily for introductory philosophy courses in colleges, so we tried to make it informative for that audience. But one doesn't have to be in college to be curious about philosophy. Many high school students wonder about beliefs, values, identity, society, and other philosophical questions. And many people develop an interest in questions about purpose and meaning after they begin their careers or after they retire. We have put together a collection of essays that is enjoyable and stimulating for anyone who begins to question the everyday routine. And we hope it gives people a "map of the territory," so to speak, so that they know where to go to find out more about a point of view that interests them. We agree with John Dewey, the American pragmatist philosopher, who said that the purpose of formal education is to learn how to learn.

The contributors to the book are just as diverse as the sixteen philosophers we discuss. We all have our own styles and interests. But we are also similar in several ways. We are all teachers, and we've been telling students about these philosophers' life projects and visions of philosophy for years. We are all convinced that the ideas in this book are important. Understanding a new way of thinking, a new vision of possibilities, or a challenge to conventional assumptions can change your life. We have all experimented with different methods in our classes over the years to make these philosophers and their ideas come alive for people. We've all reached some agreements on the best ways to teach, and we've incorporated those methods in this book. The contributors have tried to transfer the illustrations, the questions, and the excitement of their classrooms to these chapters. We all chose to be teachers because a good learning experience is a great joy, and we try to convey that in this book.

Most of us teach in the General Studies Program at New York University. Some are affiliated with other institutions. As the editor, I have been impressed by the perseverance and the creativity our contributors have shown in writing and rewriting their chapters. I think it is a reflection of their dedication to the craft of teaching. Seeing this diverse group of people bring their ideas together, and seeing this project grow from a sketchy outline into a fine book, has been a source of tremendous satisfaction. I am very grateful to all my friends in this project who have worked so hard in striving toward a high level of excellence.

The General Studies Program is a delightful place to work. We are energized every day by our contact with bright, optimistic young people. Our job is to talk with them about great books and ideas. What could be better? And we have a good balance between autonomy in our classrooms and interaction with our fellow teachers. Dean Steve Curry, the Director of the program, deserves much of the credit for creating this congenial atmosphere. From the beginning of this project he has given us consistent, practical support and has encouraged us to pursue our interests in whatever direction we chose. Without his help, we could not have written this book.

Introduction

Socrates tells an interesting story about how he became a philosopher. He was living in Athens around 440 BCE, and he says that one of his friends asked the priestess at nearby Delphi who the wisest person in all of Greece was. The priestess spoke on behalf of the god Apollo, and she answered that no one was wiser than Socrates. When Socrates heard this, he says he was baffled, because he was just an ordinary man. He knew very little. He certainly wasn't wise, he thought.

He decided to look for people who were wiser than he so that he could understand the real nature of wisdom and perhaps to show that the gods had made a mistake. So he went to the marketplace and talked to judges, generals, poets, and other authorities in Athens who were thought to be wise. But when he asked them simple questions about their specialty, like "What is justice?" or "What is courage?" or "What is beauty?" he found that they couldn't answer or that their answers made no sense. They really didn't understand justice or courage, even though everyone thought they did. In fact, citizens entrusted them with tremendous responsibility based on their supposed "expert knowledge." Even the authorities thought they themselves were wise. But they weren't, because they couldn't explain what they claimed to know.

After this discouraging experience, Socrates made two decisions. First, he decided that the gods were right after all. He still knew nothing, but at least he *knew* that he knew nothing. The authorities in Athens didn't realize that they knew nothing, or wouldn't admit it, and in this small way Socrates was indeed wiser than they were. The second decision he made was to continue searching for wisdom by asking everyone he met about justice, courage, knowledge, love, and the other basic elements of life. He became a "philosopher." The word literally means "a lover of wisdom." Socrates always insisted that he himself was not really wise (even if he might be a little wiser than some Athenian windbags). But he wanted to become wise (maybe to vindicate the gods). For the rest of his life he pursued wisdom like an ardent lover.

This is not the end of the story, which Socrates tells in his "Apology." But this episode is his explanation of how he became a philosopher.

In some ways the contributors to this book are like Socrates. Of course, we are not so arrogant as to think we can match Socrates' skill. But like Socrates, none of us knows what wisdom or philosophy is. We don't have the answer. And, like Socrates, we decided to ask some people who have a reputation for understanding the nature of philosophy just what it is. In effect, we went to a number of great philosophers and asked, "In your opinion, Plato (Aristotle, Descartes, etc.), what is philosophy?" We have tried to explain how *they* would answer the question.

The remarkable thing is how differently the philosophers see philosophy itself. The philosophers in this book are great thinkers in part because each redefined the nature of the enterprise. Each created a distinctive view of the principal goal and the proper method of philosophy. Consider some of the philosophers we discuss.

- Plato. Plato believed that philosophers can achieve a rare insight into a higher level of reality, a level of absolute justice, perfect truth, and absolute beauty. It takes years of training through dialogue and discussion with expert teachers, and most people won't succeed.
- Aristotle. Aristotle made no distinction between science and philosophy. He thought philosophers should observe the world and find the most general truths they can. He thought his version of the scientific method applied not only to nature, but to morality, politics, and art as well.
- Marcus Aurelius. The Roman emperor said that the purpose of philosophy was to bring us emotional equilibrium and peace of mind. Philosophy helps us gain control over ourselves and our lives by reminding us of basic truths about our place in the cosmos and our true nature.

- Kant. Kant believed that our minds filter and organize our experience unconsciously. If we can discover the way the mind shapes experience in general, then we can understand the universal features of the world. The key to all knowledge, he thought, is understanding the basic structures of the mind.
- Nietzsche. Nietzsche said humanity has outgrown religion and needs a new basis of values and a new sense of purpose. Philosophers take on the Herculean task of finding—or creating—meaning in a meaningless universe.
- Wittgenstein. According to Wittgenstein, we get confused about God and values and other philosophical issues because we don't pay enough attention to the language we use. Philosophers untangle these puzzles by carefully analyzing the way language actually works.

We think that our survey shows the tremendous diversity within the field of philosophy. There is no single answer to the question "What is philosophy?" There are many answers, all interesting, all viable, and all competing for adherents today.

Some people probably think that all the great philosophers agree on the nature of philosophy. Everyone agrees that the word "philosophy" comes from the Greek words for "love" and "wisdom." But what does it mean to love wisdom? When we get past these general, broad definitions and ask what philosophers are trying to do, we find a variety of different answers. In fact, a person who earns a degree in philosophy from one university today may have little in common with a person who earns a degree in philosophy from another university. More than one of the contributors to this book have seen philosophers at national conventions struggle even to communicate, like a Hare Krishna trying to talk to a conservative Republican.

Philosophy is not like the sciences, such as biology. Biologists agree on their proper field of study (living things), their goals (new knowledge, laws, theories), and the way they reach their goals (the scientific method). Philosophers don't. They not only disagree about God and morality and the mind, as one might expect; they also disagree about what it means to do philosophy.

This is not to say that one can't find answers to the question "What is philosophy?" Many philosophers offer an answer. The answers are simply different. In this book we don't offer an answer. Or rather, we offer sixteen different answers. But we don't favor one answer or another. We leave it to the readers to decide which answer or answers are most reasonable.

It may seem as if this book is a history of philosophy, but it isn't. We did not ask these philosophers "What is your theory of the universe?" or "What is the best way of life?" or "What do you think of the mind-body problem?" (although we inevitably discuss those things). Instead, we asked the philosophers what they were doing, what they were trying to accomplish, and how they saw themselves. The great philosophers were passionate about their work; they devoted their lives to philosophy. We wanted to understand that devotion, so we focused on each philosopher's conception of philosophy itself. We wanted to know what their goals were as philosophers or what they thought it meant to be a lover of wisdom. We wanted to understand their "life project," so to speak.

To understand how a philosopher conceives of philosophy, naturally we have to consider his or her ideas about reality, values, knowledge, and perennial issues. But those theories are secondary; we consider them as illustrations of the philosopher's more general conception of philosophy. Actually, we believe that if people grasp a philosopher's ultimate goal and way of thinking, then it will be easier for them to understand the more specific theories and details, because they will know what the philosopher is trying to accomplish.

If the definition of philosophy is so broad and inclusive, one might ask, then why do we limit ourselves to these thinkers? Why not have an essay on Jesus or Buddha or Hinduism? Our answer is that philosophy is not the same thing as religion. Religious leaders rely on faith and authority. Some religions are based on scriptures, or texts the worshippers believe are divinely inspired and uniquely authoritative. Some religions were founded by charismatic leaders who had the power to transform people and perhaps perform miracles. They were so impressive that their followers trust them implicitly and have faith in their goodness. Some religions place more emphasis on ritual, others emphasize compassion, others community, and so on. But the foundation of religion is faith and authority.

Philosophy is different. Philosophers do not ask anyone to accept their ideas on faith. On the contrary, they invite people to find flaws in them if they can and test the ideas themselves. Philosophers do not claim to be authorities. They try to offer reasons and evidence to support their views. Philosophers disagree on just about everything, but perhaps the one thing they can agree on is that questions are good; everything can be questioned. So, while philosophers and religious leaders often discuss similar topics (ultimate reality, right and wrong, belief, the soul), their approaches or attitudes toward those topics are different. Many people claim to be wise, but we can't discuss all of them. We are looking at great philosophers' pursuit of wisdom.

Even among philosophers we have limited ourselves. We have not discussed Epicurus, Spinoza, Hegel, or others. We wouldn't say that we have included all the great philosophers or that our sixteen are the greatest. For one thing, people have different standards for measuring greatness. That is part of what we mean when we say that philosophers conceive of philosophy in different ways. What one philosopher calls profound another calls mediocre. But the main reason we have chosen these sixteen is that each one created or promoted a distinctive, influential conception of philosophy. Each took the subject of philosophy as it existed at one point in history and reimagined it. Each envisioned a new purpose or goal and then devised new methods of reaching that goal.

William James, for example, was educated at Harvard and the best schools in Europe and was thoroughly grounded in the history of philosophy. But instead of continuing the same debates that had gone on for centuries, he proposed that all the complicated thinking and abstract theories of philosophy should ultimately improve someone's life in some tangible way. The test of a philosophy, or of any belief, he said, was its consequences in one's thoughts, feelings, and actions. What real difference will it make if I believe A or if I believe B, he asked? During his career he wrote a number of popular books explaining and applying his view. James' "pragmatic" way of thinking about philosophy was different from Aristotle's way, or Descartes', or any previous philosopher's way. James may not be a great philosopher by someone's standard of greatness, but he is certainly an original philosopher, because he created a new vision of philosophy itself. Whether or not James is great, he is one of the most fascinating philosophers. We have chosen a group of philosophers who all proposed new and attractive ways of thinking philosophically.

We've written this book for people who want to know what philosophy is. And we've emphasized the diversity within the field by describing various philosophers' conceptions of philosophy. Since philosophers have contrasting ideas about what philosophy is, that means they have contrasting ideas about how to teach someone what philosophy is. Some say that the best way to teach someone about philosophy is to let the person engage in philosophy himself or herself. First, explain some of the questions philosophers ask, such as "Are right and wrong relative to societies or are they absolute?" or "Are your choices free or are they determined by some cause?" Then let the learner try to answer one of the questions. Discuss the strengths and weaknesses of the answer and let the person try to find a better answer. Continue the dialogue. In other words, one learns the nature of philosophy by *doing* philosophy, some say. We think this is an excellent way to teach and learn philosophy. In fact, it's Socrates' way (and it's amazing how much of Western philosophy is a continuation of Socrates' practice).

But to begin philosophizing oneself, one needs to know what questions to ask and how to evaluate possible answers. This book can help one get started by showing how different philosophers raise different questions. And we try to explain how they judge proposed answers. Ideally, after getting acquainted with Confucius, Aquinas, and others here, one should go to their original works to better understand their questions and assessments of answers.

Other philosophers think the best way to understand philosophy is to study its history. One should read about the bold ideas and creative solutions to problems that philosophers in different periods have advanced. By analyzing theories and tracing the steps in a philosopher's thinking, one comes to understand not only what philosophy is but what makes some thinking excellent. Studying the history of philosophy is a little like the previous method of trying to answer a question and then talking with a teacher about the answer, except that with history one observes others in a dialogue. Philosophers propose answers, and then later philosophers criticize those answers and offer their own. For example, Plato offered answers to basic questions, and then his student, Aristotle, pointed out weaknesses in Plato's theories and offered different answers. Hume did the same with the earlier Descartes, Kant did the same with Hume, and so on.

We also think this is a wonderful way to learn about philosophy. The philosophers we discuss cover the entire range of history from ancient China and Greece through the Middle Ages and the modern period, up to the end of the twentieth century. But as we said earlier, this book is not a history of philosophy. We do not attempt to give a comprehensive survey, either of influential philosophers or of our own sixteen philosophers' ideas. We focus on different views of the nature of philosophy itself.

The history of philosophy is interesting, but it can give people a mistaken idea. We've had students who got the wrong impression of philosophy in a historical survey course. Teachers and writers often emphasize the common themes and problems in the history of philosophy. For example, near the beginning of Western philosophy, Plato raised questions about morality, knowledge, human nature, and reality, among other things. Aristotle was Plato's pupil and was a great philosopher in his own right. But it is easy to present his ideas simply as responses to Plato. One can say that he asked questions similar to Plato's but formulated different answers. In fact, one can look at many later philosophers in the same way. That is, one can interpret the history of philosophy as a long conversation, or argument, with later philosophers attempting to improve upon their predecessors' theories. John Locke proposed a theory of knowledge, Bishop Berkeley improved upon it, and Hume went further than Berkeley. Kant tackled the same problem and thought he had trumped Hume, and Hegel extended Kant's ideas in new directions.

The danger in this way of organizing the history of philosophy is that it makes students impatient with the earlier theories. If Aristotle's views really are improvements over Plato's views, then why read Plato at all? Why not just read Aristotle? And if later philosophers were asking similar questions, but saw limits in Aristotle's answers and avoided them, then why read Aristotle? This way of presenting philosophy leads some students to decide that the history of the subject is a waste of time and that they should concentrate on contemporary theories.

In this book we try to avoid giving that impression. We believe that each of our philosophers has an intriguing, completely plausible way of doing philosophy. We regard all these writers as contemporaries. We don't believe that the fact that a philosopher lived later in history means that his or her conception of philosophy is better than earlier ones. We have arranged the essays chronologically, but we could just as well have arranged them alphabetically or in some other way. Existentialism—the last philosophy we discuss—may be attractive to some people today, but then

Confucianism may seem more convincing to others, even though it appeared centuries ago. We don't know for sure what philosophy is, so we've gathered a number of answers that, to us, seem about equally plausible. Each essay in the book is independent of the others. One can understand the later essays without having read the earlier ones.

To make our case—that each of these visions of philosophy is viable and useful today—we need to present each one clearly and sympathetically. That is why this book is written by thirteen different people. By focusing on one philosopher (or two, or in the editor's case, three), each of us can try to get inside that philosopher's skin, so to speak, see things as he or she saw them, and explain that philosopher's point of view as clearly as possible. That doesn't mean that each of us accepts one philosopher's conception of philosophy uncritically. In fact, some of the essays are quite critical. But we believe that a group of different authors can give a more vigorous, vivid account of the diversity in philosophy than a single author could. We hope that this book will offer more than an introduction to a number of different views of philosophy. We hope that reading it will be like having thirteen different teachers, who all love their subject, who have different personalities and methods of teaching, but who are all committed to explaining their philosopher in an engaging and helpful way.

In the last part of this introduction, we want to define some key terms in philosophy. They come up in many of the essays, and they will be useful in discussing the philosophers' views. We have been emphasizing the diversity in philosophy, but one can also look for similarities. One similarity among philosophers is the main topics they discuss. Many philosophers think about the best way of life, the nature of reality, what we should believe, human nature, and other issues. They have names for these topics, and the names are useful to know.

One branch of philosophy is called "ethics." Ethics is the study of the best way to live. Some philosophers try to figure out what goals we should have (such as happiness, helping others, or doing our duty). Some ask what makes a particular action right or wrong. Stealing someone's money is wrong, but why is it wrong? Some focus on the qualities or virtues we should have. Like Socrates, they might ask, "What are pride and humility, and are they valuable? Can one have both qualities?"

Another branch of philosophy is called "metaphysics." Metaphysics is the study of the nature of reality. Scientists study the nature of reality, too, but philosophers ask the most general questions about the world. For example, they ask what is real and what isn't. Are souls real? Does God exist? I have two pens here, and they are certainly real, but does the number 2 exist as well, in addition to the two pens? Scientists investigate cause and effect and search for lawful connections, but philosophers ask what it means to say that one thing causes another. And is everything caused, including all our thoughts and actions?

A third part of philosophy is called "epistemology," or sometimes "the theory of knowledge." Philosophers interested in epistemology try to understand when people really know something and when they only think they know it (like Socrates again). Must you see something with your own eyes before you can be confident that you know it? Does seeing something (such as a UFO) guarantee that you know it? Do you know what's in your own mind, or do others who can observe you objectively understand you better than you understand yourself? Philosophers try to figure out the nature of knowledge in general—how we know, what we know, when we know and when we don't, whether in ordinary experience, science, religion, morality, or anywhere.

There are a number of other branches of philosophy. Political philosophy raises questions about society; aesthetics is the study of the arts; the philosophy of science, of religion, and of history all ask the most general questions about the methods and goals of those subjects. But the last branch we want to focus on here a little more fully is logic, and we would like to explain some of the key terms in more detail. We hope that after reading this much of the introduction, you are eager to move on to Confucius, Socrates, and the other philosophers, and you may think that explanations of terms in logic are irrelevant. But the words in this last section are useful in several ways. For example, the terms of logic give us a common language in which to discuss the various philosophers. They also give us the tools or tests with which we can *evaluate* the different conceptions of philosophy. And these words are essential in every area of inquiry, not just philosophy. You will encounter these terms in the sciences, literary criticism, politics, the daily newspaper, and everywhere.

So, what is logic? "Logic" is the study of correct reasoning. "Reasoning" means moving in a certain way from one statement or belief to another. For example, suppose I say, "The ashes in this campfire are still warm. Someone must have been here recently." These simple thoughts are a bit of reasoning. The first statement, about the ashes, leads me to the second, about people. (The second might lead me to a third: "They must be nearby.")

People's thought processes are very interesting. But logic is not the study of people's thinking. That's a job for psychologists. Logic is the study of *correct* reasoning. In other words, logicians ask whether a move from one statement to another is a correct move. They aren't interested in correct grammar or good manners or anything like that. They have a special definition of the word "correct." A move in reasoning is correct if the first statement makes it more likely that the second statement is true. Take the earlier example. Suppose the ashes in the campfire really are warm. Does that fact make it more probable that someone was at the camp recently? It isn't an absolute guarantee; maybe lightning struck the campfire. But even though it isn't a guarantee, it does make it more likely that someone was there recently. (It would be strange to feel the warm ashes but then decide that no one had been there for weeks.)

Here are some more interesting examples of reasoning:

Statement 1: The world exhibits the most amazing order, precision, and harmony, like a vast machine.

Statement 2: Therefore it must have been designed and created by a supremely wise Architect.

Statement 1: Different societies have different moral values and standards.

Statement 2: Therefore, no moral value or standard is superior to any other, and none has universal validity.

Is this reasoning correct, in your opinion? That is, if the first statement is true, does that make it more probable that the second statement is true? We aren't asking about proof but only about evidence. If you were considering the second statement in these examples, and you suddenly learned that the first statement was true, would that affect your opinion about the second? More precisely, *should* it affect your opinion? People can disagree about the correctness of reasoning in some cases.

These two examples are difficult, but other cases are simple and clear. Not all reasoning is correct. Someone might say the following: "The Congressman was unfaithful to his wife. Therefore none of his proposals for improving the economy are worth listening to." If you think about it, you will see that the first statement is actually irrelevant to the second. The Congressman might be dishonest and immoral, and yet his ideas for the economy could still be good ones. Criticizing a person is not the same as criticizing his or her ideas. So anyone who reasons this way would be making a mistake. Here's another example. Someone might say, "My car won't start. Now, I know that if it's out of gas, then it won't start. So it must be out of gas." This reasoning is incorrect, too. Logic is the study of the rules people must follow if they want to reason correctly.

We've described these examples so that we can introduce some terms that many philosophers use. If you make a deliberate move from one statement to another (that is, you decide that one is true because the other is), philosophers call that an "inference." Feeling the ashes and then deciding that someone was here recently is an inference. I "infer" that someone was here recently.

The parts of the reasoning have names as well. Philosophers call the first statement a "premise" and the second a "conclusion." In the reasoning about God, the first statement about order and harmony in the world is the premise, and the statement about the designer is the conclusion. Premises are starting points. They are the things that people believe are established or known. In the campfire example, I say that the ashes are warm because I feel them. I know it. In the God example, I say that the world is ordered and complex because I observe it. On the basis of the premise, I draw a conclusion; I make an inference. The premise makes it more likely that the conclusion is true (more likely than it would be if I didn't know the premise). The premise is my reason for believing the conclusion. But I'm not as sure about the conclusion as I am about the premise. (Sometimes premises turn out to be mistaken, too, in spite of our confidence in them.)

Premises and conclusions are very important because when we look for them in what a person says, that means we are looking for the main point (the conclusion) and the reasons he or she has for believing the main point (the premises). Practicing using these terms will make us more effective communicators and more analytical thinkers.

If we accept a premise that is not true, we simply have a false belief. But if we make a mistake in reasoning, philosophers have a special name for it. It's a "fallacy." In other words, if you think one statement supports another, and makes it more probable, when in fact it doesn't, then you have committed a fallacy. Making an inference from the Congressman's infidelity to the worthlessness of his economic policies is a fallacy. But fallacious reasoning is not always easy to see, and philosophers try to be very sensitive to it.

The last term from logic that we will mention is "argument." It's very common in philosophical discussions. Ordinarily the word "argument" means a dispute or fight, and while philosophers often engage in disputes, that is not how they use the word "argument." In philosophy, an argument is a bit of reasoning that has already occurred in the past. It is a premise and the conclusion it led to. For example, the two statements about the world and God constitute an argument. The two statements about moral values make up another argument. Usually more than one premise will lead to a conclusion. A well-worn example of an argument from textbooks is:

1.   Socrates is a man.
2.   All men are mortal.
3.   Therefore, Socrates is mortal.

Any time a philosopher tries to persuade people to believe something by offering reasons, he or she is presenting an argument.

Often people will apply the word "argument" simply to the premise or premises by themselves. Someone could say "His argument for opposing capital punishment is that all killing is wrong no matter who does it." The statement "all killing is wrong no matter who does it" is, strictly speaking, only a premise, or reason, not a whole argument, which includes the conclusion "capital punishment is wrong." But you will very often hear people call the premise alone an argument.

We hope these terms will be helpful as you begin your exploration of different visions of philosophy.

CHAPTER 1

Confucius

Philosophy as Interdependence

Christopher Rzonca

∿ Preview

Some philosophers look for differences among things and make fine distinctions; others look for similarities and make connections among things. Confucius was among the latter. He was concerned with the best society and the virtuous individual, but above all, with the interdependence of these two ideals. Good people require a harmonious society, but a harmonious society comes about through the efforts of good people. Furthermore, while he wanted to understand the connection between government and personal morality, he also wanted to improve them in a practical way. Indeed, a true philosopher combines theoretical contemplation with reform and honest practice. Morality includes decorum, courtesy, and respect for the family, as well as major principles. And all these complex networks depend on past traditions as much as they depend on present choices. For Confucius, philosophy means harmonizing innumerable interconnections. (The Editor)

∿ Introduction

What is philosophy according to Confucius? There is no philosophy, as we know it, according to Confucius. The Chinese word for philosophy was created only after contact with Western missionaries in the eighteenth century. There was no word because for the Chinese, there was no separation of philosophy (or religion for that matter) from the actual living of one's life. They were profoundly interconnected. Of course, the Chinese had to deal with the same basic human needs and problems as people everywhere. But because of China's unique geographical position and large population throughout history, the Chinese identified needs and envisioned solutions in very different ways than in the Western world.

Therefore it cannot be overemphasized that the great thinkers of China did more than create different answers to the same questions the Greeks and Romans were asking. In fact, the Chinese asked different questions from a very different point of view. Therefore any study of Chinese thinking must take into account the fact that not only is the outcome of what we call philosophy radically different, but so is the starting point.

Take, for example, a typical Western philosophical question—where do humans come from? This question resonates differently in China than it does in the West; it calls up different assumptions or perhaps none at all. As far as the Chinese are concerned, they didn't come from anywhere. They have always been there, in the same place, since humans have been humans. They are connected to the land in ways I'm sure few other people can understand. The notion of coming from somewhere and going somewhere else, or a feeling of restlessness, be it literal or figurative, is not often found in Chinese thought. Chinese tended to stay in the same village for many generations, learning to get along because there was nowhere to go, no escape.

Another Western philosophical question is "Who are you?" The Chinese know where they come from and therefore who they are, because they are not only connected to the province, the county, and the village but are also embedded in clans and families. They know where they belong not only geographically but also socially. They define themselves by their connections to land and family in very profound ways. Therefore the Chinese have never felt the need to establish an identity or uniqueness through myth, for instance, such as the Greeks or the Japanese have done. They are who they are and have always been confident in their sense of place and importance. Therefore philosophical questions take on a different tone in China.

The idea of radical new philosophies or ways of thinking, so prevalent in the West, are also absent from Chinese history. The past and the present are strongly connected, and so certain root traditions remain despite gradual evolutionary reinterpretation. Even the social classes, with their wide disparity in wealth, power, and education, share the same basic world view. No wide philosophical gulf separates the literati and the peasants. The educated display, in a much more sophisticated form, the same fundamental cosmology and thought system as the peasant. Therefore Confucianism, as well as Taoism and Buddhism, have both elite and popular interpretations.

What kinds of questions do Chinese thinkers ask? The primary focus is on social, political, and moral problems and not on the physical world as such. For instance, how do we live together in harmony? How can we live in harmony with nature? How can society help a person live a moral life? So when we look at Confucius, and at most Chinese philosophers, for that matter, we see more political science or sociology than philosophy. But to look at what the most influential Chinese thinker taught is to transcend the narrow categories that stem from Western views.

Kung Fu Zi (Master Kung) (551–479 BCE) is known to the West by his Latinized name, Confucius. We don't know much about his life, and what we do know is suspect because it is written by students and admirers. It seems that he was born into an aristocratic but poor family and may have been orphaned. Nevertheless, he was educated and probably held minor administrative posts in his native state of Lu (in modern Shandong province).

Confucius considered himself a teacher and not a philosopher, but we might call him one if we must, depending on what definition of philosophy we use. If by philosophy we mean love of wisdom, then he was clearly a philosopher. If we mean the study of human morals, character, and behavior, then Confucius was a philosopher because he devoted himself to those things. If, however, we use a more precise, formal, and Western-oriented definition of philosophy as the study of the processes governing thought and conduct, investigating the principles or laws that regulate the universe, including aesthetics, ethics, logic, and metaphysics, then Confucius' ideas were not always so philosophical.

He did not talk about aesthetics, logic, or metaphysics, nor was he concerned with the laws of the universe as we know them, although his followers would expound on some of these subjects. He was concerned with the right way to live, especially in relation to others in society, and this led him to think deeply about government as well, traditional concerns of philosophers everywhere.

Did he preach religion, we might ask? Was he a religious leader? Again, it depends on how we define the term. Confucius did not speak much about a supernatural power regarded as the creator or governor of the universe, but this has never been part of the Chinese conception of the Divine. At the same time, he did create an ethical system, and his students seem to have held him in the kind of esteem due more to a spiritual leader than to a simple teacher. Furthermore, in his teachings, he often spoke about issues like loving one's fellow man, reverence, and filial piety (respect for one's parents and, by extension, for all elders), which we might think more appropriate to religion. Later writers tried to claim he was the son of a god, but that idea never really caught on. However, he was so respected by scholars and the Chinese government that he became a kind of "patron saint" of education, and temples were erected to him throughout China.

Those of us trained in the Western educational system have a great desire to place thought systems into categories and to give them labels such as "philosophy" or "religion," "political science" or "sociology." Such categories are a Western invention and are important in the West. It matters and has mattered enormously throughout Western history whether the subject is called religion or philosophy. For the Chinese, such a distinction seems irrelevant.

In fact, the Chinese impulse is to seek out and elucidate the intricate *connections* in the universe and the human place in it; to promote the harmony of opposites rather than searching, as Western science does, for finer and finer ways to divide the world. Therefore the Chinese feel no need to categorize Confucius precisely. He was a great teacher who brought order, humanity, and virtue to the fore in Chinese society, creating a way of life emulated throughout Asia for thousands of years, and that is quite enough. Seen in this way, the question becomes not "What is philosophy, according to Confucius?" but "What did Confucius teach?" What we call it is not important. What the Chinese called it was the essence of being Chinese, and it shapes their society even today.

∼ Goals and Methods

In his time, Confucius thought he had something important to say to his contemporaries, particularly those in power. He felt he had some solutions that might bring about the end of the wars, instability, upheaval, and general confusion he saw all around him.[1] His greatest hope was to be hired as an advisor to a ruler and to use his ideas, wisdom, and virtue to make a better society in that state. Not wanting the power to rule, but rather the right to advise the powerful, he traveled to various kingdoms offering his services. He was rejected everywhere he went. In retrospect, it seems obvious that he would be. His call to virtue, morality, and righteousness must have seemed irrelevant, naive, and possibly even dangerous to the rulers and political philosophers of the day, most of whom stressed strict obedience to an all-powerful ruler.

The philosophers were all competing for an opportunity to put their ideas into practice. One thing setting Confucius apart was his claim that none of his ideas were his own or even new. Long before Confucius, Chinese thinkers had held the past and tradition in great esteem. History was extremely important because it kept tradition alive so that it could be used to inform, advise, or even chastise leaders in the present. In keeping with this established practice, Confucius claimed to be only transmitting and teaching the wisdom of the past.

His method might be described as teaching through the example of his life, and this may be a reason for his success; he practiced what he preached. He answered the questions put to him by his followers and challenged his students with questions of his own, liberally citing examples from legendary Chinese rulers such as Yao and Shun, as well as figures such as the Duke of Zhou, the virtuous ruler of an historical dynasty, the Zhou.[2]

Yao was a virtuous emperor said to have ruled from 2357 to 2256 BCE, and was so concerned with the welfare of his kingdom that he handed over his empire to Shun because he considered his own son unworthy to rule. Shun ruled from 2255 to 2206 BCE, and was known as a model of filial piety because he managed to live peacefully with a stupid father and a malicious stepmother. The Duke of Zhou was credited with creating a ruling system similar to European feudalism in order to rule effectively the territories he had conquered.

We can say that Confucius was a man who saw his world as flawed and had a plan for its improvement. At the time he taught, he was an outsider who thought his ideas ought to be accepted by the ruler, yet he was not willing to sacrifice his principles simply to gain power for himself. What kind of man was he? What were his teachings? In order to answer such questions, we need to turn to the most reliable source of what he actually said, a book containing conversations with his students called the *Lun Yu* or *Analects*.

Though Confucius is traditionally credited with writing many books, we have no absolute proof that he wrote anything. Probably he helped edit the chronicles of the state of Lu from 722 to 481 BCE called the *Spring and Autumn Annals*, and possibly also the *Book of Songs*, a compilation of ancient folk songs. His teachings were compiled by his disciples in the *Analects*. He had many students, and some did manage to gain administrative posts even in his lifetime.

⟶ Individual and Society

Since Confucius wanted to advise a ruler, his concerns naturally revolved around government. For instance, how does one create a perfect state? Confucius rejected the idea of harsh laws and strict punishments: "Why should it be necessary to employ capital punishment in your government?" (XII:19) He was concerned not with survival of the state or even of the ruler above all;[3] rather, he set his sights on a higher goal—following the Way, becoming a man of *ren*,[4] or humanity. For him this meant being fully human, filial, and virtuous, because by doing so the individual could actively help create a better society. That better society would in turn nurture better people.

Societies and individuals cannot exist without each other, since a virtuous person would not last long in a corrupt society and an evil person would soon be censured in a good society. In effect, one creates the other in a subtle but powerful continuous loop of interaction: man and society are necessarily interconnected.

The responsibility of the individual here is enormous; it is to be a perfect part of a perfect whole. Everyone must contribute in his or her own way, however small, to making society harmonious. Those with education and power were expected to take more responsibility in this regard by providing an example to others.

No person and therefore no state is ever perfect; problems and disputes arise, and evil exists in the world. But the Chinese notion of the source of evil is quite different from the Judeo-Christian belief. For instance, the Chinese have no idea of a God "out there," who created and is controlling the universe, and consequently no idea of sin or guilt. Evil exists in the world not through humanity's original sin or transgression of God's laws, but through human actions that contradict the harmonious workings of the universe. Although Confucius never explicitly stated that human nature was originally good, he did imply it.

Therefore the creation of a harmonious, just, and peaceful society allows people to respond to their natural inner goodness while at the same time maintaining the harmony of the universe. An ideal state is one that nurtures the individual's original goodness and does not promote evil, power, or military might. "The gentleman seeks to enable people to succeed in what is good, but does not help them in what is evil" (XXII:16).

An ideal state needs virtuous persons and an ideal government. Duke Ching of Qi asked Confucius about government. Confucius replied: "Let the prince be prince, the minister be minister, the father father, and the son son" (XII:11). If individuals accept their role and their responsibility, then the society will work. Here he clearly favors the status quo. In fact, he wanted to enforce a strict hierarchy because he believed it led directly to a harmonious society. Not unlike medieval Western views of the feudal system, Confucius believed that the order to be found in a strictly hierarchical society, unequal and seemingly unfair as it might be, was the very basis of harmony. Because the social structure was just and virtuous, all that was needed was for individuals within that society to be taught how to remain virtuous.

Every aspect of society, even humanity itself, was shaped by a profoundly hierarchical social order. Confucius was not talking about universal brotherhood when he said: "All within the four seas are his brothers" (XII:5). He was referring only to the ruling class of China, with its shared values and attitudes, not to foreigners or even to the peasants. Love for others should vary according to how closely related you are to the person, with family ties being the closest, strangers the furthest removed. Perhaps that is why, when asked "What do you think of requiting injury with kindness?" Confucius said, "How then will you requite kindness? Requite injury with justice and kindness with kindness" (XIV:36).

This is not Christianity, nor is it religion. In fact, with regard to religion, Confucius said, "We don't know yet how to serve men; how can we know about serving the spirits; we don't yet know about life; how can we know about death?" (XI:11). Clearly, he is thinking about this world, taking care of humanity and society, free of metaphysical speculation: "Devote yourself to the proper demands of the people, respect the ghosts and spirits but keep them at a distance—this may be called wisdom" (VI:20).

Confucius lived in a time of tremendous superstition and opposed it by coming down firmly on the side of rationality. In so doing, he began the strong rational tradition among the educated class of China. At the same time, he continued to advocate strict adherence to the traditional rituals and respect for the beliefs of others. He took no advice from the supernatural, but spoke of Heaven (Tian) as a silent model of a harmonious human society. "Look at Heaven there. Does it speak? The four seasons run their course and all things are produced. Does Heaven speak?" (XVII:19). Confucius was not looking for omens or portents from Heaven or from the whole pantheon of gods, goddesses, or nature deities associated with the folk traditions of another major philosophy/religion in China, Taoism.[5] For Confucius, Heaven was an abstract principle and not an anthropomorphic god, as earlier people had believed. It was the guardian of the moral order of the universe, and could only be worshipped by the king and later the emperor, also known as the Son of Heaven because of their close relationship. Neither king nor emperor was ever considered divine, however.

Confucius saw laws as unnecessary and even counterproductive, a sign of the breakdown of harmony and order. "Lead the people by laws and regulate them by penalties, and the people will try to keep out of jail, but will have no sense of shame. Lead the people by virtue and restrain them by the rules of decorum, and the people will have a sense of shame, and moreover will become good" (II:3). He seems to be talking here not about virtue or morality as something imposed from without, but rather about recognizing that it is something that must arise from within. Each person must develop his or her own sense of morality and practice it in the world, which in turn benefits society as a whole. This is especially true of members of the ruling class, since their sense of internal morality is almost the only restraint on their actions.

This idea of a government free of the need for harsh punishment and dependent on the virtue of the individual would have great appeal to the leaders of the Enlightenment in eighteenth-century Europe. But it must be remembered that Confucius, unlike many Enlightenment thinkers, strongly favored the status quo and the maintenance of a strict social hierarchy.

～ The Virtuous Gentleman

It ought to be stated clearly at the outset that in the *Analects*, Confucius rarely spoke about women, and when he did his comments were not complimentary. His notions of virtue did not apply to women. Later, ideas of what was expected of women in Chinese society would be drawn partly from his teachings but mostly from deeply ingrained cultural attitudes toward women. Since the hierarchy Confucius advocated was clearly patriarchal, the status of women tended to decline under Confucian rulers. His attitudes, however, were not so different from, say, the ancient Athenians' attitudes.

In spite of this, the values he espoused for the educated class would be appropriated in the modern era by women as well, when opportunities for higher education were opened to them. It is not unusual for contemporary Chinese women to see themselves as Confucian in outlook, minus the misogyny, of course. So his reference to the gentleman has come to mean in modern times the educated, cultivated, moral individual, male or female.

Confucius believed in government by personal virtue; the ruler ought to rule well. "If the ruler himself is upright, all will go well without orders. But if he himself is not upright, even though he gives orders, they will not be obeyed" (XIII:6). With a paternalistic, almost mystical identification between the ruler and his people, Confucius advocated rule by example. "Just so you genuinely desire the good, the people will be good. The virtue of the gentleman may be compared to the wind and that of the commoner to the weeds. The weeds under the force of the wind cannot but bend" (XII:19).

In fact, Confucius stresses the importance of individual morality throughout the *Analects*. In section IV he says: "The gentleman understands what is right; the inferior man understands what is profitable" (IV:16) and "The gentleman cherishes virtue; the inferior man cherishes possessions" (IV:11). He emphasizes the idea of virtue over profit and doing what is right over becoming rich.

Confucius says, "Having only coarse food to eat, plain water to drink, and a bent arm for a pillow, one can still find happiness therein. Riches and honor acquired by unrighteous means are to me as drifting clouds" (VII:15). Here Confucius seems to be expressing his love of simplicity and his ability to be happy with little. As so many people in ancient China and even philosophers of the day were only concerned with reward and punishment, honor or disgrace, Confucius spoke about virtue and the acceptance of poverty. He was concerned about doing the right thing and knew that doing right might not bring reward but often in fact brought disgrace. He knew there was no point in trying to convince his followers to do good in order to be rewarded. One did good for its own sake and accepted the consequences.

In the *Analects* he doesn't seem to be disparaging "riches and honor" in themselves, but rather is concerned about the means or method of attaining wealth and status. Confucius believes people ought to be righteous and moral; he introduced morality and virtue into the discussion of how one should live, much as Socrates did in his time. While the Sophists taught how to win an argument, Socrates spoke about the morality of the argument. Confucius brought morality into the discussions that were important to the Chinese. What was important at that time and for all time in China was how to govern well, how to keep a society with a very large population stable and harmonious.

"When the stables burned down, on returning from court, Confucius asked: 'Was anyone hurt?' He did not ask about the horses" (X:12). This seemingly natural reply expresses in a simple way that he cared more about humans than about material possessions. If we are animal lovers, we might berate him for his callousness, but I think that in the context of his time, when horses were not pets, but signs of wealth and power as well as modes of transportation, his answer reflects his priorities. He is a humanist because he puts human beings before possessions.

The term *junzi*[6] or prince, the gentleman, the ideal man, was a term that had once meant "nobleman," but that Confucius would transform into "noble man," thereby emphasizing that it was an ideal that could be attained by anyone who cultivated the character of the gentleman. Being born good was not enough; education was necessary to remain good and strengthen good character. A disciple asked about the character of the *junzi*, the gentleman, and by extension any member of the ruling class. Confucius answered: "He cultivates himself in reverential attention." The disciple then asked: "Is that all there is to it?" Confucius said: "He cultivates himself so as to be able to bring comfort to other people." "Is that all?" asked the disciple. Confucius said: "He cultivates himself so as to be able to bring comfort to the whole populace. Even [sage-kings] Yao and Shun were dissatisfied with themselves about this" (XIV:45). This seems to show how strongly Confucius felt about the importance of unselfish devotion not only to equals but also to the common people. He wants it to be clear that the moral individual should always be committed to helping others and the society, not to acquiring wealth and power or to saving his or her own soul.

Therefore it may be said that Confucius' method for creating a perfect society rested on making individuals perfect or nearly so. Of course, he meant that the ruling classes should study and learn the wisdom of the past to become "perfect" themselves. This also had another benefit, which was to help them maintain the connection with their heritage. For the lower classes, who could not read, following the example of their betters was enough.

∾ Humanism, Diversity, and Order

Feelings were important for Confucius because people were important, and people were more than just thoughts or even education. Confucius called the feeling between humans *ren*, one Chinese character that needs many words in English to capture his meaning. Goodness, benevolence, love, humanity, human-heartedness, and reciprocity all are found in the character. About this humanity he said, "Is humanity something remote? If I want to be humane, behold, humanity has arrived" (VII:29). If you are a human being, you can be humane because "Is there anyone who exerts himself even for a single day to achieve humanity? I have not seen any who had not the strength to achieve it" (VI:5). It doesn't take effort, but only a willingness to surrender to the feeling. Humanity arises spontaneously, automatically, unless something gets in its way.

I am reminded of an incident that happened to me many years ago when I was first struggling to understand what Confucius meant. Walking quickly down the street in New York City, as one does there, I saw out of the corner of my eye a woman next to me stumble and fall. My first reaction was to stop, reach down, and help her. I did so without thinking; it was a spontaneous, natural, human reaction. This is, I think, what Confucius meant by humanity arriving. It takes no work, no effort; it just happens.

Of course, other things can get in the way of this reaction. Since I was in New York City, my next thought was, is this wise? Is it a scam? Will someone use this opportunity to try to pick my pocket? In Confucian terms, what I had learned in my society did not encourage my humanity, but just the opposite. What I learned about life in the big city interfered with my being fully human. My education threw up obstacles to my humanity. This is a mundane example, but I believe it illustrates what Confucius meant about the powerful effects of both basic human nature and of education. *Ren* ought to be intuitive, but in order for it to function properly, it must be both cultivated by the individual and reinforced by the society.

Ren is truly the heart of Confucius' teaching. It is the meta-virtue, that which binds all his other concepts together as well as providing further motivation for right conduct. It is derived from a character depicting the way two people behave toward one another, the feeling of connection two humans share as humans. This concept is strictly natural, a part of being human, and is not bestowed by the supernatural above. It is the essence of every human and is his or her true identity. At the same time, *ren* acts like the oil that smoothes all human contact and underlies all action, even the practice of rituals, infusing all with a sense of connection with the human family.

Although *ren* is the essence of what it means to be human, it is possible for an individual to be divorced from that essence of oneself. It takes cultivation to stay in touch with it. The method Confucius recommends is called *li*, translated as ritual, ceremony, courtesy, good manners, politeness, the codes of proper social behavior. Confucius regarded such behavior not only as an end in itself, but also as a didactic tool used by ancient sages to educate the people and maintain the social order, which would lead to a moral order among humans that in turn reflected the cosmic order.

Furthermore, the knowledge of *li* gave one status in society. The more rituals and etiquette one knew, the more situations one could handle and the higher one's position. In this way, order itself acquired a cosmic significance while serving a practical purpose. Of course, courtesy in a society as crowded as China's has always made practical sense when combined, as it often was, with a more tolerant attitude toward one's personal life.

Following the social order leads to harmony but is not, as Linda Young says, "an absolute conformity of mind and body to a singular monolithic ideal but rather a harmony of behavior; your thoughts remain your own."[7] In fact, "harmony is always paired with human diversity as a basic condition of social life and the point of harmony is to minimize the conflict that comes along with diversity."[8] The Chinese understand that people may not always think the same or even behave the same, but if they follow at least the minimum requirements of *li*, they maintain harmony and peace as well as strengthen their connection with their neighbors and family. Other behavior can be overlooked if an individual does his or her duty to society. Thus *li* provides a place for tolerance.

The individual is not an isolated entity but exists in relation to others. As Joseph Wu says, "apart from one's relations with other human beings, the concept of individuality has no meaning."[9] Humans make sense only in relation to other humans. "In order to establish oneself, one has to establish others; this is the way of a person of *ren*" (VI:28). In other words, a person needs socialization to become a true individual, to realize the *ren* within; "individuation and socialization are two aspects of the same process."[10] The individual human being needs to have a web of relationships and to take care of them. One must cultivate one's connections as diligently as one cultivates one's sense of individuality. Paradoxically, only by cultivating connections with others can one fully cultivate oneself. Confucius thought the best way was through careful adherence to decorum. "He who does not know *li* cannot establish himself" (XX:3). One cannot attain self-realization without *li*, without proper interaction with others, without taking one's place in society.

∽ The Family and Manners

Since the first place one takes in society is in the family, Confucius stressed *xiao*[11] (filial piety) as a foundation of moral education and the practice of *li*. Respecting one's parents, however, was meant to be done with genuine love, and filial piety reinforced the importance of the Chinese family, imbuing it with a deep moral and ethical importance. Teaching children filial piety then becomes a moral duty that benefits the whole society.

But if the family is of primary importance, what is the role of the state? In one of his most controversial statements, Confucius says this: "The Duke of She observed to Confucius: 'Among us there was an upright man called Kung who was so upright that when his father appropriated a sheep, he bore witness against him.' Confucius said: 'The upright men among us are not like that. A father will screen his son and a son his father—yet uprightness is to be found in that'" (XIII:18). On the one hand, this quote seems to be favoring the man who protects his father from the laws of the state. But it must be said that Confucius is vague here. He is not wholeheartedly condoning either position, but rather, it seems, accepting the fact that any filial son might make some effort to protect his father in such a situation and giving him some credit for his filial piety.

Li for Confucius was not a rigid concept, but changed over time and in different situations, determined by the overarching principle called *yi*,[12] which was associated with rationality or moral reason.[13] *Yi* means doing what is right, no matter what the consequences. But how does a person determine what is right? "What is right or appropriate is constantly being negotiated," Young says; "what is important is the larger picture, the (long-term) result felicitously gained rather than the application of specific rules and principles."[14]

Decorum, manners, and proper behavior toward one's parents and others were of the utmost importance to Confucius. He felt the proper observance of *li* would uphold the social hierarchy and lead to social harmony. Following the rules of conduct made the society strong and the individuals within it happy and content. In later times, these rules would become rigid and even harmful as people forgot the importance of tolerance.

Confucius did not mean "empty ritual," or going though the motions, but rather performing the correct act because it corresponds to one's true feeling. With regard to filial piety, for instance, he says, "Nowadays a filial son is just a man who keeps his parents in food. But even dogs or horses are given food. If there is no feeling of reverence, wherein lies the difference?" (II:27). The conduct or action must have true feeling behind it, love and reverence in this case, or else caring for parents will be no different from tending animals. "Without the proper feeling, why bother to take care of your parents at all?" he almost seems to be saying. Your feelings and actions must be one and the same; therefore *li*, or right conduct, is right because it corresponds to your true feeling. There is no contradiction, no separation between feeling and action; in fact, their interdependence is the essence of spontaneity.

To live up to this ideal in practice took years of moral cultivation. "At seventy, I could follow my heart's desire without transgressing what was right" (II:4). It is only after one has thoroughly absorbed the Way (of humanity) and has become thoroughly moral that one can simply act without thinking, and that action will automatically be correct.

∿ Education

Confucius clearly cherished virtue, and he also cherished learning because he knew education and study were necessary to remain good. He felt one could learn from anyone: "When walking in a party of three, I always have teachers. I can select the good qualities of the one for imitation, the bad ones of the other and correct them in myself" (VII:21). Regarding education, he said two things that had a long-lasting impact on Chinese society: "By nature men are pretty much alike; it is learning and practice that set them apart" (XVII:2) and "In education there are no class distinctions"(XV:38), a quotation that was written over the gates of Chinese schools. All people are alike until they have been acted upon by external things. If people's environment is consistently good, they will learn to practice good so that goodness will become second nature to them; they will, in other words, become good. The opposite is also true; one who is taught to practice evil will become evil. A powerful interaction binds together the individual and his or her environment or society.

The Chinese implemented a form of equal opportunity in education long after the death of Confucius, when nationwide exams were administered to test the learning of scholars from all social classes. Those who passed were rewarded with degrees, exemption from taxes, the respect of the people, special clothing, and jobs in the government. Any male could take these exams, which were based on the Confucian Classics (the important writings of Confucius and his followers),[15] at least on the lowest level, and if you passed, your status was changed overnight. In today's world it would be like graduating from an Ivy League school, winning the lottery, and even getting the girl, because the parents of all the eligible young women were anxious to make a match with a degree holder. This system provided a modicum of social mobility, but it also provided opportunities for abusing the system for material gain.

Eventually a new class emerged, the scholar-officials, who rose in a government bureaucracy made up of those the exam system singled out as the best and the brightest. They advanced not as elected officials in a democracy, but as bureaucratically appointed administrators under a benevolent but all-powerful

Emperor, who was also expected to be moral and rule well. Thus we can say that the two lines about education helped shape basic elements of the Chinese social and political structure, as well as the respect for education still evident in China today.

Confucius himself was a demanding teacher and took on only a particular kind of student. "I won't teach a man who is not anxious to learn, and will not explain to one who is not trying to make things clear to himself. If I hold up one corner of a square and a man cannot come back to me with the other three, I won't bother to go over the point again" (VII:8). He expected that his students truly wanted to learn, that they would be active learners, willing to question, to draw out the teacher, to think and be passionate about ideas and the truth. "Those who know the truth are not up to those who love it; those who love the truth are not up to those who delight in it" (VI:18).

Confucius was as practical about learning as he was about everything in life: "Shall I teach you what knowledge is? When you know a thing, say that you know it; when you do not know a thing, admit that you do not know it. That is knowledge" (II:17). But knowledge is always more than just the accumulation of facts; rather, it implies wisdom, making the right decisions, and behaving properly in society. Confucius believed that men were born basically good but needed to work at staying good, a job he called "personal cultivation." It "begins with poetry, is made firm by rules of decorum (or *li*) and is perfected by music" (VIII:8). Personal cultivation or "growing virtue" are agricultural metaphors that must have been easily understandable to a country of farmers. Throughout history, eighty percent of the Chinese population have always lived in the countryside. Confucius' idea of education we might call "liberal arts" because he believed in training men to make wise decisions rather than to acquire specific jobs. His proposal is remarkably similar to the thoughts of Renaissance humanists in Europe.

Confucius did not take credit for these ideas about humanity and society and government. He said he was only following the example of great sage-kings and heroes of China's past. "I am a transmitter and not a creator. I believe in and have a passion for the ancients" (VII:21). He felt he was merely transmitting the wisdom of the past, reminding people of what the great rulers and thinkers of the past did. He never claimed that any of what he said was new or revolutionary; instead, he borrowed the legitimacy of the ancients.

But I think Confucius may be too modest here. He did more than merely transmit. He *chose* what he wanted to tell his generation. He edited the past for the purposes of the present and for his own purposes. He lived in a society in need of reform, and rather than look for totally new answers, he looked to the past and chose the examples that suited his needs. In this he was creative; this editing or selection was a creative act. Confucius was a reformer and wanted to change his society, not into something new, but rather creatively toward his version of the past. In doing so, he insisted on a living connection between the past and the present. That connection is in fact his greatest legacy.

He might be called a conservative reformer because he emphasized the virtue of the past in an attempt to improve the present. The times in which he lived were dominated by war and what might be called Machiavellian politics. Although he did not succeed in changing the government of his time, his ideas were modified and adapted during the Han Dynasty (206 BCE–221 CE). They became a cornerstone of Chinese life and even spread to other parts of East Asia.

Many Chinese scholars of the 1920s and 1930s chose to see him as a reformer to legitimize their own calls for reform that became necessary for national survival at that time. Of course, in looking to the past to solve the problems of the present, they were behaving in a very Chinese and Confucian way.

ᕯ After Confucius

After Confucius, the second most important Confucian thinker was Mencius (371–289 BCE). He has been called the Second Sage who consciously promoted Confucian ideas that later would be known as Confucianism. His most famous book, probably also written by his disciples, is known as the *Book of Mencius*. In it, Mencius flatly states that human nature is innately good, but that education and moral cultivation are necessary for an individual to remain good.

Mencius also emphasized the sense of duty that marked the true ruler and said that his first duty was to rule well, even stating that the governor exists for the sake of the governed. If the ruler abuses his power he is no longer a true ruler, and the people are absolved of their obligation to obey him. In Chinese political and spiritual thought, the idea of Heaven showing its approval or disapproval of the actions of the ruler was known as the Mandate of Heaven. If the ruler rules well, he maintains the right to rule, that is, the approval of Heaven. If, however, he abuses his power or is simply incompetent, Heaven will show its disapproval through such disasters as floods, earthquakes, famines, or rebellions. This shows the strong connection between the ruler and Heaven, his subjects, the land, and nature itself. Although Mencius valued the common people, he insisted on a strict hierarchy and the legitimacy of a ruling class, but one with a strong sense of responsibility.

Other interpreters of Confucius took his ideas in quite different directions. Xunzi (c. 300–c. 215 BCE) was a high official who contradicted Mencius by stating that human nature is innately evil. He felt that the natural inclination of the person is toward selfish desires and that it is only through "artificial" means—education, the guidance of rulers and teachers—that one could become good by learning to discipline those desires. He can still be called a

Confucian, however, because of his belief that anyone can become a sage through education, although his idea of education was more of a necessary, external, molding process than personal cultivation.

Confucian scholars have returned again and again to these writings for inspiration and help in solving the problems of their day while reaffirming their connection to their great tradition. Some of these scholars called for a rigid, literal interpretation of the texts, but others, like Confucius himself, used some creativity in their reinterpretation of the past. In doing so, Chinese thinkers made their great tradition live on, revitalizing Chinese philosophy and statecraft generation after generation.

Confucian thinking had many long-term effects on Chinese society. We have seen how it stressed the importance of education and brought about the examination system designed to select intelligent, moral individuals to run the government. Those officials were given wide latitude under a system we might call "the rule of men," as opposed to "the rule of law." People regarded the laws as merely normative guides for the official, who was expected to use his own judgment to make wise decisions by interpreting the laws in light of individual cases.

The importance of the rule of men can be best understood by examining its opposite in the West (the rule of law), where laws are more clearly and rigidly defined. Officials need only to follow the letter of the law to be correct; little room is left for discretion. More importantly, no individual is above the law.

Confucius also amplified the importance of the Chinese family, making it the moral core of a moral cosmos. Ritual and etiquette defined human relations and created a harmonious, hierarchical, morally ordered society, which in turn ensured human harmony with the universe.

Today, many countries of East Asia claim that they owe part of their economic success to Confucian values. Governments of widely different forms have appropriated Confucian thinking to legitimize their rule, perhaps because no other philosophy so clearly speaks to the human need for stability and harmony. It is perhaps ironic that Confucius' ideas grew out of his position as an outsider and a reformer. But Chinese rulers came to recognize the usefulness of his teachings in maintaining harmony and social order, which in turn helped maintain their power. The very variety of uses to which Confucius' thought has been put testifies to its fundamental value to the Chinese people.

∾ Conclusion

Confucius' philosophy includes many important concepts. Yet, I think, the one thing that could be said to unite all of these ideas is also powerfully Chinese: all of these concepts are interconnected and make sense only as a whole.

All of Confucius' ideas reflect the spirit of interconnectedness so important in Chinese thinking before and since. Humans are connected to nature, the cosmos, and each other. Their individual lives and the society they create must nurture those connections and not contradict them. The past and the present are connected through the maintenance of tradition. Harmony in the family comes about through respecting the proper connections as demanded by filial piety. The Confucian Classics sought to teach not only these individual concepts, but also the wisdom of seeing the subtle and profound interconnectedness of all these ideas.

All things in the universe, for Confucius and for all Chinese, must be seen as dependent on each other in ways not readily apparent from the Western viewpoint. It is impossible to talk about humanity apart from society or apart from nature. One cannot really understand the present without knowledge of the past. We all know this, of course, but in the West the trend has been to analyze, to separate and divide the world into components, like slicing up a melon. In our desire to understand this whole mass of knowledge we call the universe, we logically cut it into pieces.

The Chinese view can be seen as more holistic. There is analysis going on, of course, but the dividing lines are not only different, they are less sharp, mitigated by a powerful sense of the interconnectedness and continuity of life, nature, and tradition.

Perhaps this has something to do with the need to feel a part of something, a basic human need to belong to a family, a society, nature. The family is important to Confucius as it is to all Chinese, and a close, interconnected family is the model for Confucian philosophy and the Chinese world view. The closeness and interdependence of the family can be used by all Chinese, and by all humans for that matter, to understand and relate to the world as a whole.

Confucius fits into the context of Chinese thinking that existed long before him. He not only transmitted the past to the present, but also amplified trends and ideas that were already there. He clarified and codified to some extent the very essence of what it means to be Chinese. That may be why his philosophy is so difficult to separate from the life of the Chinese people, why Chinese sometimes don't even know when they are acting Confucian, and why the communist government could never completely eliminate his influence.

The Confucian outlook is a truly fundamental sense of belonging to something, culture as family, if you will. It is different from Western attitudes. The closest parallel in the West might be the sense of shared European roots in ancient Greece and Rome. But for modern Europeans, the thread has been broken and we tend to focus more on the ways we are different than on the ways we are connected.

China has not undergone divisive religious and philosophical splits such as the Reformation, the Scientific Revolution, or the Enlightenment. This is not to say that there have not been philosophical or religious divisions or even persecution, for that matter, but they took place upon a ground of an essential interconnectedness that continues to manifest itself. China was able to absorb

Buddhism, for instance, which both profoundly changed China and was itself changed by its integration with Confucianism and the Chinese world view. What the Chinese people will do with Western culture remains to be seen, but whatever happens, Confucius will be there to guide them.

∼ NOTES

All quotations from the Confucian *Analects* are taken from *Sources of Chinese Tradition,* vol. I, eds. Wm. Theodore deBary et al. (New York: Columbia University Press, 1960), 15–33.

1. Confucius lived during the Spring and Autumn Period (771–484 BCE), a time of great political and social disruption as several independent states fought violently for hegemony. It was also a time of intellectual growth that saw the rise of many different political philosophies.

2. Also known as Chou (1122–225 BCE).

3. Unlike another important group of philosophers known as the Legalists, who ruled by strict rewards and punishments and, like Machiavelli, put the needs of the state above all else.

4. Also spelled *jen.*

5. Taoism as a philosophy is said to have begun with Lao Tzu, who, according to legend, wrote a short mystical book called the *Tao Teh Ching (Dao De Jing)* or *The Classic of the Way and Its Power.* This philosophy is based on the "Tao" (Dao), literally meaning "Way" but metaphorically both the natural and cosmic order that a wise man could determine and strive to harmonize himself with. The same idea also led to a popular or religious tradition that espoused the search for immortality and Chinese alchemy as well as temples, rituals, and "saints"—people said to have achieve actual immortality.

6. Also spelled *chün-tzu.*

7. Linda W.L. Young, *Crosstalk and Culture in Sino-American Communication* (Cambridge: Cambridge University Press, 1994), 8.

8. Ibid.

9. Joseph S. Wu, "Confucius," in *Great Thinkers of the Eastern World,* ed. Ian P. McGreal (New York: HarperCollins, 1995), 5.

10. Ibid.

11. Also spelled *hsiao.*

12. Also spelled *i.*

13. Wu, 5.

14. Young, 111.

15. Confucian Classics are the *Yijing (I Ching),* a book of divination with commentary; the *Book of Documents* or *Book of History,* a collection of speeches dealing with ancient history and ethical principles; the *Book of*

Songs or *Odes*, 305 love songs, folk ballads, and hymns of praise to Zhou rulers; the *Book of Rituals* or *Book of Rites* containing philosophical essays, idealized descriptions of administration, and instructions on proper behavior; and the *Spring and Autumn Annals*, a chronological record. To these Five Classics were added the Four Books: *Book of Mencius, Analects, The Great Learning,* and *The Doctrine of the Mean.* This was due to the advice of the great Neo-Confucian scholar Zhuxi during the Sung Dynasty (960–1279 CE). These nine works formed the basis for the questions on the state examinations until 1905. *The Great Learning,* attributed to Zengzi (c. 505 BCE) but actually written between the third and second centuries BCE, was meant to be learning for adults or higher education. It was seen as a complete system of education and social organization and is the only book that clearly and concisely presents the Confucian ethic. It provides a step-by-step method for self-cultivation. *The Doctrine of the Mean* is attributed to Zi Si, but the actual author is unknown, and it was probably also written between third and second centuries BCE as a metaphysical justification for Confucian philosophy. Because of its religious and metaphysical elements, displaying Buddhist and Taoist influences, this book is seen as a bridge between Confucianism, Buddhism, and Taoism. It says that goodness comes from Heaven and that human beings and Heaven are an inseparable oneness.

∿ SUGGESTED READINGS

Allinson, R.E. *Understanding the Chinese Mind: The Philosophical Roots.* New York: Oxford University Press, 1989.

Creel, H.G. *Confucius: The Man and the Myth.* New York: John Day, 1949.

Fung, Y-L. *A Short History of Chinese Philosophy.* New York: Free Press, 1966 (1948).

Hall, D.L., and R.T. Ames. *Thinking Through Confucius.* Albany: State University of New York Press, 1987.

Kupperman, J.J. *Classic Asian Philosophy: A Guide to the Essential Texts.* New York: Oxford University Press, 2001.

CHAPTER 2

The Presocratics and Socrates

Philosophy as Rational Inquiry

Phil Washburn

~ Preview

When did philosophy begin? Every civilization has some kind of speculation about the origin of the world, human nature, and the good life, so there is no single answer to that question. But if we restrict ourselves to Western philosophy, the answer is clear. Western philosophy began around 600 BCE in ancient Greece. The crucial step was looking for rational answers instead of mythological answers. Rational thinking differs from mythological thinking in several ways: the Greeks looked for physical explanations rather than anthropomorphic stories about gods; they looked for natural, lawful processes rather than magic and miracles; they separated their emotions of fear and awe from their understanding; and they adopted a critical attitude toward their explanations. The Greeks also developed this new rational thinking in several directions. The most important development was the application of rational thinking to human life. Socrates tried to get his fellow Athenians to think rationally about their own beliefs and values. (The Editor)

✑ Introduction

In his play *Oedipus the King,* the Greek dramatist Sophocles described how Oedipus became the king of Thebes. Thebes was plagued by the terrible Sphinx, a cruel monster with the head of a woman, the body of a lion, and the tail of a serpent. She prowled the roads around the city and confronted travelers with a riddle. If they couldn't answer it, she tore them to pieces. The riddle was this: what creature walks on four legs, and on two legs, and on three legs? When Oedipus came to Thebes, the Sphinx sprang out and hurled her question at him, but Oedipus figured out the answer. He said that human beings crawl on hands and knees as infants, walk on two legs as adults, and use a cane as a third leg in their old age. The Sphinx was so enraged by Oedipus' cleverness that she threw herself from a cliff to her death, and the Thebans made Oedipus their king.

The ancient Greeks passed down stories about legendary heroes such as Oedipus because the heroes embodied traits the Greeks admired (and sometimes made mistakes the Greeks wanted to avoid). Oedipus' outstanding traits were his insatiable curiosity and intellectual confidence. He never stopped asking questions, and he knew he could find answers. The Greeks felt the same way. They were explorers, not only of seas and mountains, but even more of ideas, riddles, questions, and possibilities. They asked questions about everything because they were sure they could find the causes, see how things worked, and penetrate the secrets.

The Greeks' remarkable curiosity and confidence stand out clearly when we compare their way of thinking with their neighbors' ways. The Egyptians and Mesopotamians explained the world with myths, but the Greeks invented a new way of thinking, which they called "philosophy." We will examine the differences between myths and philosophy in the first part of this chapter. Philosophy is not a single, simple method or outlook, and in the second part of the chapter we will see how the earliest Greek philosophers diverged and developed along different paths. Perhaps the Greeks' most audacious venture was to turn their keen curiosity inward, and apply their new method of inquiry to human nature and the mind itself. Socrates is the best example of this humanistic philosophy, and we will look briefly at his teaching in the third part of the chapter.

◠ Myth and Philosophy

Around 3000 BCE, near the Tigris and Euphrates rivers in Mesopotamia and along the Nile in Egypt, people created what historians call "civilization." That means they mastered irrigation to grow more food, began living in large cities, learned to make metal tools, built large structures, and invented the art of writing. They also tried to understand the powerful, unpredictable world of storms, floods, crops, and diseases. Of course, men and women had been wondering about the world around them for centuries, but we know more about the Mesopotamians' and Egyptians' ideas because they wrote down their poems, songs, and beliefs.

The people of the ancient Near East tried to understand things through stories, or myths. A myth is a story about supernatural beings and often describes the beginnings of something. For example, the Egyptians believed that before the earth was formed the universe was a watery mass: dark, formless, and inert. Out of this mass the god Atum created himself. Once he existed, he spat out a son and daughter: Shu, the air, and Tefnut, moisture. Shu and Tefnut then produced their own children: Geb, the earth, and Nut, the sky goddess. Shu (air) lifted up Nut (sky) on his back and separated her from Geb (earth). In some versions of the myth, Atum was a hillock emerging from the dark waters; in other versions he was identified with the sun, Re, rising above the hill.

For ancient peoples, the sky, the air, the earth, the sun, and all parts of the world were living beings, with desires, emotions, and often tremendous power. When they looked at the sun, they not only saw a bright light, but they also realized their dependency, they felt their gratitude, and they tried to communicate with it. As Frankfort and coauthors say, for them an object was not an "it" but a "Thou."

> "Thou" is not contemplated with intellectual detachment; it is experienced as life confronting life, involving every faculty of man in a reciprocal relationship. Thoughts no less than acts and feelings, are subordinated to this experience. . . . The whole man confronts a living "Thou" in nature; and the whole man—emotional and imaginative as well as intellectual—gives expression to the experience.[1]

Living beings have personal histories, or life stories, so the natural way to understand the parts of the world was to learn their stories. Myths were their stories.

The basis of mythological thinking was the unquestioned conviction that the world was a grand society of living beings, some friendly, some malicious. Everything that happened—from a birth to an illness to a broken pot—was the result of some invisible spirit's action. According to H.W.F. Saggs, the ordinary man in ancient Mesopotamia

> saw himself surrounded by forces which to him were gods and devils. There was a raging demon who manifested himself in the sand-storm sweeping in from the desert, and the man who opposed this demon was likely to be smitten with a painful sinusitis. Fire was a god. The river was a god.[2]

The surviving Mesopotamian documents are filled with incantations and rules for neutralizing the innumerable demons haunting households and workplaces. The Mesopotamians believed that every part of their lives was controlled by the gods. The gods might be influenced by prayers, pleas, or sacrifices, but ultimately their actions had to be accepted.

To us in the twentieth century the stories of the gods may sound charming or quaint. But the ancient people's attitudes were different. Their myths expressed their deepest understanding of the world and life. The Egyptians told their children the story of Osiris, for example, with reverence and solemnity. The great king Osiris gave the Egyptians the arts of civilization, but he was treacherously killed by his jealous brother Set. Set cut up Osiris' body and spread it all over Egypt. But Osiris' loving wife, Isis, carefully gathered all the pieces together. She then conceived a son, Horus, who grew up and killed his evil uncle. Osiris partially recovered and became the benevolent ruler of the underworld, welcoming people when they died.

The Egyptians meditated upon the myth and understood it on different levels. Osiris was associated with grain and crops and represented the creative, ever-renewed power of life. His story not only explained springtime's rebirth (when Isis revived him) and everyone's life after death, but it also provided models for behavior as well. Isis was a model of loyalty and devotion, Horus a model of courage and a son's duty to his father, and Set reminded the Egyptians of evil in the world. They felt a profound reverence for their gods and their myths. The stories were passed from generation to generation for centuries, outliving governments and empires. Frankfort et al. say that they were told

> not with the playfulness of fantasy, but with a compelling authority. Myth, then, is to be taken seriously, because it reveals a significant, if unverifiable, truth—we might say a metaphysical truth. . . . It is concrete, though it claims to be inassailable in its validity. It claims recognition by the faithful; it does not pretend to justification before the critical.[3]

To ancient peoples, their myths were not amusements, or hypotheses, but were unshakable truths that gave order and meaning to all aspects of their lives.

The ancient Greeks had their own myths similar to the Egyptians' and Mesopotamians' stories. Homer's great epics, *The Iliad* and *The Odyssey,* are full of gods and goddesses and stories of their adventures, which explain various aspects of nature. For example, the earliest Greeks believed thunder occurred when Zeus threw his lightning bolts. Hesiod, a later poet, tried to bring order to the conflicting stories, and he did it in a typically mythological way: he wrote a genealogy, or family tree, for the gods, explaining who gave birth to whom.

But around 600 BCE, among a few people in the port city of Miletus on the coast of Asia Minor, a remarkable change in thinking occurred. Wallace Matson calls it "the most stupendous intellectual revolution in recorded history,"[4] and Crane Brinton says, "Western intellectual history in great measure begins with the Greeks, for they were the first to use the mind in a striking and novel way."[5] To understand the revolution, we must try to see how the Milesians' ways of thinking were different from the Egyptians' and Mesopotamians'. The first of the Milesians was Thales, who taught Anaximander, whose student was Anaximenes.

Thales said, "All is water." We do not have his explanation of this idea. We know what he taught from later writers who commented on it. Apparently he meant that everything we see—earth, plants, animals, clouds, sun, and moon—is made of water in different forms. Perhaps he was impressed by the fact that water can be solid (ice), liquid, and gas (steam). He wondered what the world was made of, and he decided it must be water.

His pupil, Anaximander, proposed a different theory. Anaximander said the ultimate basis of everything must be a different kind of element, not water or earth or fire, but "the boundless," or "indeterminate." He probably reasoned that water cannot turn into its opposite—fire—so both must be composed of some more basic stuff that we don't see, that is, the indeterminate material.

Finally, Anaximander's student, Anaximenes, asked how the indeterminate material could sometimes become water and sometimes fire and sometimes earth. He offered a more logical explanation. He said everything was made of air, and the principle of transformation was condensation and expansion. We can see air condense to fog, which further condenses to water. If water condenses further, he suggested, it becomes earth. If air is heated it expands, and if it expands enough it becomes fire, he said. Anaximenes wanted to explain not only what the world was made of, but also the process by which that basic material could change into the various things we see.

These simple ideas seem as fanciful as the Egyptians' stories, and maybe even cruder. But they are fundamentally different from earlier myths in five ways. First, Thales and his students did not assume that everything was alive or a spirit or a Thou. They offered explanations based on physical substances such as water. Water in the ocean is not a god; it doesn't have unpredictable moods or desires. It just freezes or expands. These are mechanical processes everyone can observe.

The Egyptians observed the ocean, too, but they did not carefully separate what they could see and understand from what they felt. And that is a second difference from the Milesians. The Egyptians responded emotionally to what they saw, and that made them see the ocean or the sun as a living being. Thales observed the world, but he tried to think about it in an intellectual way without allowing his personal feelings of hope, awe, disgust, or anger to shape his understanding of its true nature. He tried to compartmentalize his experience and separate thinking from wishing or feeling.

The third difference is between stories and explanations. Since water and air are not gods but physical substances, they do not have personal histories or stories. Thales wanted to understand the world and the origins of things, as the Egyptians did. And some writers have noted that Thales' idea is similar to the ancient people's myths about the beginning of the world as a watery chaos. But Thales and the other Milesians had a completely different concept of "origin." Thales said everything was made of water. Water was the origin of things in the sense that things could be broken down into water. Thales did not wonder about the beginning of the world in the sense of events in a far-distant past. Instead, he asked about the foundation (or origin) of each thing in the present. He believed in an underlying unity behind the diverse appearances. And he explained the world by suggesting that all the parts could be constructed out of one basic substance.

The Greeks' drive for a single, unifying principle of things is similar to other people's belief in a single God, but the differences are far more important. Not only was the Greeks' principle impersonal, not an object of fear or hope and not the subject of a story, but it was different from the gods in other ways. The fourth difference was in the activities or changes in the world associated with the principle. The Milesians described natural processes to explain the world, whereas myths described the decisions and actions of supernatural beings. Thales probably referred to water's transformation into ice and steam, which was a familiar process most people could see and even control. Anaximenes referred to condensation and expansion to explain the nature of things. But myths referred to magical transformations that no one can understand, such as Isis' reconstruction of Osiris. And they were about supernatural beings who can "spit out" children, lift up the sky on their backs, and do other miraculous things. This difference indicates different basic outlooks on the world. The Milesians confidently assumed that the physical world was orderly and lawful. Things operated in predictable ways, according to natural laws that we can discover. But to the people of the ancient Near East, the world was unpredictable, capricious, and arbitrary, like a crowd of spoiled aristocrats.

Finally, one of the most important differences between the Milesians and their ancient predecessors was in their attitudes toward their ideas. To the Egyptians, their myths were profound truths about sacred things, possessing tremendous authority. They learned the myths at an early age and chanted them at solemn rituals. The myths were expounded by priests, who dedicated their whole lives to preserving and teaching the stories, and who possessed the almost magical ability to read and write. The Milesians' attitudes were completely different. Anaximander criticized Thales' theory about water and proposed a better theory. Anaximenes, in turn, pointed to flaws in Anaximander's theory and tried to figure out a way to correct them. The Milesians' attitudes toward their explanations were not reverent at all. On the contrary, they were critical. Thales was not regarded as a powerful authority, but rather as a fellow investigator. His ideas were not sacred truths, but were hypotheses that should be judged by their conformity to observed facts and by their internal coherence or reasonableness.

These new thinkers wanted to explain things in terms of abstract, impersonal concepts rather than stories about powerful beings. They were critical and analytical rather than worshipful. They tested and questioned ideas because they believed the ideas could be improved. And their criteria for improvement were careful observation and logical consistency. They wanted explanations based on familiar, understandable processes, not miracles. They wanted theories that satisfied the mind and intellect, not personal hopes and emotions.

Some have called the new method "objective thinking" to contrast it with the subjective imagination of myth makers. Some say it was "rational inquiry" rather than religious speculation. The Greeks themselves called it "philosophy." They combined the word for love *(philo)* with the word for knowledge or wisdom *(sophia)*. It was the love of knowledge. The new way of thinking was different from mythological thinking, but it could not have been absolutely new. The men and women of the ancient Near East could certainly think rationally and objectively. They did so when they designed large irrigation systems, built pyramids, and charted the movements of the planets and constellations. But the Greeks began applying objective inquiry more widely, to all the questions of life—questions about the ultimate nature of reality, the organization of society, good and evil, human nature, and the nature of thought itself. The Greeks saw no limits to human understanding and accepted no restraints on their curiosity. They were not satisfied with the wishful, unverifiable myths.

Why did philosophy begin in Greece, in coastal cities of Asia Minor like Miletus? Some historians have suggested that the coastal cities were crossroads of trade where people from all over the Mediterranean and the Near East came together and exchanged ideas as well as goods. Furthermore, Miletus and other cities were close to the ancient centers of civilization in Egypt and Mesopotamia, and the Greeks may have learned from priests and scholars there. But this cannot be the whole explanation. For one thing, merchants and sailors do not normally carry abstract theories and difficult methods of thinking with them. Another problem is that the Greeks could not have imported philosophy from Egypt or Mesopotamia because it didn't exist in the older societies. The Greeks' way of thinking was different from mythological thinking.

The cosmopolitan character of the port cities and contacts with the East may have created a feeling of openness, of possibilities, and perhaps conflicts in beliefs. But probably a more important factor was the structure of Greek society itself. The Greeks lived in small city-states, which were independent, self-reliant communities of ten thousand to thirty thousand inhabitants. A few, like Athens, were much larger, but most were small. Before 1000 BCE the city-states were ruled by kings, but later the kings were replaced by councils of nobles. By 600 BCE, many city-states had replaced the councils with assemblies of citizens, where all the citizens could meet, debate policies, and vote on what actions the city should take. The Greeks called this type of government "democracy," or "rule by the people" (from *demos*, the people). Not all the city-states developed democratic governments, and Greek democracy was not exactly like modern democracy. Women were not regarded as citizens, so they had no political rights, nor were foreigners, no matter how long they lived in the city-state, nor were slaves. Nevertheless, the beginning of democracy in ancient Greece is as important for understanding Western society as the beginning of philosophy. And the two may be related.

In the assembly of a democratic city-state any citizen could stand up and propose a course of action for the whole state. The other citizens listened and debated the pros and cons of the idea. They might point out undesirable consequences, false assumptions, or internal contradictions. They might modify the proposal, accepting some parts and rejecting others. But they all had to think carefully. They had to be critical and constructive. They had to determine the facts as accurately as possible and put them together meaningfully. They had to listen carefully to many points of view and try to find a common ground, because their society depended on the quality of their understanding and their decisions. In Egypt, by contrast, the Pharaoh was believed to be literally a god, and he guided the society with the help of other gods. Only a few advisors were allowed into his holy presence. Most subjects could not imagine even speaking to the Pharaoh, much less criticizing his political policies. Therefore it is likely that as Greek society evolved toward democracy, the Greeks developed their independent thinking, their critical attitudes, and their wide-ranging intellectual boldness. When they applied these methods to understanding the world and human experience, they invented philosophy.

∾ Later Presocratics

The new way of thinking opened up virtually unlimited possibilities. In fact, people have been exploring and developing different aspects of rational inquiry ever since Thales and his students first applied it to questions about the world. Two aspects of rational inquiry stand out: careful, objective observation and creative, critical analysis of what is observed. The Milesians combined both aspects. They observed the different states of water, the process of expansion and condensation, and the different types of things around them.

They also reflected on what they saw. They put specific facts together under more general concepts and found universal processes that could explain many particular changes. They criticized some ideas as inadequate and tried to put the facts together into logically consistent theories.

Since the Milesians combined observation with rational analysis, they were both scientists and philosophers. Scientists do both, and philosophers do both. The difference is a matter of emphasis. Scientists place more emphasis on careful observation, experiment, and measurement, but they must also interpret and synthesize their observations. Philosophers begin with common experiences or observations, such as the fact that we all die, that we make choices, that we believe some things are morally wrong, and so on. But they place more emphasis on analyzing and unifying the diverse experiences, and finding some meaningful pattern among them, than on making new, more precise observations. But philosophy cannot dispense with observation and experience, and science cannot dispense with reflection and criticism.

The Greeks of the sixth and fifth centuries, after Thales, were fascinated by the new way of understanding. Some leaned more toward careful observation, and others were more interested in pure reasoning. Hippocrates, for example, described a number of illnesses very precisely. He observed the course of a disease from its onset to recovery or death. He did not speculate on unseen factors, but tried to build up a collection of careful observations of treatments and results that would be helpful to later doctors. On the other hand, a number of Greeks developed the science of geometry. By simply thinking hard about figures, they discovered a large number of theorems describing the necessary relationships among lines, angles, and areas of space. Around 300 BCE Euclid organized all the discoveries, showing the logical connections among the axioms as the foundation and numerous consequences built up from them.

Other thinkers continued the tradition of the Milesians and tried to understand the nature of the world. In general, the Greeks were more interested in speculating and reasoning about things than in observing and experimenting with things, so they produced some of the greatest philosophers and mathematicians of all time, but they did not develop science as we know it. Among the philosophers, some placed more emphasis on reasoning and others placed more emphasis on observation. An example of the latter was Heraclitus, who lived in Asia Minor around 500 BCE. Heraclitus said that if we observe the world we do not see unity, but complexity, differences, and change. He taught that the foundation of things was not water or any substance, but change and conflict. He loved paradoxes and said that the only constant is change. "Everything flows," he said. "You cannot step into the same river twice," because the second time the water is different. Furthermore, the parts of the world are in constant conflict. "The way up and the way down are the same." Sea water is foul unless you are a fish. Pain is bad unless you need a wound cauterized. Day wouldn't exist without night, or spring without winter, or hot without cold. Heraclitus summed up his paradoxical view in the expression "Opposites are the same." The apparent conflicts are actually harmonious and necessary.

At the other extreme, emphasizing reasoning, was Parmenides. Parmenides was born in a Greek colony in southern Italy around 515 BCE. Like many Greeks, he was fascinated by the process of rational thinking itself. For example, he thought about contradictions, such as "a fish is not a fish." Anaximander had criticized Thales for saying that water can become fire, its opposite. Such contradictions are impossible and any adequate explanation must be internally consistent, many Greeks thought.

Parmenides taught that "what is, is, and what is not, is not." To him, the statement "what is not, is not" meant that nothing, emptiness, or the void, does not exist. Emptiness is "what is not," and the statement says it does not exist. Today we believe that the so-called empty space inside a basketball is occupied by molecules of air. But we also believe that between the molecules there is nothing. And in outer space between the stars there is a vacuum, or emptiness. But Parmenides would say that we have contradicted ourselves. "There is nothing" means "there is what is not" or "what is not, is." We are saying that nothing exists, or that which is not exists. But then we are contradicting ourselves and speaking nonsense, according to Parmenides. If we take reason and logical consistency seriously, as Parmenides did, we must conclude that emptiness does not exist.

Parmenides was so impressed by the power of pure reason that he accepted the logical implications of his discovery. If emptiness does not exist, then the world is one solid mass. There are no spaces separating things. Everything is part of one contiguous whole. Of course, the world doesn't appear to be a single, solid mass. When we look around us, we seem to see individual objects separated by empty space. But we know, in our minds, that empty space ("nothing") cannot exist. So our eyes must be playing tricks on us. Since our eyes and ears are often unreliable, and truths like "what is, is and what is not, is not" are perfectly reliable—how could they be false?—we should believe what is logical and rational, even if it is different from what we seem to see with our eyes. Parmenides had an almost absolute confidence in the powers of the mind.

Another philosopher who emphasized reason over observation was Pythagoras, who moved from Asia Minor to southern Italy around 530 BCE. Pythagoras and his followers discovered a number of mathematical relationships among things, such as the relations among strings on a lyre that produce different musical notes. His name is also associated with the Pythagorean theorem, which describes the mathematical relations among the sides of a right triangle. Pythagoras investigated many such relationships and proposed that the basic foundation of the world was not a substance at all but number. The world is made of numbers. Apparently he meant that the constantly changing colors and smells and shapes that we see are merely superficial appearances, and the unchanging mathematical relationships beneath these appearances are the ultimate reality. (This idea is not very different from a modern physicist's world view.) Pythagoras also reintroduced a religious element into philosophy. He believed that we have immortal souls that are reborn in new bodies when our present bodies die. We should try to purify our souls through the study of mathematics and the harmonies of the world.

Later thinkers learned about the whirling flux of Heraclitus, and the unchanging One of Parmenides, and tried to find a middle way. To accept Heraclitus' kaleidoscope of contradictory sensations as the only reality was to give up on rational understanding. But to accept Parmenides' logical reasoning was to retreat from the real world into a linguistic castle in the air. One philosopher who tried to reconcile observation and reason was Empedocles, who lived in Sicily in the middle of the fifth century. Empedocles wanted to explain how one thing, like wood, might become another thing, like fire. He wanted to accept the visible changes in the world but also find an underlying factor that remained constant. He taught that the world is made of four elements—earth, air, fire, and water—but these combine in different proportions to produce the different objects we see. For example, a person is made of all four elements. A tree is also made of all four elements but in different proportions. The four elements do not change; they are eternal. But they combine and recombine in different ways to produce the changing world we see. Wood that burns simply separates into its components: fire, air (smoke), and earth (ash). Empedocles also said that two forces rule the world: love and strife. In other words, the elements are sometimes drawn together and sometimes break apart.

Democritus of Abdera refined Empedocles' approach and produced a theory that is remarkably modern. Democritus said that the world is made of atoms. The word "atom" simply means indivisible. So his idea was that if you break down anything into its smallest parts, and cannot separate them any further, you have atoms. Democritus taught that everything is made of such tiny particles, which are too small to see. There are many types of such particles, not just four. Some are smooth, some rough, some have hooks on them that make them difficult to separate. Atoms themselves are neither created nor destroyed but combine in different ways to make up all the objects we see. Democritus' theory is similar to the atomic theory of elements and matter, but he did not make experiments on different elements, as a chemist does to see how they combine and react. Democritus simply thought about how we can believe that one thing changes into another and believe in an underlying constant factor at the same time.

The dance of observation and reflection has continued to the present day, with observation taking the lead in some eras and reflection calling the tune in others. But by 450 BCE the Greeks' insatiable curiosity led philosophy into a whole new adventure. Many Greeks were becoming dissatisfied with the new way of thinking for two reasons. First, the "natural philosophers" had criticized their predecessors' ideas, proposed their own theories about the world, and then seen their ideas undermined in turn. For ordinary educated Greeks, it was difficult to know whom to believe. In the hands of some philosophers, like Parmenides, the new method seemed to be more of an intellectual game than a way of finding the truth. Second, the Greeks wanted to understand people, society, choices, and human relationships, as well as the natural world. But natural philosophers had little to say about human nature. In the fifth century BCE, a new generation of thinkers responded to these dissatisfactions and opened up a whole new world to explore.

~ Sophists and Socrates

The second half of the fifth century was a thrilling period of Greek history. As Dickens said of France during the Revolution, "it was the best of times; it was the worst of times." It was the Golden Age of Athens, when dramatists like Sophocles and Euripides presented their tragedies on the stage, when the Athenians built the magnificent Parthenon overlooking the city, and when the citizens crafted their own laws in democratic assemblies. However, as Athens' wealth and power grew, their neighbor to the south, Sparta, became increasingly alarmed. Sparta was a militaristic agricultural society, suspicious of outsiders, and afraid of change. The mutual mistrust between the two city-states grew until war broke out in 431. It dragged on, with intermittent pauses, until 404, when Athens was defeated.

In philosophy, too, it was a complex period of decline and progress. In the middle of the century, the Greeks actually began to lose their intellectual nerve. Some doubted their ability to solve any problem they could find. But by the end of the century, their robust confidence was restored by Socrates.

Frustration with the natural philosophers was one factor in the appearance of an influential group of people called "sophists." The word "sophist" comes from the same root term as "philosophy," namely, "sophia," meaning knowledge or wisdom. Sophists possessed a kind of knowledge, which they were willing to teach to pupils who could afford their fees. But they did not claim to explain the nature of reality. In fact, after listening to the philosophers criticize each other, many sophists had decided that such knowledge was impossible. Instead, they turned to the practical investigation of human affairs. They offered to teach a young man how to be successful and how to get ahead in society. In most Greek city-states, that meant learning to speak well and persuade an audience. Most city-states were ruled by an assembly of all citizens or a council of nobles, and in either case the ability to explain a proposal, defend it, and criticize opponents was the key to success. The art of persuasive speaking and writing is called "rhetoric," and the sophists taught rhetoric. The young men of Athens, Corinth, and other cities paid large fees for the instruction.

In a way, the sophists were like the philosophers. They were fascinated by the process of rational inquiry. The sophists analyzed the method of reasoning and argument itself. They classified the different kinds of reasons one could give for a position, the best order in which to give them, when to appeal to emotion, the types of audiences one faced, and so on. But in another way, they were different from the philosophers. They did not believe rational inquiry could lead to the truth. The most it could do was persuade an audience to believe something. And then a more skillful speaker could come along and persuade the same audience to change its mind and believe something else. We never find the truth. All we find are stronger and weaker arguments that persuade us to hold the beliefs we hold. Thus most sophists were skeptics. They did not believe we can find genuine, objective knowledge about the world or anything else.

They extended their skepticism to morality and politics as well. In the past, most Greeks had believe that moral rules were part of nature. They were just as objective as physical laws such as the law of gravity. But the sophists decided that moral rules were man-made and changeable. Most sophists had traveled widely, and in general the Greeks were becoming more aware of other societies and differences in beliefs, customs, and values. Herodotus, the "father of history," had visited Egypt, Persia, Scythia, and other places and had written a popular book about them around 440 BCE. The differences in moral convictions suggested that there was no truth about morality; there were only artificial standards set up by different societies.

One of the most famous sophists was Protagoras, who said, "Man is the measure of all things." He meant that the "truth" about the world is whatever human beings decide it is. When a stream feels cold to me but warm to you, we are both right. It is cold to me and it is warm to you, and that is all we can say. There is no deeper objective truth about the matter. The same applies to moral rules. It is right to hang petty thieves in Scythia and it is wrong to hang petty thieves in Athens. Different groups of people make up different rules.

The sophists were important in the development of philosophy for several reasons. They shifted attention from questions about the natural world to questions about human beings, society, and morality. Henceforth, people applied the method of rational inquiry to questions about human life as well as the natural world. The sophists also forced thinking people to examine their assumptions about knowledge. They were skeptics; they said it was impossible to understand and to know anything. They challenged the new way of thinking and claimed it was impotent. Ever since, philosophers have tried to figure out what we can know and understand and what we can't. Finally, the sophists' rejection of knowledge and objective morality inspired other Greek thinkers to defend these key ideas. One of the most important defenders was Socrates.

Socrates (469–399 BCE) was a famous fixture in Athens during the Golden Age. Almost everyone in Athens knew him, and he could usually be found in the central marketplace talking with friends or anyone else. Many called him a sophist because he said he knew nothing, he paid close attention to reasoning and persuasion, and he loved to talk about morality. But he himself rejected the label. He said he never asked for payment because he had nothing to teach. He compared himself to a midwife—a nurse who helps a woman give birth. Socrates said that by talking to people, he helped them give birth to their own ideas and beliefs.

On the outside, Socrates' life was relatively uneventful until the end. He fought with distinction in the Peloponnesian War, but for the most part he lived in a world of ideas and questions. But after Athens was defeated, some leaders of the democratic party accused Socrates of sympathizing with the Spartan enemy and the aristocrats. They could not publicly charge him with treason, however, because to keep domestic peace the government banned political trials. So the democrats charged Socrates with corrupting the youth of Athens and with rejecting the official state religion. Those were capital crimes. Socrates was tried and convicted in 399. He could have easily engineered an escape with the help of his wealthy friends, but he chose to obey the law, drink the hemlock, and die. He was seventy years old.

Socrates wrote nothing, but his most famous student, Plato, attended the trial and wrote an account of Socrates' defense of his life before the jury. It is called "The Apology," from the Latin word meaning defense. In other dialogues, Plato reconstructed conversations Socrates had earlier in life with various people. Altogether the dialogues give us a vivid picture of the man, his way of life, and his convictions. In all these accounts Socrates illustrated the Greeks' tremendous intellectual confidence. While he modestly admitted that he knew nothing, he insisted that people search for answers to the most difficult questions: questions about themselves. He applied the new methods of rational inquiry not to nature or to politics, but to ordinary everyday living. In one of the most famous passages in "The Apology," Socrates says

> to let no day pass without discussing goodness and all the other subjects about which you hear me talking and examining both myself and others is really the very best thing that a man can do . . . life without this sort of examination is not worth living.[6]

Socrates believed that "the examined life" is the best sort of life. What did he mean by "the examined life"?

In the dialogues we see Socrates talking with people, usually asking them questions. He often began with questions about their activities of the moment, but soon he came to questions about their general beliefs. For example, at court he encountered a young man named Euthyphro who was charging his father with the murder of a servant. A servant had died, and Euthyphro believed his father was responsible. A surprised Socrates asked about the case and discovered that Euthyphro believed he had a religious duty to charge his father. He would be impious if he didn't. Then Socrates asked Euthyphro what religious duty and piety were. Was Euthyphro really sure that being religious and devout required him to take his father to court?

In other words, Socrates typically asked people what they really believed and valued. People could come up with some sort of answers, but then Socrates moved on to the more difficult question of *why* they believed what they did. Most people didn't have good reasons. They fell into a tradition and simply accepted the beliefs and values of their parents. Or they conformed to the crowd because "that's what everyone believes." Or they followed someone who claimed to be an authority, such as a scientist. Or they believed whatever made them feel good at the moment. Euthyphro was sure that prosecuting his father was the religious thing to do, but he couldn't explain why he believed that. Socrates gently made people face difficult questions: What do I know? How should I live? Why do I believe something? Why do I value something? A big part of living an examined life was asking these questions.

Socrates said he himself did not have answers to these questions, but he was eager to find answers, and he was confident that we can understand ourselves. He thought the best way to find answers was to think about what we mean by certain key concepts, rather than by exploring the world or finding new facts. For example, in Euthyphro's case, Socrates learned the specific facts, but the issue was not whether Euthyphro's father was innocent or guilty. The issue was what Euthyphro should do. To explain why prosecuting his father was the pious thing to do, Euthyphro had to explain what piety was. He had to define "piety." Today someone might say that "people should have equal opportunities." Why? "Because it's fair." But what do you mean by "fair"? Or someone might say, "I want to make a lot of money." Why? "Because it will make me happy." But what do you mean by "happy"? The answers to these basic questions do not depend on acquiring more information. They depend on understanding what we mean in the first place.

In most of the dialogues, Socrates asked people questions such as "What is piety?" or "What is courage?" or "What is right conduct?" His friends offered tentative explanations, but by asking more questions, Socrates showed that the explanations wouldn't work. The definitions were either too broad, and included things that shouldn't be included, or too narrow, and left out important cases. People thought they understood what it meant to be courageous or religious, but they discovered that they really didn't. For Socrates, examining one's life was trying to understand the meaning of important concepts such as friendship, justice, and happiness.

Socrates thought that the best way to understand one's own beliefs and values was to talk about them with other people. Trying to explain our beliefs to others forces us to think clearly. And our friends bring up common experiences and facts that we overlook. They correct our narcissistic bias. In the dialogues, the friends get closer and closer to understanding a key concept, with the help of Socrates' questions, even if they never reach a precise, final answer.

Or at least they uncover the confusion in their ideas, and that is a kind of progress as well. Socrates himself never offered answers. It's possible that he held back because he wanted young people to discover their own answers for themselves. Or perhaps he believed that the interdependent web of concepts and beliefs that make up our world view is so intricate and subtle that we can never map it completely. We can make progress in philosophy, as we do in science, but in neither pursuit do we ever find ultimate, final answers. The human world of beliefs and values is just as vast and intricate as the natural world, and there is always more to learn. Socrates believed that each of us is so complex and so deep that we can always improve our self-knowledge. Examining one's beliefs and values with the help of others is a never-ending task.

The examined life, then, is the reflective life or the thoughtful life or the conscious life. It is thinking about what we believe and why we believe it. It is trying to understand the central concepts of happiness, fairness, respect, excellence, knowledge, and many others that make up our world view. It is investigating these ideas in an honest, open way with others.

Socrates' conception of philosophy is different from Thales', but there are continuities as well. In the two hundred years between them, the Greeks explored many of the basic themes and directions opened up by their new method of rational inquiry. They tried to understand nature as a whole, some tried to see what pure observation would reveal, and others tried to follow the severe demands of logic alone. The sophists turned to the world of politics and persuasion, and Socrates applied rational inquiry to ordinary life, morality, and self-knowledge.

It is an interesting challenge to try to pick out some continuities among all these creative minds, which link them together as philosophers. One possible commonality is the search for rational explanations, as opposed to stories, intuitions, or revelations. A rational explanation is one that is based on objective evidence or reasons that anyone in principle can understand. However, the sophists denied that people ever have rational explanations for anything. They questioned the whole idea of rationality. And the debate over the nature of philosophy has raged on ever since. Should we say that the sophists were not philosophers at all? Or that the continuity linking all these inquirers—including the sophists—is their willingness to question absolutely everything? Or should we expand our understanding of what it means to be rational? I can imagine the voice of Socrates saying, "My friend, you say you are searching for answers you can understand. But what is an answer, after all, and what do you really mean by 'understand'?"

〜 NOTES

1. Henri Frankfort, H.A. Frankfort, John A. Wilson, Thorkild Jacobson, William A. Irwin, *The Intellectual Adventure of Ancient Man* (Chicago: University of Chicago Press, 1946), 6.

2. H.W.F. Saggs, *The Greatness That Was Babylon: A Survey of the Ancient Civilization of the Tigris-Euphrates Valley* (London: Sidgwick and Jackson, 1962), 302.

3. Frankfort et al., 7.

4. Wallace I. Matson, *A History of Philosophy* (New York: American Book Company, 1968), 1.

5. Crane Brinton, *Ideas and Men: The Story of Western Thought* (New York: Prentice-Hall, 1950), 32.

6. Plato, *The Last Days of Socrates,* trans. Hugh Tredennick (New York: Penguin, 1954), 70–71.

∿ CHRONOLOGY

c. 750 BCE	Homer composes epic poems, *The Iliad* and *The Odyssey,* based on oral traditions
c. 600	Thales teaches in Ionia
540–480	Heraclitus
515–456	Parmenides
500–428	Anaxagoras
493–433	Empedocles
460–370	Democritus
490–480	Persian wars, Greece defeats Persia, Athens gains wealth, power, prestige
480–430	Golden Age of Athens
447	Parthenon begun
440	Protagoras and sophists teach in Athens
431	Peloponnesian War between Athens and Sparta begins
430	Sophocles' *Oedipus Rex*
404	Athens surrenders to Sparta, reign of the Thirty Tyrants
399	trial and execution of Socrates

∿ SUGGESTED READINGS

The Presocratics

Cornford, F.M. *From Religion to Philosophy: A Study in the Origins of Western Speculation.* Princeton: Princeton University Press, 1991 (1912).

Kirk, G.S., and J.E. Raven. *The Presocratic Philosophers: A Critical History with a Selection of Texts.* Cambridge: Cambridge University Press, 1962.

Long, A.A., ed. *The Cambridge Companion to Early Greek Philosophy.* Cambridge: Cambridge University Press, 1999.

Taylor, C.C.W., ed. *Routledge History of Philosophy, Vol. 1: From the Beginning to Plato.* London: Routledge, 1997.

Wheelwright, P., ed. *The Presocratics.* New York: Odyssey Press, 1966.

Socrates

Benson, H.H., ed. *Essays on the Philosophy of Socrates.* New York: Oxford University Press, 1992.

Brickhouse, T.C., and N.D. Smith. *The Philosophy of Socrates.* Boulder, CO: Westview Press, 2000.

Colaiaco, J.A. *Socrates Against Athens: Philosophy on Trial.* New York: Taylor and Francis, 2001.

Reeve, C.D.C. *Socrates in the Apology.* Indianapolis: Hackett, 1989.

Seeskin, K. *Dialogue and Discovery: A Study in Socratic Method.* Albany: State University of New York Press, 1987.

Stone, I.F. *The Trial of Socrates.* Boston: Little, Brown, 1988.

Taylor, C.C.W. *Socrates.* New York: Oxford University Press, 1998.

Vlastos, G., ed. *The Philosophy of Socrates: A Collection of Critical Essays.* Notre Dame, IN: University of Notre Dame Press, 1980.

CHAPTER 3

Plato
Philosophy as an Ideal

Phil Washburn

～ Preview

For Plato philosophy is many things, but primarily it is a search for a better world than the world we see around us. Plato believes that we can sometimes glimpse perfection, and philosophers spend their lives pursuing and trying to understand that perfection. To Plato, perfection means reality and truth—clear, unchanging, eternal, universal. One example is a geometrical form such as a perfect circle, which we can glimpse amid imperfect drawings of circles. But Plato believes we can comprehend other aspects of reality that are better than what we have now: a better kind of knowledge, a better kind of person, a better kind of society. Philosophers seek the ideal through dialogue—questions, answers, further questions—in a never-ending approach to perfection. The fact that we can envision true justice,

absolute beauty, and unquestionable truth, untainted by the impurities of
ordinary life, convinced Plato that part of us belongs to a higher realm and
longs to return to it. (The Editor)

∾ Introduction

Why are people drawn to philosophy? For many reasons. Some have a sense
of wonder about the world or a desire to see the pattern of things. Some want
to know how to live and what makes life worthwhile. Some have a passion to
find the ultimate foundations of things.

Plato had all these motivations, but above all he was disappointed by the
world as he found it. For Plato, philosophy was a search for a better world.
The main events in the first thirty years of his life were war, defeat, the moral
decay of his country, and the execution of his beloved teacher, Socrates. But he
didn't become cynical or apathetic. The early disappointments energized him
to search for a better way to live, a better society, and a better understanding
of things. The central concept in his philosophy is the concept of the ideal: the
ideal person, the ideal education, the ideal society, the ideal wisdom. Plato
observed the actual world very carefully, but it was not enough. He devoted
his life to the exploration of perfection.

Some hard-nosed realists might dismiss Plato as a mere dreamer or a
starry-eyed idealist. They might say that imagining an ideal person or an ideal
society is a waste of time, and in any case, everyone's ideal is different. But the
concept of the ideal is complicated. Even realists admit that everyone *has* an
image of an ideal job, an ideal life, an ideal spouse, maybe an ideal person or
society. It is possible that if we compare the highest ideals, we can find some
agreement. And which talent is more valuable: the ability to see what is actually there or the ability to imagine something better that might exist? It's an
interesting question. Plato believed that pursuing the ideal was more important than accepting an uninspiring reality.

The beginning of his life gave few hints of later disappointments. He was
born in Athens in 427 BCE into one of the most illustrious families of that
famous city. His mother was descended from Solon, the original architect of
Athens' democratic government, and his father traced his lineage back to
Poseidon, the god of the sea. The family was wealthy and influential. Plato
was a very successful athlete and was honored as the victor at two important
Olympic-style games. In fact, the name "Plato" was a nickname meaning
"broad-shouldered." He was tall, handsome, charming, and brilliant, an aristocrat in every sense of the word.

But there was a cloud on the horizon when Plato was born. Four years
earlier, in 431, Athens had gone to war against Sparta, the second most powerful city-state in Greece. The two states and their allies continued fighting as

Plato grew up, and it is likely that he commanded troops as a young man. But in 404, after twenty-seven years, Sparta finally defeated Athens. It was a disaster for both sides. Both were exhausted, and neither ever recovered its former strength.

Plato blamed the democratic Assembly in Athens for the defeat. He believed that the citizens had tried to manage military affairs they didn't understand, and that they were fickle and easily swayed by ambitious speakers. He had considered a career in politics, but the incompetence and arrogance of the Athenians discouraged him. The enemies of the democrats were no better. Sparta set up an oligarchic government in Athens after the war. (The Athenians called it the "Thirty Tyrants.") In fact, Plato's uncle was one of its leaders. But Plato was disgusted by the oligarchs' brutality and greed. So were the Athenians; the government was overthrown after eight months.

As a member of an influential family and an intelligent young man, Plato must have spent many hours discussing the decline and humiliation of his city with its leading citizens. Why was the democratic government so short-sighted? He decided that one of the root causes was the failure of the educational system. Traditionally Greek children learned from their parents, and then from craftsmen and professionals. For higher levels of education they studied with tutors. In the fifth century most tutors were known as "sophists," a term derived from the Greek word for wisdom or knowledge. The sophists offered to teach young men how to speak well in the assembly, and how to make an impressive argument and refute others' views, because in democratic Athens persuasive speaking was the key to political power and success. Well-known sophists traveled from place to place and charged high fees for their instruction.

Many sophists were also moral relativists. In their travels they had learned about different societies and customs, and they decided that right and wrong were relative to society. What the Persians called "right" the Greeks called "wrong," and vice versa. There is no true right or wrong; there are only different societies' traditions, they said. An enlightened man, therefore, will take whatever he can get and do whatever pleases him, because there is no real reason he shouldn't. Plato believed the sophists were mistaken, and that they had a terrible influence on Athenian politics and society. The military defeat was part of a broader decline in morals and intelligence.

The final straw for Plato was the trial of Socrates. Socrates was Plato's teacher, but he was an unusual kind of teacher. He was trained as a stonecutter, but he spent most of his time in the central marketplace of Athens, talking with friends and acquaintances and others. He talked about the affairs of the day, but he guided the conversation toward deeper questions. He tried to get his fellow Athenians to examine their own opinions and values and think about their real reasons for holding them. Socrates lived by the command at the religious shrine at Delphi: "Know thyself." The command sounds simple, but Socrates made people realize, by simply asking questions, that they didn't know themselves at all.

For many people, looking in the mirror and seeing a baffling stranger was very disorienting. For others, such as Plato, Socrates held a magnetic attraction. He clearly wanted to help people, and his questions were the kind that keep one awake at night. There is no doubt that Plato loved Socrates very much. But in 399, some fervent democrats in Athens accused Socrates of corrupting young people and of rejecting the official gods of the city. The democrats believed that Socrates had supported Sparta during the war. But Athens had banned political trials, so they had to find another charge. Socrates defended himself at his one-day trial. Plato was there, and he later wrote an account of it called "The Apology," from the Latin word meaning "defense." Socrates gave the jury of five hundred a moving explanation of why he lived as he did, and he was clearly innocent of the charges. But the jury convicted him and condemned him to death. He was executed by having to drink poison. He was seventy years old, and Plato was twenty-eight.

Plato called Socrates "the wisest, the most just, and the best of all the men whom I have ever known." His execution by the Athenians must have been a crushing blow to him. Plato lived to the age of eighty and he wrote many books, but all of them reflect the direct influence of Socrates. All are in the form of dialogues, or questions and answers, just like the conversations Socrates had in the marketplace. Moreover, the main speaker in almost all the dialogues is Socrates himself. For example, in an early dialogue called "Crito," Socrates talks with his friend Crito about whether it would be right or wrong to escape from the jail where Socrates is waiting to be executed. In other words, almost everything Plato wrote was part of his portrait of Socrates' philosophical activity. He was by far the most important influence on Plato, and his unjust execution was a bitter disappointment for him.

After Socrates' death, Plato left Athens. The military defeat, the irresponsible teachings of the sophists, the democracy's travesty in killing its best citizen, and the loss of his mentor were more than he could bear. For the next twelve years he lived in southern Italy, Cyrene in north Africa, Egypt, and probably other places. The Pythagoreans in Italy had a strong influence on him. They believed that the world was made of mathematical forms and relationships. They also believed in reincarnation and lived in a small community of dedicated philosophers. He also lived with the ruler of Syracuse in Sicily for a time and may have offered the king political advice. Plato spent these years studying the traditions and philosophies of all the people around the Mediterranean world. Perhaps he was trying to understand all the failures he had seen so far in his life after the great promise of his youth. How does a person respond to tragedy and loss? It was probably during these travels that he wrote "The Apology" and other dialogues representing Socrates' conversations.

In 387 he returned to Athens. He was no longer a student but was now a mature thinker of forty-one developing and extending Socrates' ideas. He was convinced that the political and moral failures of his city were partly due to the corrupted educational system, which was dominated by sophists. In response, he opened his own school of higher learning called the Academy. Over the entrance was the inscription "Let no one ignorant of mathematics enter here." He wanted students to recognize the difference between personal opinion and rigorous knowledge. While he was teaching at the Academy he wrote what are known as "the middle dialogues," including *The Republic,* "The Symposium," "Phaedo," "Phaedrus," and "Cratylus." Socrates was still the main speaker, but Plato probably put more of his own ideas into these works than into the early dialogues.

∽ The Ideal Person

In all his works Plato continued his pursuit of perfection, and in incomparable prose he described his vision of the ideal. His starting point was Socrates. Socrates was the ideal human being. He was kind, gentle, fearless, absolutely honest with himself and others, dutiful, and rational, among other things. But Plato wasn't satisfied with a list of traits. He wanted to understand the ideal human being in a deeper way. He wasn't satisfied with one example, however admirable, but wanted a general theory of the ideal person.

We have all faced some form of Plato's question at one time or another. What is a perfect game or an ideal race horse or the best way of life? Baseball fans know what a perfect game is. When a pitcher allows no hits, no walks, and no runs, he has pitched a perfect game. If a tennis player wins with a score of 6–0, 6–0 and makes no errors, we might say she played a perfect match. Horse breeders have a mental image of the ideal race horse even if they have never seen a horse that was actually ideal. They will pay more for a young horse if it comes closer to the ideal. At dog shows the judge picks the best working dog, the best terrier, and so on based on the standards and the ideal that dogs conform to. Plato applies this process to a much more important subject: how can we discover the ideal human being?

The sophists ridiculed Plato's quest and said that there is no ideal human being. All standards are subjective and arbitrary, they said. Some people prefer one thing and others prefer another, and one person's preferences are no better than another's. The sophists were called "relativists" because they believed standards were relative to a society or an individual. But the relativists' point of view does not apply to baseball or tennis. Some players really are better than others, depending on how closely they resemble the ideal player. Some horses really are better than others. A person can *say,* "I like this dog, it's an ideal golden retriever," even if the poor dog is lopsided, losing its hair, and walks with a limp. But people who have studied dogs for years and know all about golden retrievers will not agree that it is an ideal retriever. However, it's still an open question whether being human is like being a tennis player or an animal or something else. Is there an ideal for human beings?

Plato believed there was. He based his view on a broad theory of human nature. He believed there were basically three types of people. The majority of people simply want to be comfortable. They want good food, a soft bed, and sex. They want to satisfy their physical desires, and they pursue money as a means whereby they can do that. But other people are different. While everyone has physical needs, some people care more about reputation and esteem. Their most important goals are social rather than physical. They want to earn the respect of others, to be the best, to win the race. They take on difficult challenges and enjoy competition. And there is a third type of people who are the rarest of all. They want to know the truth about things. Of course, they need to survive, and they must cooperate with others, but what they really value is understanding. They pursue knowledge in all its forms and keep digging through loose opinions until they find the bedrock of solid knowledge.

Plato believed there are three types of people because there are three parts of the soul, and an individual's personality depends on which part of the soul is dominant. A person's soul consists of reason, emotion, and appetite. Reason is the part of us that can see similarities and differences, consider consequences, weigh pros and cons, and think rationally. Emotion is the feelings of pride, anger, joy, sadness, determination, and their variations. Appetite is the desire for things that satisfy the body. Most people allow appetite to guide their lives. They define happiness in terms of eating, drinking, watching TV, and generally enjoying pleasurable sensations. They use the other parts of their personalities only to serve their appetites. Other people are dominated by emotion. Their ego and feelings of pride and anger are the strongest part of their personalities and therefore guide their lives. They are most concerned with how other people see them or what others think of them. And in a few people the reasoning part is strongest. They are curious. They want to see through illusions to the truth. They look for causes, always seek to understand, and think before they act. Their reasoning or intelligence guides their feelings and desires.

An ideal person like Socrates is one of the small group of people whose souls are dominated by reason. Integrating one's personality so that reason guides emotion and appetite is ideal because it is the natural function of reason to consider possibilities and choose the best. Emotion is unstable and extreme. Appetite is shortsighted and single-minded. An ideal person doesn't attempt to deny emotions and physical needs. He or she simply subordinates them to understanding and calm analysis. The rational type of person is one who not only has the intellectual ability to understand difficult concepts, but who also has the desire to understand. In other words, the ideal person is a philosopher, a lover of wisdom. Philosophy is the *love* of wisdom, not merely intelligence. Like a lover, a true philosopher will pursue wisdom continuously, be dedicated to it, endure hardships for it, and struggle to be worthy of it. The attitudes are rarer than the ability.

Plato's theory of human nature illustrates his great faith in reason and intelligence. Choices based on knowledge and clear understanding are better than choices based on whim, craving, instinct, or strong emotions. In general, the more one's reason controls one's emotions and appetites, the better one's life will be, he believed. That doesn't mean ascetic self-denial or cold isolation from people. It means one recognizes the proper place of emotion and appetite in one's personality. Plato called the proper control of emotions "courage." A courageous person is one who can organize her emotions in a way that drives her toward difficult goals. The proper control of appetites is "moderation" or "self-discipline." It means satisfying needs for the purpose of health and not allowing them to interfere with more important matters. The proper use of reason is "wisdom." It is understanding the true nature of things, their essences and proper functions. A person who exercises all these virtues—moderation, courage, and wisdom—is a "just" or morally good person, according to Plato. She allows each part of her personality to perform its proper function, she has her priorities in order, she has internal harmony. She is not only the happiest kind of person but the best in every way. She is ideal.

⌒ The Ideal Knowledge

Plato realized that sophists would question his vision of the ideal and ask, "How do you know?" He based his view on a careful examination of human nature and the three parts of the personality. But he was also searching for the ideal *knowledge*. Some people claim to know something when in reality they do not. Plato had probably been disappointed by political leaders and teachers who had claimed to know but had turned out to be mistaken. And he realized how central and essential the concept of knowledge was. Before we can be sure that we understand anything—photosynthesis, computers, politics—we must have a clear definition of knowledge itself. Before we can say we know what the ideal human being is like, we must be able to explain how we know anything, that is, what it means to know. Plato responded to the skepticism and relativism of his age with a sophisticated vision of ideal knowledge.

He says we all recognize the difference between knowledge and opinion, and examining that difference will help us understand what knowledge is. So, suppose you and I have a mutual acquaintance, Susan, and someone asks us what Susan looks like. You have met her a few times, and you say, "I think she's sort of tall." But suppose I measured her height yesterday, and I say, "She's tall, five feet, ten and a half inches." What is the difference between our two statements? For one thing, you aren't sure. You haven't observed Susan carefully or compared her with other people. But I am sure; I just measured her yesterday. So one difference between knowledge and opinion is certainty. To know something, you must be certain that it's true, and if you are not sure, then you have an opinion, a belief, not knowledge.

There are other differences between knowledge and opinion as well. Plato says that knowledge is universal and precise. Though Susan may seem tall to you, she may seem short to people in another country. Therefore you cannot know that she is tall; you only have an opinion. But knowledge is the same for everyone. When I say Susan is five ten and a half, I will probably claim that I have knowledge, because everyone can agree about the statement. It is universal. And my statement is exact and definite. I can say precisely what I know. But "Susan is tall" is vague. It does not convey a clear, definite idea. Most people are satisfied with such foggy, unfounded opinions, but Plato sought perfect knowledge. He wanted information that was precise, true for everyone, and beyond question.

But these characteristics of knowledge lead to further complications. Is it really beyond question that Susan is five ten and a half? No, because she may have been slouching or the tape may have stretched. Is she exactly five ten and a half or a thousandth of an inch taller? Plato decided that no matter how care-ful I am, I cannot acquire real knowledge about the physical world, so if I say I *know* Susan is five ten and a half, I am exaggerating. I may feel certain, but I can't really be certain. Physical objects are too complex, too variable, to appre-hend with complete certainty. But in thinking about measuring things, Plato real-ized that we can acquire some knowledge. I know that five feet is more than four feet. Five is more than four, and six is more than five. Here is a statement—"five is greater than four"—that is certain, precise, and universal. There is no chance that I could be mistaken, the relation is exact, and it is true for everyone. In other words, Plato said that we can have real knowledge of numbers and mathemati-cal relations even if we can only have opinions about physical objects.

What are numbers? Are they real? Are they just ideas in our minds or are they part of the world? Plato's answer to these questions is the most famous part of his philosophy. He said that there are levels of reality. Some things are more real than other things. Numbers are definitely real, they are not just human inventions, and in fact they are more real than physical objects. A num-ber, such as five, is a sort of pattern. Think about a set of five apples on a table. Then replace each apple with a cup, and now replace the five cups with books. Apples are different from cups, but the pattern—five—is the same. We can all recognize numbers by ascending to a higher level of generality. We ignore the particular physical objects in a group and think about the pattern that the group has in common with other groups of five. A pattern is not a physical object, but it is certainly real.

Most people will say they know that Susan is tall and apples are sweet. And on a practical level, they can get through life with such vague, unreliable statements. But Plato wanted perfect knowledge, not "good enough" knowledge. In analyzing what we can know perfectly, he realized that there is an ideal level of reality, beyond the colors and sounds of the physical world around us. But to reach the ideal level, we must realize that we encounter it with our minds, not our eyes or ears or fingers.

Consider another example. I can take four buttons and arrange them in a square, with one button at each corner. I could then take away each button and replace it with a raisin. Now I would have different physical objects but the same pattern, a square. Is the pattern real? It isn't the same as the physical objects because they can change. But we all understand the pattern and can describe it. It may be ten centimeters on each side, it is two-dimensional, each corner is a right angle, and so on. In fact, there is a whole science—geometry—based on such patterns. We also recognize patterns in time. I notice that when water boils, steam lifts the lid on the pot. And a large gas flame makes the air in a hot-air balloon expand. After observing a number of examples like these, physicists recognized the pattern: gases expand when they are heated. The general law is not about any particular objects; it is about relations among events in time. Science is about patterns (laws), not physical objects.

Plato claims that patterns such as squares are actually *more* real than buttons or raisins or lines on paper. One reason is that the square lasts longer. The buttons will break and disintegrate eventually, but the square shape will not. It will last forever. The pattern, or shape, is an abstract object, outside of space and time. It is not physical. The buttons are at a particular place, but the square they help us think about is not in any particular place. The same applies to numbers. Five apples may be on the table, but the number five is not on a table or in a room or anywhere at all. Things that last forever are more real than things that appear for a while and then cease to exist.

Furthermore, we can be certain about the square, but we cannot be certain about the buttons or lines on paper. One can be certain that the square has four sides and each side is equal, that the angles are exactly ninety degrees, and so on. If I put a button in the wrong place or draw curved lines, then I have not represented the pattern "square." I am absolutely certain that squares have equal sides. And everyone agrees. Everyone who understands what a square is agrees that its angles are ninety degrees. Geometry is the same in every society. But I cannot be absolutely certain about physical objects. A button may look blue to you and green to me, shiny to you and dull to me. We can never pin down physical objects with precision. We can never acquire real knowledge about them. That means they are less real than things we can know.

Plato believed there was an even higher level of reality than mathematical objects. He called the higher level the "Forms." We can begin to understand what he meant if we think about how a child learns the meanings of words. When we teach a child the meaning of the word "five," we show her five fingers, five people, five cookies, and she recognizes what the groups have in common. We teach her other concepts in the same way. She learns the meaning of "cat" when we point to our cat, the neighbors' cat, and pictures of cats. It may take some time. At first she may think that all four-footed, furry animals with tails are cats, and she may call dogs "cats." But with help she comes to grasp the concept. She understands the pattern that all cats share and that nothing else has. These patterns, or defining features, are the Forms. For each general term, such as "cat," "dog," "animal," "living," "walking," "human," and so on, there is a Form. The Form is a sort of ideal cat, ideal dog, or ideal animal. Understanding the general word means comprehending the Form. Forms are like numbers in that they are abstract objects, outside space and time. Therefore we can have genuine knowledge about them.

Plato said that philosophers are people who try to understand the Forms. The most important Forms are those applying to human life. Like Socrates, Plato wanted to understand the nature of courage, happiness, justice, wisdom, and other moral concepts. He wasn't satisfied with opinion but wanted certain, precise, universal knowledge. By examining a wide range of courageous acts, we can see what the acts all have in common (just as we understand the term "cat" by seeing what all particular cats have in common). We can rise up to the level of the Form of courage, the abstract essence, outside space and time, and understand what makes an act courageous.

Plato's theory of Forms is about knowledge, meaning, and reality, so it is difficult and controversial. Most people believe physical objects are the ultimate reality, and seeing them with our eyes is the highest kind of knowledge. But Plato said that some facts are inescapable, and those facts lead logically to a different conclusion. The patterns that we see—in scientific laws, in concepts such as "cat," and most clearly in numbers and shapes—are undeniable. They are not the same as the particular physical objects that exemplify them. And by the standards we normally use to measure knowledge—certainty, universality, precision—they rank higher than physical objects. Plato was willing to break away from the majority and "common sense" and conclude that the patterns exist on a higher level of reality.

Plato found an ideal world, better than the ordinary world of trees and tables and human bodies. The world of Forms does not change. Two has always been half of four and will always be half of four. But the physical world changes. We can know the Forms perfectly, but we make mistakes and chase illusions in the physical world. Forms are universal and eternal. But the physical world is full of conflicts, and everything in it will die. The patterns or Forms are the structure of the world. Individuals come and go, but the structures remain the same.

∽ The Ideal Education

Plato's vision of the ideal person, ideal knowledge, and ideal reality led him to propose a better kind of education than the sophists' training in rhetoric. An ideal person is a philosopher, and he or she seeks genuine knowledge. Plato said that becoming a philosopher is like climbing an intellectual ladder. The first step is mathematics because anyone who studies mathematics seriously realizes two things: first, there is a difference between a vague, unprovable opinion and precise, certain knowledge; and second, there are realities, like numbers, that are abstract, perfect, timeless, and universal.

After mathematics a person would investigate the Forms. Through discussion and dialogue, people propose descriptions and definitions of all the Forms, particularly Forms of moral qualities; they analyze and criticize the proposals, and gradually achieve better and better understanding. Philosophers do not gather more facts about animals or societies or human behavior. We already recognize fairness and unfairness when we see them; the question is, why do we say an act is fair or unfair? What makes an act fair? Philosophers try to understand the basic concepts we have now, the categories and patterns in the world that make it meaningful.

In a dialogue called "The Symposium," Plato describes the intellectual ascent philosophers make. The dialogue is about the Form of love. He says a young person begins by loving the beauty in another individual. But she will see that other people are beautiful as well; she will see that the beauty is the same in all beautiful individuals (as five is the same however it is embodied). So she will grow to love the beauty in many people. Then she will rise above bodies to the level of minds and personalities, and learn to love beautiful souls even more ardently than bodies because souls are more real. Continuing her flight, she will begin to see the beauty of certain ideas, thoughts, laws, and understandings. Finally, after a long, dedicated search, she will reach the highest stage of love when she comprehends the Form of beauty itself, the pure essence, unlimited by any particular expression. Our love for people and other things is really our confused, misguided search for perfect beauty. Thus our love can be truly satisfied only when we find the highest kind of beauty, which is the Form of beauty itself. Plato included a more famous description of the philosopher's intellectual ascent in *The Republic*. He says most people believe ordinary physical objects like tables and chairs and trees are real and that visual perception is knowledge. Most of us are not aware of the higher levels of reality. He says we are like prisoners in a deep cave, chained to the floor from birth, facing the rear wall of the cave. Behind our backs is a large fire. Between the fire and the prisoners, other people carry objects over their heads, so that the fire projects shadows of the objects on the rear wall of the cave. All the prisoners ever see are the shadows of things moving back and forth. That is the life most of us lead.

But occasionally one person will break free from the chains, although it is difficult and painful. He will turn around and observe the fire and the moving objects. The scene will be confusing at first, but eventually he will understand. Then he will climb to the mouth of the cave and emerge into the daylight. The bright light will hurt his eyes, but if he has the strength and courage to persist, he will see real tables and chairs and trees and people. Eventually he will look at the sun, which makes it possible to see everything else. The contrast between the world outside and the dark world of the prisoners in the cave is so stark that he will return to help his friends. But they will not be able to understand him. To them he will sound like a fool or a madman with his talk of a "higher reality." They will laugh at him or ignore him, and if he tries to pull them out of their chains, they will probably kill him. The story is clearly an allegory of the philosopher's ascent to the Forms and of his relation to society. And it is a reminder of the execution of Socrates.

Plato described the process of becoming a philosopher as an ascent, a climb from the level of the physical world to a higher level. But the relation between the physical world and the Forms is one of the most problematic parts of Plato's theory. A particular cat is not the Form of cat; a square drawn on a blackboard is not the Form of squareness. So how are physical objects related to the eternal Forms that define them? Plato said an object "resembles" a Form or "participates" in a Form. But he insisted that the two levels were distinct. We do not see Forms in objects. For example, we do not see the Form of squareness in the square on the blackboard, because the physical drawing is not perfectly square. The lines are not exactly straight, not exactly equal, and so on. A particular cat is not a perfect example of the Form of cat. Plato rejected the commonsense belief that we look at a lot of examples of something, find what they have in common, and thereby acquire general ideas. But if we do not learn about Forms in this way, how do we learn about them?

Plato's answer was that we have always known the Forms. He said that our souls are immortal, and before we were born into our present bodies we existed in the higher world, where we learned the exact nature of all the Forms. But when our souls were united with our bodies at birth, our bodily senses and desires clouded our minds, and we forgot what we knew. Thus understanding the Forms is closer to remembering than it is to observing or generalizing.

Plato wanted to emphasize the difference between our opinions based on sensory experience and the true knowledge we have about the Forms. For example, in math class you might learn that if you draw a straight line through the center of a circle you get equal halves. You can look at an illustration on the blackboard to get the idea, but if you just think about what is involved— straight line, center, circle, equal—you will see that the principle *must* be true. In math there is a sort of "click" of understanding when your mind suddenly grasps the necessity and certainty of things. We never have the same kind of certainty about physical objects. Plato said the certainty of true knowledge is more like memory than generalization. His theory about the soul existing before birth was a way of emphasizing the different kind of knowledge we have of the Forms. Becoming a philosopher, therefore, means remembering what one already knows. One uses physical objects as reminders, but ultimately one turns away from the physical world to the knowledge within one's soul, the legacy of a previous existence, the understanding of a higher reality.

∾ The Ideal Society

Plato's theory of remembering the Forms shows that it is difficult to describe an ideal. An ideal world is different in crucial ways from the imperfect, material world of the senses, so Plato could not describe it with the same language we use to describe the material world. He had to use metaphors, images, myths, and other ways to suggest perfection. The same problem arises in his masterpiece, *The Republic*. Plato brought together his ideal human beings, ideal knowledge and education, and ideal reality in a unified vision of an ideal society called the Republic. But how much of his description did he intend to be taken literally and how much was only metaphorical? It's difficult to know for sure.

He began with the assumption that a good society must be based on human nature. Since the soul has three parts and there are three types of people—appetitive, competitive, and rational—society should have three classes. The largest class is made up of appetitive people, called "Producers," who produce goods for consumption. They are concerned with satisfying needs, so they are happiest working to produce and distribute all the things people need. The second class is the defenders: the police and the army. This class, which Plato called "Auxiliaries," consists of people who strive to excel, who seek difficult challenges, and who want to be respected. Finally, the smallest class is the "Guardians," who guide society and make political decisions. They are the rational people, the philosophers.

Thus a good society perfectly mirrors an individual personality. It has three parts, and its happiness depends on each part doing the task it is best qualified to do. In such a well-ordered society, Plato said, everyone benefits. Each individual will be happier doing what he or she can do best—produce, protect, or lead—and the society as a whole will benefit from such an efficient use of resources. The Producers and Auxiliaries recognize the wisdom of the Guardian-philosophers, and they have no interest in politics anyway, just as most people in the United States have no interest in politics.

The functions of producing and defending are simple and clear, but the job of leading society is complex, so Plato spent more time discussing the Guardians. Once we accept the principle of three classes, the next step is to find and prepare those rare people who have the natural ability to understand things and to make good decisions. Democratic elections are not the way to find wise leaders. Plato believed that people's basic psychological orientations are evident at an early age. He thought that people are either natural leaders or natural followers, and they begin to stand out in kindergarten and elementary school. To find good Guardians, we should look for children who put the welfare of the group above their own selfish interests; they are natural leaders. And they are as likely to be girls as boys. Plato held the view—unheard of in the ancient world—that women could be political leaders and philosophers (and even soldiers), just as men could.

Then these potential Guardians go through a long period of education. Plato believed that educating young people to leadership was as important as finding those with natural ability. First, their character and values must be shaped. Plato said young children learn from the stories they hear, so these future leaders should hear only stories that make them brave, confident, compassionate, and fair. They should not hear stories about people terrified of death or gods who tell lies. In fact, Plato extended his censorship to the whole state. He thought that artists of all kinds have an undesirable influence on people. They excite and strengthen the emotions, and if that happens repeatedly, the emotional part tends to take over the personality. Dramatists in particular encourage spectators to identify with characters on the stage, including evil characters, and that makes it easier for people to be evil in reality. Besides strengthening the emotions, artists undermine reason and the love of truth. Artists create images, fictions, and stories that are not true. They make it easier for people to live in a fantasy world and imply that it is good to withdraw into the imagination. But their images are even less real than the observable world, which is less real than the world of Forms. They draw people in the wrong direction, away from the higher world. Consequently, Plato said, philosopher-rulers would ban artists from the ideal state.

After the potential Guardians' moral character has been formed in their early years, they undergo rigorous physical training until they are about twenty. Then comes several years of university education, followed by several years of philosophical study with other philosophers attempting to understand the Forms. After this long academic preparation they should spend another fifteen years gaining practical experience in the world of Auxiliaries and Producers. Only then are they ready to become Guardians. They are tested all along the way to see if they retain their love of truth and their dedication to the good of society. Plato believed that true philosophers loved justice, wisdom, courage, and moderation in all their forms, so they would love the well-ordered society. They would gladly work to create those virtues in their society, even if it meant sacrificing the personal pleasure of philosophical discussions with friends.

Nevertheless, the task of the philosopher-rulers was surrounded by distractions and pitfalls. Plato proposed that the Guardians live together in something like dormitories, taking their meals together and sharing everything. He said they should have no money and no private property, but should have all their needs supplied by society. In such a system they would not abuse their power, become greedy, or lose sight of their primary obligation. Besides this communism of property, Plato also proposed a communism of family. The Guardians should form one large family, with all the women regarding all the men as their husbands, all the men regarding all the women as their wives, and adults regarding all the children as their own. Plato didn't eliminate families among Guardians; he only redefined the family and extended it.

He argued that such an arrangement would have a number of benefits. Children would have many caregivers and role models instead of just two, would receive more love, and so would grow up happier and healthier. Jealousy and possessiveness would be reduced. Guardians wouldn't restrict their strongest loyalty to a few people, but would feel affection for the whole group, and therefore could more easily care about the good of society as a whole. Another advantage, in Plato's view, would be the regulation of reproduction. He said that, while all the male and female Guardians were husbands and wives, they would arrange for the best males among them to mate with the best females more often to produce the best children. Such controlled reproduction among humans is called "eugenics." If the best life is one in which every aspect is guided by reason rather than instinct or emotion, then eugenics makes more sense. Plato said that the decision to have children is perhaps the most important decision we make, and therefore it should be based on the best knowledge and aimed at the best possible outcome. Especially since the Guardians are devoted to the welfare of the society instead of their own personal pleasures, they would welcome such family planning.

How much of this scheme did Plato believe was really possible? It may be that he described this three-level society led by philosophers as an ideal, or an extreme, which we can never fully achieve but toward which we can continually strive. The Republic may be a kind of Form of society. The philosopher-kings' communistic way of life is an ideal for philosophy as well. In less perfect societies, philosophers pursue truth and goodness but must compromise on practical necessities. Or perhaps Plato had more faith in human reason. He said in *The Republic* that none of his plan was strictly impossible, though it would be difficult to implement. The fact that ordinary people would be shocked meant little to Plato. Ordinary people believe that if something has been done for centuries, then it must be natural and good. But, of course, slavery lasted for centuries until thoughtful people began to question it and educate others to see that it was not natural or good. Plato believed that we can ask questions and use our intelligence to decide the best way to live, and we might discover that the present way is not the best way. Perhaps a major cause of failure and decline is simply the lack of courage to look for the ideal.

In fact, late in life Plato ventured into practical politics. In 367, after he had written *The Republic* and had been teaching at the Academy for twenty years, he received a flattering invitation from the new king of Syracuse. Plato had visited Sicily in his early travels and had become acquainted with the king, Dionysus. Now Dionysus had died and his son, Dionysus the Second, had assumed power. Plato went to Sicily, perhaps with the idea of transforming the teenage ruler into a philosopher-king. But the youth was not ready for philosophy. Plato even went back a second time four years later but had no more success. Shortly afterward, Dionysus was overthrown in a violent coup. It is difficult to believe that Plato was surprised, since he had lived through the upheavals in Athenian politics and had written about corrupted governments. But apparently he never gave up hope.

In the last years of his life he wrote what are known as "the late dialogues." In them he raised difficult questions about his own theory of Forms. He was one of his own toughest critics. He also wrote his longest book, *The Laws,* in which he presented a more moderate blueprint for society than the one in *The Republic.*

Plato continued his search and revised his ideas even into his seventies. He was a visionary, and he kept striving to understand his vision more completely. He conceived of a more demanding standard of knowledge, a higher level of reality, an inspiring model of human excellence, and a harmonious society. He perceived perfection, and earnestly tried to help others see it as well. Like Socrates, he was a passionate lover of wisdom. He thought deeply about all areas of life, and like Socrates, he taught by example as much as by explanation. In his work and in his life he presented an ideal of philosophy that few have matched. He was never satisfied, he continually searched for a better way, he was completely honest, even about his own work, and he respected the truth. Among all the numerous lessons that Plato has taught later philosophers, one of the most important is that philosophy is open-ended: we can always improve our understanding, our selves, our conduct, and our society.

∿ CHRONOLOGY

431 BCE	Peloponnesian War begins between Athens and Sparta
427	Plato born to a wealthy, influential family in Athens
404	Athens surrenders to Sparta
403	rule of "the Thirty Tyrants," one of whom was Plato's uncle, overthrown after eight months
399	trial and execution of Socrates, Plato leaves Athens to travel and study for twelve years
387	returns to Athens and opens the Academy, the first university in Europe
367	goes to Sicily to visit the king, Dionysus the Second
363	returns to Sicily for another visit
347	dies in Athens

~ **SUGGESTED READINGS**

Armstrong, A.H. *An Introduction to Ancient Philosophy*. London: Metheun, 1965.

Crombie, I.M. *An Examination of Plato's Doctrines*. New York: Humanities, 1962.

Cross, R.C., and A.D. Woozley. *Plato's Republic: A Philosophical Commentary*. London: Macmillan, 1964.

Dilman, I. *Philosophy and the Philosophic Life*. New York: St. Martin's Press, 1992.

Durant, W. *The Story of Philosophy*. New York: Pocket Books, 1953 (1926).

Gill, C. *Greek Thought*. New York: Oxford University Press, 1995.

Hare, R.M., J. Barnes, and H. Chadwick. *Founders of Thought*. New York: Oxford University Press, 1991.

Irwin, T. *Classical Thought*. New York: Oxford University Press, 1989.

Lavine, T.Z. *From Socrates to Sartre: The Philosophic Quest*. New York: Bantam, 1984.

Reeve, C.D.C. *Philosopher Kings: The Argument of Plato's Republic*. Princeton: Princeton University Press, 1988.

Rice, D.H. *A Guide to Plato's Republic*. New York: Oxford University Press, 1998.

White, N.P. *A Companion to Plato's Republic*. Indianapolis: Hackett, 1979.

CHAPTER 4

Aristotle
Philosophy as Science

Phil Washburn

～ Preview

Aristotle sees philosophy as continuous with science, but his idea of science is slightly different from the modern idea. Philosophy, like science, is an attempt to understand the whole—the universe, humanity, and culture. It tries to find basic principles that will reveal the underlying pattern in all the changing, conflicting aspects of the world. Just as modern science is founded on a few basic concepts—mass, force, element, evolution—Aristotle proposes the concepts of function, classification, and hierarchy to explain virtually everything. While modern science emphasizes the search for laws, Aristotle emphasizes the search for accurate definitions of things in terms of their essential properties. He thinks philosophers can find definitions through careful observations of things. But where modern science sees the world as a machine, Aristotle sees it as an organism. Everything has a function or pur-

pose, and its essential nature is to grow and achieve its purpose. Aristotle believes his scientific method applies to ethics, politics, and art, as well as to the natural world. (The Editor)

∼ Introduction

One historian says that Aristotle was the greatest biologist before Darwin. St. Thomas Aquinas, the medieval theologian, said that Aristotle was the greatest philosopher ever; he was "*the* Philosopher." So was he a scientist or a philosopher? Of course, a person can be both, just as a person might be a lawyer and a painter. Wallace Stevens was an insurance executive and also a great poet. But not at the same time. If he had tried to write poems about insurance policies, they would probably have been boring poems, and if he had tried to sell insurance by reciting poetry, he probably wouldn't have sold much.

But Aristotle believed he could be a scientist and a philosopher at the same time. He wanted to understand the nature of things, and he didn't make a sharp distinction between a scientific understanding and a philosophical understanding. It is possible to do science and it is possible to do philosophy, but is it possible to combine the two kinds of investigation? Aristotle believed it was, and by examining his ideas, perhaps we can enlarge our views of science and philosophy.

Aristotle was probably the most prodigious and comprehensive philosopher in history. He wrote on virtually every topic, from astronomy to biology to psychology, from ethics to rhetoric to art. And after he had mastered and contributed to every discipline, he invented the science of logic. But in spite of the diversity of his interests, he created a unified, systematic point of view. Even more amazing than his wide range was his ability to tie everything together. He found several key concepts that he believed explained almost everything he studied. His method and key concepts are in some ways scientific and in some ways philosophical. They are an exciting blend. Today philosophy seems to many to be a sterile exercise in semantics, divorced from the real world. And science seems overwhelming, divided into mutually unintelligible parts and moving in frightening directions. Perhaps Aristotle's conception of philosophy can suggest a new synthesis in which all the confusing discoveries of science can be organized, and philosophy can be informed by the best knowledge of the real world.

Aristotle's life was divided into three stages. He was born in 384 BCE in a small town called Stagira in northern Greece. His father was the court physician for the government of Macedonia, Greece's powerful neighbor to the north. In 367, at age seventeen, he came to Athens to study with Plato at the famous Academy. He remained as a student and as a teacher for twenty years, until he was thirty-seven. His experience in the Academy was the first stage of his career.

When Plato died in 347, Aristotle left Athens and went to Asia Minor, beginning the second stage of his intellectual odyssey. He spent several years on the island of Lesbos studying marine life. In 342, King Philip of Macedonia invited Aristotle to his court to serve as the personal tutor to his son, Alexander. Thus the conqueror of the entire world of knowledge instructed the future conqueror of the entire political world. In 336 Philip was assassinated and the twenty-year-old Alexander ended his academic education and took command of the government.

A year later, when he was forty-nine, Aristotle began the third period of his career when he returned to Athens and opened his own school called the Lyceum. He supervised researchers in all the sciences and taught courses himself. According to legend, he liked to stroll as he lectured; his followers, therefore, were known as the *peripatetics,* which is Greek for "walkers." Most of the works we have were probably written during this period, although some were based on observations and ideas from earlier periods. When Alexander died in 323, anti-Macedonian riots broke out in Athens. Aristotle was in danger, since he had been Alexander's tutor. He decided to return to his home in northern Greece "to prevent Athens from sinning twice against philosophy." (Its first sin was the execution of Socrates.) He died a year later of natural causes at age sixty-two.

∼ First Period: At the Academy

To understand Aristotle's idea of philosophy, it is helpful to review Plato's teachings, since Aristotle absorbed some of them and rejected others during the first period of his career. The foundation of Plato's system was the theory of Forms. Plato taught that the ordinary world of trees and tables that we can see and touch is actually an illusion. It is not completely real. If we see a square brown table, it is the squareness and brownness that are fully real, not the particular physical object. Plato thought physical objects were too elusive to be entirely real. They change over time, different people perceive them differently, and we can't be absolutely sure about their nature. Squareness, on the other hand, is not a physical object but a Form. We can understand squareness with clarity, precision, and certainty—we know exactly what it is—but we cannot achieve the same level of precision with ephemeral particular objects. Plato believed that squareness, brownness, and other Forms were completely real, eternal, and unchanging. Particular objects only resemble these Forms more or less adequately.

Aristotle studied Plato's theory thoroughly, and he produced some striking criticisms of it. He was convinced that reality is what we can observe. He rejected Plato's "transcendental" vision of a higher realm, grasped only through the mind. As he gradually decided that Plato's theory was flawed, he was faced with some basic questions. What is real? What kinds of things exist? What is the world made of? Is this table real or is its squareness more real? And how can one find out what is real and what isn't? Aristotle came up with an ingenious, and characteristic, solution. He examined all the things we can say about a table and classified the statements. We can say the table is three feet wide, it is brown, it is larger than a desk, it is in the office, it was made last year, it is standing upright, it is polished, and several other things. Aristotle thought there were ten basic types of statements about objects, or ten "categories." These fundamental ways of talking about things give us an insight into the nature of reality because they all involve the word "is." The table *is* brown, *is* larger than a desk, and so on. The ten categories are:

1. quantity (three feet wide)
2. quality (brown, square)
3. relation (larger, half)
4. place (in the office)
5. time (last year, Tuesday)
6. position (upright, lying down)
7. state or condition (polished)
8. action (cuts, burns)
9. affection (is cut, is burned)
10. substance (man, table)

The categories show us the types of things that exist; places exist, times exist, numbers exist, properties, relations, actions, and so on exist.

But the category of substance is different from the others. It is more basic. There is something, some substance, that is brown, three feet wide, and polished. There is a subject that has these properties. In other words, if we examine the ways we actually talk and think about the world, we see that the world consists of individual substances and their modifications. Both substances and modifications exist, but not in the same way. The table itself is the basic reality, and its quantity, quality, and position are secondary. Aristotle makes individual substances basic because they are "separable," whereas the other categories are "inseparable." He means that a substance can exist without being brown, but brownness cannot exist except as a modification of some particular substance.

A substance, therefore, is a particular thing and its properties. We can distinguish the underlying subject and its properties in our minds, but they are never actually separate in reality. We can think of the table remaining the same table while its color, position, and relations to other things change, but the table never exists without some properties. Aristotle calls the underlying subject the "matter" and the properties the "form." Thus a substance consists of matter and form, and to understand something one should analyze it into matter and form. Form, for Aristotle, is not a separate realm, as it was for Plato.

The forms of things are their properties, relations, positions, and so on, but the form of a substance never exists apart from the substance itself. The primary reality is a particular substance.

Aristotle probably formulated his basic ideas about the nature of reality—his metaphysics—while he was still teaching at the Academy. Later he expanded them and applied them to other subjects. But his theory of substance as matter and form is crucial for understanding his views, and it illustrates three fundamental features of his thought. First, to solve a philosophical problem, Aristotle carefully studied what others had thought about it. He surveyed past theories. In all his books he consistently follows this method. He describes a problem and then summarizes the different solutions other philosophers have proposed. But he goes further, because philosophical problems arise from ordinary, everyday experience. So, in addition, he examines what average people believe or say about an issue. He does not see himself as a prophet, or even a solitary genius, but rather as an investigator who can build upon previous discoveries and clarify matters, as a scientist does. This is not to say that he is uncritical. Most of what others believe is self-contradictory or confused, as Aristotle incisively demonstrates. But common beliefs provide the basic data and the starting point for understanding.

Second, he often finds a compromise among conflicting views or a synthesis of them. In metaphysics, Plato had taught that unchanging, nonphysical Forms were real and physical objects were illusory. On the other hand, earlier philosophers called "Atomists" had claimed that only atoms were real and properties like brownness and squareness didn't exist. Aristotle tried to combine Plato's idealism and the Atomists' materialism in his own theory of matter and form. He believed that if serious philosophers reach some conclusions about reality, there is probably some truth in what they say. The prudent course is to try to reconcile the different theories. Aristotle sifted all the theories and tried to separate the insightful wheat from the unfounded chaff.

Finally, Aristotle's treatment of the problem of reality illustrates his method. He began with particular cases or facts and worked his way up to broader generalizations based on them. He carefully examined scores of specific statements people made using the word "is." Then he noticed that the statements could be classified into ten general groups or categories. At a higher level, he recognized that all the statements depend upon the idea of a subject and its properties, or matter and form. The process of making generalizations about a group of particular cases is called "induction." Once he had a broad generalization, like "substances consist of matter and form," he could apply it to new areas and figure out their basic structure. Applying a generalization to new particular cases to learn something about them is called "deduction."

Aristotle's philosophy is similar to science in several ways. Like a good scientist, Aristotle begins with experience—his own and others'. He examines various theories and explanations of our experience and tries to find a general law that describes all the different things people have observed. So is he a scientist rather than a philosopher? For Aristotle, there is no difference. But a scientist today might point out that his theory of substance as matter and form is not based on experiments. Aristotle does not offer a test of his theory. That is, we cannot go into a laboratory and break apart substances into matter and form. But a scientist can break apart water into hydrogen and oxygen, and can break apart any material into atoms. A scientist's claim that water is H_2O can be tested.

In response, Aristotle might say that matter and form are never separated. We can break them apart in our minds, but not physically, so any test of his theory has to occur in the mind. Moreover, since he is talking about all of reality, we can see examples everywhere to support his theory, not just in a laboratory. He is trying to explain the nature of reality itself, not just parts or aspects of it. Thus his thinking is like science is some ways and different in others.

∼ Second Period: Biologist

When Plato died in 347, his nephew Speusippus was appointed as the head of the Academy. Aristotle and some colleagues left and began a twelve-year period of traveling, teaching, and research. Some have speculated that he was offended because he wasn't selected as the head of the school, but there is no evidence of that. He might have left for any number of reasons.

What is more important is his shift in interests. Aristotle wrote several books on biology in which he described and classified plants and animals. Many of the examples in those books came from the upper Aegean and from the coast of Lesbos, where he lived for several years. The evidence suggests that during this second stage of his life, Aristotle was actively engaged in research on plants and animals. He was always interested in an astonishing range of subjects, but it seems that during his forties he spent much time collecting, observing, and dissecting animals.

He made a number of important discoveries. For example, he carefully described the step-by-step development of a chick embryo from conception until hatching. He must have designed a kind of experiment: he opened and examined an egg that was one day old, another that was two days old, another that was three days old, and so on. He also described the difficulties of observing veins, arteries, and other organs, indicating that he had fairly extensive experience with dissection. At the same time, he made some simple and glaring errors. For example, he reported that men have more teeth than women and that the mammalian heart has three chambers instead of four. But the accurate observations far outnumber the mistakes, which were probably the result of trying to do too much in a limited amount of time.

Aristotle's biological investigations were the major influence on his philosophy. They were even more important than studying with Plato, because they shaped the distinctive and unique aspects of his philosophy. Three central themes, or concepts, can be traced to Aristotle's close study of the living world. The concepts are function, definition, and hierarchy. These concepts are not only distinctive but also central, in the sense that Aristotle uses them to explain a very wide range of phenomena. In fact, he thinks they apply to virtually everything. As a result, his philosophy is coherent: all the different parts revolve around these basic concepts. He gives us a unified world view.

Function

The concept of function seems to apply to man-made artifacts, not living organisms. For example, in an automobile the function of the brakes is to allow one to stop, the function of the battery is to supply electricity, and the function of the camshaft is to open valves in the cylinders. To understand an automobile, one must recognize the parts' functions. But Aristotle discovered that the same is true of plants and animals. To understand an animal, it isn't enough to describe its parts or the stages of their growth. One must understand what the parts are for. For example, Aristotle could observe the little pads on the underside of an octopus' arms. But to understand them, he had to recognize their function: they are suckers. They enable the octopus to hold shellfish and other things in a tight grip. The roots of plants aren't just a branching growth. They have a purpose, a goal, which is to absorb water and nutrients from the soil.

Wherever one looks among living things, one sees purpose. In the human body, the function of the teeth is to tear and grind food. That explains their shape and extraordinary hardness. The function of the stomach is to dissolve the food in powerful acids. That explains its unusual lining, its muscular action, and, when things go wrong, its ulcers. Aristotle found that the question "What is its function?" was like a master key to the living world; it opened all the doors and explained all the parts. When faced with an unknown, puzzling specimen dredged up from the ocean, all one had to do was examine the parts and ask, "What does this do?" "Why is this shaped this way?", and "What is the purpose of this," and the strange creature gradually became comprehensible.

For Aristotle, function meant natural development. He tied the concept of function to the concept of growth. When something exercises its function, it is fulfilling its nature, and when it grows, it is fulfilling its nature. Growth is a universal characteristic of living things, and Aristotle said that an organ's growth was its attempt to fulfill its function. Each part of an organism strives (unconsciously) to fulfill its function. Whole organisms do the same. An acorn, he says, aims at being a full-grown oak tree, and its growth can be explained as its blind attempt to realize its true nature. The function of a thing is more important than its color or shape. The purpose of the stomach is to digest food. But different organisms might have slightly different organs with different colors or shapes, made of different tissues, to do this. The organs are all stomachs, however, because their essential nature is to digest food, not to be shaped in a certain way.

Is Aristotle's notion of function a scientific theory? He was so impressed by the pervasive roles of function and purpose in living things that he extended these concepts to the whole world. Just as Newton used the idea of gravity to unify a wide range of facts, Aristotle used the idea of function to explain an even larger range of observations. He believed everything that exists has a function or goal and attempts to achieve it. Even the elements—earth, air, fire, and water—have functions. Earth and water tend to move toward the center of the earth, and air and fire tend to move away from the center. Their function explains their behavior. On the other hand, the gravitational attraction described by Newton is a measurable force, and Newton even stated a precise law involving mass and distance to describe it. Objects' functions, in Aristotle's sense, are much more difficult to observe and measure. Perhaps the function of a bear's fur is to keep it warm. (Or is it to camouflage the bear or protect its skin?) But what is the function of the bear itself? It's hard to say. Aristotle did not emphasize measurement and quantification as much as modern scientists do.

In a sense, Aristotle's way of thinking was exactly the opposite of ours in the twenty-first century. We often assume that to understand something, one must discover the cause. "Why did it happen?" "What made it that way?" we ask. Aristotle recognized that things are shaped by causes. But he thought that the much more important questions were "What is its purpose?" "What is it aiming at?" "What is the direction of its growth?" We look to the past; Aristotle looked to the future. Aristotle's point of view is called "teleological," from the Greek word *telos,* which means "goal."[1] Aristotle was searching for general, lawful explanations for why things happen, as all scientists do. He simply believed that the direction in which something was moving or developing was more useful for understanding than the past causes of change.

When Aristotle wrote his book on physics, he brought together his earlier metaphysical ideas with his later biological ideas. He proposed that to understand any part of the world, one must find its four "causes," or explanations. At the beginning, one must understand its matter and form, since all substances consist of matter and form. But one must also discover its "final cause," which means its function and goal. And one must discover its "efficient cause," which means the prior events or agent that made it what it is now. Aristotle gives the example of a house. Its matter is wood or brick and its form is normally rectangular. Its function and goal is to provide shelter, and its efficient cause is the builder who made it. A house is artificial, but we can also look for the four explanations for natural objects, such as a boy. His matter is bone, muscle, hair, and so on; his form is two-legged with hands; his function is to become an adult and do all the things men can do; and his efficient cause is his parents.

Definition

The second main theme that Aristotle developed in his biological investigations was definition. As he was observing and surveying the world of living things, he naturally had to organize his research. He was probably supervising a number of assistants, and he wanted to learn as much as possible. So he had to proceed systematically rather than haphazardly. But what is the system of nature? Where does one begin? How does one know one has surveyed everything? The obvious solution is to divide the material into parts and then subdivide each part into smaller parts. Living things can be divided into plants and animals, animals into those that lay eggs and those that give birth to live young, and so on. Actually, such a project is not easy. Aristotle considered classifying animals by their means of locomotion—four feet, two feet, wings, fins, and so on. But that division cuts across other important characteristics. He decided that the best basis was reproduction and proposed five major divisions: giving birth to live young, three types of eggs (such as bird, reptile, and fish eggs), and larvae (for insects). Each of these groups can be further divided.

Classifying animals gives us a good way of understanding their nature. When we encounter a particular animal, we can ask where it fits in the general scheme of things. And the most specific classification will be the most illuminating. For example, if we encounter a creature unfamiliar to us, it is helpful to know that it is an animal rather than a plant, but even more helpful to know that it is a mammal (live young) and even more helpful to know that it is a four-footed, grazing, antlered animal. The best description gives the object's genus and specific difference. That means it tells us what class the object belongs to and what specific differences distinguish that object from others in the same class. So one might describe a deer as a grazing animal that has antlers. The genus "grazing animal" includes cattle, bison, and sheep, as well as deer, and the specific difference "has antlers" distinguishes deer from other grazing animals.

Aristotle extended this notion of classifying living things beyond biology and applied it to everything. He developed it into his concept of definition. To define something is to state its genus and specific difference. A chair, for example, is an article of furniture (genus), which is used to sit on (specific difference). One could be more precise and define a chair as an item used to sit on (including couches, benches, stools, etc.), which has four legs and a back.

The concept of definition may seem trivial, but in fact it is extremely important to Aristotle. The goal of philosophy is to understand the nature of things, and understanding the nature of a thing means defining it. We can try to define a human being and say exactly what makes us human. We can try to define happiness or society or art. To define something is to understand it, and until we define it, we haven't really understood it. As the case of living things shows, to define something is to figure out what class it belongs in and how it is also different from other members of that class. It is to see its proper position in a broader system of categories. To define something we must examine its properties, and that means we employ the four explanations. In approaching any subject, Aristotle often tries to analyze it into parts (material), see the structure, or relations among the parts (formal), discover the highest development, or purpose of the whole (final), and find the source of changes that occur (efficient). When we can answer these questions, we can define whatever we are studying. We can see how it fits into a larger pattern.

Scientists today ask these same questions. They try to discover the real nature of genes, black holes, superconductive metals, insect societies, and numerous other fascinating phenomena. And they try to find relations among different phenomena so that they can classify them by genus and specific difference. But definitions and classifications are still controversial. For example, we know a great deal about the matter and structure of human beings, but are human embryos human beings? Does the definition of "human being" include embryos? Some say yes and some say no. As for classification, should we regard human groups as one type of society, along with wolf societies, insect societies, and fish societies? Can we explain features of all these societies with similar evolutionary principles? Some scientists say yes and some say no.

It is not easy to classify things, although it is an important part of science and philosophy. The task is to organize what we know into categories and subcategories. That means beginning with particular cases and looking at similarities and differences for the purpose of classifying the cases. The goal is to find the inherent structure in things, whether it is living things, societies, the heavens, or human values. The structure is expressed in definitions that are more and more general and that explain the nature of the particular parts. For Aristotle, philosophical understanding means grasping the structure of the whole and seeing where each part fits into a larger whole. We understand the whole by seeing the parts, and we understand each part by seeing the whole. Aristotle was not only a scientist, but also a philosopher, or a scientific philosopher, because his main goal was to understand the whole: the world and our place in it.

Hierarchy

The two concepts discussed so far—function and definition—when joined together produce the third idea that Aristotle took from biology and applied to everything else. That is the idea of hierarchy. A hierarchy is an arrangement of things in a scale from the least valuable up through ranks to the most valuable at the top. Aristotle believed that nature is a hierarchy. Everything has an essential nature, expressed in its definition. Moreover, the most important property of each thing is its function or goal. Its goal is its full development, its final stage of growth, the complete exercise of its powers. Some things have a higher function than others, in the sense that the goal of the higher things includes the goals of the lower things. A house ranks higher than an umbrella because a house can not only protect one from rain but can do other things as well. An insect ranks higher than a worm because an insect can eat, reproduce, and move, as a worm can, but it can also sense its environment through sight and hearing, which a worm cannot do.

The best illustration of Aristotle's concept of hierarchy is presented in his book *On the Soul*. The Greek word for soul is *psyche*, but psyche is very broad. A better translation might be "life," since plants as well as animals have a psyche. Plato had taught that the human psyche was the most important part of a person, that it was a different kind of thing from the body, and that it was immortal. That position is called "dualism" since it sees the mind and body as two things, separate and distinct. Aristotle rejected dualism. He proposed that a living being is a substance, consisting of matter and form, and the psyche is the form of the body. The psyche is not a separate thing inside a body, but is just the principle of life, of activity, that animates a body.

Not all living things have the same type of psyche. Aristotle said that the four types of psyche are the nutritive, the sensitive, the locomotive, and the rational, and they form a hierarchy. The nutritive psyche exists by itself in plants. Plants absorb food and they reproduce. Simple animals possess a nutritive psyche, but they also have a sensitive psyche. They absorb food and reproduce, but they also sense their environments. All animals possess the sense of touch. Some can also taste; some can also smell, hear, and see. Higher animals have a locomotive psyche. They move from place to place, and there are levels of this ability. At the highest level, human beings can do all the things plants and animals can do, but in addition, we can think rationally. We have a rational psyche. Aristotle says that the gradations are very fine and gradual; it is impossible to draw sharp lines between different levels. Nature is so various and subtle, he says, that even between plants and animals one cannot point to a specific place as the dividing line. Nevertheless, there are unmistakable differences in complexity as one ascends the hierarchy.

Aristotle also applied the concept of hierarchy to the physical world. He believed the earth was the center of the universe, and it was encased in a series of larger and larger transparent spheres. The moon was embedded in one sphere, the sun in a larger one, the planets circled the inner spheres in their own individual spheres, and the stars encased the whole series. But why are the heavenly bodies higher in the scale of nature? Well, as one ascends the scale from plant to animal to human, one sees an increase in the power of mind, from simple sensitivity to limited awareness to conceptual consciousness to theoretical understanding. The highest development (on earth) is human reasoning or intellectual contemplation. Aristotle believed the heavenly bodies were conscious beings—"gods"—with greater powers of understanding and thought than humans possessed. They were made of a fifth element, called "ether," and did not eat, reproduce, perceive the environment, or feel pleasure and pain. They only thought. They achieved in a greater degree what the whole ladder of life was clearly aiming at: pure mental activity. Living beings have the potential to be conscious, and human beings realize that potential most completely on earth. But the gods made actual and active what humans only have the potential to be.

A hierarchy has a highest point, and Aristotle believed there was a highest god located in the outermost sphere. The highest god was pure thought, with no potential at all. He, or it, was completely actualized. It was the highest stage of growth, the last possible development, what all things were striving for. Even the lesser deities continually strove to become more like the highest god. Their impulse was expressed as motion, a pilgrimage to god. But as lesser beings, they never reach god. Their motion is eternal. In a finite universe (as Aristotle believed ours to be), an eternal motion must be circular. That explains the orbits of the moon, sun, and planets. The revolutions of the heavenly bodies are an expression of their innate desire for perfection.

All the activities of living things are also attempts, in one way or another, to reach the pure actuality of god. Everything an animal does is aimed at the fullest development of its potential. Eating, reproducing, learning, and working are all motivated by a desire for a state of eternal consciousness. Therefore Aristotle's name for god is "the unmoved mover." It is the ultimate cause of everything, the source of all change and motion. But not in the modern sense of "cause." God did not create the world at some moment in the past. Aristotle's view is teleological; he explains things by their purpose. The unmoved mover causes everything in the sense that it is the goal of every change. It draws everything continuously toward itself. Things change because they are attempting to reach god.

Aristotle's picture of the universe was tremendously influential for many centuries. In the sixteenth century, Copernicus challenged the picture with his heliocentric model of the solar system. But the most profound change was gradual. After Copernicus, philosophers and scientists such as Bacon, Galileo, Hobbes, and Descartes began to think of the universe as a huge machine, or a series of machines within machines. In this modern view, greater complexity does not imply greater value. Nor does development toward a goal imply any value. An oak is no better or worse than an acorn. A mammal is no better or worse than an insect. In this respect, Aristotle's outlook is different from the neutral, mechanistic outlook of modern science. Aristotle believed that values (better or worse, higher or lower, healthy or unhealthy, more developed or less developed) were inherent in nature, whereas many scientists today believe that values are human responses to the world or personal projections onto the natural world.

∽ Third Period: The Lyceum

When Alexander ascended to the throne of Macedonia in 336, Aristotle returned to his hometown of Stagira. A year later he went back to Athens and opened his own school, called the Lyceum. He taught there for twelve years. It was probably during this third period that he wrote the treatises that have survived, although he had been working on the theories for many years. Philosophically, the significance of the third period is that Aristotle applied the key concepts of his view of nature to the human world of ethics, politics, and art. Human beings are part of the natural world, and therefore the concepts of function, definition, and hierarchy should help us understand human behavior and culture as much as they help us understand the earth, animals, and the heavens.

In fact, Aristotle approached culture using the same methods he used to study nature. Today most colleges have departments called "political science," but can there be a science of ethics or art? Aristotle said yes, but we should remember two qualifications. First, for Aristotle, science meant understanding the essential nature of things by classifying them on the basis of their function. He did not attempt to measure human behavior or perform laboratory experiments. And second, he recognized that we cannot achieve the same level of precision about human culture as we can about the natural world. But he did believe that we can understand human societies, what is good for people, and art, in a systematic, organized, and objective way.

Ethics

Aristotle's predecessors had asked, "What is the best way of life?" "What is mankind's highest good?" Socrates had taught that a life of simplicity, dialogue, and reflection was best. Plato defended a view of justice as harmony among intellect, emotion, and appetite. And some sophists had proposed that the highest good was power. Aristotle approaches the subject in his usual way, by considering the prevalent opinions. The most common belief is that happiness is the highest good, and Aristotle agrees. When sophists talk about power or wealth or reputation as the highest good, they are mistaken, because people want these things for the sake of happiness. Power and wealth are stepping stones that will lead one to happiness (some say). But happiness is always an end in itself. People want happiness for its own sake, not as a means to something else. Therefore happiness is the highest good for mankind.[2] But what is happiness? The claim that happiness is the highest good doesn't help us because it is very difficult to explain what happiness is. Is it different for different people? Is it an individual's free choice, ultimately arbitrary? Aristotle says no. Human happiness is based on human nature. Of course, we are all different and have different tastes and preferences, but we are also all human. Our deepest needs and fulfillments are based on our nature as human beings.

And what is our nature? In other words, what is the definition of human being? Enjoying sports is certainly a trait some people have. But it isn't essential to being human. A person can know nothing of sports and still be human. So what is essential? All humans must eat, sleep, and navigate through the environment, so perhaps satisfying basic needs is our defining property. Indeed, some philosophers said that pleasure is the highest good. Aristotle agrees that humans are animals and that pleasure is one good. But "animal" is not the definition of human being because it doesn't distinguish us from other animals.

To understand the essential nature of anything, according to Aristotle, one must discover its function. Its function is its highest development, or what it aims at. For human beings, eating and sleeping are not our highest development. What distinguishes us from other animals is our ability to think rationally and understand. That is our highest development because it is beyond the capacities of other animals. It sets us apart and makes us human. It is our unique function, our purpose in life. Thus the definition of human being is "rational animal." We are animals, and Aristotle says that fulfilling our animal nature is part of happiness. He disagrees with Socrates and Plato on this. But he also agrees with their emphasis on reason. He says that a higher level of happiness, or complete happiness, consists of the active use of our minds.

Thus Aristotle believes that ethics has a rational basis in nature. By studying human beings objectively, we can discover what is good for us and how we should live. Fulfilling our human potential is good, and thwarting our nature is bad. Ethics is like nutrition. Some things to eat are healthy and good for us and others are harmful. Of course, different cultures prepare foods in different ways, and individuals develop preferences based on childhood experiences. But the basic laws of nutrition are the same for all human beings. No culture or individual can develop a taste for arsenic or completely avoid protein. Aristotle claims that the laws of happiness and the good life are the same for all people as well.

Politics

For Aristotle, ethics is inseparable from politics, because the most complete happiness depends on living in a community and interacting with others. One who lives alone is "either a beast or a god." Politics is about society, or the state. Can there be a science of politics? How would a scientific philosopher study society? Aristotle tries to define the state in terms of genus and species, and he searches for the four causes.

A state belongs in the general category of associations, that is, groups of people joined together for some purpose. But there are many types of associations. What makes a state different from the others? To find out, Aristotle surveys various types. For example, a man and a woman form the simplest association, and they join together for the purpose of reproduction. Relatives join together in families to ensure food, clothing, and shelter, and families join together in villages to acquire some luxuries. Villages form military alliances for the sake of security and trading alliances for the sake of prosperity. Aristotle claims that all these associations form a hierarchy, from the simpler to the more complex.

The most complex association of all is the state, which results when villages and towns join together. For what purpose? Aristotle says self-sufficiency and independence. The distinctive function of a state is to be independent. None of the simpler associations can exist by itself, but when they all join together, the resulting complex association can be self-sufficient. A state is a natural system, like an organism or a forest, except that it is made up of people. And if we study the hierarchy of associations in nature, we can see how they all grow in the direction toward greater self-sufficiency and independence. The highest development is the state.

The purpose of a thing is the most important clue to its definition, and so Aristotle emphasizes the final explanation, or function, of society. He also bases his theory of society on an examination of its parts, including families, villages, and other associations. In other words, he also emphasizes the material explanation of society. What is the formal explanation? The form of a state is the arrangement of political offices in it, that is, its constitution. In the United States, for example, the offices are divided into legislative, executive, and judicial. Aristotle said that the most important part of the constitution was the final authority, the office with the power to overrule others and make the final decision. He classified different states on the basis of whether the final authority was held by one person, a few people, or many people.

Finally, Aristotle investigated the efficient explanation of states, that is, the causes of change or revolution. He was thoroughly familiar with the history and politics of the Greek world, and based on his extensive observations, he describes twelve types of causes. They include loss of wealth, a rise to power by an individual or a group, election fraud, unequal growth of parts of a state, large differences between parts of a state, and so on. But the purpose of observation is to make inductive generalizations, and so at a higher level Aristotle says that all these causes illustrate one general cause, which is equality and inequality. Some people (aristocrats) feel that there should be less equality, and some (democrats) feel that there should be more. The perception of injustice makes people resort to violent change.

Aristotle's approach to political theory was based on observation and classification, but he made some glaring errors. He notoriously believed that some people were incapable of self-determination and were slaves by their very nature. They were only capable of manual labor and would be happier if they were supervised by a more rational person. Barbarians and women were natural slaves, in his opinion. It is surprising that such a careful observer as Aristotle could believe that some people were incapable of making decisions for themselves. On the other hand, people who are silenced and abused and driven like animals may, after a time, lose some of their humanity. Aristotle may have believed that they never had it. Moreover, besides observing, Aristotle's method was to begin with the accepted beliefs about a question.

Most ancient Greeks felt certain that slavery was natural and inevitable. Usually Aristotle's method was helpful, but sometimes there is a fine line between "common sense" and blind prejudice.

Drama

Aristotle approached the subject of art and drama the same way he had approached politics: as a scientist. He observed a large number of plays, searched for their essential properties, and summed up the properties in a definition. On a more specific level, he discussed the four explanations, as he had for the state.

Aristotle said art is representation or imitation. Human beings have an instinct to mimic sounds and speech, to draw pictures, to make statues (such as dolls), and to imitate behavior. Any time we engage in a natural activity we feel pleasure, so art is enjoyable. Drama is one type of art. That is, in defining drama we put it in the genus art. The specific difference is that drama is a representation of action. That distinguishes it from painting, music, and sculpture.

Aristotle also analyzes a drama into its parts and discusses the material, formal, and final explanations. (The efficient explanation is the writer.) What is a drama made of? He says speeches, not recited like a poem, but acted out. So he includes the gestures, tone of voice, and movements that actors use to represent people and their lives. Dramas also consist of characters, music, and scenery. What is the form of a drama? It is the arrangement or organization of the parts, which is to say the plot. Aristotle said that the plot is the soul (psyche) of a drama. A drama succeeds or fails with its plot, and Aristotle discussed some features that good plots should have.

What is the purpose of a drama? When we watch characters like Oedipus or Hamlet struggle with the most urgent questions of identity, good and evil, and survival, and the suspense builds, we get emotionally involved and vicariously experience the tragedy ourselves. Aristotle says that we feel fear as we realize that something similar could happen to us. And we feel pity when we see the suffering and loss that afflict the characters. Afterward, we feel relieved and more in control of our own lives; we feel that we have a better perspective on things. Aristotle says that the purpose of drama is to purge the emotions of fear and pity, so that we are more calm and rational. His word is *catharsis*.

Aristotle's "Poetics" is important not only for the extensive influence it has had on drama, but also because it provides a counterweight to Plato's theory of art. Where Plato said that art was false and misleading, Aristotle claimed that art was natural and pleasant. It was thought-provoking. He said poetry was "more philosophical" than history because it dealt with what might happen, not with what had actually happened. Where Plato condemned art for stimulating the emotions, Aristotle claimed that art was valuable just because it stimulated the emotions. However, they were not completely at odds. He agreed with Plato that strong emotions interfere with clear thinking and should be defused or controlled. They disagreed on whether art intensifies or moderates emotions in our daily lives. Is it a stimulant or a release?

∼ Conclusion

Viewed as a whole, Aristotle's thought has three main characteristics. It is empirical. That is, Aristotle believed that observation and experience are the basis of all knowledge. It is also synthetic. Aristotle not only relied on his personal observations, but also considered the widest range of experience he could. And he often finds a compromise position between conflicting views. Finally, his thought is systematic, in the sense that he employed a relatively small number of concepts—matter and form, function, definition, hierarchy— to make sense of a tremendously wide range of knowledge. He shows how many different things fit together on the basis of these concepts. These are also characteristics of science. We limit ourselves if we think of science only as an experimental search for specific causal laws.

People today are still asking the questions Aristotle asked, and more importantly, many people are persuaded by the answers he gave. In *The Future of Philosophy,* Harry Lesser says that of all the philosophies of the ancient world, Aristotle's will probably have the most influence in the twenty-first century. "The strength of this tradition is that it provides an alternative to what appear to some people to be 'dead ends' in modern philosophy. The next century will determine whether they really are dead ends. Platonism could also do this job, but Aristotelianism makes fewer metaphysical demands, or at any rate makes metaphysical demands more in line with common sense."[3]

Or perhaps Platonism and Aristotelianism will both continue to win adherents. Someone said that all Western philosophers are either little Platonists or little Aristotelians, and these two giants do represent the major alternatives on many philosophical issues: rationalism versus empiricism, transcendentalism versus naturalism, dualism versus monism, radicalism versus conservatism. In some eras, one view is more popular; in other eras, the other is more popular. As one of the enduring ways of interpreting the world and human experience, Aristotle's thought is of permanent value.

∼ NOTES

1. However, in his book *How the Mind Works,* Steven Pinker advocates a teleological approach to understanding the mind and brain. He says we should practice "reverse engineering" to understand how the parts of the mind and brain evolved and for what purpose. Modern science still employs the concept of function in some areas.
2. The Greek word for happiness is *eudaimonia,* which is very broad and general. It is sometimes translated as "well-being."

3. Oliver Leaman, ed., *The Future of Philosophy: Towards the Twenty-First Century* (London: Routledge, 1998), 21.

CHRONOLOGY

384 BCE	born in Stagira, northern Greece
367	enrolls in the Academy, Plato's school of higher education in Athens
347	death of Plato; Aristotle begins biological research in Asia Minor and on the island of Lesbos
342	becomes the tutor of Alexander, prince of Macedonia, age fourteen
336	Philip, Alexander's father, is assassinated, Alexander becomes king, Aristotle returns to Athens to open his own school, called the Lyceum
335	Alexander destroys Thebes, subdues Greek states
323	Alexander dies in Persia, anti-Macedonian riots break out in Athens, Aristotle goes to Stagira
322	dies in Stagira of natural causes

SUGGESTED READINGS

Ackrill, J.L. *Aristotle the Philosopher*. Oxford: The Clarendon Press, 1981.

Allen, D.J. *The Philosophy of Aristotle*. Second Edition. New York: Oxford University Press, 1970.

Copleston, F. *A History of Philosophy*, vol. 1. Westminster, MD: Newman Press, 1963.

Durant, W. *The Story of Philosophy*. New York: Simon & Schuster, 1933.

Ferguson, J. *Aristotle*. New York: Twayne, 1972.

Hare, R.M., J. Barnes, and H. Chadwick. *Founders of Thought: Plato, Aristotle, Augustine*. New York: Oxford University Press, 1991.

Irwin, T. *Classical Thought*. New York: Oxford University Press, 1989.

Jaeger, W. *Aristotle*. New York: Oxford University Press, 1948 (1923).

Lloyd, G.E.R. *Aristotle: The Growth and Structure of His Thought*. Cambridge: Cambridge University Press, 1968.

Magee, B. *The Great Philosophers: An Introduction to Western Philosophy*. New York: Oxford University Press, 1987

Pinker, S. *How the Mind Works*. New York: W.W. Norton, 1997.

Randall, J.H., Jr. *Aristotle*. New York: Columbia University Press, 1960.

Ross, D. *Aristotle*. Fifth Edition. London: Methuen, 1949.

CHAPTER 5

Marcus Aurelius
Philosophy as Consolation

David J. Rosner

∿ Preview

The Stoicism of Marcus Aurelius and his predecessors is probably the most popular school of philosophy in European history. When people speak of "being philosophical," in the sense of being strong in the face of disappointments, they are referring to Stoicism. For Marcus, the purpose of philosophy is to help us cope with the difficulties of life. His central doctrine is the idea that wisdom consists of recognizing the difference between what we can control and what we cannot. We cannot control events in the world, but we can control our feelings and responses to events. We may not be able to avoid illness or poverty, but we can decide how we will feel about those things, Marcus says. This doctrine is embedded in a larger theory of the universe, according to which everything is governed by natural law and divine reason. Our ability to reason is a spark of the divine providence guiding the universe. Since all people are endowed with reason, we should recognize the common family of humanity. Meditating on these truths will bring us peace of mind. (The Editor)

⌒ Introduction

This chapter discusses Marcus Aurelius' version of Stoic philosophy. Marcus Aurelius was an unusual philosopher for a number of reasons. For one thing, he was a Roman emperor, the most powerful man on earth at the time, with all the responsibilities that position entailed. Most philosophers are not public officials, much less emperors. For another thing, he wrote his famous book, *Meditations,* as a private diary, and originally did not intend to publish it. Not many people's personal notes to themselves have endured for eighteen hundred years as profound philosophy. Finally, while most great philosophers appeal only to specialists, Marcus' Stoicism has always attracted a wider audience. Today, under the heading of "philosophical counseling," some philosophers are using Marcus' vision of philosophy in a practical way to help people make sense of their lives.

I explain some of the basic ideas and themes of Stoicism, as formulated by Marcus, and I emphasize the conception of philosophy itself put forth by the Stoics. For the Stoics, philosophy offers consolation for the reflective individual as he or she deals with the many trials and tribulations of everyday life. However, I argue that ultimately, given some ordinary facts about human nature, it may be impossible for real people in real life to put the teachings of Stoicism into practice.

Marcus Aurelius was born in the year 121 AD. His parents both died young, and the boy was adopted twice. The adoptions had significant consequences. The first adoptive parent was his grandfather, who provided him with his education. This education must have been excellent, since Marcus spends much of Book 1 of his *Meditations* extolling its virtues. The second adoptive parent was Aurelius Antoninus. Antoninus was Marcus' uncle by marriage, but he was also the emperor of Rome. Marcus in time married Faustina, the daughter of his uncle. She had five children, but none of these survived except Commodus, whom history does not remember favorably. Upon the death of his uncle, Marcus shared the throne with Verus, another adopted son of Aurelius Antoninus. When Verus died in 169, Marcus was left as the sole emperor.

During Marcus' rule, a number of powerful tribes were engaged in warfare with the Romans, and Marcus spent much of his career as a soldier with the Roman legions along what is now called the Danube River near what is now Hungary and Austria. To console himself during these harsh times, he wrote the *Meditations,* a sort of diary that he kept for his personal reflections and consolation. Marcus died of disease at his military camp in 180.[1] In *The*

Decline and Fall of the Roman Empire, Edward Gibbon said that the age of the Antonines (from about 100 to about 200 AD) was the high point of Roman history, but others argue that Rome at this time was tired militarily and spiritually, certainly not a nation with an optimistic, forward-looking outlook.[2] I discuss this issue later with respect to the *Meditations* themselves.

∾ Basic Ideas

Marcus Aurelius is generally known as a Stoic, though Stoicism took slightly different forms over time, stressing different aspects at different times. The movement originated in Greece in the second century BCE, but it flourished especially during the Roman Empire. Stoicism is a complete philosophical system, with its own foundational logic, metaphysics, and epistemology. That is, the Stoics developed theories about the best way to think, about the nature of reality, and about how we can know anything. The *Meditations* presuppose some of these basic assumptions, although they are not the primary focus of the book. Marcus' interests were more existential and ethical. He was preoccupied with larger questions, such as the meaning and purpose of human life, how to live, and what is important and what is not, and he considered metaphysics and epistemology only insofar as they helped him find answers to the human questions. The *Meditations* were not intended as a rigorous philosophical system for academic audiences or for public consumption, but rather as a diary offering consolation to Marcus after trying days fighting the barbarian tribes on the Danube. In this view of philosophy, abstract theories about reality and knowledge can be interesting, but their real value lies in helping us to lead better lives. Other consolation philosophies of the Hellenistic period, such as Epicureanism, flourished at around the same time as well, and they offered similar therapeutic perspectives in a time of brutal warfare and spiritual decline.

For the limited purposes of this essay, we need to understand the basic ideas of the Stoic cosmology. The word "cosmology" is related to the word "cosmos," which means universe. Cosmology is the study of the structure of the universe as a whole. The Stoics assumed that everything in the universe can be reduced to a single unifying principle. That is, the universe is essentially monistic. The Stoics applied many names to this principle, often referring to it as "God," "Fate," "Necessity," or the "World-Soul."[3] The Stoics believed that, although this universe as a whole is perpetually in a process of change, every event unfolds in an orderly, rational manner; there is nothing chaotic, random, or incoherent about it. Every event that unfolds is therefore a manifestation of the divine order.

Marcus writes: "Whatever happens, happens rightly. Watch closely, and you will find this true. In the succession of events there is not mere sequence alone, but an order that is just and right, as from the hand of one who dispenses to all their due . . ." (Book 4, sec. 10, p. 66).

Much of the *Meditations* emphasizes humanity's small place in the universe and our ultimate insignificance. Even if an individual life seems chaotic, we should remember the larger orderly whole of which it is a tiny part. Marcus often discusses the brevity of life, naming many famous emperors, kings, philosophers, orators, politicians, and civilizations of the past that have simply vanished into the abyss of oblivion. He exhorts the reader to consider the vast eternity of time and space, and to consider, compared to this eternity, how small and insignificant an individual human life is. Indeed, when contrasted with this big picture, how many of the things we think are so important really are not?

Marcus writes, "Most of what we say and do is not necessary, and its omission would save both time and trouble . . ." (Book 4, sec. 24, p. 69). And

> The great river of Being flows on without a pause, its actions forever changing, its causes shifting endlessly, hardly a single thing standing still; while ever at hand looms infinity stretching behind and before—the abyss in which all things are lost to sight. In such conditions, surely a man were foolish to gasp and fume and fret, as though the time of his troubling could ever be of long continuance.
>
> *(Book 5, sec. 23, p. 86)*

Thus an essential feature of Stoicism is the connection Marcus and others see between the nature of the universe as a whole and our personal attitudes and values. Marcus doesn't simply counsel acceptance and modesty as a wise outlook. He believes these attitudes are required by the structure of the world we live in.

One interesting thing about these aphorisms is that they can be viewed as both depressing and comforting. They are depressing insofar as the shortness of human life and the insignificance of much human activity are facts that many do not wish to confront. In actuality, much human energy is spent in the service of denying these facts. Marcus emphasizes, in the spirit of twentieth-century existentialists like Heidegger, that authentic human behavior consists partly in coming to terms with the shortness of life, and somehow living and acting in accordance with this brutal fact on an everyday level. However, these aphorisms could also be seen as comforting if they could somehow give us the freedom to distinguish between those things we can control and those things we cannot. After all, why become angry and upset about things in the world that we cannot control and that ultimately are not our doing? We are only small parts of a larger whole that exists prior to us and independently of us. Our everyday concerns are not especially important in the grand scheme of things.

Furthermore, Marcus asserts repeatedly that the universe is not merely orderly and rational, but essentially good. This is another fact about the nature of reality that has implications for our lives on an individual level. Since the universe as a whole is good, we ought to follow nature and accept whatever happens to us without complaint. Everything that happens is right and for the best. Traditional religious answers to the problem of evil often assert that although events may appear to us to be terrible and unjust, God has good reasons for the apparent tragedies in the world. This is what is traditionally known in the philosophy of religion as "theodicy," or the rational justification of God's actions. Marcus' attitude seems to be similar to the religious point of view. Indeed, Marcus believes that since whatever happens according to nature is for the best, nothing that happens is ultimately bad.

Even death fits into this perspective. Marcus writes: "Everything that happens is as normal and expected as the spring rose or the summer fruit; this is true of sickness, death, slander, intrigue, and all the other things that delight or trouble foolish men" (Book 4, sec. 44, p. 73).

And "Death, like birth, is one of Nature's secrets; the same elements that have been combined are then dispersed. Nothing about it need give cause for shame. For beings endowed with mind it is no anomaly, nor in any way inconsistent with the plan of their creation" (Book 4, sec. 5, p. 65).

According to the Stoic cosmology, birth is defined as the process in which certain elements in the universe come together, and death is defined as the inevitable process in which these elements in the universe disperse into the larger whole from which they came. Insofar as the universe unfolds in an orderly, rational, and ultimately good way, death is to be seen as a necessary and natural event in the universe, one that certainly should not produce negative reactions (such as fear, anxiety, or denial) in us. It is as natural and as necessary as day turning into night. Indeed, one of the purposes of philosophy is to help us put death into its proper perspective. Stoicism offers consolation insofar as it shows us how events in life should not cause worry or dread, but should simply be accepted as inevitable parts of the unfolding of a larger, orderly, and ultimately good universe.

Stoicism is not the only philosophy to recognize the importance of death. Dealing with death is a project central to philosophers from Socrates to Heidegger. Some philosophers provide consolation. For example, Plato offers arguments for the immortality of the soul. Certain religions stress an afterlife, and this, depending upon one's ultimate convictions, may also offer consolation to many. On the other hand, some philosophical conceptions offer nothing whatsoever in the form of consolation. An example is Heidegger's stark definition of death as the possibility of the end of all possibilities. Whether or not one finds Marcus' account convincing is, of course, up to the reader.

Marcus also believes that since we are all part of the universe and that the universe is ultimately good and rational, we all, as individuals, partake of the divine reason governing the universe. Marcus writes, "Always think of the universe as one living organism, with a single substance and a single soul; and observe how all things are submitted to the single perceptivity of this one whole, all are moved by its single impulse, and all play their part in the causation of every event that happens . . ." (Book 4, sec. 40, p. 73).

In this sense, we are all brothers and sisters, all citizens of a world community. We are all subject to the same laws and necessities of the universe and must face the same existential issues. We are all endowed with reason, and therefore we all deserve a minimum of sympathy, empathy, and respect from each other. This insight reveals Marcus' belief that all human beings are ultimately "in the same boat." We are all equal in the ways that matter. Realizing this will enable us to view all our fellow human beings as metaphysical brothers and sisters. When it comes to human behavior, most faults, foibles, and follies can be understood as deriving from the same basic misunderstandings about the nature of the universe and our limited, finite place in it. In light of people's misunderstandings, Marcus emphasizes an attitude of forgiveness toward the mistakes of others—hence the quote "Leave another's wrongdoing where it lies" (Book 9, sec. 20, p. 142). It is more important to keep one's sights focused on one's own life and its formidable demands than to involve oneself in petty arguments founded, more often than not, on an arrogant overestimation of our (and others') ultimate importance in the grand scheme of things.

On all these topics—relations with others, death, the significance of one's decisions, and so on—Marcus assumes that our feelings depend on our thoughts. In other words, our beliefs about things determine our feelings and responses to them. Studying philosophy helps us find the truth and see our place in the world, and that clarity dispels frustration, anger, depression, and other negative emotions.

◯ Evaluation

Whether one accepts Marcus' perspective on these matters will perhaps depend on whether one ultimately accepts the cosmology that it is based on. If one does not believe that the universe is rationally ordered and good, then one may not find Marcus' meditations about accepting one's fate very persuasive or comforting. Are there good reasons for accepting the Stoic cosmology? Is there any hard empirical evidence for this cosmology? I'm not sure that such evidence can be found or even what could possibly count as evidence for it. Experiments and discoveries do not imply that the world is good or that it isn't good. Scientists do not discuss fate, or a World-Soul, or universal reason. From a strictly scientific point of view, there is room for a healthy skepticism regarding any such metaphysics.

But people might have other grounds for accepting some of Marcus' pronouncements. Statements about good and evil cannot be verified scientifically, but that doesn't mean they cannot be supported at all. Stoic cosmology may not seem any more or less convincing than many other ancient cosmologies—

for example, the biblical story of creation. But there may be good ethical or existential reasons for believing in the validity of propositions such as the Ten Commandments even if one is an atheist.

Many other important philosophical issues arise when we try to evaluate Marcus' philosophy. A major issue is freedom and determinism, and their alleged compatibility or incompatibility. Determinism is the doctrine that events essentially consist of causes and effects. Each effect is determined necessarily by a previous cause, which itself was determined necessarily by an even earlier cause, and so on backward in time forever. An event is thereby defined in terms of a cause necessitating a particular and specific effect. In this view, events necessarily occur exactly the way they do (and cannot occur in any other way) because there is a previously existing specific and determinate causal nexus. This leads to one of the perennial problems of metaphysics: if everything is determined, are we, as human beings, really free and responsible moral agents? In other words, when I make a decision, am I really deciding for myself, or is my decision predetermined by earlier causes? I believe that Marcus' views on this matter are interesting but problematic. The problems are that (a) Marcus' views may not be internally consistent and (b) they may not be true to human nature and the lived human experience. Let's look a bit more closely at Marcus' views.

Marcus stresses throughout the *Meditations* that each person's place in the universe is small and insignificant. But what are we then to make of the aphorisms exhorting us to urgently make the most of life, since it is short, and to take one's stand nobly, to be an upright and just individual?

For example, he says:

> Think of your many years of procrastination; how the gods have repeatedly granted you further periods of grace, of which you have taken no advantage. It is time now to realize the nature of the universe to which you belong, and of that controlling power whose offspring you are; and to understand that your time has a limit set to it. Use it, then. . . . or it will be gone, and never in your power again.
>
> *(Book 2, sec. 4, p. 46)*

While this is one way to view the matter, it seems the entire Stoic cosmology could just as easily lend itself to an attitude of existential apathy and ennui. After all, if everything happens of necessity, why bother doing anything at all? Why not just stay at home and watch TV all day? The great stream of existence is going to flow according to its prescribed, determined path, regardless of our actions or nonactions. Furthermore, regarding ethics, why be moral at all? Why bother trying so hard to be an upright and just individual? If everything is determined and our lives are only moments in an eternity, why not act in a completely egoistic manner? Why not just "take the money and run"?

Indeed, the thoughtful reader may ask here: Is it just an evasion to believe in any sort of fate, determinism, even God (or any preordained order)? Is it an excuse to avoid taking responsibility for oneself? Some thinkers (perhaps the most famous being Sartre in the twentieth century) believe that when we are born, it is entirely up to us to make our lives whatever they are. Any deterministic account detracts from our facing up to this radical freedom and responsibility, and leads us to make excuses for our actions or nonactions. It is interesting that Marcus accepts deterministic assumptions but still holds to a strong sense of existential freedom and responsibility nonetheless. That is, he reaches some conclusions similar to Sartre's, even though he starts from radically different (perhaps diametrically opposed) premises. One must wonder if Marcus can, logically, believe in determinism and freedom at the same time.

The issue of determinism is central to Stoicism as a consolation philosophy. Marcus says we should distinguish between the things we can control or change and the things we cannot. External events cannot be controlled, but the way in which we deal with them internally can be. Marcus explains his view this way: "It lies in my own hands to ensure that no viciousness, cupidity, or turmoil of any kind finds a home in this soul of mine: it lies with me to perceive all things in their true light, and to deal with each of them as it merits" (Book 8, sec. 29, p. 127). And "If you are distressed by anything external, the pain is not due to the thing itself but to your own estimate of it; and this you have the power to revoke at any moment" (Book 8, sec. 47, 131).[4]

For example, let's say we are caught in the middle of a terrible (and completely unexpected) three-hour traffic jam. We know that being in the traffic jam is not something we can control. But how we react to it is within our control. It is up to us whether or not we are going to let it bother us or cause us stress and anxiety. We cannot control the world, but we can control our own emotional reactions to the world, according to Marcus. If this is true, nothing can really hurt us. When things look bad, all we need to do is remember this part of Stoicism, and we can free ourselves from life's burdens and pains.

However, one could object to this concept of self-control in the following way: if everything is regulated by reason and happens according to necessity, then aren't our internal reactions to things determined as well? If we should simply accept tragedies and calamities in the outer world as inevitable, then shouldn't we accept anger or sadness within ourselves as inevitable? It appears that Marcus' doctrine is logically inconsistent on this point, and if so, then it is a fairly serious problem in the Stoic philosophy. Is there some qualitative difference between external events (occurring in the physical world) and internal or mental events (presumably occurring in our minds), such that internal events are somehow outside of the determinism that (according to Stoic cosmology) characterizes the universe? If so, I don't see how Marcus has explicitly made a provision for this fundamental difference in the *Meditations*. And self-contradictory ideas cannot comfort people.

Moreover, if a Stoic says that the mind or soul is fundamentally different from the natural world—it is free, whereas the world is causally determined—

then it seems that people are not integral parts of the universe. We are set apart. But then the objective nature of the universe is not particularly relevant to human life, contrary to one of the fundamental Stoic assumptions.

Let's return to the terrible traffic jam. Perhaps we could refrain from becoming panicky or angry in the traffic jam for the first hour or two. But isn't it a natural and understandable human reaction, after sitting in traffic for two hours, to finally get annoyed and frustrated during the third hour, perhaps even to curse the fates that somehow arranged for us to be caught up in such a mess? Perhaps this reaction isn't going to change anything, but it is human nonetheless. Is the Stoic acceptance of fate or circumstances without complaint always a sincere, authentic human response, or does one really have to work at it? And if one has to work so hard at it, what does that say about its ulti-mate grounding in reality and human nature? It may be that Stoic resignation sounds attractive but is completely unrealistic.

Of course, many extremely influential and popular doctrines have con-tained some perspectives that seem foreign to human nature. Consider Jesus' famous Sermon on the Mount, so central to Christianity. One could say that the Christian doctrines of "turn the other cheek" and "loving one's enemies" are completely contrary to human nature. Perhaps some of the Eastern reli-gions, with their focus on "nonattachment," also seem difficult to apply in practice for the same reason. Does a philosophy have to be true to the way life really is in order for it to be valuable and helpful on the existential level? Most philosophers, I believe, would say yes. A doctrine filled with idealistic assump-tions may sound good on paper, but if it is impossible to put into practice, given human nature, then what good is it ultimately? It is irrelevant to real life.

However, a Stoic might still defend this view of philosophy. Marcus' pro-posals about controlling one's emotions can be conceived as ideals to strive for, even if we as imperfect human beings cannot achieve these ideals very often, or even ten percent of the time. Striving to be better is what life should be about. It gives us a purpose to live for. Perhaps one must train oneself to act nobly and rationally, even when (and especially when) the world around us is often ignoble and irrational. One shouldn't necessarily succumb to the baser elements of human nature or act in accordance with what is, in terms of behavior, the lowest common denominator. Perhaps that is what philosophy (and religion) are teaching. Hence the Talmud offers the following bit of wis-dom: "In a place where there are no men, strive to be a man." Human nature contains many elements, good and bad. Marcus exhorts us to nourish the good and resist the bad, however difficult that may be.

In examining possible contradictions in Marcus' philosophy, we may be asking the wrong questions. Perhaps we are asking him to provide us with detailed explanations of the world and human nature, when what he intended was to console people in a time of decline and uncertainty. If the purpose of philosophy is to provide consolation, then perhaps it should not dwell on everyday comings and goings, but should remind us of the larger world and what is possible. One can easily picture Marcus, after a brutal day of fighting barbarian tribes on the Danube, returning to his tent to take consolation in writing, reading, and rereading his diary. When the pressures of life (large and small) seem too much to bear, philosophy, in this view, has the value of putting them in perspective, reminding us how unimportant so many of these pressures and problems ultimately are.

> In the life of a man, his time is but a moment, his being an incessant flux, his senses a dim rushlight, his body a prey of worms, his soul an unquiet eddy, his fortune dark, and his fame doubtful. . . . Where, then, can man find the power to guide and guard his steps? In one thing and one thing alone: Philosophy. To be a philosopher is to keep unsullied and unscathed the divine spirit within him, so that it may transcend all pleasure and all pain, take nothing in hand without purpose and nothing falsely or with dissimulation, depend not on another's actions or inactions, accept each and every dispensation as coming from the same source as itself—and last and chief—wait with a good grace for death, as no more than a simple dissolving of the elements whereof each living thing is composed. . . .
>
> *(Book 2, sec. 17, p. 51)*

One might accept Marcus' inspiring vision of the purpose of philosophy even if one questions some of his particular assumptions. It is interesting to note that today, at the beginning of the twenty-first century, this conception of philosophy has, in some quarters, taken root again. There is today a fledgling movement called "philosophical counseling," that takes its therapeutic model not from psychology (e.g., psychoanalysis or behaviorism) but from philosophy. A philosophical counselor would see patients in a face-to-face situation and discuss their lives, their relations with others, and their feelings about these things. One of the founding practitioners of philosophical counseling, Lou Marinoff, says:

> you need a conception of how everything fits together—all the elements of your situation, all the elements of your world, all the elements of your philosophy. Finding that unity is what allows you to put a problem behind you. If you're stymied by a problem what you need is a conceptual breakthrough. Your habitual responses aren't enough.[5]

Can philosophy be of use in helping people cope with everyday problems? If, for example, someone is depressed or anxious much of the time, can philosophy be of use in helping him or her? Many schools of thought fashionable at the end of the twentieth century may not be very useful in this context. For example, some strains of contemporary analytic philosophy in the Anglo-American tradition do not raise questions about coping with the frustrations of life. Often the concerns of this movement have been with logic and language, and have been intelligible only to an academic audience.

How does Stoicism as a school of thought fare for this purpose? It is a complex matter. Many of the Hellenistic schools of thought, including Stoicism and Epicureanism, certainly appear to have valuable insights to offer in this connection. Are the insights ultimately useful? Let's examine the issues more closely. Can Stoicism guide philosophical counselors and help relieve the anxieties of contemporary life? Exactly how does Stoic philosophy offer consolation? Part of the answer is that it helps us realize the difference between things we can control and things we cannot, and it emphasizes the doctrine that everything that happens is for the best. Stoicism helps put things into perspective, so that the patient could perhaps try not to be troubled by concerns and issues he or she has no real control over anyway. The patient could learn not to be overly upset or overjoyed at the ups and downs of life, but rather to cultivate an indifferent acceptance of the day's happenings.

This viewpoint would provide consolation because if we realize that we cannot control external events, maybe we will stop trying to do so. Often it seems that we spend much time and energy trying to force the inevitable to be other than it is, and then fuming and fretting when it doesn't turn out the way we want it to. (The frustration caused by unrequited love is an example that comes to mind in this context.) Stoicism exhorts us just to "let things happen," and this acceptance dissolves the frustration and anxiety. Of course, it is still up to us to react to events in a rational rather than an irrational way, and this is not always easy. But if so much human energy is spent in a futile attempt to bend reality to our expectations, any viewpoint that suggests that this is pointless will perhaps provide comfort to our already overburdened souls.

However, Stoicism as a philosophy to live by faces some problems. My main objection is this: we may convince ourselves intellectually that we shouldn't be anxious about life's problems, big and small. But such anxiety may be something that doesn't go away so easily. Worry, fear, anger, and sadness are not propositions or theorems that one can prove or disprove, assent to or deny. In fact, sometimes the little frustrations of life (flat tires, broken toilets, and so on) can upset us the most, even while we know rationally that they are insignificant on the cosmic level. Worrying about things you cannot control or change may be futile, but it is human and everyone does it to varying degrees. Some nineteenth- and twentieth-century existentialist thinkers (such as Kierkegaard and Heidegger) have even speculated that anxiety in general is in fact rooted fundamentally and basically in the human condition itself. Existentialists discuss the concepts of dread and anxiety because they believe that we are thrown into the world and must live our entire lives in the face of impending death. We honestly can know nothing of death except that it is most certainly coming closer for us and our loved ones every day. Anxiety in the face of such a condition is the only possible response.

If this is true, then some of the insights of the *Meditations*, however rational and laudable, may be difficult to put into practice in everyday life. Can we just accept without complaint all that life throws at us? I think not.

Although the insights offered by Marcus may make us feel better as we are reading them, in the long run these insights may not be believable, reasonable, or even (as far as we can tell) true. Marcus certainly does not shy away from describing the brutal facts of life, and he may be right that we really have no choice but to accept life's ups and downs. But perhaps we have no choice but to accept our own anxieties and frustrations as well. In light of the inevitable problems we encounter and our fragile human nature, it is difficult to see how Stoicism can provide consolation. I'm afraid that the truth doesn't exist to dull our pain or to make our lives more bearable. Sometimes discovering the truth only makes us feel worse. These considerations, in conclusion, may delineate some of the limitations of Stoicism as a practical philosophy for actual living, breathing, imperfect human beings.

◠ NOTES

1. Marcus Aurelius, *Meditations,* translated by Maxwell Staniforth (London: Penguin, 1964), inside cover note.
2. Bertrand Russell, *A History of Western Philosophy* (New York: Simon & Schuster, 1945), 262.
3. Marcus Aurelius, *Meditations,* translated by Maxwell Staniforth (London: Penguin, 1964), translator's introduction, 13.
4. Alain de Botton makes the same point in discussing Seneca's version of Stoicism: "Though the terrain of frustration may be vast—from a stubbed toe to an untimely death—at the heart of every frustration lies a basic structure: the clash of a wish with an unyielding reality." Alain de Botton, *The Consolation of Philosophy* (New York: Pantheon Books, 2000), 110.
5. Lou Marinoff, *Plato, Not Prozac! Applying Philosophy to Everyday Problems* (New York: HarperCollins, 1999), 43.

◠ CHRONOLOGY

300 BCE	Zeno of Citium creates the Stoic school of philosophy in Athens
106	birth of Cicero, Roman statesman who helped bring Stoicism to Rome
44	assassination of Julius Caesar
31	Octavian (Augustus) defeats Anthony and Cleopatra at Actium, becomes emperor of Rome
3	birth of Seneca, Stoic philosopher, playwright, tutor of emperor Nero
50 AD	birth of Epictetus, former slave, whose Stoic teachings influenced Marcus Aurelius
64	Rome burns, Emperor Nero blames Christians

121	birth of Marcus Aurelius
138	adopted by emperor Antoninus Pius
165	plague spreads throughout the empire
180	death of Marcus Aurelius on the Roman frontier, near Vienna
235–285	years of civil war and turmoil throughout the empire
325	Emperor Constantine convenes the Council of Nicaea, consolidates the influence of Christianity in the empire
476	last Roman emperor overthrown, empire broken up into barbarian kingdoms

∿ SUGGESTED READINGS

Aurelius, Marcus. *Meditations*. Translated by Maxwell Staniforth. London: Penguin, 1964.

de Botton, A. *The Consolation of Philosophy*. New York: Pantheon Books, 2000.

Long, A.A. *Hellenistic Philosophy: Stoics, Epicureans, Skeptics*. Second Edition. Berkeley: University of California Press, 1986.

Long, A.A., and D.N. Sedley. *The Hellenistic Philosophers: Translations of the Principal Sources, with Philosophical Commentary*. Cambridge: Cambridge University Press, 1987.

Marinoff, L. *Plato, Not Prozac! Applying Philosophy to Everyday Problems*. New York: HarperCollins, 1999.

Nussbaum, M. *The Therapy of Desire*. Princeton: Princeton University Press, 1996.

Rist, J.M. *Stoic Philosophy*. Cambridge: Cambridge University Press, 1969.

Russell, B. *A History of Western Philosophy*. New York: Simon & Schuster, 1945.

CHAPTER 6

St. Thomas Aquinas
Philosophy as the Handmaid of Theology

Ronald Rainey

~ Preview

St. Thomas Aquinas sees philosophy as useful but limited. All people by nature desire to understand, and philosophy is one way to discover the truth, but it isn't the best way. Revelation based on faith is the best way. Philosophy can help us understand the complex truths that we know through revelation. For example, we know from Scripture that God created the world, Aquinas says. He believes we can also prove, rationally, that a Creator exists. Philosophy employs reason and observation, without relying on any religious assumptions, to show why the scriptural lesson must be true. But we need Scripture to learn more about God's character and plans. Aquinas wanted to show that philosophy is not a threat to religion. On the contrary, truth is all one. If reli-

gion possesses the truth and philosophy possesses the truth, then religion and philosophy cannot be in conflict, although religion can give us truths that are beyond the reach of philosophy. (The Editor)

∾ Introduction

It should be noted from the outset that St. Thomas Aquinas occupies a special place in any survey of Western philosophers, but it is also an odd place. When telling the story of Western philosophy, historians often take a chronological approach, and Aquinas is important because he is the representative of medieval thought in a chronology that tends to emphasize the thinkers at the beginning (since the roots of philosophical discourse are to be found among the ancient Greeks) and the end (since the most direct influence on modern thought has been made by more recent philosophers who flourished since the Enlightenment). In such a chronological arrangement, therefore, which attributes great significance to the ancients and to the moderns, the special place occupied by Aquinas might be described as the connective tissue. He might be seen as a representative of all the thinkers in between, in the so-called Middle Ages, who held the philosophical tradition together in an age of confusion and turmoil, and who were thereby able to transmit that tradition from the ancients to the moderns. If this were Aquinas' only virtue, it would be enough to qualify him as an important player in the continuum of Western philosophy and it would certainly win for him a boldface bullet on the timeline of Western philosophers. Aquinas, however, was also a saint[1] of the Catholic Church, and herein lies his real distinction among Western philosophers.

Not that Aquinas was the only saint to come down the philosophical turnpike. He was preceded by such outstanding luminaries as St. Augustine of Hippo, St. Anselm of Canterbury, and St. Albert the Great (Aquinas' teacher), among others. Historians often make the point that the medieval period was a time of deep religious faith, sometimes explained as a search for order in reaction to the chaos caused by the decline and fall of the Roman Empire. The Middle Ages are populated in our imaginations by monks and nuns and pilgrims and penitents; the dominant institution in medieval Europe was the Church; and the same religious fervor that sparked the Crusades, the Inquisition, the founding of the Franciscan and Dominican orders of monks, the building of great cathedrals in every major city of Europe and countless roadside chapels, the writing of Dante's *Divine Comedy,* and the outbreak of the Protestant Reformation and the religious wars of the sixteenth and seventeenth centuries also inspired the scholars of medieval universities. Aquinas stands out among them because he practiced philosophy in the service of theology. The "Angelic Doctor" is what he was called, and he is equally revered by students of the Middle Ages as both a philosopher and a theologian. It is only fitting that medieval philosophers should be represented here by a saint.

A story told by some of Aquinas' biographers, perhaps more of a legend than anything else, illustrates clearly how medieval religious fervor inspired Aquinas in his twin vocations as a theologian and a philosopher. Aquinas was born around 1225 in the castle of Roccasecca, near Aquino in southern Italy, the son of a nobleman and, through his mother, a relative of the Emperor Frederick II. At around the age of five, Aquinas was sent to the famous Benedictine Abbey of Monte Cassino, which had been founded by St. Benedict in the sixth century, to begin his education in the liberal arts taught by the Benedictine monks. He remained there for about nine years, studying the basic subjects of grammar (how to write), rhetoric (how to speak), and logic (how to think), which comprised the so-called *trivium*, or three-part way to learning. After these basic liberal arts were mastered, the more difficult *quadrivium*, or four-part way to more advanced learning, would be pursued, comprising arithmetic, geometry, music, and astronomy. Altogether, the three subjects of the *trivium* and the four subjects of the *quadrivium* added up to the Seven Liberal Arts, which served as the basic training of every educated person in the Middle Ages.

At around the age of fourteen, Aquinas began his studies at the University of Naples, founded by his imperial relative, and there he is known to have studied Aristotle's philosophy. Somewhere along the line, Aquinas decided to become a monk, and he informed his parents of his decision to join the Dominicans, an order of mendicant preachers founded by St. Dominic Guzman in 1215, but his parents were apparently unhappy with his decision. They were not opposed to an ecclesiastical career for Thomas, but perhaps their aspirations for their well-educated son were more elevated than the life of a begging friar was likely to satisfy. Perhaps they envisioned a more lofty ecclesiastical career, helped along with important family connections. But Thomas was stubborn, and he insisted on becoming a Dominican friar.

As he was about to embark on his journey to Paris to join the Dominicans at the university there, his own older brothers wrestled him to the ground, carried him off to a tower in the family castle, and imprisoned him there for about a year. He was eighteen years old. One might have expected a lot of whining and self-pity, demands to be released, perhaps some willingness to alter his plans in order to soften the hardened position of his family against his desire to become a monk. We are told, however, that Aquinas spent his time reading the Bible from cover to cover and the *Metaphysics* of Aristotle. One night (and it is said that his mother was behind this caper), a voluptuous young woman was admitted into Thomas' chamber, willingly or not it is hard to say, apparently in the hope that his solitude would have made his flesh weak and lusty and an easy mark for temptation, perhaps in the hope that a sexual encounter with the woman would change his mind about becoming a celibate monk. Thomas is said to have pulled something out of the fire, perhaps a burning ember or a hot poker, and brandishing it before him, he chased the frightened young girl out of the tower chamber, terrified, leaving a charred sign of the Cross on the inside of the door as it closed behind her, an emblem of his rejection of this lusty world and the symbol of Jesus Christ, whose servant and disciple Thomas would become as a friar. Upon his release from the tower, he set off for Paris, undeterred in his monastic vocation, where he would become the leading theological scholar, teacher, and writer of his day. Aquinas' life provides an excellent example of medieval religious fervor.

∾ The Medieval and Modern World Views

And yet it must seem odd, to contemporary college students at any rate, to read about a philosopher who is also a saint. The scholars of our own age have compartmentalized philosophical speculation and the study of religion to such an extent that we moderns tend to think that the two are completely different and incompatible enterprises. Philosophers are guided by pure reason, while theologians tend to be believers who are guided by religious faith. Philosophers are lovers of wisdom who may or may not be on the lookout for truth, but they are led to whatever truths they find through the use of reason and dialectic; theologians, on the other hand, already accept the Truth, as they understand it, through their religious faith in revelation, and their theological studies are designed to confirm what the believer already accepts through religious faith. The contemporary college student, who is encouraged to be skeptical about religion, may well be inclined to ask how a theologian, or for that matter any religious believer, can be engaged in what we think of today as philosophy. That is because we moderns have a view of the world in which philosophical speculation, as well as scientific inquiry, are supposed to be open-ended inquiries, guided by rational processes or methods that do not have fixed outcomes. Both philosophers and scientists, according to this world view, should arrive at conclusions that are valid because they are based on the evidence they find in the course of a process or method by which they proceed. Conclusions should come at the end of that process and should not be influenced by any preconceived ideas. To the modern mind, nothing is true until it is proven to be true.

There are some dramatic differences between the medieval Catholic world view of Thomas Aquinas and the more skeptical and materialist world view shared by many of those who teach and study at contemporary universities, and the greatest difference of all is the modern-day emphasis on the material world. Modern intellectuals tend to be much more interested in things they can see and touch, as opposed to underlying spiritual or religious truths, and this is certainly true of the scientific community. While Thomas Aquinas would have believed that the existence of God was an objective truth, for example, modern scientists would insist that since there are no scientific proofs of God's existence, the question of the existence of God is moot from the point of view of science. Scientists might concede that the existence of God could be accepted by a believer as a subjective truth, and indeed, some scientists themselves are believers, but they would certainly not accept the existence of God or any other religious belief as an objective truth.

We need to keep in mind that in the centuries between the age of Aquinas (c. 1225–1274) and our own times, there were several major intellectual movements that redirected the attention of Western thinkers away from the spiritual world for which Aquinas had so much regard and toward a greater emphasis on the material world. The Italian Renaissance (1300–1600), for example, encouraged renewed interest in the study of humanity, using the works of the ancients as models, and Renaissance humanists were more famous for their interest in human beings than for their interest in the divine. The Scientific Revolution (1600–1700) focused attention on the physical world, as opposed to the metaphysical, and demanded physical evidence in order to prove every hypothesis; scientists believe in what they can measure and observe; they tend to be skeptical about everything else and, faced with such skepticism, Church leaders during the period of the Scientific Revolution became overly suspicious of scientists (the case of Galileo comes quickly to mind).[2] The philosophes of the Enlightenment period (1700–1800) placed reason on a pedestal, while denouncing superstition, and sometimes implied that religion was the same thing as superstition. And both the French Revolution of the late eighteenth century and the *Communist Manifesto* of the mid-nineteenth century, inspired by Enlightenment ideas, declared war on religion and created a serious divide between believers and nonbelievers.

Emerging from this intellectual rebellion against the metaphysical and the spiritual was the modern world's emphasis on the physical and the material. Both capitalism and Marxism, for example, were the products of this intellectual climate. Religion was considered the enemy of the Enlightenment "idea of progress," and it is no coincidence that it was in this period that the "separation of church and state" became the preferred political ideal among such enlightened thinkers as the authors of the U.S. Constitution. University curricula evolved slowly during these centuries, reflecting some of the changes noted here, from the medieval European university, where theology was considered the "queen of the sciences," to the contemporary American university, where undergraduate degrees in business and the natural sciences are far more coveted nowadays than degrees in religious studies. Religion still exists in the modern world, of course, but those in charge of contemporary secular universities tend to consider religion as something of an embarrassment (at best) or as entirely irrelevant to the questions addressed by a modern university (at worst). In our more skeptical and materialistic age, philosophers and scientists have very little to say about God.

Aquinas would not have shared this modern view of the world. His medieval Catholic world view placed God at the center of everything that was worth studying, which included the natural world and human behavior. The purpose of learning, the very reason that universities existed, was to know as much about God as possible. To focus only on the material and the visible would have been considered absurd by Aquinas, since the spiritual and invisible forces that animate and govern the physical world are of much greater importance. Aquinas believed that there is a very close connection between the spiritual and the material, the invisible and the visible. Everything that is material (and visible) was created by God (Who is invisible); every human body (which is visible and also mortal) is animated by a soul (which is invisible and immortal); the Christian community, also known as the "communion of saints," was composed not only of living Christians, both clergy and laity (visible to one another), but also of angels, saints, and the souls of those being purified in purgatory, as well as the immortal souls of those in heaven. (Angels and souls could not be seen by mortals on earth under ordinary circumstances, although there are recorded "visions" of spiritual beings by some mortals, a famous example being the visions of St. Joan of Arc,[3] who had visions of several saints and who heard their voices encouraging her to lead the French forces to victory.) Aquinas believed that there were communications and interactions between the visible and invisible realms, through the prayers of mortal Christians on earth and the intercessions of the saints in heaven, for instance, and through God's answers to those prayers delivered ordinarily in everyday and unseen ways, and extraordinarily and only on rare occasions through miracles. Being unable to see some aspect of the spiritual world, such as an angel or a soul, was the function of the limitations of a human being's senses and not a valid reason for ignoring the spiritual world; a later Dominican friar would pray, "Lift me up, Strong Son of God, that I might see further," as if religious truth were just beyond one's ordinary field of vision. Just because a human being could touch and see a rock did not make the rock more "real" than the person's soul, which he or she could not touch or see. Both the rock and the soul are creations of God, although since the soul is immortal, it is therefore more significant, and Aquinas would not have had much respect for the work of modern-day geologists, for example, who are interested in rocks but not in souls.

One knew for certain that God had created the world because Scripture had revealed this to be the case. It was the duty of human beings to learn as much as possible about God during one's life, and it was the hope of every Christian that his or her soul, after death, would be judged worthy to live through eternity in the presence of the Divine Creator. Human beings had at their disposal a variety of means by which they could learn about God, but the two most important were the disciplines of theology and philosophy.

Theologians would study the Scriptures, the revealed Word of God, as well as the interpretations of Scripture by the "authorities," in order to discover what God revealed about Himself and how serious students of Scripture in the past, some of them divinely inspired, explained some of the more mysterious truths. The Truth about God, according to the Catholic Church, was arrived at by the combined study of both Scripture (the Old and New Testaments) and Tradition (the interpretations of Scripture by the "Fathers of the Church"). Philosophy, however, could be helpful to theologians as the "handmaid of theology," and the medievals would have used the word "philosophy" in the most inclusive sense, involving every kind of intellectual activity, including the sorts of questions that we moderns generally associate with both philosophy and the natural sciences. Aristotle had divided the study of philosophy into several categories, giving the name "natural philosophy" to the branch of philosophy that studied the physical world (Aristotle's *Physics* was the textbook for this branch of philosophy) and giving the name "metaphysics" to the branch of philosophy that focused on things "beyond the physical" (Aristotle's *Metaphysics* was used as the textbook for this branch of philosophy). Therefore, theologians could employ natural philosophy as well as metaphysics as aids in understanding the truths revealed in Scripture.

Aquinas believed that God revealed Himself to human beings in Scripture. He also believed that reason was God's gift to human beings and that this gift naturally enabled them to inquire about the world around them and to come to rational conclusions about the human condition. Arriving at the Truth was the essential aim of scholarly enterprise. Aquinas believed that human beings could accept religious Truth blindly through faith, but he also believed that human beings could use reason to come to an understanding of that Truth and they could observe the world around them. And in learning more about God's Creation, they would learn more about the Creator as well. Aquinas would have thought that physics and metaphysics were both helpful to the scholar who wanted to know more about God's Creation, and they were helpful for the same reason, namely, that God had given these gifts (the senses with which to observe and touch the physical world, and reason with which to inquire about the world and find answers) as tools for investigating the world that He had created. It was for this purpose that he studied philosophy.

Aquinas the theologian would have considered philosophy, the handmaid of theology, to be a supplement to theology in a coherent and unified quest for knowledge about God. He would not have considered theologians and philosophers to be in competition with one another, nor would he have thought that the findings of either theology or philosophy (including natural philosophy, or what we think of in modern times as science) could contradict or disprove anything that was revealed in Scripture. Theology and philosophy were means toward the same end, namely, the study of God and His Creation. Separating them, and building walls between the disciplines of theology and philosophy, and even taller walls between religion and science, would be left to a later era. Aquinas sought the Truth, and he was convinced that both the faith of the theologian and the reason of the philosopher were helpful means of achieving that end. The aim of this essay will be to describe the method used by Aquinas in his work and to examine some of the topics he addressed, with a view to explaining how a theologian of such intense religious belief could also be one of the greatest philosophers of his day.

~ Aquinas' Method

Thomas' reading list during his year of captivity in that tower at the age of eighteen, the Scriptures and the philosophy of Aristotle, set the stage for his later career as a teacher and a writer. Professors in medieval universities gave "lectures" or readings of texts, combined with their own "commentaries" offering explanations of difficult passages and solutions to thorny problems. Aquinas' prolific career as a writer would mirror his teaching experience and interests. Among his many writings, Thomas' first major theological work was a commentary written between 1254 and 1256 on the *Sentences,* a major compendium of theological opinions and judgments compiled by Peter Lombard a century earlier that served as something of a textbook for students of theology. This commentary by Aquinas was followed by three theological compendia compiled by him, borrowing some of the organizing techniques of Peter Lombard and other earlier authors. His encyclopedic *Summa Contra Gentiles* (as it is known to us nowadays, but which Aquinas himself called "On the Truth of the Catholic Faith") was produced between 1259 and 1264 at the request of Pope Gregory X. Aquinas was by this time a world-renowned theologian, and the pope had asked him to produce a set of arguments to be used in the conversion of the Muslims in Spain; the work therefore assumes a reading audience of Muslim intellectuals, although it is more likely that his actual reading audience was composed of other Catholic theologians. Aquinas' most famous work, the *Summa of Theology* (officially known as the *Summa Theologiae* and more popularly as the *Summa Theologica*), was written between 1265 and 1272, but it was unfinished at the time of Aquinas' death in 1274.[4] Aquinas also produced the *Compendium of Theology* in 1273. His other writings included a political treatise, *On the Government of Rulers,* written between 1265 and 1267 at the request of the king of Cyprus, who had asked Aquinas for his advice on the best form of government; Aquinas obliged the king, who died before the work was completed, by expressing his opinion that the best government was provided by a virtuous king who obeyed the Ten Commandments. Aquinas was also the author of many theological works on particular topics, such as his treatises *On Truth, On the Power of God, On Evil, On Spiritual Creatures,* and *On the Soul,* just to name a few of these works in order to indicate the breadth of his interests.[5]

In his careers as a teacher and a writer, Aquinas employed a method known as the "scholastic" method, developed in the schools (the *scholae*) of the Middle Ages and used in medieval universities by the schoolmen (who were known as "scholastics") as both a teaching method and a tool for organizing their written works. During the twelfth century, the scholastic method was developed by theologians and canon lawyers looking for ways to juxtapose different opinions, and sometimes contradictory statements, by authorities in either theology or canon law, for the purpose of finding the truth or at least some middle ground between extremely different opinions and judgments. Peter Abelard (c. 1080–1142) was a pioneer in this development. In his book *Sic et Non (Yes and No)*, written in 1123, Abelard compiled theological judgments on a variety of topics from leading authorities in Church history, with the particular purpose of pointing out that different authorities gave different answers to the same theological questions. Abelard collected theological arguments on both sides of an issue and lined them up in columns to point out the differences in opinion.

In the 1150s, Peter Lombard (c. 1095–1160) compiled his *Sentences* along similar lines, but he added a step to what would become the scholastic method; whereas Abelard in *Sic et Non* indicated that some authorities answered a theological question in one way and other authorities answered the same question differently, Peter Lombard in the *Sentences* indicated his preference for a particular set of answers by a particular set of authorities. Likewise, the canon lawyer Gratian, whose *Decretum* was compiled around the year 1140, organized his work on canon law in a similar fashion, stating a question of canon law and then finding different authorities, among the Church Fathers, popes, council pronouncements, canon law cases from earlier times, or eminent bishops and canon lawyers, who gave different answers to canon law questions. Gratian compiled the authorities in a pro and con fashion, depending on how they approached the legal question, and he sought a resolution to the problem by examining the variety of opinions and finding some sort of consensus or reconciliation.

It was in this tradition that Aquinas perfected the scholastic method. The scholastic method consisted of a three-part process: posing a question (the *Quaestio*), offering some opposing arguments (the *Disputatio*) advanced by a variety of authorities, and then finding some resolution (the *Sententia*) to the arguments and thereby allowing Aquinas to express his own opinions or judgments. Definitions were very important to Aquinas, and the scholastic method relied on precise definitions of words and careful distinctions to resolve conflicting opinions on the same topics by different authorities. The most important element of the scholastic method, however, was the disciplined use of logical thinking in analyzing the problem at hand, and the brand of logic preferred by Aquinas was Aristotelian logic. During his teaching and writing careers, Aquinas posed and published thousands of questions. He was a wide-ranging scholar, and the scholastic method allowed him to pose a variety of questions, exhibit his extensive readings in the works of the authorities, and express his opinions on any number of issues, both abstract and concrete, both eternal and contemporary.

In providing the arguments in the second step of the scholastic method (the *Disputatio,* or conflicting opinions), Aquinas was able to explore the many sides of a problem and to allow his readers to understand the complexity of an issue. The authorities from whom he quoted represented the whole body of learning that a medieval scholar would have had at his disposal. Of course, in theological matters he quoted from Scripture, the revealed Word of God in both the Old and New Testaments, but he also relied on the interpretations of Scripture expressed in the works of the Church Fathers. The official "fathers" of the Latin Church were St. Augustine (from whom Aquinas quoted extensively), St. Ambrose, St. Jerome, and St. Gregory the Great, but he would also cite, when it was useful for him to do so, many other medieval theological authorities such as Boethius, Isidore of Seville, and the Franciscan theologian St. Bonaventure. He cited the opinions of popes across the timeline of Church history and, for legal questions, the most famous canon law collections such as Gratian's *Decretum* and the *Decretals* of Pope Gregory IX. Two of his most frequently cited authorities were St. Paul (to whom he referred simply as "The Apostle") for theological questions and Aristotle (to whom he referred simply as "The Philosopher") for philosophical matters. Whenever he mentions The Apostle, the reader should understand that he means St. Paul, and whenever he refers to The Philosopher, the reader should understand that he means Aristotle.

A close examination of one of the questions posed by Aquinas in his *Summa of Theology* will illustrate Aquinas' reliance on the accepted authorities of the day and provide an example of his use of the scholastic method. This particular example has been chosen, from among countless possibilities, because of the diversity of authorities cited and because it underscores the importance of definition to Aquinas in his handling of theological and philosophical questions. This example serves as an interesting point of entry into the mind of a medieval scholar. In one of the many volumes of the *Summa* (volume 41), Aquinas identifies the "virtues of justice in the human community," and in this list of virtues he includes piety, respect, and obedience.[6] Aquinas is aware that the word "piety," or *pietas* in Latin, has a diversity of meanings; to be pious is to be dutiful, reverent, devoted, and loyal; one might picture in one's mind the famous statues of Michelangelo and other artists of the medieval and Renaissance periods, known as *pieta* statues, using the Italian form of this word, in which Jesus is depicted in the arms of his grief-stricken Mother, and get an idea of the way in which the word *pietas* is meant to convey the relationship between them. Among the ancient Romans, the word *pietas* connoted the attitude one was to have toward one's family, and it was contrasted with the word *fidelitas,* which connoted the attitude one was to have toward outsiders. Piety was also the proper attitude that a believer was to have toward God.

Aquinas examines the issue of piety by posing the *Quaestio* "Whether piety is directed towards certain people?" with a view to identifying the range of people to whom piety was owed. He provides quotations from three different authorities, all of whom use the word "piety" in the passages cited, but all of them use the word in quite a different way, and it is certain that Aquinas chose his examples to underscore the complexity and richness of this issue. He begins with a quotation from St. Augustine's *City of God* and goes on to express an opinion based on Augustine's comment:

> The range of piety does not seem to be a particular class of people. For Augustine observes that *pietas* "is usually taken in its strict sense to mean the worship of God." The worship of God, however, refers to acts offered not to human beings, but to God alone. So the special reference of *pietas* is not to human beings at all.

Next, Aquinas provides a passage from St. Gregory the Great's *Moralia*, in which he uses the word *pietas*:

> Further, Gregory states that *pietas* has its days of feasting, for it fills the heart's desires with works of mercy. Works of mercy, as Augustine points out (in *De Doctrina Christiana*) are to be shown to all. The reach of piety is, therefore, not to be narrowed down to special individuals.

And thirdly, Aquinas offers a comment by Aristotle, which does not seem at first glance to have anything to do with piety:

> Further, as The Philosopher notes (in his *Ethics*), in human affairs there are many relationships other than those between blood relatives or fellow countrymen, each of them being the basis of some form of friendship. And a gloss on II Timothy—"having an appearance of godliness" seems to identify friendship with piety—the range of piety, therefore, is wider at least than relatives and compatriots.

Based on these three quotations, therefore, the question as to the range of piety, that is, to whom piety is owed, becomes rather complicated. Augustine uses the word in such a way as to suggest that we do not owe piety to any human beings at all, since it is owed only to God. St. Gregory the Great, however, uses the term in such a way as to suggest that we owe piety to everyone we meet. And if one were to equate "piety" and "friendship," as one medieval glossator on Scripture apparently has done, then what Aristotle has to say about friendship may also apply to piety, according to Aquinas.

Things get more complicated now, when Aquinas adds to the mix another authoritative statement from Cicero. He gives the definition of piety provided by the famous Roman orator, which seems to suggest that piety is owed to particular persons:

> On the other hand [this is the way in which Aquinas introduces the *Disputatio*, or argument] Cicero maintains "this is *pietas*, to fulfill one's duty and conscientious service towards our own flesh and blood and those having the interests of our country at heart [which is to say, to our relatives and to our countrymen].

In what we have seen so far, Aquinas has given the reader a lesson in the variety of usages of the word "piety."

In the next section of his presentation on this topic, the *Sententia*, Aquinas demonstrates how the various meanings of the word are related to one another, and explains how the different ways in which the three authorities quoted above used the word "piety" can be reconciled with one another. Aquinas first gives his opinion as to the best way of understanding the concept of piety. He says that indebtedness to others depends on their superiority, or the benefits one receives from them. By these standards, God is supreme and we owe the greatest piety to Him. Next come parents, relatives, and countrymen, to whom we owe a degree of piety, but not as much as to God.

Aquinas now returns to the original three statements by Augustine, Gregory, and Aristotle to resolve how the different ways in which they used the same word can be understood as part of the same discussion of this virtue. To St. Augustine's assertion that piety has only to do with God, Aquinas now replies that Scripture teaches us to honor our parents. "The kind of homage owed to God," he says, "already embraces as but a partial form of itself the kind owed to parents," so the two expressions of piety are not in conflict. In answer to St. Gregory the Great, who connects piety with works of mercy due to everyone, Aquinas replies that since it is God who urges us to perform acts of mercy toward all people, being pious toward God is easily joined with being pious toward others. And perhaps to justify the glossator's equation of friendship and piety, Aquinas concludes this presentation by tying together Cicero's definition of piety with Aristotle's comments about friendship:

> Ties of blood and native origin have a more direct bearing upon the sources of our existence and development than do other human relationships; this is why the term "piety" has a more apposite application here.

In examining this single question, Aquinas brought into the discussion the voices of two Fathers of the Church, a distinguished Roman orator, and the great Greek philosopher. Aquinas' medieval Catholic world view allowed him to conclude that all of these authorities, some of them Christians and some of them pagans who flourished before the Christian era and without the benefit of having read the Scriptures, really had similar ideas in mind when speaking about piety, although each authority expressed only part of the truth in each of his comments. It was Aquinas' task to fill in what was left unsaid, to tie it all together for them. It was in this way that Aquinas attempted to demonstrate in his work that conflicting views could be understood to be in complete harmony with one another. The scholastic method was a tool that was useful to Aquinas in his attempts to reconcile faith and reason.

ᕽ God, Nature, and Humanity

Aquinas had not even celebrated his fiftieth birthday when he died in 1274, during a journey from Italy to France, where he was planning to participate at the invitation of the pope in a church council being held in Lyons. His scholarly career, if we consider his entry into the Sorbonne as a student in 1245 as the starting point, consisted of about a decade of study and reading and then about twenty years as a teacher and writer. It is therefore all the more remarkable that in the course of this relatively short career, Aquinas managed to produce such a prodigious amount of work on so many different topics. While it would be impossible in a brief essay to discuss all of the topics considered by Aquinas throughout his career, or even to list all of them, we can get some idea of the scope of Aquinas' work by examining three major areas of interest to which all of Aquinas' works were related. Aquinas was most interested in inquiring about God, nature, and humanity, and he was especially interested in pointing out how all three of these topics related to one another, demonstrating the harmony of God's creation. It will be under these three headings, and with a view to discovering Aquinas' use of philosophy in his inquiries about God, nature, and humanity, that we examine some of the topics treated by Aquinas in his many writings.

As a theologian, of course, Aquinas was interested in learning as much about God as possible. Theologians are interested in defining God, discovering His nature, uncovering His plan of creation, and speculating on the relationship between God and humanity, asking such questions as what God expects of humans and how humans are supposed to behave if they are to live according to the Laws of God. That God exists is taken as a given by theologians, belief in God's existence being the starting point of religious faith, and Scripture providing all that a believer really needs to know about the mysteries of revealed truth. Philosophers, on the other hand, are more interested in determining how the human faculty of reason can be used in the discovery of God and how reason can serve as an aid in understanding the mysteries of faith. Long before Aquinas, there were many Christian philosophers, such as St. Augustine of Hippo and St. Anselm of Canterbury, who employed philosophy in the service of religious belief; to express it in the elegant words of St. Anselm, these philosophers used philosophy in the service of "Faith seeking to understand" (*"Fides quarens intellectum"*).

Augustine and Anselm belonged to a school of Christian philosophers who attempted to use philosophy to explain the mysteries of religious faith, in the hope that the natural faculty of reason could be used by all human beings to come to a better understanding of God and His mysteries as revealed in Scripture. Some mysteries of the Christian faith, such as why God took on flesh (the Incarnation) or how it was that one God could be described as being composed of three Persons, the Father, the Son, and the Holy Spirit (the theological concept known as the "Trinity"), or why God chose to suffer in the Person of Jesus Christ (the Redemption), were truths revealed by Scripture that the Christian believer was expected to accept on faith. These truths were outside the personal experience of believers and were not demonstrable through any sort of physical evidence such as the evidence that might be required by a scientist in a scientific investigation, for example. Nor could these theological truths be proven through any kind of evidence that would be accepted in a court of law to meet the standard of proof beyond a reasonable doubt. Human reason, however, can provide some help in trying to understand these theological concepts, even though this understanding would be incomplete and imperfect precisely because human understanding is incomplete and imperfect. Religious Truth in its entirety is more than the human mind can comprehend; theologians sometimes argue that although the human mind may have been originally designed to comprehend God's truths, one of the consequences of the Fall of Adam and Eve was to forfeit the easy knowledge of God, and one of the penalties of the Fall would henceforth be humanity's struggle to come to know and understand God. But the human mind could use the natural faculty of reason, which was one of God's gifts to human beings, to understand some of that truth. For Christian philosophers such as Augustine and Anselm, however, faith had to come first. St. Anselm used the motto *"Credo ut intelligam"* ("I believe in order to understand") to indicate that a believer could use his or her natural faculty of reason to come to some understanding of the mysteries of faith. To Augustine and Anselm, philosophy could be helpful to believers as a tool for understanding more clearly what the believer already believed.

St. Anselm was most famous for his celebrated attempt to prove the existence of God through the use of human reason or, more particularly, through the use of logic and dialectic. Anselm offered several different proofs of the existence of God, but he is most celebrated for his "ontological argument."[7] (He did not call the argument by this name, but modern philosophers adopted this name for the argument following the eighteenth-century philosopher Immanuel Kant, who used the word "ontological" in his work to connote the study of "being"). Anselm made use of philosophy in order to explain to a believer why belief in the existence of God made sense. He began his argument with a definition of God, asserting that "God was understood by all believers to be that Being greater than which no other being could be conceived." This was a rather simple statement that all those who already believe in God can readily accept, namely, that there is no being greater than God. God is perfect Being. To suppose that some other being could be greater than God would mean that God was not perfect, which would contradict the definition of God with which we started. Indeed, God introduces Himself to Man in one passage of the Old Testament by saying, "I am Who am" (see Exodus 3:14), and one could therefore argue that God is Being itself, the source of all other being(s).

Anselm goes on to say, however, that the very definition of God as that Being greater than which no other can be conceived implies the very existence of God. And this is how he proves it. Anselm asserts that the biblical fool who claims that he does not believe in God [Psalm 14:1: "The impious fool says in his heart 'There is no God'"] must have an understanding of what the term "God" means, which is to say that in his mind even the fool can conceive of a Being greater than which no other being can be conceived. Even if the fool claims not to believe in this Being, he can conceive of such a perfect Being in order to deny its existence. Anselm points out, however, that if the concept of God were merely an idea in the mind of the fool, a "Being greater than which no other being can be conceived" that actually *existed* would be *greater* than the idea of God in the mind of the fool; greater because He exists; greater because of His being or existence. And therefore, if the fool recognizes the possibility of a Being greater than which no other can be conceived, by having a an idea of such a Being, then God must truly exist, because the Being who truly exists is greater than the idea.

Does Anselm really prove the existence of God through his ontological argument? Or does he perform some philosophical sleight of hand, as some of his contemporaries and many moderns think he does? For starters, Anselm probably did not expect nonbelievers to pay any attention to his argument. His reading audience would have been his fellow monks and theologians, Christians who already accepted the existence of God through faith and who sought to articulate, through language (the definition used by Anselm at the beginning of the argument), and to understand, through reason (using the natural faculty of reason to draw out the logical implications of the definition). Anselm was perfectly convinced that God existed, and he probably did think that he had used philosophy to demonstrate that what the believer already believed to be true could also be demonstrated to make logical sense.

Thomas Aquinas, however, belonged to another school of Christian philosophers who turned Anselm's motto, "I believe in order to understand," on its head. Aquinas was interested in proving that in the search for Truth, one could arrive at religious faith because of philosophical inquiry. He introduced the motto *"Intelligo ut credam"* ("I understand in order that I might believe"). And he set out to prove through Aristotelian logic that believing in God not only made sense, as Anselm had demonstrated to believers in an earlier century, but that an honest philosopher, properly considering the logical arguments that Aquinas would present, would have to admit the necessity of believing in God. Early in his *Summa of Theology,* Aquinas poses the question "Does God exist?"[8] and he offers several answers to the question through philosophical reasoning in both the *Disputatio* section of the presentation, where he offers conflicting arguments on the topic, and in the *Sententia* portion of the presentation, where he offers his own opinions. After posing the question, Aquinas discusses conflicting points of view, including denials that God exists. The first objection to the proposition that God exists arises from the fact of evil. Since God is all good, there should be no evil in the world, inasmuch as perfect goodness should be able to destroy any evil that happened to get in its way. But we all know that there is evil in the world, Aquinas asserts; and therefore there is no God. In the second objection, Aquinas appeals to a philosophical axiom, namely, that "what can be explained by a few causes should not be explained by many." He observes, however, that just about everything we see around us can be explained by immediate causes without ever assuming that God exists, since "natural things are explained by natural causes." If this is true, who needs supernatural explanations? There is, Aquinas allows here, "no need to suppose that God exists."

However, Aquinas points out, Scripture positively says that there is a God (he provides the passage from Exodus cited previously as evidence). And since Scripture is recognized as an authority of the first rank, a serious Christian philosopher is obliged to try to understand how the two objections can be reconciled with the fact that Scripture definitely says that God exists.

Aquinas goes on to offer five different philosophical arguments in favor of the existence of God. As we shall see later, these five "proofs" do not assume a belief in God, as Anselm's ontological argument assumes (Anselm, after all, began with a believer's definition of God); rather, the starting points for these five arguments are philosophical in nature and rely on observation and logical reasoning to lead in the direction of accepting the existence of God. A close examination of the first of these five proofs of the existence of God presented by Aquinas in his *Summa of Theology* allows us to get a better understanding of how Aquinas found philosophy to be a useful tool in pursuing theological truth.

Aquinas begins his first proof of the existence of God by citing a scientific assertion from Aristotle's *Physics,* namely, that "it is certain and evident to our senses that things are in motion in this world." This is a statement that could be made by anyone who uses his or her senses, and there is certainly no need at the beginning of this argument to assume that God exists. He continues in the Aristotelian vein by reasoning that everything that is in motion is moved by something else, "for nothing can move unless it has the potentiality of acquiring the perfection of that towards which it moves." Moving is an action, inasmuch as moving something is to make actual what is potential; one could say that something that can be moved has the potential to be moved; by moving it, the potentiality becomes actuality. What is potential cannot make itself actual. Aquinas says:

> Therefore everything that moves must be moved by something else. If that by which it is moved also moves, it must itself be moved by something else and that by something else again. But things cannot go on forever because then there

would be no first mover, and consequently no subsequent mover since interme-
diate things move only from the motion they receive from the first mover. . . .
Therefore it is necessary to go back to some first mover who is not moved by
anyone, and this everyone understands as God.[9]

Has Aquinas proved the existence of God in this so-called proof? Unlike
Anselm, he did not begin with a definition of God that believers already
accept; rather, he began with a common observation about the world, the
observation that things move. In order to bolster the reader's confidence in his
or her own observations of motion, Aquinas thinks that he strengthens his
argument by noting that Aristotle makes the same observation that things
move; and this observation is authoritative precisely because it is made by The
Philosopher himself. Aristotle's observations come in handy now and again
when considering some philosophical proposition, and one can apply those
observations, definitions, and axioms to the case at hand. This is what
Aquinas does, for example, when he relates his own remarks about actuality
and potentiality to Aristotle's principle about actuality and potentiality
expressed in his work on metaphysics. In his roundabout way, Aquinas asserts
that if one begins with a simple observation about the motion of things, and
then begins to wonder about the source of motion, one will eventually arrive,
step by step, at the ultimate question about motion, and that is, "Where does
it all begin?" The only possible answer is the unmoved mover, "and this everyone understands as God."

Some critics will argue that Aquinas' attempts to be scientific fail because
of his antiquated understanding of physics and that his ignorance of modern
science tarnishes his philosophical conclusions. Other critics will complain
that Aquinas puts too much faith in his authorities; scholastics in general are
faulted for attributing too much weight to an author's opinion simply because
the author happens to be considered an authority. But Aquinas used the tools
at his disposal, the science of his day coupled with Aristotelian principles, to
pose questions about the world around him in order to arrive at deeper and
more penetrating answers than one could experience through the senses. Now
it may be true that only someone who already believes in God will equate the
first mover with God. Perhaps a nonbeliever will prefer to call this first mover
by a different name, perhaps the "Prime Mover" or some other name, and not
give the name of "God" to the first mover. But Aquinas has argued that any
reasonable inquirer will arrive at the point in this argument about motion that
there has to be an ultimate source of motion. While Aquinas may not have
proved to a nonbeliever's satisfaction that there has to be a God, he has made
a fairly strong case for the necessity of a first mover. And to a believer, as well
as to a Christian philosopher such as Aquinas, what better name for that first
mover can there be than God?

In his other proofs of the existence of God, Aquinas again begins his
arguments with philosophical rather than theological assertions. In his second

proof, for example, Aquinas begins with the assertion that there is a sequence of efficient causes in the world. Aquinas leads the reader through a series of steps (similar to the first proof) in which he asserts that everything that happens must be caused by something else until he arrives at the point in his argument where he declares that the first efficient cause of all things is God. The third proof also begins with a nontheological premise, namely, that there is a difference between possibility and necessity, and therefore a difference between what can exist and what must exist. The things we see in the world have the possibility of existing and the possibility of not existing, since things that exist did not always exist and nothing that exists will exist forever. But does this mean that everything that exists has the possibility of not existing all at once? Could there be nothing in existence? If this were true, nothing would exist now, because nothing can come from nothing. But things do exist now, and so at least one thing exists that does not have the possibility of not existing; that is, it exists necessarily. That Being is God. We don't observe His existence; we deduce it from what we do observe.

The fourth proof produced by Aquinas begins with sensory perceptions. Everyone can see that in the real world there are different gradations of things. Among hot things, for example, some are hotter than others. Among things that one perceives as beautiful, one can differentiate between things that are more beautiful and things that are less beautiful. But the degrees "more" and "less" are relative terms; they depend upon a standard. Something that is hotter is said to be hotter not just because there is something that is less hot than it, but because the hotter thing is approaching what we suppose to be the hottest thing, the most superlatively hot thing of all, which in the case of hotness would be fire, since Aquinas believed it to be one of the four elements of the physical world. Without a standard, nothing would be hotter or cooler. The same could be said of beauty. The most beautiful of several things is that thing that is measured not only against those things that are less beautiful, but against the standard of the most beautiful thing of all. Some things are more just, more wise, and more powerful than others, and therefore there must be an absolute standard of these qualities as well. Aquinas concludes that "there is something that is the cause of being and goodness and whatever perfection has, and this we call God."

His final proof offered in the *Summa* is based on the order that Aquinas perceives in the universe. He notes that things that lack consciousness function with a purpose ("purposively"); they function in a particular way, as if there is an end to be achieved for all things, which is to say that all things seem to have been created for a purpose. The rabbit's fur keeps it warm, and the seeds inside the green pepper allow it to reproduce. Aquinas suggests that things achieve their purpose, or end, not by chance but by design. "But things that do not possess consciousness tend towards an end only because they are directed by a being that possesses consciousness and intelligence, in the same way that an arrow must be aimed by an archer . . . therefore there is an intelligent being who directs all things to their goal, and we say that this is God."[10] In this fifth proof, Aquinas posits the need for a governing intelligence in the world, something that designs or plans everything that happens in the world. We have learned enough about Aquinas to understand that this governing intelligence will turn out to be God.

In studying this fifth proof, we also find the root of Aquinas' interest in nature. Unlike earlier medieval theologians and philosophers, such as St. Augustine, Aquinas did not exhibit contempt for the natural world in his written work. Earlier medieval thinkers found the world to be a dangerous place, an enemy of the soul, a fleshpot of temptations that distracted the Christian from the true purpose of life, which was to contemplate God, to observe His commandments, and to look forward to happiness in the eternal life after death. "Contempt of the world" was the proper Christian attitude toward this agent of distraction and sin. Aquinas, on the other hand, saw the world in a more positive light and celebrated the natural world as the result of God's handiwork and as the most tangible evidence in favor of the Creator's existence. For Aquinas, an appreciation of the natural world was tied very closely to one's reverence for God Himself. God was, after all, the Creator of all things. Humans were incapable of knowing God directly or experiencing Him through the senses, since God is not a material being, but they could come to know something about God through their own experience of the natural world. Aquinas would spend a good deal of time writing about God's Creation, devoting an entire volume of the *Summa of Theology* and a whole book of the *Summa Contra Gentiles* to the subject, as well as a section of his commentary on Peter Lombard's *Sentences* ("The Work of the Six Days of Creation").

Aquinas began Book II of the *Summa Contra Gentiles* with a quotation from Psalm 142, "I meditated upon all Thy works; I meditated upon the works of Thy hands," in order to reinforce the connection between God and Creation but also to reinforce the connection between faith and reason. For he asserts that "this sort of meditation on the divine works is indeed necessary for instruction of faith in God."[11] How could human beings learn about God through careful examination of God's Creation? In the first place, they could admire the beauty of nature through their senses and minds. Humans could then use their faculties to contemplate nature and come to an appreciation of the harmony in nature. Ultimately, however, human beings would have to recognize that there was an overall design to nature that was the masterpiece of the Creator's handiwork. For the symmetry of dry spells followed by rainy days, the darkness of night followed by the light of day, the rotation of the four seasons, and the cycle of life and death will point toward a grand design or program. And in the quest to understand that program of nature, human beings will be amazed and humbled into recognizing that nature cannot possibly be a random enterprise by any stretch of the imagination, but is a well-ordered system designed by a master architect with a master plan.

Aquinas and other medieval theologians would have referred to this master plan as "Divine Providence," and Aquinas would have considered it the proper aim of both theologians and philosophers to learn as much as possible about that plan.

Perhaps it is a bit surprising that Aquinas would take such an interest in the natural world. This is not the sort of interest that a modern student would automatically expect of a medieval theologian or philosopher, since what we know of them so often pertains to spiritual and metaphysical matters, and here Aquinas is taking a great interest in physical matters. Modern students may be more accustomed to thinking of matters concerning the physical world as being entirely separate from metaphysical matters, more in the province of the "natural sciences," as we call them, and, indeed, physics and metaphysics are separate branches of inquiry today. On most college campuses today, the professors of physics and metaphysics are housed in different buildings, they rarely encounter one another professionally, and they do not share a common vocabulary, methodology, or set of interests. But to Aquinas, there was not so sharp a separation between the physical and metaphysical, or even between the visible and invisible, since his medieval Catholic world view encompassed a unified and continuous Creation, some of which could be observed and perceived through the senses and some of which was hidden from our senses.

Learning about nature, therefore, involves more than simply looking around. Sensory perception might be an appropriate starting point, and the five senses would enable human beings to recognize that such things as rocks and rivers and trees and animals exist. Even among visible things, however, there is an invisible element. For while rocks and rivers might be said to be inanimate, trees and animals are very definitely animate, living things, animated by their own individual *animae,* or souls. There are different types of souls, according to Aquinas. Plants and other living things have what Aquinas identifies as "nutritive" souls, which give them life; animals have "sensitive" souls, which give them feelings; and human beings have the highest type of soul, the "intellective" soul, which enables him to reason. One could not understand God's Creation without knowing something about these spiritual, invisible elements, and this is why the physical and metaphysical categories could not be kept entirely separate. Understanding God's Creation called for more than sensory perception, even more than rational inquiry, since reason too had its limits. But reason, and the tools of philosophy, could assist human beings in their search for an understanding of the invisible but guiding hand of God, and one of the vehicles for coming closer to such an understanding was what Aquinas called "natural law."

Just as all living things have been designed by Divine Providence and made subject to God's eternal law, human beings have been endowed with a natural capacity to know what is expected of them. "Rational creatures are under divine providence in a more excellent way than the others since by providing for themselves and others they share in the action of providence themselves. They participate in eternal reason in that they have a natural inclination to their proper actions and ends. Such participation in the eternal law by rational creatures is called the natural law."[12] Reason is the tool that human beings use to decipher the specifics of the natural law, but human nature is naturally inclined toward observing natural laws, such as doing what is required to survive (since everything naturally loves itself and seeks to preserve itself), to reproduce (since nature has taught all animals how to reproduce), to educate children (since human beings have a natural inclination to avoid ignorance), and to live in society (since human beings are naturally inclined to do so). Reason further enables humans to deduce specific natural laws from the more general set of natural laws to which humans are inclined, as outlined above. For example, since human beings are naturally inclined to live in society, natural law inclines them to behave in ways that are conducive to living in society, such as living peacefully with one's neighbors and avoiding offensive behavior toward others. Reason, however, is not foolproof. While all human beings are rational creatures, capable of deciphering the natural law, not everyone is equally adept at using it. Reason can be fine-tuned through education and experience, which also means that the undereducated or inexperienced are less skilled in using reason. Reason can also be ignored altogether, if a person chooses to ignore it, and therefore human laws, also known as "positive" laws, are necessary so that human beings will know exactly how to behave in society. However, even these human laws must be enacted with the natural law in mind. Aquinas' work on natural law would inspire legal and political writers for centuries.

The great bulk of Aquinas' many works was devoted to the topic of humanity. As we have already learned, his interest in humanity was entirely interrelated with his interest in God and nature, inasmuch as the human being is a creature of God, but unlike the rest of nature, human beings are made in God's image, each individual being an imperfect reflection of the Creator Himself. To study the creature is to study the Creator, and Aquinas was interested in every facet of the human experience, from human nature to the every thought, intention, desire, and activity of human beings. By posing thousands of questions about humanity in his various works, Aquinas inquired into a broad spectrum of moral, legal, social, and political issues. In surveying the variety of topics touched upon in Aquinas' writings concerning the human experience, one discovers a rich treasury of opinions and judgments made by this medieval scholar on topics of universal interest and importance. Questions are posed about the most grave issues ("Is someone who kills a man by accident guilty of murder?") and about seemingly trivial matters ("Whether mock modesty is sinful?" followed by "Whether it is less sinful than boasting?"). A student of Aquinas can survey the *Summa of Theology* for answers to questions about what makes human beings happy (happiness, which does not come in this life, consists of the vision of the Divine Essence) to whether or not it is sinful to charge interest when lending money to someone (usury was deemed sinful by Aquinas, and it was forbidden by canon law in his day, but canon lawyers later in the Middle Ages would relax restrictions on usury by suggesting that it was sinful to charge "too much" interest, as opposed to charging any at all). The works of Aquinas provide a window into the medieval mind as no other medieval source can do, but they also present a treasury of moral reflections and judgments made with clarity and precision that many people, even in the twenty-first century, continue to admire and affirm.

Thomas Aquinas made a particular use of philosophy, as a supplement to theology in his quest to know as much as possible about God, the source of being, goodness, truth, and love. Aquinas relied on the cool reason of the pagan Philosopher, Aristotle, to demonstrate the rationality of the truths of Christianity and to prove that nothing that Scripture teaches us about God can be contradicted by rational analysis. The truth was revealed in Scripture, but also in nature and in the workings of the human mind. Aquinas the theologian was a student of God; Aquinas the philosopher was a lover of wisdom. This believer in a unified and harmonious Creation, with a common purpose and a common goal, would have understood the study of God and the love of wisdom to be two different ways of expressing the same enterprise, of finding one's way back to the source of all being and wisdom, namely, God Himself. As a sign of respect, but also as an acknowledgment of the success he achieved as both a theologian and a philosopher, the Catholic Church canonized Thomas Aquinas as a saint in 1323. In doing so, the Church paid a compliment not only to this man of religion, but also to the philosopher. For Aquinas believed that philosophy, the "handmaid of theology," was a vehicle that could bring one home to God. Aquinas, now certified by the Church as a saint in heaven enjoying the Beatific Vision of God, is believed to have found his way home, and the Catholic world reveres him as much for the journey as for his success in arriving at his final destination.

∽ NOTES

1. Thomas Aquinas died in 1274 and was canonized as a saint in 1323. A saint is a deceased individual recognized posthumously by the Catholic Church to be in heaven in the presence of God because of that individual's heroic virtue during his or her lifetime or because of martyrdom. As a member of the "communion of saints," a saint continues to participate in the life of the Church through his or her intercession with God on behalf of those who request his or her help.

2. Galileo accepted the Copernican theory of the solar system at a time when the Church continued to accept the Ptolemaic theory. The Church ordered the sixty-nine-year-old scientist to refrain from teaching the new heliocentric view. But in 1633 Church leaders decided he had disobeyed. They brought him to trial, threatened him with torture, convicted him, and confined him to house arrest, where he died nine years later.

3. A famous painting of St. Joan of Arc (c. 1412–1431) by Jules Bastien-Lepage at the Metropolitan Museum of Art in New York, dated 1879, depicts Joan walking in the woods near her home in Lorraine, with images of St. Michael the Archangel, St. Margaret, and St. Catherine hovering in the sky.

4. St. Thomas Aquinas, *Summa Theologiae,* Latin text and English translation, introductions, notes, appendices and glossaries (London: Blackfriars, 1972), 60 vols.

5. St. Thomas Aquinas, *Summa Contra Gentiles,* translated, with an introduction and notes, by Anton C. Pegis (Notre Dame, IN: University of Notre Dame Press, 1975; originally published by Doubleday, 1956), vol. I, 15–19. Pegis provides a chronology of Aquinas' writings, which I have used here.

6. Ibid., vol. 41, 2–19. All quotations related to this *Quaestio* on piety are found here.

7. David Knowles, *The Evolution of Medieval Thought* (New York: Random House/Vintage Books, 1962), 101–106, provides a very insightful account of Anselm's ontological argument, which I have followed closely.

8. In the following section of this essay on Aquinas' five proofs, I have used the translation and quoted extensively from Paul E. Sigmund, translator and editor, *St. Thomas Aquinas on Politics and Ethics* (New York: W.W. Norton, 1988), 30–32. All quotations in this section of my essay are from Sigmund's translation.

9. Ibid., 30–31.

10. Ibid., 32.

11. Aquinas, *Summa Contra Gentiles,* vol. II, 30.

12. Sigmund, *St. Thomas Aquinas on Politics and Ethics,* 46.

∾ CHRONOLOGY

374	St. Ambrose becomes the bishop of Milan
380	St. Jerome translates the Bible into Latin
412	St. Augustine begins writing *The City of God*
590	St. Gregory the Great elected pope
762	Muslim invasion of Europe halted at battle of Tours by Charles Martel
800	Charlemagne unites a large part of Europe; crowned by the pope in Rome as Holy Roman Emperor on Christmas day
1093	St. Anselm becomes archbishop of Canterbury
1123	Abelard publishes *Sic et Non (Yes and No)*

1155	Peter Lombard's *Sentences* further develops the scholastic method
1225	Thomas Aquinas born near Aquino in southern Italy
1239	attends the University of Naples
1243	kidnapped by his family and held in the family castle to prevent him from carrying out his intention to become a monk
1245	begins studying theology at the University of Paris
1256	receives master of arts degree and license to teach
1264	*Summa Contra Gentiles*
1265	begins the *Summa Theologiae,* unfinished
1267	*On the Government of Rulers*
1274	dies at age forty-nine on a journey to attend a Church council in France
1320	Dante, *The Divine Comedy*
1323	Aquinas canonized by the Catholic Church
1300–1600	the Italian Renaissance
1600–1700	the Scientific Revolution
1700–1800	the Enlightenment
1879	Pope Leo XIII declares Aquinas' system to be the official philosophy of the Catholic Church

∾ SUGGESTED READINGS

Aquinas, St. Thomas. *Selected Writings,* edited and translated with an introduction and notes by Ralph McInerny. London: Penguin Books, 1998.

————. *Summa Contra Gentiles,* 5 vols., translated with an introduction and notes by Anton C. Pegis. Notre Dame, IN: University of Notre Dame Press, 1975 (originally published by Doubleday, 1955).

————. *Summa Theologiae,* 60 vols., Latin text and English translation, introductions, notes, appendices, and glossaries. London: Blackfriars, 1972.

Catechism of the Catholic Church. Vatican City: Libreria Editrice Vaticana/Paulist Press, 1994.

Chesterton, G.K. *Saint Thomas Aquinas: The Dumb Ox,* with an introduction by Anton C. Pegis. New York: Doubleday/Image Books, 1956 (originally published by Sheed & Ward, 1933).

Copleston, F.C. *Aquinas: An Introduction to the Life and Work of the Great Medieval Thinker.* London: Penguin/Pelican Books, 1955.

Honderich, T., ed. *The Philosophers: Introducing Great Western Thinkers.* Oxford: Oxford University Press, 1999.

Knowles, D. *The Evolution of Medieval Thought.* New York: Random House/Vintage Books, 1962.

Parker, F.H. *The Story of Western Philosophy.* Bloomington: Indiana University Press, 1967.

Sigmund, P.E., translator and editor. *St. Thomas Aquinas on Politics and Ethics.* New York: W.W. Norton, 1988.

Strathern, P. *Thomas Aquinas in 90 Minutes.* Chicago: Ivan R. Dee, 1998.

Stumpf, S.E. *Philosophy, History and Problems.* Fifth Edition. New York: McGraw-Hill, 1994.

Tomlin, E.W.F. *The Western Philosophers: An Introduction.* New York: Harper & Row, 1963.

CHAPTER 7

Descartes

Philosophy as the Search for Reasonableness

Michael Shenefelt

 Preview

The sixteenth century was an age of religious wars and fanaticism. Descartes (born in 1596) sees the philosopher's task as finding a way out of these difficulties, and other forms of irrationality, too, by discovering a standard of reasonableness. He wants a method for distiguishing what we really know from what we only believe. The starting point is doubt, or questioning authority. We must have the courage to admit that most of the things we believe are simply prejudices, without any sound basis. He then describes a special kind of certainty, illustrated by mathematical certainty, that is the mark of genuine knowledge. The most certain thing that each person knows is that he or she is conscious and therefore exists. Descartes thought that he could build up all of our other knowledge on the basis of that firm starting point. For Descartes, philosophy is testing beliefs for their certainty and examining how some beliefs support others. (The Editor)

∿ Introduction

In 1586, a decade before René Descartes was born, the Archbishop of Trier, in Germany, ordered some one hundred twenty alleged witches burned to death for interfering with the weather.[1] Another sixty-three were burned at the stake in Bavaria a few years later for having caused hail, thunderstorms, and a plague among cattle.[2] Some years after that, in 1609, hundreds of people in southwestern France came to believe that they had been possessed by devils, and many, thinking they had become dogs, barked.[3] None of this was improbable for the period. People all over Europe believed themselves surrounded by demons and fiends. As a book of the time put it, "everywhere the whole universe, inward and outward, water and air, is full of devils, of wicked, invisible spirits."[4] And many people concluded that the only way to escape these wicked spirits was to execute their neighbors.

Executing neighbors was nothing new. For more than half a century, pious Christians throughout Europe had been killing one another in a vast struggle over whose version of Christianity was theologically correct—a paroxysm of blood and rage that makes the current excesses of radical Islam look timid by comparison. Catholics killed Protestants with zest, Protestants killed Catholics with equal zest, and when Catholics got the upper hand in France with the massacre of St. Bartholomew's Day, a Jesuit priest at Bordeaux explained that the slaughter of the Huguenot Protestants had been especially arranged by the Archangel Michael.[5]

This is the background against which Descartes tried to figure out the difference between reason and fanaticism. Descartes exalted reason in a way that is not always readily comprehensible today, but it makes much more sense if we remember just how unstable and unreasonable his own world was. Intellectually, the world of his youth was far less secure than ours. Europe was still staggering through the last phases of the Wars of Religion, during which many ridiculous claims of spiritual certainty produced much useless bloodshed. Deep forces, political and economic, had profoundly disturbed the region's peace, and the resulting antagonisms often took the form of religious conflict. One group often claimed to know *for sure* that God was on its side, and it would then invoke this supposed knowledge as a reason for sending thousands on the other side—sometimes tens of thousands—to their death. The effect of these tactics, then, was to make thoughtful observers in many countries ask just how many of these claims of knowledge were really valid.

More generally, they asked, "How do we know what we know?" And again, "How much of what we believe is really well founded and how much is just nonsense?" And, "Is there anything we can know for certain?" And,

"When is it reasonable to believe and when is it reasonable to doubt?" These are now the central questions of epistemology—the theory of knowledge—but for Descartes's generation they were never mere theory. On the contrary, they were matters of life and death. Modern epistemology was born at a moment of particular pain and paranoia in the development of early modern Europe. Philosophers often make their greatest contributions not by supplying answers but by supplying questions, and this was certainly the case with Descartes, because the implicit question in all his philosophical musings is one that returns whenever the calm of social peace gives way to hysteria, cruelty, or chaos: What distinguishes a reasonable person from a fanatic?

⌒ Intellectual Independence

Philosophy for Descartes was in many ways a search for reasonableness, and the underlying assumption of such a search is that reason is indeed something objective. That is, the search assumes that certain things are reasonable independently of whether we judge them so—since, otherwise, even fanaticism counts as reasonable from the standpoint of the fanatic. Still, the modern reader is sometimes tempted to wonder whether this assumption is altogether justified, and its legitimacy is worth a moment to consider. After all, if "reasonable" people sometimes disagree, a phenomenon we often encounter today, then why suppose that reason is anything more than a fiction?

One approach to this question is to liken reasonableness to twilight. If we ask, "Where does twilight end and darkness begin?" we may well reply, "Nowhere in particular." The distinction between twilight and darkness is vague. Just so, if we ask, "Where does the reasonable end and the unreasonable begin?" the distinction sometimes seems vague. Many things are matters over which "reasonable" people differ, and even if there *is* a sharp line between reason and its contraries, sometimes it is just too fine a line to draw. Still, it is quite another thing to say that there is no distinction at all, or to say that the difference between reason and unreason is merely arbitrary. This further move is certainly one that Descartes would resist.

After all, a distinction can indeed be vague yet no less real and objective. By analogy, though the distinction between twilight and darkness is vague, it is by no means nonexistent. *Some* hours are clearly in twilight, *some* hours clearly in darkness. Just so, it may still be the case that *some* things are clearly reasonable and *some* things are clearly unreasonable. Put another way, it is simply a non sequitur to say that a vague distinction is, therefore, always an arbitrary one. This point may be easily overlooked in societies that are generally shielded from frenzy and tumult, but the thing to remember about the societies of Descartes's era is that this security was largely missing. The great fear of his contemporaries was of a backward slide into the religious zealotry of the recent past; in consequence, the whole idea of reasonableness had a kind of urgency for his generation that it sometimes lacks now. Thus, were Descartes alive today, he might well accuse some of his modern critics of over-looking an obvious point—that the vagueness of *some* things in no way diminishes the clear rationality, or clear irrationality, of other things.

Still, what made Descartes most interesting to his contemporaries was not merely his belief in the reality of reasonableness. Rather, it was his equally firm conviction that the societies of his own time were profoundly *un*reasonable. And this further conviction also deeply affected his conception of what philosophy ought to be. Descartes's attitude toward these further matters was in many ways radical, and his radicalism is still bold and amusing.

Four years before the publication of his first major work, the *Discourse on Method* (1637), Descartes learned that Galileo had been condemned by the papacy for insisting that the earth moves around the sun. What caused Galileo's arrest was not merely his opinions, which he had already made perfectly clear in a series of earlier works, but the fact that he was now publishing these opinions in Italian rather than Latin—the language of the learned. In Italian, his opinions could be understood by a growing assortment of middle-class readers, and they were thus far harder to suppress. But when it came time for Descartes to publish his own views, he, too, chose to write in the vernacular, in French, so that he could be understood by the widest possible audience. His choice of French was deliberate and confrontational. Descartes mocked the intellectual authorities of his age, yet he always managed to do so with such subtlety and cleverness as to stay out of harm's way.

A good example is the story of his own life as he depicts it in his *Discourse*. Descartes disclaims any political meaning in his *Discourse* and says his only interest is in reforming his own ideas. Yet he notes that he has been educated in one of the best schools in Europe—where he says he was by no means an inferior student—and he then goes on to say that most of his ideas upon graduation from that school were entirely worthless. Thus, the inference left to the reader is that even the best education then available in Europe was still essentially worthless.

This was not his only dig at the intellectual authorities of his time. He also explains in the *Discourse* how he decided to educate himself in a new manner. He gave up his earlier studies, he says, "as soon as I reached the age when I was no longer under the control of my teachers."[6] Then he struck out on a new path: "I resolved to seek no other knowledge than that which I might find within myself, or perhaps in the great book of nature."[7]

Now the thing to notice here, however dubious Descartes's claim of a new method of education may really be, is his implicit theme—the theme of intellectual independence. Throughout, Descartes insisted on thinking for himself. If the received learning of Europe was essentially worthless (as his remarks on his own schooling seemed to imply), then he had to discover whatever truths were to be had on his own. And the effect of this example was to encourage others to do the same.

This, more than any other doctrine or argument, is what most appealed to Descartes's contemporaries, especially to middle-class burghers, who often saw themselves as self-made men with no particular debt to traditional author-ity. Descartes encouraged them to think for themselves. And it was precisely this same group to which Martin Luther had appealed a century earlier by encouraging them to read the Bible for themselves. But whereas Luther had effectively taken the Bible rather than the pope to be infallible, Descartes attrib-uted infallibility to nothing and nobody. He never explicitly *denied* the infalli-bility of Scripture or the pope—his sense of political danger was much too keen for such a misstep—but he said, nevertheless, that he chose to doubt everything that might be doubted, even the existence of his own body. Thus, whereas Luther and his adversaries had stressed faith, Descartes stressed doubt.[8]

This idea of intellectual independence is perhaps one of the best ways to understand Descartes's famous conjecture that the whole physical world might be merely an illusion or a dream. Perhaps, Descartes suggested, I have no hands or feet, no body, and no physical surroundings. Instead, perhaps every-thing I see is merely a dream, and all evidence I might invoke to prove that it *isn't* a dream is merely part of the dream itself. How, then, can I verify the exis-tence of the physical world without taking for granted the very point at issue—that the evidence does indeed come from a world that is more than illusory?[9]

Of course, Descartes's conjecture is theoretically interesting in itself; how *do* I know that life isn't a dream? Many subsequent epistemological theories take this very question as their starting point. And the conjecture also plays a subtle but critical role in Descartes's claim that our minds are demonstrably different from any part of our bodies. In fact, many of the positions that Descartes will defend in answer to this conjecture will turn out to have a decid-edly medieval flavor, and many studies have shown his deep indebtedness to medieval predecessors in all these investigations.[10] Still, beyond these points, the conjecture has a further crucial effect that was new for his time, though frequently overlooked today: it expresses in the most dramatic way possible the fundamental theme of his age—the theme of thinking for oneself.

After all, if I doubt whether I have a physical body or physical senses, then I must certainly doubt the infallibility of the pope, of Scripture, and of every secular authority, since my knowledge of these other things comes strictly from physical sensation. If I don't know whether I even have a body, then neither do I know whether anyone else has one or whether anyone else even exists; thus I must solve all my theoretical difficulties for myself, with-out relying on anyone else's opinion. This challenge to the existence of the physical world arises in Descartes's writings out of a quest for absolute cer-tainty, a quest I shall discuss further in a short while. But for his contempo-raries, what made the quest attractive in the first place was a widespread popular feeling that all the *old* certainties, propounded by the old authorities, were untrustworthy. Thus, they could see at once that an effect of the con-jecture, one of its apparently logical consequences, was to call into question every authority of the period. Indeed, it was precisely this effect that gave the conjecture its stunning impact. Nor is the effect especially difficult to repro-duce today.

In particular, if it really makes sense for a high school or college student, reading Descartes for the first time, to doubt the existence of the physical world, then it certainly makes sense to doubt whether everything now coming from the teachers of the school is gospel truth. Such attitudes in a student can appear threatening, perhaps even dangerous and disruptive. But in due measure they can also be liberating. And it was just this sort of liberation for which Descartes's contemporaries longed. Even if his strange conjecture had been merely a literary pose, it would still be a pose of genius because it expresses the idea of intellectual independence taken to its logical extreme.

The whole thrust of his approach, then, was to renounce any attempt at argument by authority. Since he relied for proof only on himself, he never argued that something must be true because so-and-so says it is. Instead, he always demanded that the reader decide the case on its own merits, and it was this spirit, above all, that made him the founder of modern philosophy.

The contrast with earlier times could hardly be starker. Throughout the Middle Ages, philosophical writers had often circulated ideas very like Descartes's, but their style of argument had been different. Though they had often put together highly original demonstrations, they had also made a point, usually, of showing how their results agreed with those of Plato or Paul, Aristotle or Augustine, Anselm or Aquinas. The idea was to find shelter for one's theories under the reputation of some famous ancient worthy. A celebrated name, annexed to your opinions, was supposed to make them more credible. And even today, academic writers sometimes make a point of asserting how their opinions flow from those of Russell or Wittgenstein, Heidegger or Kuhn, Derrida or Foucault. But Descartes would have none of this: "I do not claim that I am original in these ideas, but only that I have never accepted them because they were maintained by others . . . but only because reason persuaded me of their truth."[11] If an idea is true and well founded, Descartes supposed, then no great name should be needed to prop it up. Let it rise or fall on its own merits.

Of course, this contempt for intellectual authority can be easily overdone. In fact, we all rely from time to time on the testimony of experts. But the feeling of Descartes's contemporaries was that it was this reliance on the supposed experts that had been overdone, not contempt for them, and that many of the supposed experts of the day were really just charlatans. What was needed above all, they thought, was greater independence of mind. Thus, they supposed that the true path of reasonableness lay in trusting one's own "good sense." Or, put another way, they felt that being reasonable *required* this kind of independence. In effect, then, Descartes arrived like a breath of fresh air. He seemed to be freeing philosophy from a tyranny of past reputations and making it once more the possession of anyone with gumption to follow a reasoned argument.

∾ The Quest for Certainty

The Descartes I have described so far is the Descartes of the *Discourse on Method*, and the spirit of this book has clung to philosophy, to a greater or lesser degree, ever after. Independence of mind is something that the discipline has generally come to prize, and in a way that the medievals would have found peculiar. Nevertheless, there is also a later Descartes, the author of the *Meditations on First Philosophy*, and this later Descartes is equally intriguing. The *Discourse* had been brash and daring, and this was half its charm, but the *Meditations*, which appeared four years afterward, and in Latin, were cautious and studied, and they threw into high relief many of the special problems of his outlook.

Among the most imposing of these problems is a difficulty I touched on a moment ago—his insistence on certainty.

Descartes believed that our reasonableness depends inescapably on finding something certain, something "entirely certain," something "metaphysically certain." And he tells us that it was precisely his relentless pursuit of certainty that first led him to the study of mathematics,[12] which then becomes for him a paradigm of knowledge. Still, his attitude toward certainty is often the very point that today's readers find most strange. After all, why should being reasonable have anything to do with being certain? Why can't we be reasonable *without* being certain?

Let me try for a moment to put this criticism as forcefully as I can.

In some sense, no doubt, the existence of our own bodies is *already* as certain as anything needs to be, or could be, and this complaint against Descartes's preoccupations was pushed with great force not only by the English commonsense realist G.E. Moore but also by the famous Scottish philosopher David Hume. Doubting the existence of our bodies, Hume thought, was not only silly, it was also psychologically impossible: "The Cartesian doubt . . . were it ever possible to be attained by any human creature (as it plainly is not) would be entirely incurable; and no reasoning could ever bring us to any assurance and conviction upon any subject."[13] In Descartes's defense, it is sometimes argued that his extreme doubts here were never really "practical" anyway, but merely "methodological"—meaning that they had no purpose except to help him discover absolute certainties. And Descartes does indeed describe his doubts as an element of "method," and he insists in his First Meditation that "the end I now seek is not action but knowledge." Still, to a critic such as Hume, distinctions of this sort were always a sham. For Hume, doubt is simply a psychological fact, and you either have doubts or you don't. So, from Hume's point of view, Descartes had merely confounded doubting the existence of his body with *imagining* that he was doubting it.

In fact, Descartes's intentions on this point are by no means obvious. On the one hand, his doubts about the physical world often seem, at least to the naïve reader, sincere: "Yesterday's Meditation has filled my mind with so many

132 CHAPTER 7 DESCARTES

doubts that it is no longer in my power to forget them."[14] On the other hand, he sometimes seems to admit that they strain credulity: "that there is a world, that men have bodies, and other similar things . . . have never been seriously doubted by anyone of sound mind."[15] The great temptation for the commentator is to assume that Descartes's professed "doubts" are really meant to be something else—suppositions, imaginings, perceptions of logical possibility, and so on. On this view of the matter, then, his "methodological doubt," a term coined by the commentators themselves, is not really doubt at all but some other psychological state, traveling under a fictitious name. (Merely *supposing* I have doubts is no more a sort of doubting than supposing I can fly is a method of traveling from place to place.) The chief trouble with this reading, however, is that Descartes clings to the language of doubt even when replying to critics—which is precisely where we should expect him to drop any false pretense of doubting, if, indeed, his doubts *are* a pretense. For example, he remarks, "before we can decide to doubt, we need some reason for doubting; and this is why I put forward the principal reasons for doubting in my First Meditation."[16] More generally, the theoretical problems he troubles himself with are sometimes ones that arise precisely over doubting in the proper sense of the word, and, in consequence, it may well be wondered whether his language ever wholly lends itself to any of the alternate interpretations that have been suggested for it. Again, it is possible that sometimes Descartes is simply of two minds about these matters.

However this may be, the larger and more troubling question remains: Whatever Descartes means, exactly, by the terms "doubt" and "certainty," why should the rest of us bother with such investigations at all? Put bluntly, either his doubts are intended seriously or they are not. If not, why should serious people spend time on things that aren't serious? But if they *are* intended seriously, then who can really share these doubts in the first place?

David Hume expresses this sort of criticism very ably: "For here is the chief and most confounding objection to excessive scepticism, that no durable good can ever result from it. . . . We need only ask such a sceptic, What his meaning is? And what he proposes by all these curious researches? . . . The first and most trivial event in life will put to flight all his doubts and scruples, and leave him the same, in every point of action and speculation, with the philosophers of every other sect."[17]

There is a long and respectable tradition of dismissing Descartes's analysis of certainty as being not worth the time required to puzzle it out. Still, before giving in to this sentiment (and personally, I think it mistaken), there are two points that ought to be recognized in his defense. And the first is the special meaning of doubt and certainty for the seventeenth century—a meaning that is not always readily apparent today. In fact, the seventeenth century was tormented by ideas of doubt and certainty because it was probably the period of greatest intellectual uncertainty in modern history.

Seldom had the usual verities of life been less clear. Not only had the medieval age of faith just given way to a new age of doubt. Not only had Martin Luther undermined the authority of Catholicism. Not only had religious warfare steeped the European states in blood. The seventeenth century also witnessed the greatest revolution in physics in nearly two millennia—championed first by Galileo and Kepler and then, after Descartes's death, by Newton. Descartes lived in the midst of these upheavals and was keenly attentive to them. His enthusiasm for science, in particular, was unbounded. He was filled with optimism about the power of science to remake the world, but he was also especially concerned that the reigning feeling of intellectual drift be replaced with a new feeling of intellectual security. And this anxiety is perhaps best understood by contrasting it with the outlook of the earlier French essayist Michel de Montaigne—whose influence on Descartes's whole generation was immense.

Montaigne shared Descartes's contempt for argument by authority. ("I do not speak the minds of others, except to speak my own mind better."[18]) And he was equally convinced that the claims of spiritual certainty expressed by all sides during the Wars of Religion were hollow. ("We are Christians by the same title that we are Perigordians or Germans. . . . We happen to have been born in a country where [our religion] was in practice."[19]) But Montaigne had no certainties of his own to offer in their place. Instead, he embraced universal doubt. His personal motto, which he had struck on a medal, became "What do I know?" This attitude was in many ways a reaction to the age, but for Descartes it was quite unacceptable. Universal doubt, if left unmodified, would be just as useless, he thought, as universal certainty. Being told that all things are doubtful is just as unavailing as being told that all things are certain. What we need to know, instead, is which things are *more* certain than others (and thus which things are more doubtful), and Descartes hoped to answer this question by finding some primary certainty from which all other genuine certainties might flow.

In short, the seventeenth century did indeed require a general reexamination of doubt and certainty, *genuine* doubt and certainty, as a means to the restructuring of its opinions. Given their recent past, thinkers of the period might be forgiven for erring on the side of too much doubt rather than too little. Still, even if we now feel inclined, perhaps, to reject many of Descartes's answers, this is still very different from rejecting the fundamental importance of his questions: "When is it reasonable to doubt?" and "When is it reasonable to feel certain?" These questions were vital to the seventeenth century, and they remain of no small consequence to our own. And in the end, Descartes's inclination to doubt, though surely radical and in his own telling "hyperbolic," was *not* universal—not quite. Instead, he sought to disclose some sort of exception to Montaigne's sweeping doubts, something beyond all doubt: "I think, therefore I am."

To doubt my own existence, Descartes argued, is simply incoherent. After all, if I doubt whether I exist, then there must still be some "I," some self, to do the doubting, and this remains true even if the self in question turns out *not* to be a physical object. Put another way, I can never be merely nothing "so long as I think that I am something . . . this proposition, I am, I exist, is necessarily true every time that I pronounce it or conceive it in my mind."[20]

Thus, the individual's knowledge of his own existence was to be the primary certainty, the "metaphysical certainty," from which all other real certainties would derive, and the rest of human knowledge was then to be reconstructed so as to stand on this single pillar, this self-evident truth, as a house might be reconstructed to stand on a new foundation. And just as important, the striking new discoveries of seventeenth-century science were to be a vital part of this reconstruction.

Now, so far as the proposition "I exist" is concerned, most readers have always found it difficult to see how anything else of significance can really be deduced from it, and this was the case even when Descartes first published. On the other hand, his assumption that science would play a vital new role in the reconstruction of our opinions has turned out, for better or worse, to be largely correct.

More precisely, despite the many misgivings and apprehensions we often feel now over the results of science, it still exercises enormous authority over our ideas, and its current role in society still expresses something like the old Cartesian quest for a new security. Few of our customs, laws, or beliefs actually follow, in the logical sense, from modern science. Yet they are surely influenced by science. As a culture, we probably attribute a greater degree of certainty to science than to anything else, and this has remained true for the vast majority in modern societies, despite various efforts by many philosophers over the centuries to show that this certainty is somehow misplaced. For good or ill, science has become our new security—much as Descartes had anticipated.

The second thing to remember about Descartes's approach to certainty—and a point that may even help to vindicate him, if we stop to consider it—is his role as mathematician. In fact, Descartes was one of the great mathematicians of history, the creator, or perhaps one should say the discoverer, of analytic geometry. Most high school students have had at least a passing acquaintance with his "Cartesian coordinates," the x, y, and z axes that turn geometrical shapes into equations of numbers. Descartes understood mathematics as a professional, and its influence on his philosophy is everywhere profound.

Most important, Descartes believed that mathematical propositions throw special light on certainty because they are verified in a way quite unlike our beliefs about the physical world.

For example, to know whether the sea off the beaches of New York is at present stormy, I must go and look at it. But to know whether all triangles are divisible into at least two right triangles, I need not look at any triangle in particular. In fact, no sort of physical looking at triangles will actually prove the theorem. I can hardly look at *all* triangles, though the theorem applies to all, and no triangular object in the physical world is perfectly triangular anyway. Yet the theorem applies only to perfect triangles. Descartes believed that physical sensations might *acquaint* me with the propositions of mathematics, and perhaps suggest possible solutions, but they could never confirm or verify those propositions. Instead, mathematical propositions had to be confirmed or verified by thinking itself, and no possible physical sensation could ever refute them, because nothing to which they really apply is ever truly observable in the physical world.

Thus, Descartes believed that mathematical propositions had a special kind of certainty in that their truth was impervious to physical disproof. No physical event could ever refute them, because the objects of geometry and arithmetic were never physical. And it was precisely this kind of certainty that he tried to replicate in philosophy.

Part and parcel of this project, moreover, was his attempt to convince his readers of a further grand claim—that our most important philosophical ideas are precisely the ones we can never imagine. This further contention strikes many modern readers as absurd, but it makes much more sense, I think, if we turn once more to mathematics.

If we ask how many integers there are between four and six, the usual answer is one—the number five. Yet what happens if we try to imagine this number? I can easily imagine, for example, a tall sailboat or a yellow motorcycle, but if I try to imagine the number five, I usually find myself imagining a symbol—"5." Yet there are *many* symbols for the number five—"5," "V," "five," "ⵏⵏⵏ ," "cinq," "cinque," and so on, whereas there is only *one* integer between four and six. This suggests that the symbol is not the number. Still, when I do mathematics, I do indeed reason about numbers. Thus, it seems, I reason about things that I never really imagine. In fact, mathematicians reason about whole infinities of numbers, but who can imagine infinities? Descartes's position was that some things can't be imagined at all even though we *do* reason about them, and the point to notice here is just how natural this assumption is for someone steeped in mathematics. When we reason about numbers, we often visualize the symbols, which are surely an *aid* to our reasoning, but they are not, therefore, the *subject* of our reasoning. Instead, the subject seems to be *un*imaginable. Such, at least, is one theory of what numerical analysis is all about.

It is no objection to Descartes's position, I think, to complain that such things as imagining, visualizing, or mental picturing are vague and poorly understood processes. Though we can't always analyze these processes, we may still be able to experience them, and Descartes's view is that his main point *is* something we can experience. When we reason about mathematical entities, we often reason abstractly, but when we reason about sailboats, we reason concretely. And however vague the distinction between the abstract and the concrete may be, the Cartesian still insists that the two experiences *are* different and that we can feel this difference. The distinction in question, according to Descartes, is evident to introspection. My ideas of numbers *appear* to me very different from my idea of a sailboat. Part of what separated Descartes from his empiricist rivals—those who stressed physical sensation in accounting for human knowledge—was his view that sound philosophy must inevitably be abstract like mathematics, rather than concrete like our imaginings of a sailboat.

This is why he dwelled so lovingly on what he called "clear and distinct ideas." Contrary to what one might initially think, these clear and distinct ideas were never intended to be vivid in the way that a stunning, sunny morning is vivid. Instead, they were to be vivid only in the way that the Pythagorean theorem is vivid—vivid, that is, to a mathematician. They were usually pure abstractions, and for the most part they were unimaginable. (I say "for the most part" because Descartes sometimes allowed for exceptions. For instance, he said that a triangle might be both imagined and conceived abstractly.) Like many earlier thinkers, Descartes supposed that our imaginings are but manipulations of our remembered experience, and he supposed, likewise, that anything we can physically experience we can also imagine. But since these so-called clear and distinct ideas were mostly *un*imaginable, he inferred that they had to come from a source *other* than physical experience. He called them "innate." He thought that we are simply born with the capacity to entertain them, quite independently of particular physical sensations. My ideas of color, for example, come from physically seeing colors, but my ideas of substance, the soul, perfection, and God come to me independently of any particular sensory stimulus—or so Descartes asserted. This is not to say that infants are born prattling of "substance," "the soul," and so on, but only that their capacity to do so in later life hinges on no specific sensory influence. (If ideas such as substance and the soul now sound too ethereal or superstitious for modern readers to entertain, one might still try reverting to the idea of the number five. If, as Descartes's analysis suggests, we never really imagine numbers, then how do we come up with the idea of numbers at all?) To lift a page from Immanuel Kant's *Critique of Pure Reason,* "though all our knowledge begins with experience, it does not follow that it all arises out of experience." In meaning, Descartes's "clear and distinct ideas" were very like Kant's "a priori concepts."

In essence, then, Descartes's approach is a prime example of what has since become known, in epistemology, as "rationalism" (as opposed to "empiricism")—that is, a theory of knowledge that stresses what is instilled, implanted, confirmed, or verified in ways *other* than physical sensation.

Descartes had many other ideas and took many other positions, and though often highly controversial, they were rarely simply foolish. Among other things, he believed that mind and body were different substances and that the one could never be reduced to the other. He believed that the existence of God could be proved and, apparently, that any genuine knowledge of the physical world always depended on such a proof. Most notoriously, he asserted that animals have neither thoughts nor consciousness, and he implied that when injured they do not suffer. Descartes effectively conceded that the bodies of animals *react* to such injuries and that their bodies may even scream, but he implied that since the animal's body contains no soul, the scream represents no real awareness.[21]

This last contention was probably the least defensible and most detestable thing Descartes ever suggested. But none of his other views necessarily entails it, and the other views are the ones that have had the deepest philosophical impact.

Descartes's greatest influence, historically, is likely to lie not so much in his doctrines as in his questions, and in the bold and independent way in which he tried to investigate them. Many of his solutions turn out, on examination, to be medieval and scholastic, but what was new was his willingness to rethink and recast them without regard to philosophical tradition. He made himself, in essence, an apostle of independence, and all subsequent philosophy has traveled to a greater or lesser degree in his wake. Even his empiricist adversaries caught this aggressive and renovating spirit, and however much they disagreed with him, they almost always made a special point of reading him. And, inspired by his daring and panache, they often imitated him.

∼ NOTES

1. H.C. Lea, *History of the Inquisition in the Middle Ages* (New York: Macmillan, 1922), Volume 3, 549.

2. Johannes Janssen, *History of the German People After the Close of the Middle Ages* (St. Louis: B. Herder, 1910), Volume 16, 414–416; Wolfgang Behringer, *Witchcraft Persecutions in Bavaria,* translated by J.C. Grayson and David Lederer (New York: Cambridge University Press, 1997), 135–136.

3. Jules Michelet, *Œuvres Complètes* (Paris: Flammarion, 1971–1982), Volume 9, 168–169.

4. Published in 1585 at Heidelberg, the book was called *Christian Ideas on Magic.* See Janssen, Volume 12, 346–347.

5. Jules Michelet, *Histoire de France,* Volume 5, in *Œuvres Complètes,* Volume 8, 265.

6. *Discourse on Method,* 1, AT VI, 9. In this, as in most other instances, I quote from Laurence J. Lafleur's translation, published by the Library of Liberal Arts. The first number after the title refers to the part or meditation of the work in question. The subsequent numbers refer to the volume and page number of the relevant text as it appears, either in French or in Latin, in the authoritative *Œuvres de Descartes,* ed. Charles Adam and Paul Tannery (Paris: Librairie Philosophique J. Vrin, 1996).

7. Ibid.

8. As a matter of diction, writers of Luther's day preferred to ask whether the pope could "err" in matters of faith and morals. But by the close of the seventeenth century, this same controversy had been transformed, in

phrasing, into the question of whether the pope was "infallible"—an adjective also applied to statements in Scripture. The doctrine of papal infallibility was then formally defined by the first Vatican Council in 1870.

9. Descartes introduces this strange possibility in Part 4 of his *Discourse* and also at the end of the first of his *Meditations on First Philosophy*.

10. Among these studies is Zbigniew Janowski's recent *Index Augustino-Cartesian: Textes et Commentaire* (Paris: Librairie Philosophique J. Vrin, 2000), which pairs key passages from Descartes with strikingly similar ones from Augustine.

11. *Discourse*, 6, AT VI, 77.

12. Ibid., 1, AT VI, 7.

13. David Hume, *Enquiry Concerning Human Understanding*, Section 12, Part 1.

14. *Meditations*, 2, AT VII, 23.

15. *Meditations*, Synopsis, AT VII, 16.

16. AT IX, 204.

17. *Enquiry Concerning Human Understanding*, Section 12, Part 2.

18. "Of the Education of Children" in Donald Frame, ed., *Selections from the Essays* (Arlington Heights, IL: Harlan Davidson, 1973), 9.

19. "Apology for Raymond Sebond" in *Selections from the Essays*, 58, 57.

20. *Meditations*, 2, AT VII, 25.

21. Descartes allows that animals have "sensations" and "passions," but he seems to use these terms only to indicate physical processes, not a mental awareness of the processes. His view of animals is elaborated in his Letter to the Marquis of Newcastle, November 23, 1646, AT IV, 573–576.

∾ CHRONOLOGY

1572	St. Bartholomew's Day massacre, in which thousands of French Protestants were slaughtered by French Catholics, intensifying religious warfare in France
1596	birth of Descartes, son of a local official, at La Haye, near Tours, in France
1604	enters the celebrated College of La Flèche at Anjou, run by Jesuit priests, though the exact dates of his attendance are disputed. He studied there eight or nine years
1616	receives degree in law from the University of Poitiers

1618–1648	The Thirty Years War, initially religious but later a struggle for supremacy among great powers, visits more destruction on central Europe than any previous event since the Black Death
1618	joins the army of Prince Maurice of Nassau during first phases of the Thirty Years War
1619	after a day of intense reflection (November 10), Descartes has a series of dreams that convince him that he must establish a new, unified science of nature
1628	back in France after further travels, Descartes argues with other intellectuals that certainties rather than probabilities must be the foundation of human knowledge. He sells his French properties and eventually moves to Holland, where he lives for the next twenty years
1633	Galileo is forced by the Catholic Church to "abjure, execrate, and detest" his view that the earth moves around the sun
1637	publishes the *Discourse on Method,* some of which had been written ten years earlier, and attaches to it three essays on scientific subjects, including one that lays the basis of analytic geometry. He becomes a hero to reformers but is deeply suspected by conservatives
1640	death of Descartes's five-year-old daughter, born out of wedlock
1641	publishes his *Meditations on First Philosophy,* which had already been circulated in manuscript among intellectuals living in France, and to it he adds six sets of objections and replies, later followed by a seventh
1642	outbreak of the English Civil War (or Puritan Revolution), leading to the beheading of King Charles I (1649)
1644	publishes his *Principles of Philosophy,* devoted mainly to physical science
1649	publishes *The Passions of the Soul*
1649	after repeated invitations, Descartes goes to Sweden to become tutor to the monarch, Queen Christina. But the climate and taxing schedule wear down his health
1650	dies in Sweden of pneumonia, February 11
1651	publication of *Leviathan,* by the English philosopher Thomas Hobbes, empiricist, materialist, absolutist, and one of Descartes' chief philosophical rivals
1677	death of Benedict Spinoza, Dutch philosopher of Jewish heritage, influenced by Descartes, proponent of rationalism

1714   publication of *Monadology* by G.W. Leibniz, a German philoso-
              pher influenced by Descartes

〜 SUGGESTED READINGS

Cottingham, John, ed. *The Cambridge Companion to Descartes*. New York: Cambridge, 1992.

Kemp Smith, Norman. *New Studies in the Philosophy of Descartes*. London: Macmillan, 1966.

Kenny, Anthony. *Descartes: A Study of His Philosophy*. New York: Random House, 1968.

Williams, Bernard. *Descartes: The Project of Pure Enquiry*. Atlantic Highlands, NJ: Humanities, 1978.

Wilson, Margaret Dauler. *Descartes*. London: Routledge, 1978 (1993).

CHAPTER 8

Locke

Philosophy as Moderation

John Barna

~ Preview

Locke lived during a time of dramatic discoveries in science and revolutionary changes in government. His goal as a philosopher was to keep his head while others were losing theirs. In other words, he wanted to understand what was happening in science and society in the most realistic, objective, and systematic way that he could. He tried to understand what kind of knowledge the new science provided and decided that it was substantial but limited. He analyzed the impressive powers of the mind but also its limits. In politics, he worked out a theory of society that supported the democratic revolution of his day by basing government on natural rights. Individuals have rights, he said, but they must give up some of them for the sake of a peaceful society. Above all, he thought philosophers should be fair and balanced. They must look at both sides of every issue and find the most reasonable compromise. (The Editor)

∾ Introduction

"Why, man, he doth bestride the narrow world like a Colossus. . . ." One cannot aim an ironic zinger at Locke in quite the way Cassius does at Julius Caesar in Shakespeare's play. But like the Roman leader, the British philosopher is both part of his epoch and at the same time transcends it. And, like Julius Caesar, Locke witnessed tremendous political upheaval in his country. The civil unrest forced him to leave England for Holland and to go "underground" with other refugees, in fear for his very life.

England changed fundamentally during Locke's lifetime. When he was ten years old, in 1642, a civil war broke out between the king and his supporters on one side and Parliament and its Puritan supporters on the other. Seven years later, the victorious Puritans publicly beheaded King Charles I. Oliver Cromwell instituted a strict "Protectorate" government, following Puritan principles. When Cromwell died in 1658, the Puritans were unable to maintain their control, and Parliament invited the former king's son, Charles II, to come back from exile and assume the throne in a grand "Restoration."

Charles II tried to balance the different groups and interests of the society. But he died in 1685 and was succeeded by his brother, James II. James was a Roman Catholic, which disturbed some, and personally he was arrogant and intolerant. He filled many government posts with Roman Catholics, and it seemed he might try to impose his religion on the country. In response, Parliament passed the "Bill of Rights," accusing James of adopting laws without Parliament's consent. Parliament further declared him a traitor to the nation and invited Prince William of Orange (in Holland) to come and take power in England. When William accepted the Bill of Rights, Parliament conferred the crown on him and James fled to France. The peaceful transfer of power in 1688 is known as the "Glorious Revolution." It abolished absolutism in England and established the first constitutional monarchy in Europe.

Locke participated in these events in a small way, and his writings express their spirit of liberal rationalism. He wrote an *Essay on Toleration*, in which he argued that sincere religious belief cannot be forced on anyone and that such a policy would be contrary to Christian ideals. In general, he promoted moderation and compromise in all things. He was a devout Christian himself, and he thought others should be as well, but he said he was not so certain of his beliefs that he could impose them on anyone. He was a strong believer in the rights and liberties of the individual, but he also said that people must voluntarily surrender some of those liberties for the sake of a peaceful society. He believed the new scientific method enabled people to understand the world as never before, but he also recognized its limits.

Locke's intellectual and political reach extends from the historical movements of the Renaissance and Reformation to the eighteenth-century Enlightenment (that is, from about 1500 to about 1800), a transitional period that is marked by the progressive emancipation of the individual from outer authority and a growing independence from supernatural beliefs. During these centuries, people came to believe that they could govern themselves and that they were more directly related to nature than to God. Locke lived during a period when the former directing role of philosophy and theology was being increasingly displaced by science.

Locke not only summed up these trends of his time, but the elegance and lucidity of his thinking gave them an additional impetus. He was able to communicate the most complicated ideas and make them intelligible; in short, he was a popularizer, but without the intended negative connotations of the word. Locke's fundamental ideas are found in two treatises that were among the most widely read books of his own day. First, the *Essay Concerning Human Understanding* tries to show that experience is the basis of human knowledge.[1] The second book, the *Second Treatise of Government,* tries to show that political liberalism is the foundation of the individual's life in society.[2] Both books demonstrate Locke's twofold purpose: to limit the excesses of some continental thinkers, such as Descartes, but at the same time to defend the basic intellectual powers of people. We can know the world, but not with the certainty or to the extent that Descartes and others said; and we can know the natural law, which regulates society, but not with such certainty that we can enforce it ourselves, individually. We therefore need government to do that. And if we accept those limits on ourselves, we enlarge the sphere of liberty for everyone. Thus the purpose of philosophy for Locke is to discern both the powers and the limitations of human beings.

Locke broke the centuries-old precedent of the philosopher-as-university professor by getting involved in the political life of England and Europe. He was what may be called a "public philosopher," not only intellectually engaged and engaging, but very much involved in political and commercial affairs. These activities influenced his philosophical thinking. His writings were easily understandable by educated people, and his ideas circulated more widely than those of some others of his profession. Nowadays, in contrast, philosophy is communicated chiefly among professionals who are highly specialized.[3]

As a student at Oxford University, Locke found the prevailing instruction of Scholasticism uninteresting and inadequate in providing answers to the "big questions" of modern life. Scholasticism was the philosophical movement dominant in Western Christian civilization from the ninth to the seventeenth centuries. Scholastic philosophers assumed that the basic beliefs of Christianity were true and, as philosophers, tried to develop a rational understanding of those beliefs. So they tried to explain the concepts involved—for example, defining the word "soul"—and through strict, careful reasoning, they drew out the logical consequences of the beliefs. This medieval philosophical pursuit prevented the expansive questioning and experiential investigation that interested Locke. A career in either the church or the university did not attract him, and he trained for a while to be a medical doctor. Always fascinated by science, Locke became friendly with members of the Royal Society, an organization founded in 1662 for the purpose of scientific discussion and experimentation. The chemist Robert Boyle and especially the physicist Isaac Newton became his close friends. Newton's stress on observation and slowly building up generalizations from data influenced Locke's thinking for the *Essay Concerning Human Understanding*. In the late 1660s, Locke took the position of physician and advisor to the Earl of Shaftesbury, a prominent political leader, and became more interested in politics and public service.

Locke, as a public philosopher, was following the philosophic tradition that is perhaps best exemplified in the last century by John Dewey (1859–1952). Like Locke, Dewey in his philosophy reflected the inevitable tensions of a society wracked by upheaval—in Dewey's case, the upheavals of World War I. And by commenting on the chaos, he articulated what it is that philosophy does. Dewey believed that "the distinctive office, problems and subject matter of philosophy grow out of stresses and strains in the community life in which a given form of philosophy arises, and that, accordingly, its specific problems vary with the changes in human life that are always going on and that at times constitute a crisis and a turning point in human history."[4] It is the task of the philosopher, therefore, to relate philosophical investigation to contemporary social problems and to attempt to offer possible solutions. The initial task of a genuine philosopher (like Locke and Dewey) is to identify the most fundamental and pressing problems of his or her own society. Just as forceful and highly influential is the philosopher Richard Rorty, who has openly criticized his professional colleagues for abandoning this role of public debate on actual problems of contemporary society that previous philosophers traditionally embraced.

One problem with philosophy in this connection has been the development of a jargon that cannot easily be understood; most professionals nowadays are content to communicate with other initiates. Granted, philosophers have usually stood apart from ordinary people, but the distance has been increasing. To fill the void, specialists of all sorts have taken over the counseling and informing tasks that philosophers (and Church clerics) used to perform.

On the other hand, interestingly enough, philosophy has been given a "shot in the arm" by the wedding of what used to be called "high culture" with popular culture. Stanley Cavell of Harvard University has seen the possibility of understanding culture through the application of a philosophical concept to, for example, Alfred Hitchcock's films *North by Northwest* or *Psycho*. Philosophers have the perhaps unique ability to fuse the many streams running through culture that many other people perceive only partially or in a segmented way. Their special brand of wisdom might help people grapple with troubling technological advances such as cloning or the problem of an increasingly computer-controlled world. Although the times were vastly different, Locke employed some similar intellectual procedures and habits of mind.

☙ Agenda for Modern Philosophy

Because of the dramatic discoveries in the natural sciences during Locke's lifetime, he wanted to understand how these advances were possible and what they meant for the future. He wanted to understand the nature of the human mind and how we can know the world around us. After surveying a large range of well-known facts about sight, memory, reasoning, and other mental activities, Locke decided that the mind is a sort of receptacle that stores experiences. All knowledge is derived from experience, he said. So it is through our senses (seeing, hearing, tasting, etc.) that we acquire knowledge, and Locke introduces his famous idea of a *tabula rasa*, usually translated as "blank slate" or "tablet." (Actually, it is Latin for "scraped tablet.") He claimed that the human mind at birth is blank, a "white paper" he called it, upon which nothing is inscribed. Modernizing a bit, we could say that the mind is like a strip of photographic film, its chemicals ready to receive light and images at the click of a camera. Experience is like music or a movie burned onto the surface of a digital disc.

This view is called "empiricism," from a Greek word that means "experience." Locke explained and defended this theory in the *Essay Concerning Human Understanding*. The *Essay* was the first comprehensive exposition of empiricism, which was to become the foundational method of the modern natural and social sciences. Locke paved the way for later thinkers such as Berkeley, Hume, Kant, Bentham, and Mill, among others. After reading the *Essay*, Mill called Locke the "unquestioned founder of the analytic philosophy of mind."

But before he could make a case for empiricism, Locke had to deal with other theories and show that they were not acceptable. The most influential philosopher of the seventeenth century was Rene Descartes (1596–1650), who claimed that the mind is not shaped and filled by experience, but at birth is already equipped with basic ideas and concepts, which allow us to interpret the world. According to Descartes, the physical world is one vast mechanism, a "Newtonian world-machine." He believed that the parts, including the bodies of animals and humans, plus objects such as the stars and the earth itself, were propelled by a force arising from the original motion given to the universe by God. He did insist, however, that man is distinct from all other creatures in possessing a reasoning faculty. The mind is not a form of matter but an entirely separate substance implanted in a human body by God. Thus Descartes was a dualist; he believed reality was composed of two distinct types of things: material objects (such as the human body) and minds. Objects are made up of parts that have size, weight, and position in space, but minds are made up of thoughts, feelings, memories, beliefs, and so on. A thought is not two inches long; it doesn't weigh three ounces, and it isn't located inside one person's skull. Mental things are not physical at all.

But then how does the mind come into contact with the physical world and acquire knowledge? Descartes said, first, that mind and body can interact in the brain. Sound waves impacting my eardrums affect my mind, and when I decide to move my arm, my mind can affect the physical world. However, that interaction is not the source of knowledge. Descartes proposed that all people possess certain basic concepts, such as the concepts of substance, self, cause and effect, number, and perhaps others, from birth. They are inborn and innate. They have only to be stimulated to become evident; they are already and automatically present in all individuals. Putting it another way, Descartes taught that self-evident truths having no relation to sensory experience must be inherent in the mind itself. We do not learn them through the use of our senses, but rather understand them instinctively, because they have been part of our mental equipment from birth.

Descartes believed some ideas were innate because he made absolute certainty, grasped by the intellect, his criterion of knowledge. Anything that he could doubt, anything that might be false, fell short of genuine knowledge. The most certain knowledge is a person's knowledge of himself or herself. After doubting virtually everything, Descartes arrived at the absolute certainty of his own consciousness: "I think, therefore I am." The mind, the intellect, must therefore contain innate ideas that are prior to experience, because it is experience that brings doubt.

Descartes continued the Copernican revolution and the revolution of the "mechanical philosophy," both of which drove home the startling realization that things are not what they seem to our senses to be, and neither are they what they have been taught to be. Sensory experience, as well as doctrinal or other authoritative teaching, was shown to be misleading. Descartes rejected the senses as a source of knowledge because they can fool us. And he rejected religious and philosophical authority because, being secondhand information, authoritative teachings can be false or misleading. Only the rational mind with its clear and distinct ideas can be trusted, according to Descartes.

Locke offered a different view of the mind. He believed that knowledge does not exist prior to experience and that there is no innate knowledge. Rather, our knowledge originates in sense perception. As he says, whatever idea "was never perceived by the mind, was never in the mind." It is true that an idea may appear to be innate, and Locke explains how. Whatever was perceived by the mind at one time (for example, a math problem) can be stored in the memory, and a person might even forget that he perceived it earlier. If the person remembers the math example, but doesn't remember where he learned it, it might appear to him to be innate. But it only appears to be innate. There are no ideas in infants' minds that they aren't aware of. For, as Locke affirms, "what is not either actually in view, or in the memory, is in the mind no way at all" and is "as if it never had been there."

It must be added that the mind, as a blank tablet at birth, does not even contain the idea of a God or any notions of right and wrong. For Locke it is only when the newborn child begins to have experiences, to perceive the external world with its senses, and to feel pleasure and pain, that anything gets registered in its mind. Empiricism means that we do not have these moral or religious ideas in our minds from birth.

Locke asks the logical question that if the mind is blank and without any ideas, "how comes it to be furnished?" Or as he puts it more poetically: "whence comes it by that vast store, which the busy and boundless fancy of man has painted on it, with an almost endless variety?" The answer he gives is "from experience," upon which, he asserts, "all our knowledge is founded; and from that it ultimately derives itself." Seeing gives us knowledge of colors and shapes and motion; hearing gives us knowledge of sounds; touch gives us knowledge of hardness and smoothness and heaviness; and so on.

But the simple ideas that result directly from sense perception are merely the foundations of knowledge; no human being could live on the basis of them alone. These simple ideas must be integrated and fused, according to Locke, into "complex ideas." For example, a baby who encounters a red color, a round shape, and a sweet taste over and over can combine the simple ideas into a complex idea of an apple. Complex ideas are made up of combinations of simple ideas. This is the broad function of reason or the understanding (the two equated by Locke), which has the power to combine, coordinate, and organize the impressions received from the senses with the ultimate task of building a usable body of general truth. Such combinations may result in complex ideas that have no corresponding reference to the real world. For example, a person might combine simple ideas to form an idea of a square apple, even though square apples do not exist. Sensation and reason are both indispensable to this scheme—the sensations for furnishing the mind with the raw materials of knowledge and reason for working them into meaningful form. Locke's influence here was enormous for the thought of the Enlightenment: this combination of sensationalism and rationalism became one of the hallmarks of the period.

The acquisition of knowledge can take place internally as well as externally. As Locke puts it, "our observation employed either about external sensible objects; or about the internal operations of our minds, perceived and reflected by ourselves, is that which supplies our understandings with all the materials of thinking." People are aware of their own memories, imaginations, reasoning, emotions, and decisions. The internal operations or internal sense is an answer to anyone who might accuse Locke of oversimplifying or seeing only external sources of knowledge. The internal sensation Locke names "reflection," or introspection, or what the mind gets "by reflecting on its own operations within itself." Or as he puts it, reflection is what is understood as "that notice which the mind takes of its own operations." Locke is here referring to the reflexive awareness of our mental operations, which Cartesians treated as a way of accessing innate ideas but which Locke calls "internal sense." To have ideas before the mind is to be perceiving given or constructed sensory images, including images of the internal sense. In addition, Locke adds a pre-Freudian notion when he acknowledges that the dream state can also reflect experience: "The dreams of sleeping men, are, as I take it, all made up of the waking man's ideas, though, for the most part, oddly put together."

When Locke examined simple ideas, he decided that we have two different types. We have ideas of primary qualities and ideas of secondary qualities. The difference depends on whether the idea actually resembles the object in the world that caused the idea or does not resemble the object. For example, heat and cold are secondary ideas. A cup of tea may feel warm to one person but cold to someone else. Is it actually warm or cold? It's neither. Something in the tea causes the feelings in the people, but whatever causes the feelings is not itself hot or cold (it can't be both at the same time). The ideas of heat and cold exist in our minds but do not resemble the objects that cause them. A fruit may taste sweet to one person and sour to another. Even colors are secondary properties. Under different kinds of light an object may appear to be different colors. On the other hand, if a box is square, then it is square for everyone who sees it and handles it. Being square is a primary quality because our idea of square really resembles the objects that cause the idea. The objects are square. Locke said that being solid or liquid and being in motion are also primary qualities. Thus primary qualities are objective, and secondary qualities are subjective. Secondary qualities exist only in our minds. Some of our ideas are reliable representations of the world, while others are good enough for practical purposes but do not accurately reflect the external world.

Locke's doctrine of substance also illustrates his compromising, moderate view of the knowledge we can have. When I think of an apple, for example, I think of primary and secondary qualities: round shape, a certain weight, red color, sweet taste. Those are qualities of an apple. But what has the qualities? If I leave an apple on a window sill, all those qualities can change over time, and yet it is the same apple. What remains the same? Locke said qualities inhere in a substance. The substance remains the same, even if the qualities change. But I never experience the substance. All I experience are the primary and secondary qualities. Thus we can know that substances exist, because something must support the qualities, but we cannot know the substance directly. We can have knowledge, but it is limited.

In Book IV of the *Essay,* "Of Knowledge and Opinion," Locke identifies three distinct sources of knowledge: intuition, reason (or "demonstration"), and experience. By intuition Locke means that we know that black is not white and that a square is not a triangle. By demonstration we can know geometrical truths through intuitive steps of reasoning. Finally, by experience we can know that physical objects exist and possess certain qualities that are easily observable. Again, for Locke, knowledge ordinarily demands certainty, but he reminds us that ultimately we have a narrow scope of knowledge.

Locke criticized Descartes, but on some issues he agreed with his predecessor. He accepted Descartes' assumption that genuine knowledge is absolutely certain. Where certainty is absent, he thinks we have at most only probable belief or opinion. For this reason, Locke thinks that the scope of our knowledge is "very narrow." Locke did not have Descartes' confidence that through reason alone people could understand the true nature of the world. But he did believe that if people learn to extend and interpret their experience in the right ways, they can build up a significant body of highly probable beliefs, which are perfectly adequate.

Empiricism, initiated by Locke, was perhaps the most influential philosophy during the following three centuries, but it has not been without its critics. John Dewey, for example, says that the empirical mind is always an attacking one, a fragmenter, by its nature. Locke very perceptively breaks up experience into its parts and analyzes it into sensations of colors, sounds, touch, and so on. He describes the processes of remembering, imagining, and reasoning. But in taking apart consciousness in that way, what happens to the self? A person's mind is filled with sensations, and reflection reveals mental activities. But if that is the only knowledge she has, then what knowledge can she have of herself, her identity? It seems that empiricism is a philosophy that—to borrow a line—cannot see life "steadily" or see life "whole."

William Barrett, another twentieth-century philosopher, has argued that modern philosophy's insistence upon the empirical-rational point of view, to the exclusion of the irrational side of human nature, has been disastrous. Many writers, artists, and philosophers have sought out a "metaphysical"—that is, above, or beside, the physical—dimension to resuscitate a connection that has been neglected. They believe we have other ways of acquiring knowledge besides the five senses. Locke's empiricism gave a strong boost to science and technology, but the tremendous growth of science and a materialistic outlook in the modern era has been a mixed blessing. Humanity's increasing dependence on machines brings wealth, but we should try to remember what we lost as we gained that power.

✑ Transition to Political Theory

The empirical system of knowledge in the *Essay* is Locke's brilliant development of what could be called a new psychology for his time. He analyzes the conscious mind as it acquires and builds up truth perceived through the senses. Locke believes that the types of ideas and reasoning he describes are universal for every human being. The *Essay* had a wider significance for several fields besides the theory of knowledge. For example, Locke used the new psychology to strengthen one of the chief arguments he put forth in his *Second Treatise of Government*—the argument against absolute monarchy. Defenders of political and religious absolutism had contended that the inclination to submit to authority was present in the conscious mind from birth. This belief was nourished by the Cartesian theory of innate ideas, which Locke had obliterated in the *Essay*. Rather than heredity and faith, Locke believed that the environment and reason were the two "foundations of knowledge." The environment supplies the building blocks, and reason assembles them. Reason enables us to see relations among ideas, but the ideas must be furnished by experience.

Since Locke believed that human intelligence, though perhaps unable to account for everything in the universe down to the last detail, could at least explain all that one needs to know about reality, he said the same kind of thinking could be applied to a critical examination of the current government. Existing social and economic institutions could be submitted to the judgment of common sense, and one could show how many of these institutions were both unreasonable and unnecessarily complex. Locke's *Second Treatise of Government* (1690) provided the theoretical justification for the contractual view of monarchy as a limited and revocable agreement between ruler and ruled, which had triumphed in England in 1688.

Locke's life changed when he met Sir Anthony Ashley Cooper, the Earl of Shaftesbury, in 1666. For fifteen years Locke served Shaftesbury as physician, secretary, and counselor. It was Shaftesbury's most productive period; he was one of the commissioners sent from England to bring back Charles II as king, and he became a close advisor to the monarch.

But Shaftesbury argued with the king and fell from grace, and all attention was turned to the rumors of a plot to assassinate Charles II in order to replace him with his brother, the future James II, a Roman Catholic. Shaftesbury, a Protestant, proposed a law excluding Catholics from the throne. His political opponents countered with the old argument of the divine right of kings, stipulating that the monarch could choose his own religion. To bolster their side, they resuscitated an old study of divine right monarchy, *Patriarcha*, by Sir Robert Filmer, a vindication of absolutism in the monarchy. A poorly constructed argument, it nevertheless revived old fears of bloody civil wars over the question of absolutism. Shaftesbury turned to Locke for a formal reply to Filmer. Locke's *First Treatise of Government* demolished Filmer's arguments for absolutism. Locke decided on his own to write a second *Treatise*, which presented a plan for government in general terms with more universal applicability.

Shaftesbury, too, had been stimulated by Locke's thinking. He challenged the king on matters of succession and was subsequently imprisoned, briefly, in the Tower of London. Parliament was dissolved and Shaftesbury was without a political base. He was released, but he knew that self-imposed exile was his only option. He fled, taking Locke with him, to Holland, where eventually the *Second Treatise* saw publication.

Locke's stay in Holland, although fraught with danger, permitted him the leisure to write his political philosophy. It was with the perspective that geographic distance can permit that he was able to draw up on a more universal plane the justification before world opinion of the Glorious Revolution of 1688 and the placing of William on the throne of England. The Preface, written two years after the revolution, summarizes his purpose:

> Reader, thou hast here the beginning and end of a discourse concerning government. What fate has otherwise disposed of the papers that should have filled up the middle, and were more than all the rest, it is not worth while to tell thee. These which remain, I hope, are sufficient to establish the throne of our great restorer, our present King William—to make good his title in the consent of the people, which, being our only one of all lawful governments, he has more fully and clearly than any other prince in Christendom; and to justify to the world the people of England, whose love of their just and natural rights, with their resolution to preserve them, saved the nation when it was on the very brink of slavery and ruin.

As with most classical philosophy, Locke formulates his views in response to conditions of his day. He therefore appeals to the consent of the people and presents the separation of legislative and executive powers as a solution to the struggle of monarch and parliament in the England and Europe of his time. The emphasis placed on the protection of private property, too, reflects the interests of Whig landowners, the class that Locke depended on for patronage. On the other hand, and to be fair, Locke never intended monopoly on land for these landowners.

～ The State of Nature and the Natural Law

Locke's general aim and purpose in the *Second Treatise* is to explain the "true, original and extent, and end of civil government." Locke presents a series of definitions of the elements of society and government, starting with political power. "Political power, then," Locke says, "I take to be a right of making laws with penalties of death and, consequently, all less penalties for the regulating and preserving of property, and employing the force of the community in the execution of such laws, and in the defense of the commonwealth from foreign injury, and all this only in the public good." To understand this definition, Locke says that we must first consider "what state all men are naturally in," and that is "a state of perfect freedom" and "perfect equality." By nature, before governments and societies are created, people are free and equal.

So Locke's state of nature has a built-in state of liberty, but he qualifies this: "Yet it is not a state of license. . . . The state of nature has a law of nature to govern it which obliges everyone." The natural liberty of man is not to be understood as meaning that men are under no laws whatever, for "in all the states of created beings, capable of laws, where there is no law, there is no freedom. The natural liberty of man is . . . [t]o have only the law of nature for his rule" and "to be under no other restraint but the law of nature." The law of nature is not the laws that governments make but is more fundamental. He says, "The state of nature has a law of nature to govern it, which obliges everyone; and reason, which is that law, teaches all mankind who will but consult it, that, being all equal and independent, no one ought to harm another in his life, health, liberty, or possessions." Thus the natural law is a kind of moral law, informing us of what we may and may not do. Moreover, since people are equal, "the execution of the law of nature is, in that state, put into every man's hands, whereby everyone has a right to punish the transgressors of that law." Everyone can understand the law of right and wrong and can enforce it.

In discussing the state of nature, Locke is not limiting the idea to the original prepolitical condition of man. In fact, he himself asks whether it actually ever existed in the first place, and he gives an example that applies to political society.

> It is often asked as a mighty objection, where are or ever were there any men in such a state of nature? To which it may suffice as an answer at present that, since all princes and rulers of independent governments all through the world are in a state of nature, it is plain the world never was, nor ever will be, without numbers of men in that state.

The rulers of England, France, and Russia are in the state of nature because there is no government over them. Locke gives another example of a Swiss and an American Indian, at least one of them experienced politically, meeting in the woods of America. Of them Locke says, "they are perfectly in a state of nature in reference to one another." The state of nature, then, is more comprehensive than a description of the condition of humans prior to the advent of civil society. It is not based on any historical record, in addition, but rather is an artificial construct, an abstraction to be used by Locke for his theoretical purposes.

The ancient Greeks had had their notions of certain eternal laws unwritten and directing the actions of all natural beings, and built into the very structure of the universe, including the gods themselves. Sophocles' *Antigone* dramatizes the conflict between these timeless eternal laws, in this case burial rights, which Antigone holds, and the assertion of civil authority in the person of Creon. The complication comes from their similar claims for Divine justice and the clash of the religious with the secular, which are not easily reconciled.

Roman Stoicism continued the tradition of natural law with its ideas of unity among all humans, animals, and nature, connected ultimately to the Deity. The Christian theory of morality and politics absorbed those earlier principles and held that moral goodness could be known by reason. The most influential natural law theorist was St. Thomas Aquinas. For him, God's eternal reason is at the root of laws directing all things. Obeying the natural law would promote the good of the commonwealth. Natural law here shares with eternal law the aim of guiding us toward our eternal goal.

Locke changed the direction of natural law from the common good to personal, individual goals. Locke's emphasis was always on individual rights, especially the individual's right to life, liberty, and property. More recent natural law theories tend only to augment the secularized and fragmented world view by stressing the obedience to man-made laws.[5] The only binding laws nowadays are those evolved in an increasingly relativistic system of jurisprudence. Or as Irving Babbitt puts it, with regard to the idea of materialism and the stress on the "law for things" (that is, property), "Man's capacity for concentration is limited, so the price he has paid for material progress has been an increasing inattention to facts of an entirely different order—those, namely, of the human law" (that is, the moral law that makes us human).[6]

For centuries people assumed that the basis of all political authority was the connection with God and eternal law. But in the seventeenth century, as science progressed, fewer people wanted to appeal to God's direct intervention in human affairs, and without divine providence, divine right monarchy became only usurpation. Locke proposed the notion of a social contract as an alternative basis for legitimizing government. But the idea of a social contract was vague and could be interpreted in different ways. Forty years earlier, Locke's fellow countryman, Thomas Hobbes (1588–1679), had used the terms "state of nature," "natural law," and "social contract" in his book *Leviathan,* but Hobbes had defined them differently from Locke. In fact, Hobbes used his concepts to argue for absolute monarchy, the opposite of Locke's proposal.

Although both Hobbes and Locke start with the concept of the state of nature, in Hobbes' conception of nature the human race is in a perpetual "war of all against all," "and the life of man [is] solitary, poor, nasty, brutish, and short." Anything is better than the state of nature, and in fact, an all-powerful government is necessary to curb aggression and keep the peace. Locke, in contrast, has an optimistic view of human nature. People are naturally peaceful and respect the law of nature. Occasionally, a few people do not respect it, and that is why governments are created.

Fundamental to these two opposing views of human nature is the doctrine of Original Sin, which was on the minds of seventeenth-century writers like Locke and Hobbes. The biblical story of Adam and Eve, who disobeyed God and were tempted by "forbidden knowledge,"[7] illustrates the doctrine. Because of this sin, humans tend to commit evil unless some sort of authority, religious or civil, intervenes. The doctrine is related to the political spectrum. A "conservative" generally acknowledges the possibility of this tendency toward evil, while a "liberal" (such as Locke) sees things more optimistically. Human nature is essentially good, Locke says, but individuals can fall victim to social, environmental, or psychological pressures, which can result in bad conduct. Another liberal was Jean-Jacques Rousseau (1712–1778), the French political theorist, who rejected the sinfulness and fallibility of the individual and substituted the doctrine of "natural goodness."

∼ The Social Contract

How does the state of nature end and society begin? Locke says in Chapter Eight of the *Second Treatise* that people agree to form governments.

> Men being, as has been said, by nature all free, equal, and independent, no one can be put out of this estate and subjected to the political power of another without his own consent. The only way whereby any one divests himself of his natural liberty and puts his hands on the binds of civil society is by agreeing with other men to join and write into a community for their comfortable, safe, and peaceable living one amongst another, in a secure enjoyment of their properties and a greater security against any that are not of it. This any number of men may do, because it injures not the freedom of the rest; they are left as they were in the liberty of the state of nature.

A person in the state of nature, Locke holds, is not noticeably different from a person in organized society. Why would anyone give up freedom and equality for the restraints of society? The problem is that the law of nature is not always clear to everyone. As political scholars such as William Ebenstein have written, human beings are biased by their interests and not guided by pure reason to all see the same law.[8] In addition, who would settle disputes? No third party or judge exists, leaving room for passion and revenge as guides. And because the injured party might not possess the wherewithal to defend himself, he is forced to enter into society: "Thus mankind, notwithstanding all the privileges of the state of nature, but being in an ill condition while they remain in it, are quickly driven into society."

The social contract thus has a purpose: to counteract the very real dangers, or at least the precariousness, of the state of nature. Uncertainties can then be replaced by the predictability of legal precedents and stable institutions. Here we see Locke following his moderate instincts in political philosophy, as he did in his theory of knowledge. We are free and independent but unsafe. We are inherently able to understand the law of nature, but our passions interfere with that understanding.

Locke reflects the continuity of tradition, using the idea of a social contract to restate ancient political ideas. Greek and Roman writers, such as Plato and Cicero, discussed the social contract, as did writers in the Middle Ages. The medieval emphasis on communal interests or the commonwealth, where government authority depends on doing what would benefit the community, most attracted Locke. Government is subordinate to the wishes of the people and to natural law.

One may ask whether Locke really was drawing upon authentic history in the first place, and the answer is, probably not. He proposed a set of principles basing government on consent, not because of historical precedent but because for his times this seemed the reasonable thing to do. Locke wished to preserve the natural freedom of the individual, and the idea of a social contract allowed him to do that. Thomas P. Peardon points out that there is indeed no historical perspective presented in the *Second Treatise,* but rather that Locke is arguing by reason alone. He is really concerned with "the inner logic of society." Locke is saying that "relations between men in society and between individuals and society are as if there had been a contract made between them whereby men surrendered certain rights in return for protection of the rest."[9]

⁓ Property

Among the rights discussed throughout the *Second Treatise,* the reader cannot fail to observe that the idea of property receives the most attention. Indeed, preserving the right to property is the primary reason for and function of government. Locke transformed in this way the dominant trend of natural law thinking, especially when in Chapter Five he makes property a natural right, preceding even civil society. Everyone has a natural right to his or her own body, he says.[10] And one's labor is a kind of extension of one's body. Thus, "Whatsoever he removes out of the state that nature has provided and left it in, he hath mixed his labor with it and joined to it something that is his own and thereby makes it his property. It being by him removed from the common state nature placed it in, it hath by this labor something annexed to it that excludes the common right of other men. . . ." Locke does recognize some restraints on owning property. One can own as much property as one can use without anything spoiling, and no more. However, since people have consented to the use of money, which does not spoil, they have consented to unlimited accumulation, Locke says. The labor theory of property worked well for the settling of the American wilderness; it was a seal of ownership for the hardy pioneer. No one who hadn't cleared his own could usurp a settler's plot. Such a concept when applied to Europe, however, was sheer fantasy. Yet the sanction of inviolable private ownership of property brought on ruthless accumulation as an inevitable consequence. Locke's theory benefited the middle class but led to further deterioration in the condition of the poor.

Locke's idea of property rights once again shows the limits he placed on the state. In other words, Locke intended to show that the legitimate power of the state to regulate the rightful possession of property was limited. The state cannot, according to Locke, dispense with all forms of private property, because natural law requires that there should be some system of private property rights. Furthermore, anyone in the state of nature may have rights to acquired property under natural law as well. This property, it follows, can also be taken with the person when he or she joins civil society. A citizen's right to property must in this case not be violated. Locke had to allow exceptions, and he does mention that a state in certain circumstances can appropriate property (in the form of taxes, for example). But such appropriation can occur only with the consent of the majority, and thus the power of government is limited after all.

Property for Locke becomes in fact so absolute a right that it transcended even the dictates of government or religion, beyond social obligation for the common benefit. Under this system, principles of equality were an illusion. Government's *laissez-faire* economic policy and its "umpire role" in governing had the effect of vindicating the middle class, assuring its prosperity and ultimately its cultural dominance. Property rights would eventually come to displace human rights because government acts merely as an impartial referee between dubiously equal haves and have-nots. The result is the strengthening of competitive, extreme, and ultimately dehumanizing individualism.

⁓ Revolution

The ultimate purpose for writing his *Second Treatise* was to justify the Revolution of 1688. Revolution for Locke can occur when the government, set up as a protector of natural rights, becomes tyrannical. The people have the right to revolt, to overthrow the tyrant. As Locke puts it, they can exercise their right "when the governor, however entitled, makes not the law, but his will, the rule, and his commands and actions are not directed to the properties of his people, but the satisfaction of his own ambitions, revenge, covetousness, or any other irregular passion." This is a violation of the social contract, a betrayal of the trust given to the government by the people. In this case, those governed have a right to rise up and change their government when they believe that such action is for their own good as well as for the benefit of the community at large. Revolution will almost always be avoided, however, because the right of the people to rebel is "the best fence against rebellion."

~ Locke and Burke

Locke's ideas had a tremendous influence on later political thinkers. It is interesting to see how a writer such as the Irishman Edmund Burke (1729–1797), who wrote a century after Locke on the political revolutions in America and France, uses Locke's concept of a social contract but changes it at the same time. Although often thought of as opponents in political philosophy, Locke and Burke actually share more similarities than one might expect. Hobbes, Locke, and Burke all stressed that society was founded on a contract or compact or even, with religious connotations, a covenant. Both Locke and Burke were in agreement in criticizing unchecked royal absolutism. Both believed in the rightful dominance of parliamentary government and the gradual evolution of more democratic government. Although Locke justified revolution, he and Burke both favored gradual change. During the French Revolution, Burke openly decried the use of the guillotine as the way to change a government. Locke established the theoretical framework for the American Revolution, and Burke opposed Great Britain's war to suppress the colonies' defiance of the crown.

Both Locke and Burke believed that some form of divine intent really did guide society and that rights were for those who performed their moral duty. Burke presents an interesting extension of the notion of a social contract in his *Reflections on the Revolution in France* (1790). Its message fills in details that Locke's readers would probably have taken for granted. The words are so stirring and forceful that their perusal can prove enlightening:

> Society is indeed a contract. Subordinate contracts for objects of mere occasional interest may be dissolved at pleasure—but the state ought not to be considered as nothing better than a partnership agreement in a trade of pepper and coffee, calico or tobacco, or some other such low concern, to be taken up for a little temporary interest, and to be dissolved by the fancy of the parties. It is to be looked on with other reverence; because it is not a partnership in things subservient only to the gross animal existence of a temporary and perishable nature. It is a partnership in all science; a partnership in every virtue; and in all perfection. As the ends of such a partnership cannot be obtained in many generations, it becomes a partnership not only between those who are living, but between those who are living, those who are dead and those who are to be born.

Burke here shows reverence and affection for the variety and mystery of tradition. His social partnership is not a mere commercial enterprise to guarantee private profit or property; all persons, as Locke holds, have rights, too, by virtue of their humanity. And just as Locke attacks Continental philosophy, Burke attacks Continental political thought, especially Jean-Jacques Rousseau's. Burke believes Rousseau's abstract slogans and insufficient attention to the concrete details of governing had contributed to the excesses of the French Revolution.

Burke also reaches back to find connections with the roots of a living civilization and is a conserver of its values. Burke sees a societal and cosmic harmony in this deeper tradition that prescribed the pattern for human dignity and the norm for political direction. Indeed, the roots grew deeply enough to withstand the devastation of the French Revolution. Burke goes back for his appeal to the idea of community far richer than a commercial agreement. For Burke the true compact is eternal: it unites the dead with the living and with the unborn, all participating in a spiritual as well as a social partnership.

⟿ Locke and the American Revolution

We have seen that one of Locke's main purposes in writing his *Second Treatise of Government* was to defend the right of revolution. So, colonists in America who were contemplating a rebellion against Great Britain would certainly be interested in Locke's work. When Thomas Jefferson wrote the Declaration of Independence, he defended the Americans' actions by portraying King George III as a tyrant who had betrayed the trust of his loyal subjects.

Jefferson drew upon Locke not only to justify the revolution, but to explain the fundamental values of the new American commonwealth. "We hold these truths to be self-evident," he wrote: "That all men are created equal; that they are endowed by their Creator with certain unalienable rights; that among these are life, liberty, and the pursuit of happiness." In Chapter Two of the *Second Treatise,* Locke had written that "being all equal and independent, no one ought to harm another in his life, health, liberty, or possessions." The ideas were so close, in fact, that Richard Henry Lee suggested that the Declaration had been "copied from Locke's treatise."[11] Jefferson denied the charge and said that he had only been trying to harmonize the views he found in various books of political philosophy. And one should not overemphasize Locke's influence on the Declaration or the Constitution. Jefferson, Madison, Hamilton, and the other Founding Fathers were all classically educated, and a careful examination of these documents reveals that their conception of democratic principles came from traditions going back to the Middle Ages, Rome, and Greece. Jefferson certainly knew the works of Aristotle and Cicero well.

Historian Charles Beard has argued that Locke's emphasis on the right to property was just as important to the Founding Fathers as his notions of revolution, equality, and other natural rights. Jefferson and other representatives at the Constitutional Convention owned large estates, including slaves, and wanted to protect their economic interests, Beard says.[12] On the other hand, Paul Elmer More has suggested that as far as civilization goes, the right to property might in the end be more important than the right to life.[13]

A problem arises, however, in comparing Locke's and Jefferson's appeal to self-evident rights with the empiricism in the *Essay Concerning Human Understanding*. Locke had rejected Descartes' notion of innate principles and said that the mind at birth is a blank tablet. But then can he believe in self-evident rights, such as the rights to life, liberty, and property? If it is self-evident (not dependent on experience) that people have basic rights, then it seems that our knowledge of these rights is innate.

To resolve this apparent conflict, Locke distinguishes between the effects of innate ideas and self-evident rights. He says that the notion of innate principles discourages people from thinking for themselves, whereas the notion of self-evident rights has exactly the opposite effect. People must use their intuition to grasp the self-evidence of natural rights. They must test the principles by the light of their own reason. As Morton White says:

> To use one's own intuition, Locke held, was to use a faculty that God had given to all men for their use whereas, according to the doctrine of innate principles, one would be forced to swallow, as he put it, a lot of principles without checking them oneself. . . . Locke's main political point is that because innate principles are allegedly stamped by God on man's mind at birth, and hence not arrived at by the exercise of man's reason, the doctrine of innate principles is, or certainly can be, a tool of dictators.[14]

Whether Locke can maintain this distinction, the idea of self-evident rights, or human rights, has inspired countless people and continues to change the world.

Locke may not have been wholly original in his political ideas, just as in formal philosophy his talent was to synthesize magnificently some very disparate ideas from the work of other thinkers. He was a main theorist of the English Revolution of 1688 and a chief source of the ideas guiding the American Revolution of 1776. The credit received was due to his clear and reasonable expression of ideas already circulating in his time and his ability to assimilate and articulate centuries of actual political experience. This elaborate foundation coupled with the love of individual freedom, which Locke knew was endemic to Englishmen and Americans alike, helped promote and give shape to his reasonable and apt expression. The philosopher and the philosophical vision can here be likened to a seismograph for political revolutionary eruptions.

Locke writes plainly and avoids technical terms and jargon. He reins in extremism of all kinds and sees philosophy as moderation. He displays a sober reasonableness, weighs all the evidence, exhibits very little bias, and refuses to accept blindly anything based on authority alone. Locke's very style of writing promotes a feeling of security, of a certain rightness in a proposal, of a genuine confidence in rationality itself. Indeed, what was most real for Locke—from simple ideas to revolutionary action—was also most real for the majority of his readers. More importantly, in the expressive words of Basil Willey, the "very limitations of his mind fitted him to be the accepted thinker of an age which had lost the taste for spiritual exploration."[15] In reading Locke, we are aware of being in the presence of a mind that has "come to rest" in the world view of science and rationalism. It is a world of complacency, of self-sufficiency. No longer is divine revelation the guiding spirit. As for philosophy, its method and mode become less transcendent and speculative. Through Locke's colossal synthesis, the vision of philosophy thereby shifts to a new direction.[16]

∿ NOTES

1. John Locke, *Essay Concerning Human Understanding,* edited by A.C. Fraser (New York: Dover, 1959). I will refer to this book as the *Essay.*

2. John Locke, *Second Treatise of Government,* edited by C.B. Macpherson (Indianapolis, IN: Hackett, 1980). I will refer to this book as the *Second Treatise.*

3. See William Barrett, *Death of the Soul: From Descartes to the Computer* (Garden City, NY: Anchor, 1986), for a sensitive and perceptive handling of this controversial view.

4. John Dewey, *Reconstruction in Philosophy* (Boston: Beacon, 1957).

5. That moral arguments are put in more positivist, or "scientific," language nowadays attests to the ultimate failure of Locke's and the Enlightenment's program of supplying moral principles that no rational human being could dispute. In attempting to rid the culture of too much tradition and superstitious forms of morality, what they necessarily left was a secular morality wholly removed from the interconnections of man and nature to God—a concept that Europeans had taken for granted in Aquinas' time, for example, but that no longer obtained in the eighteenth century. For a highly readable introductory assessment of what the author calls "the New Cosmology," see Crane Brinton, *Ideas and Men: The Story of Western Thought* (Englewood Cliffs, NJ: Prentice-Hall, 1967).

6. Irving Babbitt, *Democracy and Leadership* (Boston: Houghton Mifflin, 1924), 15.

7. The notion of "forbidden knowledge" is a fascinating one and typically Western in its link to the idea of progress. It is enlivened and transformed in each successive epoch by what Harry Levin calls a renewed "thematic charge." The Faustian theme continues the notion in the modern world, and science often operates in the area of the "forbidden" nowadays: the threat of terrorist atomic warfare, genetic engineering, cloning, and so on. For a book-length analysis, see Roger Shattuck's interesting *Forbidden Knowledge* (New York: St. Martin's Press, 1996).

8. William Ebenstein, *Great Political Thinkers* (New York: Holt, Rinehart and Winston, 1965), 388.

9. Thomas P. Peardon, ed., *The Second Treatise of Government* (New York: Bobbs-Merrill, 1952), xvii.

10. Locke's assumption has been used in recent discussions of abortion rights. Just as Locke stressed that human beings not only own property, but also own their own bodies, some women have claimed that since they own their bodies, abortion must ultimately be a woman's decision. Kevin Knight presents an interesting debate over this issue in *The McIntyre Reader* (South Bend, IN: Notre Dame University Press, 1998).

11. Morton White, *The Philosophy of the American Revolution* (New York: Oxford University Press, 1978), 64.

12. Charles Beard, *An Economic Interpretation of the Constitution of the United States* (New York: Macmillan, 1913).

13. Russell Kirk, *The Roots of American Order* (LaSalle, IL: Open Court, 1974).

14. White, op. cit., 15, 19.

15. Basil Willey, *The Seventeenth Century Background* (London: Chatto & Windus, 1934), 266. Willey's book is one of the most brilliant assessments of the impact of the Age of Reason on our culture.

16. I am incalculably indebted to my friend, Professor John Danisi (of Wagner College), whose instruction through conversation, philosophical and otherwise, has had my rapt attention for years. I thank Professor Ronald Rainey for his confidence in requesting that I write this essay and also for his spontaneous lessons in history and philosophy. Professor Robert Gurland has been continually supportive and inspirational as a teacher–scholar, very much in the admirable tradition of the "public philosopher." Special thanks to Robin Belcher-Timme and Daniel Golden, without whom this project would have been impossible.

∼ CHRONOLOGY

1620	Pilgrims land in Plymouth, Massachusetts, and write the Mayflower Compact
1632	Locke is born in England
1642	Civil War breaks out between Royalists and Parliament, King Charles I is defeated and beheaded in 1649, Parliament rules England
1651	Thomas Hobbes' *Leviathan*
1652	Locke enters Christ Church, Oxford, remains there as a student and teacher until 1667

1660	Charles II invited back to England from exile to rule
1661	Louis XIV, the "Sun King," takes control in France, strengthens absolutism
1662	the Royal Society is founded, devoted to the exchange of scientific ideas; Robert Boyle discovers mechanistic law of gases
1667	John Milton's *Paradise Lost*; Locke joins the household of the Earl of Shaftesbury as physician and advisor
1670	writes the "Fundamental Constitution of Carolina," a colony in America
1681	Shaftesbury tried for treason but acquitted
1682	Shaftesbury flees to Holland, dies two months later
1683	the Rye House plot to kill Charles II exposed, Locke flees to Holland, members of the Whig political party arrested
1685	Charles II dies, succeeded by his brother, James II, a Roman Catholic
1688	Parliament invites William of Orange to come to England and take the throne
1689	Isaac Newton's *Mathematical Principles of Natural Philosophy*; Locke accompanies Mary, Princess of Orange, to England, meets Newton
1690	*Essay Concerning Human Understanding, Two Treatises of Government,* published
1696	becomes a commissioner of the Board of Trade, advising the government on economic policy
1704	Locke dies in England

∿ SUGGESTED READINGS

Audi, R., ed. *The Cambridge Dictionary of Philosophy*. Cambridge: Cambridge University Press, 1999.

Ayers, M.R. *Locke*. London: Routledge, 1991.

Babbitt, I. *Democracy and Leadership*. New York: Henry Holt, 1920.

———. *Rousseau and Romanticism*. New York: Henry Holt, 1919.

Beiner, R., and W.J. Booth, eds. *Kant and Political Philosophy*. New Haven: Yale University Press, 1993.

Brown, A. *Modern Political Philosophy*. Harmondsworth: Penguin, 1986.

Copleston, F. *History of Philosophy*. New York: Doubleday, 1960.

Cranston, M. *John Locke: A Biography*. London: Longmans Green, 1957.

Dewey, J. *Reconstruction in Philosophy*. Boston: Beacon, 1957.

Ebenstein, W. *Great Political Thinkers.* New York: Holt, Rinehart and Winston, 1965.

Kirk, R. *The Roots of American Order.* LaSalle, IL: Open Court, 1974.

Lowe, E.J. *Locke: On Human Understanding.* London: Routledge, 1995.

Oliver, M. *The History of Philosophy.* New York: Barnes and Noble, 1999.

Sabine, G.H. *A History of Political Theory.* New York: Henry Holt, 1937.

Simmons, A.J. *The Lockean Theory of Rights.* Princeton: Princeton University Press, 1992.

Strauss, L., and J. Cropsey. *History of Political Philosophy.* Chicago: University of Chicago Press, 1974.

Thomas, D.A. Lloyd. *Locke on Government.* London: Routledge, 1995.

Willey, B. *The Seventeenth Century Background.* New York: Doubleday, 1953.

CHAPTER 9

Hume

Philosophy as an Intellectual Game?

Angelo Juffras

~ Preview

Thinking is a distinctly human activity. Not only can human beings think, we can watch ourselves as we do it. In other words, we can examine the process of thinking itself. That is the philosopher's job, according to Hume: to analyze the process of thinking. Hume's goal was to understand the nature of ideas themselves and their interactions. But when Hume broke down ordinary ideas into their elements and traced them back to their origins in perception, he discovered that many of our normal beliefs are illusory. He said that we have no rational reason to believe the sun will rise tomorrow or that something called "the self" exists. His starting point and his reasoning seem persuasive, but his conclusions are outrageous. They are so strange that we must wonder if he was serious. What was the real purpose of philosophy? Did Hume expect us genuinely to believe that the self does not exist? Or do philosophers examine the process of thinking to show how limited and untrustworthy it is? Or, finally, do philosophers such as Hume play elaborate intellectual games simply for the pleasure of juggling ideas with amazing skill?

(The Editor)

∿ Introduction

The eighteenth century is known as "the Enlightenment" or "the Age of Reason." It was an age of social and political criticism guided by the belief that what was true ought to be reasonable and what was reasonable ought to be true. However, the meaning of "reasonable" was not clear, nor was it the same for Hume as it was for others. Hume's writings seemed to show that being reasonable led to unreasonable results.

Although his family did not possess great wealth, Hume came from the Scottish upper class and bore the traces of his class—a good classical education in Greek and Latin writers,[1] a taste for literature, a desire to write, and a hunger for fame. That is, Hume came from a privileged class; he was a gentleman with all the tastes of gentlemen. In philosophy and in literature, he preferred elegant writing and disliked "abstruse" and complex argumentation, especially "school metaphysics." Ironically, his own writing turned out to be quite abstruse.

His writing was influenced by a tradition of skeptical writing—a kind of sport that had engaged leisurely gentlemen in the past few centuries, a style to be found in Montaigne, Descartes, Bayle, and others. In this sport one can ask how one knows anything *for certain*, a question that can undermine anyone's claim to know. Persistent questioning—questioning everything—can lead to doubts about scientific laws, the external world, even one's own mind. Because Hume adopted this skeptical style, no one knows reliably whether his skeptical conclusions were part of a game, an intellectual tease, or whether he really meant what he wrote. Did Hume believe that philosophy was a set of entertaining puzzles that people might pursue in their spare time? Or did he agree with Socrates and others that philosophy leads us to the most profound truths just because it goes beyond ordinary ways of thinking and "common sense"? One can find evidence of both attitudes in Hume's writing.

∿ Locke's Influence on Hume

Like all philosophers, Hume responded to various influences. The skeptical tradition was one. An equally important influence was John Locke (1632–1704), an English philosopher who wrote at the end of the seventeenth century. Locke is famous for his influence on the framers of the U.S. Constitution. He exploited the skeptical fashion in thinking and used it to undermine political institutions.

He questioned the common belief that kings ruled by divinely ordained right and proposed the consent of the people as the basis of government. But on the issue of how we know anything, Locke disliked skeptical writing and spoke with distaste about such "disputatious wranglers."

Locke believed that we could understand knowledge by looking for its sources, and he said that the source of all knowledge was *experience*. He thought the mind at birth was like a blank slate (in Latin, a *tabula rasa*), ready to be written on by experience. All our ideas and knowledge come from what we see, hear, taste, touch, or feel; no ideas are innate or inborn. Locke's point of view about the sources of knowledge is called "empiricism." It is contrasted with "rationalism," which lays emphasis on reasoning and the innate powers of the mind as sources of knowledge.

Hume agreed with Locke that experience was the source of all our knowledge. But he went beyond Locke by inquiring into our ideas of substance, causality, and personal identity and searched for their origin in experience. Unlike Locke, Hume thought that empiricism led to skeptical doubts about our knowledge in these areas.

Although British empiricism has flaws, it has managed to weather criticism because it has been the foremost intellectual tool for criticizing political and social institutions. Despite its weaknesses, philosophers have been reluctant to abandon testing ideas according to their origin in experience. Hume followed Locke in this empirical tradition and thought he had improved it.[2]

∿ Hume's Problem

When Hume was twenty-eight (in 1739), he published his first major work. The full title of the book is *A Treatise of Human Nature: Being an Attempt to Introduce the Experimental Method of Reasoning into Moral Subjects.* As this title suggests, Hume was trying to establish a *science* of human nature based on careful empirical observation. This emphasis on science is significant because before Hume's time the study of human nature had never been actually treated as a science. The goal of applying the scientific method to human beings takes its cue from Francis Bacon (1561–1626), an English philosopher and statesman who was a contemporary of Shakespeare. Bacon wished to avoid speculative reasoning in general and wanted to replace it with conclusions derived from observation and experiment. This was to be the new method of scientific inquiry. Hume agreed, and wanted to extend the method to social and moral questions as well. He says:

> 'Tis evident, that all the sciences have a relation, greater or less, to human nature. . . . 'Tis impossible to tell what changes and improvements we might make in these sciences were we thoroughly acquainted with the extent and force of human understanding, and could explain the nature of the ideas we employ, and of the operations we perform in our reasonings.[3]

In other words, if we can understand how we think, the nature of our ideas, and how we know anything, then we can explain the nature of our moral and political ideas. In fact, we can improve all the sciences. Hume's plan is evident in the three parts of his *Treatise*. Book 1 is subtitled "Of Human Understanding," Book 2 is "Of the Passions," and Book 3 is "Of Morals."

～ Themes in Hume's Empiricism

The Origin of Ideas

Hume's *Treatise of Human Nature,* where he discusses ideas, is deceptively simple. First, he distinguishes "impressions" from "ideas." An example will illustrate his terminology. As you are looking at a ripe apple, you have an "impression" of red. The next day when you remember the apple, you have an "idea" of red. As you bite into the apple, you have an impression of a sweet taste. The next day you have an idea of sweetness. Now, if you adopt a questioning attitude and ask people "Where did you get that idea?" Hume's answer is that our ideas are exact, but less vivid, copies of our sensory impressions. All our ideas originate in sensory impressions. If you cannot trace an idea back to an impression made upon the senses, then the idea is meaningless.

However, while the theory seems simple, Hume tended to add complications and admit exceptions. He says ideas are either simple or complex. Complex ideas are composed of simple ideas. For example, the complex idea of a golden mountain is created by combining the simple ideas of golden and mountain. The complex idea of a winged horse is composed of the idea of a horse and the idea of wings. Broadly speaking, you cannot have an idea of anything without first having had a sensory impression of it.

But some ideas, which according to his standards should be considered meaningless, were acknowledged to be meaningful. He acknowledged that Blacklock the poet, who was born blind, had ideas of color that he used correctly and beautifully. He also thought that you could have an idea of a shade of blue, for which you had no prior impression, if that shade lay between two adjacent shades for which you did have prior impressions. Moreover, he thought some ideas are derived from reflecting upon other ideas. He says, "We can form secondary ideas, which are images of the primary [ideas]," formed by "reasoning concerning them."[4] In other words, some ideas are not only copies of impressions but copies of other ideas.

Abstract or Universal Ideas

Among the exceptions Hume admitted were universal ideas, that is, general ideas. Various colors such as maroon, scarlet, crimson, carmine, and pink are all examples of the color red. Red stands for all of them and is considered a universal idea. We all have the general idea of red, but how did we acquire it?

We can't have experienced a red that is no particular shade of red. What kind of a red is a red that is no particular shade? All our impressions are of particular shades: maroon, scarlet, pink, and so on. But if all our ideas come from experience, how is it that we have an idea of a red that is no particular red, a red that has never been experienced, but stands for all the various shades of red? Or consider another example. I remember Bill, Sue, Mr. Jones, and other people I've met, so I have ideas of those individuals. I also have an idea of a human being in general. But I've never met a human being in general; I've only met particular individuals who were either tall, short, male, female, old, or young. How can we have general ideas?

Hume's answer is, "If ideas be particular in their nature . . . tis only by custom they can become general in their representation, and can contain an infinite number of other ideas under them."[5] That is, your idea of red is a particular shade of red—one among the many shades you have experienced—but it stands for all of the shades. Although it is a particular shade, say maroon, it represents all reds. It functions as a general idea.

The Association of Ideas

Our memories and imaginations are continuously filled with ideas. But these ideas aren't "loose and unconnected," Hume says. They exhibit a pattern that we can observe and chart. An idea of a dog normally calls up an idea of barking, while an idea of a duck calls up an idea of quacking. In general, some ideas are naturally associated with others. Hume writes:

> It is evident that there is a principle of connection between the different thoughts or ideas of the mind, and that in their appearance to the memory and imagination, they introduce each other with a certain degree of method and regularity. . . . To me there appear to be only three principles of connection among ideas, namely *Resemblance, Contiguity* in time or place, and *Cause* or *Effect*.[6]

For example, a photograph of a friend automatically makes you think of the person herself, since it resembles her. If something reminds you of your TV, you naturally think of the table it sits on, since they are contiguous in space. And if someone comes to class on crutches, you inevitably wonder what caused the injury. Some ideas are just naturally associated with others, based on these three principles.

These associations reflect our experience. But some connections are not based on what we experience. Hume distinguishes between what he calls "relations of ideas" and "matters of fact." An example of a relation of ideas is "three times five is equal to half of thirty." You can understand the truth of such a belief intuitively, without the need of experience, if you understand the ideas involved (three, multiply, five, equal, and so on). You can see in your mind's eye the relations among the ideas and the truth of such a belief. It is certain. It is inconceivable that three times five could *not* be equal to half of thirty. Matters of fact, in contrast, are to be understood as relations between objects rather than between ideas. Gold is softer than iron, for example. Matters of fact originate in experience, are based on probability, and are not certain. It is conceivable that matters of fact could be false. We can imagine a world in which gold is harder than iron. It just happens that our world is different. If you threw a brick at your neighbor's window, as a matter of fact you would break it. But it is not necessary that it should break. That fire burns is a matter of fact, but it is conceivable that on some occasion it might not. It would be highly unusual and surprising if fire were not hot to the touch, but it is possible. It is not necessary that fire should burn, whereas it is necessary that three times five is equal to half of thirty. Relations of ideas are necessarily true (or necessarily false), but matters of fact are only more or less probable.[7]

Cause and Effect

We have seen that a fundamental principle of empiricism is the belief that all our ideas are derived from sensory impressions. But we have also seen that Hume allows exceptions to this principle. The idea of cause and effect may be another exception. Hume acknowledges the idea to be meaningful, but he also says that the idea of cause and effect, as it is sometimes interpreted, is not a copy of any impression. "Am I here possessed of an idea, which is not preceded by any similar impression?" Hume asks. Should one question the basic empiricist principle? To understand our idea of cause and effect, we should look at some examples.

Consider three pairs of statements. First, if I apply a sharp, sudden force to an egg, it will break. And if I take an egg from a chicken's nest, the chicken will lay another one. Second, if I change the position of a light shining on a houseplant, the leaves will turn to face the light. And when children begin school in the fall, the leaves on the trees soon turn brown. Third, if I heat some water over a hot stove, it will boil. And if I turn the heat off and go to a movie, the water will disappear by the time I return. In each of these three pairs, the first is a causal relation (applying force to an egg causes it to break), but the second is not. Going to a movie does not cause water to disappear. The question is, "What is the difference between causal relations and what we might call coincidental relations?" What exactly is our idea of cause and effect?

Hume approaches the question from an empiricist point of view. He says:

> 'Tis impossible to reason justly, without understanding perfectly the idea concerning which we reason; and 'tis impossible perfectly to understand any idea, without tracing it up to its origin, and examining that primary impression, from which it arises. The examination of the impression bestows a clearness on the idea; and the examination of the idea bestows a like clearness on all our reasonings.[8]

To understand our idea of cause and effect, we need to find its origin in sensory impressions. Hume says that if we think of examples of one thing causing another, we see two relations. First, we see that the cause is close to the effect in space and time. (Hume calls this "contiguity.") And second, the cause is always prior to the effect in time. But tracing the idea of cause back to those impressions doesn't answer the question of how causes are different from coincidences, because the coincidental relations are based on the same impressions of contiguity and priority. When kids go to school in September, the trees in the neighborhood soon turn brown; the first event is contiguous with the second and prior in time. So what is the difference between cause and coincidence?

Some have said that there is a *necessary connection* between a cause and its effect. In other words, when the cause occurs, the effect *must* occur. But with coincidences, the first event can occur and the second event may not occur. I can take an egg from a chicken's nest and it may not lay another. I can go to a movie and the water may not evaporate. But if I heat the water to the boiling point, then it *must* boil. According to this view, then, our idea of a causal relation is the idea of a necessary connection between two events.

But Hume disagrees, because he says we have no impression of a necessary connection between events. No matter how closely I examine the act of causing an egg to break, I never see a necessity. I see the close connection in space and time, but there is no impression of necessity. In fact, I can easily imagine that when I hit the egg with a spoon, the egg says "ouch!" or changes color or doubles in size. It isn't *necessary* that the egg should break. It just turns out that way. Hume says that necessity exists in the relations of ideas, not in the relations among objects or events. For example, it is necessary that a bachelor be unmarried or that two plus two is equal to four. The ideas are logically related. But events in space and time display no such necessary connections. It is not necessary that an effect should follow a cause, even though it always does.

But if that's true, then what is the difference between cause and coincidence? Hume's answer is that the difference is in people, not in objects. After seeing eggs break over and over again, we *expect* a sharp force to lead to a broken egg. As Hume puts it:

> For after a frequent repetition, I find, that upon the appearance of one of the objects, the mind is *determined* by custom to consider its usual attendant, and to consider it in a stronger light upon account of its relation to the first object. 'Tis this impression, then, or *determination*, which affords me the idea of necessity.[9]

So there is an idea of causal necessity, but it is based on custom. Hume says that the mind is "determined" by custom. Shall we allow Hume to get past us without raising an eyebrow? It appears that he is acknowledging another source of ideas besides sensory impressions. Everyone has an idea of cause and effect, and it is a kind of necessity (although not logical necessity). But the idea is not derived from any impression of necessity in nature. Or is Hume playing a game by drawing out more paradoxes of the empiricist principle? Is he saying that there really is no difference between causal relations and coincidence besides a subjective feeling? But that would mean that there is no such thing as cause and effect in the external world, no objective cause and effect, and therefore no scientific laws. Can he be serious?

Substance and Personal Identity

Hume inherited a notion of substance from Descartes (1596–1650). In Descartes' *Meditations* (1634), he looked at a piece of wax and described all its qualities. It had a certain shape and size, it was brownish in color, hard, and cold to the touch. But then he put the wax next to the hearth and heated it. Gradually it changed. It began to melt and change its shape. It became more transparent, soft, and warm. Originally fresh from the beehive, it had the scent of flowers. Now, after heating, the scent was gone. In fact, every one of its qualities changed. Was it the *same* piece of wax? Descartes said yes. But what was the same about it? Not the shape or color or feel. Why call it the same? Descartes' answer was that it was the same because the underlying substance was the same. Substance was supposed to be something in which qualities such as color inhere, like a sort of ethereal pincushion. You can change a thing's qualities, but if the thing's substance remains the same, then the thing remains the same, no matter how much its qualities have changed.

Hume applied the empiricist principle and asked, from what impression did you get the idea of substance? Is it derived from the impressions of sensation or from reflection? And he says it is derived from neither. All we know of the wax is what we can see, feel, smell, and so on. Nor does reflecting on these ideas give us a notion of substance. In fact, we can't imagine what a substance is supposed to be like, because by definition it has no color, no shape, no texture, no smell, or any other perceptible quality. Hume concluded that "We have therefore no idea of substance distinct from that of a particular collection of qualities, nor have we any other meaning when we either talk or reason concerning it."[10] Our idea of an object is an idea of a bundle or collection of qualities that usually go together, but we have no idea of what holds them together.[11]

The ordinary notion of a self is similar to Descartes' notion of substance. As the substance of the wax is supposed to have the qualities of heat or cold, hardness or softness, so your self is supposed to have qualities of friendliness, love of music, memories of swimming in the lake, and so on. But a perverse outcome of Hume's belief in the origin of ideas was that we, as individuals, have no idea of a self. Your idea of your self is an illusion. Hume says:

> It must be some one impression, that gives rise to every real idea. But self or person is not any one impression, but that to which our several impressions and ideas are suppos'd to have a reference. If any impression gives rise to the idea of self, that impression must continue invariably the same, thro' the whole course of our lives; since self is suppos'd to exist after that manner. But there is no impression constant and invariable. Pain and pleasure, grief and joy, passions and sensations succeed each other, and never all exist at the same time. It cannot, therefore, be from any of these impressions, or from any other, that the idea of self is deriv'd; and consequently there is no such idea.[12]

Certainly you are aware of your qualities, Hume says. You feel your aches and pains, your anticipations and satisfactions. You are aware of your thoughts and memories. But when do you ever encounter your self? In fact, you never do. "For my part, . . ." Hume says, "I can never catch *myself* at any time without a perception, and can never observe anything but the perception."[13] The notion of a self is like the notion of a substance, a bare "something" that is supposed to hold certain qualities together and endure through change. But since we never experience this "something," we have no real idea of self.

Was Hume serious or is this an example of an intellectual tease? Hume's starting point—the empiricist principle that all our ideas originate in sensory experience—seems plausible, at least initially. And his reasoning seems valid. We really do not experience within us an object we would call a self. So Hume could regard his conclusion as an important discovery. On the other hand, it's hard even to imagine how Hume or anyone else could give up his or her idea of self. He believed that he, not someone else, wrote his book. When he ordered a suit of clothes, he expected it to be delivered to him, not to Italy. How could anyone not believe in a self? It's possible that Hume was playing an elaborate game that has no relevance to real life.

Whatever Hume's intentions, his analyses of cause and effect, substance, and personal identity gave birth to a new, critical way of thinking. When considered carefully, they have liberated many minds, especially with regard to what beliefs are necessarily true. Applied to new proposals, Hume's philosophy has provided people with a new attitude: "It ain't necessarily so." This was especially liberating to persons who chafed under traditional ways of feeling, thinking, and acting. Coupled with this came a vision of new possibilities—a vision that was not limited to the readers of his generation but that continued to stimulate minds centuries later.

∿ Questions about Hume's Empiricism

Hume has been both admired and criticized. Some philosophers consider him to be the most important modern philosopher in the West. Others have been more critical. The criticisms have been of two main types. First, critics say that Hume is very difficult to interpret. For example, Kenneth R. Stunkel complained:

> [Hume's] work lends itself to numerous conflicting interpretations. What does one call him—mitigated sceptic, naturalist, crypto-rationalist, Newtonian, irrationalist, Pyrrhonian, liberal, conservative, amateur philosopher, professional historian, or intellectual wag leading us on until he wearies of the game?[14]

Some go so far as to say that his ideas are inconsistent, and we will examine some alleged examples. The second main type of criticism is that Hume is not serious, that his conclusions are so preposterous that no one can believe them. And Hume deliberately fashioned such shocking claims. We will examine several ways to decide when a philosopher is being serious and when he or she isn't. But first, consider the difficulty in interpreting Hume.

Interpretations and Inconsistencies

In 1888, L.A. Selby-Bigge edited and published Hume's *Treatise of Human Nature*. In his introduction, Selby-Bigge was decidedly cautious, if not derogatory, in his estimate of Hume:

> Hume's philosophical writings are to be read with great caution. His pages, especially those of the *Treatise,* are so full of matter, he says so many different things in so many different ways and different connections, and with so much indifference to what he has said before, that it is very hard to say positively that he taught or did not teach, this or that particular doctrine.

Pall S. Ardal claims there is a clear example of Hume's "indifference to what he has said before" in his doctrine of self. Ardal says that in Book I of the *Treatise* Hume emphasized the impossibility of finding an impression of the self, but in Book II, where Hume discusses emotions, "the impression of the self plays an indispensable part."[15] Ardal says that Hume is guilty of many such errors.

John Herman Randall, Jr., is very critical of Hume and points to several inconsistencies. The first occurs in Hume's analysis of knowledge.[16] According to Randall, Hume's analysis contains two separate positions, "the attempt to introduce the experimental method of reasoning," which Randall called "observationalism," and the view that the only objects of knowledge are our ideas, which Randall called "subjectivism." Observationalism means that people know objects and the relations among them *only* by means of experience or observation. We have no other way of knowing the world. Subjectivism means that all knowledge is knowledge of the contents of our own minds, that is, our impressions and ideas. What we know are our own ideas *rather than* the real world. In observationalism, experience is taken as a method of knowing. In subjectivism, experience is taken as the subject matter of knowledge. For the former, experience is *how* we know; for the latter, it is *what* we know. In some places, according to Randall, Hume defends observationalism and says that through experience we can know what the world is like. But in other places, he takes a subjectivist position and says that all we really know are impressions and ideas, that is, the contents of our own minds.

This inconsistency leads to another, in Randall's view. Hume says that in order to understand a belief, you must trace it back to its sources in sensory impressions. To understand what you mean by "Roses are red," you must recall the impressions that gave you the idea of roses and the idea of red. Only then do you clearly understand what the belief means to you. But Hume (and other empiricists) *also* claims that the source of a belief is a test of its truth. In other words, if one of your beliefs can be traced back to some sensory experience, then the belief is *true*. For example, how do you know that roses are red? You've seen them. You base the belief on sensory impressions you've had, and that guarantees that the belief is true.

But Hume can't have it both ways, Randall says. The origin of a belief cannot at the same time serve as the test of a belief's truth. Because if originating in experience were proof that a belief is true, then all beliefs should be true, since all the contents of our minds come from experience. That is the fundamental principle of empiricism. But of course, many beliefs are not true. Business partnerships and marriages require beliefs about the other partner's honesty, but sometimes such beliefs are mistaken. Not all our beliefs are true, even if they are based on sensory impressions. As Randall says, "The 'evidence that assures us' of a belief is the impression that causes it. If all beliefs [the true and the false] are thus similar in their origins, how can their origin in impressions possibly be the *test* of their validity?"[17] It can't. How you came to believe something, whether by experience or by some other means, has nothing to do with whether that belief is true. According to Randall, Hume's inconsistency reveals "the futility of the basic principle of empiricism, that beliefs are to be tested by their origins in experience; this origin is the cause of all beliefs, but it is not enough to justify any one of them."[18]

Randall sees yet another inconsistency in Hume's empiricism. He asks us to compare Hume's procedure in the belief in cause and effect with that in the case of belief in the continued existence of objects, that is, belief in objects distinct from the mind that thinks them and the senses that perceive them. Hume begins by asking, "What causes induce us to believe in the existence of body?" He will supply the answers, but before proceeding, he warns us, "But 'tis vain to ask, Whether there be body or not. That is a point which we must take for granted in all our reasonings."[19]

This is because the impressions that give rise to the belief in body are as discontinuous as those that proved inadequate to support belief in the self. Like the idea of self, the idea of body is not a copy of any one impression, but rather that to which our several impressions and ideas are supposed to have a reference. If an impression were the source of the idea of body, that impression would have to be unchanging and permanent, since that is how we think of physical bodies. But, as with the self, there is no constant and invariable impression of body. Bodies are nothing but a bundle or collection of different perceptions, which are perpetually changing and moving. The reason "'tis vain to ask whether there be body or not" is that it would be impractical not to. Yet, strangely, Hume does not find it impractical to doubt the belief in the self. It appears that his procedure in dealing with external objects is not consistent with his procedure in dealing with the self.

Is Hume Serious?

Not everyone agrees with Randall, of course. Defenders of Hume might be able to explain how his views are really consistent after all. But everyone agrees that his conclusions are paradoxical or even outrageous. If you accept what Hume says about the source of our ideas, and you accept the consequences he draws from that starting point, then he has upset your notions of cause and effect, scientific law, substance and objects, and your sense of identity. He says causal necessity is nothing more than constant conjunction; he says there is no substance underlying appearances, and the self is an illusion. Was he serious? Perhaps. Many writers have taken him seriously. They have debated his views on cause and effect and on substance for centuries. But who can be serious about his discussion of personal identity? Can you doubt that you exist, that you are the same person you were yesterday, or that you are different from your friend? Many people cannot take Hume seriously on these matters.

This brings us to the doubt that is supposed to arise from skepticism. Skepticism is valuable because it questions outmoded tradition and unwarranted assumptions. It operates by creating doubt. But some doubts are serious and some are part of a type of game.

Philosophical game-playing can be compared to a chess problem. In the game of chess, you play against an opponent; there are certain pieces positioned on a chess board; each piece can move in certain ways; and if you are clever, you can checkmate your opponent and win the game. Philosophy, similarly, can be an engrossing, puzzling intellectual pastime. Some philosophers think of philosophical problems in terms of "moves" and "countermoves," thrust and parry. They attempt to trap or defeat their opponent by revealing contradictions in the opponent's position, or showing that the position leads to absurd consequences, or that it is inconsistent with accepted facts, or in other ways. This sort of discussion leaves the person in the street wondering whether philosophy is serious.

One way to begin a philosophical game is to ask, "How do you know?" For example, one of the most famous skeptical questions was Descartes' question "How do you know that you are not dreaming at this very moment?" No one who considers this question sincerely doubts that he or she is awake; the point is to play the game well, move the pieces according to the rules, escape from the traps, or block one's opponent. (Philosophy is more complicated than chess because philosophers sometimes change the rules or introduce new pieces.) Hume asks similar skeptical questions that are hard to answer: "How do you know that smoking causes cancer and isn't just frequently followed by cancer?" "How do you know that you are a single, unified self?" Perhaps Hume's doubts were part of a game or perhaps they were serious.

Doubt can be genuine—a result of a genuine problem—or doubt can be pretended, as part of a game. How can you know if a philosopher's doubts are genuine or pretended? There are three ways of dealing with skeptical arguments and doubts. First, consider the answer given by C.S. Peirce, an American philosopher of the nineteenth century. Peirce says that a genuine doubt is irritating. It persists to the point where, in order to get rid of the irritation, you are driven to inquire. You ask questions, make observations, or think through the matter until you have some sort of answer. In contrast, a pretended doubt can easily be ignored. It may be interesting, and you may think about it, but it is easy to put it aside and forget about it. In Shakespeare's great tragedy *Othello*, Iago suggested to Othello that his wife, Desdemona, might be unfaithful. He simply planted a seed in Othello's mind. Othello wanted to ignore the doubt, but he couldn't. It persisted and grew until Othello couldn't think of anything else. Real doubts demand attention; pretended doubts do not. Peirce says Descartes' doubt about dreaming is not real. We can ignore it.

Is Hume's doubt about the self a real doubt or a pretended doubt? Even though genuine doubts are said to be sufficiently irritating so as to provoke inquiry, and even though this would seem to separate serious philosophers from game players, the latter can insist that they are provoked and irritated by the problem of personal identity. They have devoted considerable time and attention to the problem. They call their doubt serious; they write books about it. (Or could they simply enjoy taking part in a fascinating game?) Peirce's test for distinguishing real from pretended doubts may not be very easy to apply.

A second possible way to distinguish serious from whimsical puzzlement is the following. The irritation of doubt that gives rise to serious inquiry is created when you sense an anomalous situation, something that should not be, something out of the ordinary. For example, suppose one January morning you wake up and discover that it has snowed, but the snow is red. That would be an anomaly. You would inquire, ask questions, think about causes. You would have real doubts about your belief that snow is white, and you would wonder what to think about the event. Compare that situation to the alleged problem of the self. Has Hume pointed to anything *out of the ordinary* to make you doubt that you are a unified self? No. He only says that you do not perceive a self in the way you perceive physical objects or particular thoughts.

On the other hand, some philosophical problems seem real, even if they are not as dramatic as a red snowfall. During the past century, philosophers and mathematicians have investigated the possibility of using language and mathematics consistently, without self-contradiction. For example, is it possible to say that nothing exists without attributing existence to *nothing*? Or when I say "This statement is false," can my statement be true? (Suppose it is true. Then what it says is correct, i.e., it is false. But suppose it is false. Then what it says is incorrect, i.e., it is not false.) How many whole numbers are there? An infinite number. The series beginning one, two, three, . . . never ends. Half of the series is even numbers and half is odd numbers. So how many even numbers are there? An infinite number. But how is it possible for there to be as many *even numbers alone* as there are both odd and even numbers *together*? These problems don't arise from some surprising, bizarre event, such as a red snowfall. They are not out of the ordinary. But they are interesting, real problems, and the doubts people have about how to solve them are real doubts. So perhaps we need another way to distinguish serious issues from intellectual games.

We can return to Randall's critique of Hume to find a third test of serious doubts. Randall took Hume's stated intentions at face value. He says, "Hume wrote for two purposes; to make money, and to gain a literary reputation. Hume acknowledged, 'My ruling passion is the love of literary fame.'"[20] Hume's major works, then, were designed to gain attention, and he succeeded by challenging common beliefs and defending preposterous conclusions. But Hume wrote on religion as well as academic philosophy, even though he declined to publish his book on religion while he was still alive. (It was published after he died.) He raised skeptical doubts about religion, but Randall says the doubts are different from the doubts about causation and the self:

> Hume's practical skepticism, as distinguished from his literary skepticism, is a religious skepticism. . . . Hume's posthumous *Dialogues on Natural Religion* are his masterpiece; they are quite free from the intentional confusions of the *Treatise* and the *Enquiry*.[21]

Here Randall is proposing practicality as a guide for judging whether a skeptical philosophical conclusion is serious or not. We can interpret practicality as consequences for behavior. A practical doubt has an effect on the way you lead your life. A pretended doubt does not. For example, you may have a practical doubt about the consequences of smoking or about the statements "Smoking causes cancer" and "Smokers can be healthy." A practical doubt will make you give up smoking or smoke less. You may also have a doubt about the nature of causation and coincidence. But that theoretical doubt won't have any effects on your behavior. Or consider Hume's theory of the self. If Hume is right that the self does not exist, what difference in your behavior will it make? None. Whether Hume is right or wrong about the self won't affect your day-to-day life, although it may be an impressive move in an intellectual game. According to Randall's test, Hume's doubts about the self are not serious.

Is Randall's criterion for distinguishing serious doubts from pretended doubts adequate? It's difficult to say. One can imagine various objections and replies, moves and countermoves. Will Randall's criterion lead you to change your behavior in some way? Does it arise from an anomalous situation? Or does it persist and make you investigate the issue of when philosophers are serious again and again? Of course, in asking these questions, we are applying the tests of seriousness to them. We are thinking about the process of thinking. And in fact, that is precisely what Hume did. He asked where our ideas come from, how they interact with each other, and what we can know about them. Was he serious? Each of us must decide for ourselves. Perhaps the answer depends on whether we take thinking seriously.

∾ NOTES

1. He was especially well read in the Hellenistic skeptics and Cicero, who was part Stoic, part skeptic.
2. David Hume, *A Treatise of Human Nature* (Oxford: Clarendon Press, 1888). Originally published in 1739. Book 1, Part 1, Section 1, 2, note 1.
3. Ibid., Introduction, xix.
4. Ibid., Book 1, Part 1, Section 1, 6.
5. Ibid., Book 1, Part 1, Section 7, 24.
6. David Hume, *An Inquiry Concerning Human Understanding*, Section 3.
7. The distinction between relations of ideas and matters of fact has been taken to be an anticipation of Kant's distinction between analytic and synthetic propositions. However, this is mistaken. See Angelo Juffras, *Hume's Theory of Meaning* (Ann Arbor, MI: University Microfilms, 1969), 38–47.
8. *A Treatise of Human Nature*, Book 1, Part 3, Section 2, 74–75.
9. Ibid., Book 1, Part 3, Section 14, 156.
10. Ibid., Book 1, Part 1, Section 6, 16.
11. However, one should be aware that this notion of substance is a seventeenth-century notion—a notion that has been with us only since then; for two thousand years before that, the world had a different notion of substance. In the ancient world, to be a substance, a thing had to be something about which you could talk. In the Cartesian notion, to be a substance—something that remained apart from and that underlay all qualities—was to be something indescribable, ineffable. In the ancient world, a substance was something that one must be able to point to—a "this." It was a particular thing. In the Cartesian world, substance, instead of being particular, was universal; it underlay all matter. In the ancient world, and for centuries afterward, to be a substance was to be the outcome of a process of change; in the Cartesian notion, to be a substance was to endure unchanged through a process of change (as in the case of the wax). The idea that a substance was the outcome of a process of change was modified when it was noticed that the moon and other heavenly bodies were eternal and unchanging. Substance then became "energia," something that operated or functioned.
12. *A Treatise of Human Nature*, Book 1, Part 4, Section 6, 251–252.

13. Ibid., 252.
14. Kenneth R. Stunkel, "Montaigne, Bayle, and Hume: Historical Dynamics of Scepticism," in *The European Legacy,* vol. 3, no. 4 (1998), 43–64.
15. Pall S. Ardal, *Passion and Value in Hume's Treatise* (Edinburgh: Edinburgh University Press, 1966), 17–40.
16. John Herman Randall, Jr., *The Career of Philosophy* (New York: Columbia University Press, 1962), 636.
17. Ibid., 641.
18. Ibid., 643.
19. *A Treatise of Human Nature,* Book 1, Part 4, Section 2, 187.
20. Randall, 631
21. Ibid., 635–636.

∾ CHRONOLOGY

1620	Francis Bacon's *Novum Organum*
1687	Isaac Newton's *Principles of Mathematical Philosophy*
1690	John Locke's *An Essay Concerning Human Understanding*
1710	George Berkeley's *Treatise Concerning the Principles of Human Knowledge*
1711	birth of David Hume in Scotland
1723	enrolls in the University of Edinburgh, leaves after three years without a degree
1726	*Gulliver's Travels* by Jonathan Swift
1734	moves to France for three years, partly for his health, begins writing
1739	publishes his *Treatise of Human Nature* anonymously
1744	employed as tutor for the insane Marquess of Annandale, perseveres for two years
1746	becomes secretary to General James St. Clair; travels in France, Italy, and Austria
1748	publishes *Enquiry Concerning Human Understanding*
1749	J.S. Bach's "Art of the Fugue"
1751	publishes *Enquiry Concerning the Principles of Morals*; in France, Denis Diderot begins publishing the *Encyclopedia*
1754	publishes volume 1 of his *History of England*
1759	Hume's friend, Adam Smith, publishes his *Theory of Moral Sentiments*; Voltaire publishes *Candide*

1763 becomes secretary to the British ambassador to France, popular in Paris

1766 returns to London with Jean-Jacques Rousseau and secures a pension for him, but Rousseau accuses Hume of betrayal and leaves England

1776 dies in Edinburgh

1779 *Dialogues Concerning Natural Religion* published posthumously

⁓ SUGGESTED READINGS

Ayer, A.J. *Hume*. New York: Hill and Wang, 1980.

Capaldi, N. *David Hume: The Newtonian Philosopher*. Boston: Twayne, 1975.

Flew, A. *Hume: Philosopher of Moral Science*. Oxford: Basil Blackwell, 1986.

Green, T.H. *Hume and Locke*. New York: Thomas Y. Crowell. Reissued with an introduction by Ramon Lemos, 1968 (1834).

Hume, D. *An Enquiry Concerning Human Understanding*. Oxford: Clarendon Press, 1975.

————. *A Treatise of Human Nature*. Oxford: Clarendon Press, 1965.

————. *Dialogues Concerning Natural Religion*. Introduction by Norman Kemp Smith. Indianapolis: Bobbs-Merrill, 1947.

Kemp Smith, N. *The Philosophy of David Hume*. New York: Macmillan, 1941.

Noonan, H.W. *Hume on Knowledge*. London: Routledge, 1999.

Norton, D.F. *David Hume: Common-sense Moralist, Sceptical Metaphysician*. Princeton: Princeton University Press, 1982.

————, ed. *The Cambridge Companion to Hume*. Cambridge: Cambridge University Press, 1993.

Passmore, J. *Hume's Intentions*. Revised Edition. New York: Basic Books, 1968.

Pears, D. *Hume's System: An Examination of the First Book of His Treatise*. New York: Oxford University Press, 1990.

Penelhum, T. *David Hume: An Introduction to His Philosophical System*. Indianapolis: Purdue University Press, 1962.

Randall, J.H., Jr. *The Career of Philosophy: From the Middle Ages to the Enlightenment*. New York: Columbia University Press, 1962.

Stroud, B. *Hume*. London: Routledge, 1977.

CHAPTER 10

Kant

Philosophy as Mapping the Mind

Ellen Freeberg

~ Preview

Kant created a revolution in philosophy because he proposed that the world we all experience is created by the human mind. At the most basic level— space, time, causality—our minds work in similar ways, he says, and orga- nize raw sensations to construct a common, objective world. We all have hearts and kidneys and similar bodies, and we all have concepts of space and time and similar minds. Two plus two is necessarily four, always and everywhere, because our minds create that kind of world from chaotic sen- sations and cannot comprehend any other kind. The key, therefore, to understanding the ultimate structure of reality is not to study things but to study the mind. "What are the basic parts of the mind, and how do they work together?" Kant asks. Just as reason creates the structure of the world, it also creates the laws of right and wrong. They are objective because they are the same for every rational being. Morality depends on leading a principled life and recognizing other people's basic capacity to do the same. (The Editor)

∼ Introduction

Kant stands as a formidable practitioner of philosophy for three reasons. First, he was a great synthesizer. He analyzed the strengths and weaknesses of the most important competing views on philosophy during the eighteenth century (for example, those views focused on epistemology, or how we know what we know) and then constructed a distinctive alternative to them. With the 1781 publication of his magnum opus, the *Critique of Pure Reason,* Kant unsettled but also creatively synthesized claims by well-known competing philosophers such as Descartes and David Hume. Kant was often considered a revolutionary, not to mention the most original philosopher to emerge from the end of the German Enlightenment. He made no effort to overthrow governments and lived a quiet, even uneventful eighty years from 1724 to 1804. However, by successfully tackling problems unsolved by several major currents in European philosophy, Kant changed what it meant to do philosophy.

Second, Kant demonstrated a distinctive way of linking certain philosophical dilemmas. Specifically, he offered ways to link questions about what we can know of the observable world to questions about whether God exists and how, in this life, human beings *ought* to behave with one another. Kant offered an original way of synthesizing answers to these questions, and he made a point of avoiding extremes. For example, some thinkers, such as Hume, were highly skeptical about claims to know anything more about our world beyond what we could observe; and they linked this to a skeptical view about God's existence and rational foundations of morality. But others, such as Descartes, believed that humans could not only observe and collect data about what their senses told them, but could understand, in advance, abstract "innate" ideas—ideas about mathematics, for example—and so could grasp the necessity of God's existence. Kant did share much with insistent skeptics like Hume, but he also stood apart from them by claiming that to achieve a *unified* understanding of the experienced world, we should still seek some prior ideas available to us: ideas of God, the soul, and the cosmos. Such ideas could serve as regulative ideas of reason that would help guide the way our minds work and filter information from the senses.

Kant believed that the task facing philosophy in the eighteenth century was to find the right balance between the insights of previous philosophers, such as the empiricists and the rationalists. Like most people of his time, Kant was tremendously impressed by the progress of natural science, represented most dramatically by Isaac Newton's synthesis. He wanted to explain how the human mind was capable of discovering universal, certain knowledge, despite Hume's skepticism. But for Kant personally, a second task was even more important. He wanted to lay a foundation for our sense of morality and our experience of moral duty. The same general principles that justify scientific knowledge, he believed, also justify our undeniable sense of moral obligation. Kant said, "Two things fill me with awe: the starry heavens above and the moral law within."

Finally, few philosophers in subsequent centuries felt untouched by Kant's work. Kant was rejected by many anti-Enlightenment thinkers of the early nineteenth century. But ignoring him was impossible. He had become an essential part of the conversation about how to do philosophy systematically and well, and he offered critical explanations for understanding the way we think, the way our minds interact with our world, and how we should act as moral beings. Readers of Fichte, Schelling, or the formidable Hegel required some knowledge of Kant.

Students of philosophy today often find Kant's work difficult and his terminology perplexing. Several factors may contribute to this. First, doing philosophy for Kant required criticizing others but then establishing a clear foundation for how humans' rational thought processes could develop secure knowledge about a variety of questions. Kant felt that his explanations needed to rival, if not supersede, those of his predecessors, and he often developed his own complex terminology to explain what he believed were his original observations. He invented new terms for his new ideas. Simultaneously, however, Kant remained influenced by eighteenth-century German philosophy, which showed a continuing preoccupation with weighty system-building. So Kant's new terms were set within a logically structured, highly complex "system" for explaining relationships between various faculties of the mind and their interactions with the observable world and its laws of nature. The terms depend on each other. In addition, we might note that Kant wrote during a time when the natural sciences and mathematics were establishing their own secure basis for laws of nature. A desire to legitimate the way philosophers explained the human faculty of reason, its relation to other faculties of the mind, and how those faculties had their own necessary rules and principles likely prompted Kant's ongoing interest in supporting a technical, "scientific" vocabulary for philosophical investigations. Although further use of Kant's more technical language will not be pursued here, suffice it to say that once readers are willing to unearth Kant's basic ideas, they find valuable questions and lessons that preoccupied (and continue to preoccupy) much of modern Western philosophy.

∼ Early Influences: Natural Science and Philosophy

Kant's early years as a student, writer, and teacher are worth reviewing here briefly because they do provide a useful backdrop for what we would call Kant's most important mature reflections. Interestingly, in his early years of study, Kant avoided the topics we tend to associate with philosophy. For several decades (from the 1740s through the 1760s) Kant focused his work primarily on the natural sciences. Natural scientists were generally interested in conducting experiments in a lab using observation and the human senses, perhaps with the augmentation of instruments, and then collecting and quantifying the results. In contrast, philosophical investigators were likely to ask whether or not human observations could count as real knowledge or what to make of certain concepts used by the scientist in the course of conducting experiments. Eventually, like many of his predecessors, Kant would use his early preoccupations in the natural sciences to challenge traditional questions posed by philosophers. But if Kant's early views about the natural sciences had not been cultivated, his later questions and concerns about philosophy would have looked quite different.

Western scientific and mathematical developments during the seventeenth and eighteenth centuries had led to new tools for empirical investigations, and those appeared to provide the necessary proofs for true "laws of nature" (about gravity, energy, and the like). Thinkers during this period were also determined to distance their scientific engagements from the medieval past. They spoke less of reason as the "handmaid of faith," refused to see true knowledge as the gift of divine beneficence, and often insisted on their ability to understand the world through their own perceptions and calculations. Claims had even been advanced (by thinkers like Thomas Hobbes and Isaac Newton) about how the world could be analyzed as a system of bodies in motion in which every event had a specific determined cause and such causes could be investigated, demonstrated, and fully understood by the human mind. Early on, Kant found these views especially compelling.

When Kant entered the University of Königsberg at age sixteen, he worked under the tutelage of Professor Martin Knutzen and was influenced by a number of continental thinkers, especially those we call "rationalists." Rationalists believed that all genuine knowledge was absolutely certain and beyond doubt. Their ideal or model for knowledge was mathematics and geometry. From this perspective, seeing, hearing, touching, and observing the world do not give us real knowledge, because those experiences can be mistaken and are not absolutely certain. Instead, rationalists said, we were born with important innate ideas, such as the ideas of substance, number, and God, and we gain knowledge by examining those ideas and their implications. In his early work, Kant showed a preoccupation with rationalists like Descartes and

Leibniz. In 1746 he published "Thoughts on the Correct Evaluation of Life Forces," a treatise that addressed their ideas in relation to physics, specifically the problem of how to measure kinetic energy. Kant saw Descartes and his followers presenting one view (claiming that it was directly proportional to speed) and Leibniz and his companions another (claiming that it was the square of speed). In the end, he aimed for a reconciliation between the two while generally remaining sympathetic to the rationalist project overall.

Kant left Königsberg shortly after this time. He worked throughout East Prussia as a tutor and continued to pursue his interests in natural science. He returned to his native home several years later with a manuscript on astronomy and soon coupled this with an essay on the earth's aging process. Eventually he put both together to produce *A Universal Natural History and Theory of the Heavens, or, An Attempt to Explain the Composition and Mechanical Origin of the Universe According to Principles of Newtonian Physics* (1755). The book received favorable reviews, and in the same year Kant took his masters examinations and began lecturing at the University of Königsberg.

However, by the 1760s, Kant's preoccupations with these scientific problems shifted. Many lessons from early writings were retained, but Kant looked to tackle questions more distinctly philosophical, for example, questions revolving around how the gathering of experimental data was related to the way humans develop concepts, use their reason, and come to organize and understand what they investigate about their world. Scientists associated with the rationalist tradition had concerned themselves with these questions, too. But Kant now began to explore these ideas and, on this front, he did challenge his rationalist predecessors.

Before the winter semester of 1762, Kant prepared a booklet entitled *On the Proof of the False Subtlety of the Four Syllogistic Figures,* and while he did not pull down or abandon rationalism completely, he did open up new engagements and propelled himself toward his later efforts to think about an alternative system for how we come to think and know anything stable about our world. Kant acknowledged that logic should investigate the formation of concepts and that judgments did proceed from concepts. For example, if a person understands the concept of an apple and the concept of a fruit, then the person can form the judgment "an apple is a fruit." But what made our judgments possible and secure? In trying to answer this question, Kant claimed that judgments depend on our ability to convert sense impressions into objects of thought. And he rejected what rationalists staunchly defended, namely, that we can establish certainty from innate ideas, from self-revealing, pure concepts (about mathematics, for example) given to the mind by reason.

In this instance, Kant began to side more closely with the empiricist point of view, a view that rejected the doctrine of innate ideas. Empiricists, such as Hume, preferred to look at the acquisition of knowledge in relation to information received from sense experience. John Locke, another famous empiricist, created a memorable image when he said that the mind at birth is like a blank tablet (or *tabula rasa* in Latin), and sensory experience writes on the tablet. Every idea in our mind must have entered originally through the senses, Locke said. As Francis Bacon, an even earlier proponent of the empiricist project, had noted, "empiricists are like ants; they collect and put to use, but rationalists, like spiders, spin thread out of themselves." Kant's thoughts on these subjects were somewhat preliminary, but they started a critical turn away from rationalism and cultivated an attraction for empiricism.

Kant then wrote a response to a competition announced by the Berlin Academy of Sciences, and again, this became an opportunity to broaden his interests. Are principles of natural theology and morality at all susceptible to the proofs that seem to produce certainty? the Academy asked. How are they impacted by the latest scientific methods or approaches to mathematical proof?

Kant answered in *An Inquiry into the Clarity of the Principles of Natural Theology and Morality* and increased his doubts about the rationalist method. He explored why philosophy understandably was a lesser science than mathematics and how the former should now turn to the natural sciences to find a new method for analysis. Kant also addressed the plausibility of belief in God, although he stressed the importance of the inner, unmediated experience humans may have with a divine being. As for principles of morality, these might seem especially difficult to derive, but Kant began stressing the likelihood of some kind of compulsory grounding for morality. All of these topics would be developed in much more detail in Kant's later works. But the trajectory of such works showed Kant taking his engagements with natural science into discussions about epistemology and metaphysics.

If Kant had never written anything else beyond the works noted, he would have remained an admired teacher and a respectable contributor to the intellectual conversation of his time. His answer to the Berlin Academy competition did not win first prize but was published nonetheless. Kant subsequently wrote essays outlining more fully his ideas about the existence of God and the faulty promises of metaphysics. His new works had only begun to initiate charges against significant philosophers. Kant was claiming that others misunderstood the proper ways to explain how we secure real knowledge and misunderstood metaphysical speculation. One could scarcely say as much without further elaboration. Moreover, if prominent philosophical systems possibly should be abandoned, what new system should replace the old ones?

In his forties, Kant began to formulate the central issues of his philosophy. He had broken free from his earlier rationalist assumptions, but he now began to question the empiricist point of view as well. If one expected to ground truth claims on techniques that relied on data from empirical observation *only,* how far could this go without undermining our ability to answer any other important questions? In other words, if science was to remain our paradigm of knowledge, then how could we acquire genuine knowledge about topics that science could not investigate, such as God, the origin of anything, or moral values? And if science showed us a world of strict laws, where did this leave our freedom of choice? If philosophy should follow science in seeking more secure universal truths, what could this imply about our ability to affect the world through unpredictable choices? Is our freedom an illusion? In attempting to push himself further to answer these questions, Kant would come to craft what we consider his mature philosophy. In doing so, he would finally demonstrate his appreciation for empiricism and yet demonstrate its limits. He would emphasize the importance of natural science but avoid the corroding skepticism of those who believed that metaphysical questions and our capacity to freely choose (right from wrong, especially) were either impossible or simply the product of subjective human conventions.

∽ Rethinking Philosophy

Not surprisingly, Kant took time to sort through the philosophical concerns noted earlier. In 1781 the *Critique of Pure Reason,* the culmination of Kant's original answers to his engagements with philosophy, finally reached the public.

Unfortunately, however, reception of the *Critique* was mixed. The text was demanding, often misunderstood, and this led Kant to summarize his efforts and rewrite sections for a second edition. In time, Kant did receive attention for his work, and it became a recognizably brilliant contribution to how to think and do philosophy. What exactly did Kant accomplish?

Kant presented in the *Critique* not only his most thorough, convincing attack on rationalists and empiricists, but a systematic, new way of thinking about how we know anything. He reinforced his criticisms of major schools of thought in eighteenth-century philosophy that had struggled to identify the scope as well as the limits of the human knower and the human mind. And then he presented a new approach to analyzing the faculties of the mind and to characterizing specifically what the human faculty of reason could do and know apart from, but in relationship with, sense experience.

Some of Kant's general concerns about his predecessors have been noted. But these are worth expanding upon. To understand them more fully helps highlight the distinctiveness of Kant's contributions to the philosophical enterprise and, more precisely, why they received such attention.

By the time Kant wrote his philosophical works, he had become skeptical about how objective knowledge and certainty could emerge from a system of deductions built upon self-evident premises. Rationalists had made it difficult to understand the way their supposedly self-evident, reason-based starting points could be so divorced from empirical observations. They also went too far, Kant believed, in divorcing humans as knowing subjects from the world of knowable objects that they were striving to know. On the other side were empiricists, who had, rightly from Kant's perspective, helped reemphasize the importance of direct observation and the difficulties of acquiring knowledge from innate ideas. But Kant decided that empiricism by itself was not the answer to rationalism's dilemmas. Empiricists too often tried to produce reflections about knowledge that claimed that the human mind never needed to make *any* significant conceptual leaps beyond and more distant from observations in order to know reality. This seemed implausible. True, rationalism was "rotten dogmatism," as Kant put it; and through his study of the work of the empiricist David Hume, Kant admitted being awakened from his own "dogmatic slumbers." But the culmination of empiricism, especially in work by Hume, presented too many difficulties.

For example, while Hume recognized how experience bombarded us with data that formed simple sensations and impressions on the mind that humans then stored in various ways, he also remained skeptical of stronger claims about the active character of human cognitive capacities. The mind only passively arranged impressions garnered from objects; it did not actively create more abstract ideas (distinct from sensations). True, empiricists admitted, humans did form associations, note similarities, and infer causal relations between objects, and these were not always directly observable. However, most empiricists strove mightily to show that even such complex ideas still originated in the inherent qualities of sensations. It was this empiricist effort to explain away an active role for the human mind—including, for example, the way the mind characterizes certain causal relationships—that was especially troubling to Kant.

For Kant, Hume presented possibilities but also puzzles. Of special interest was Hume's explanation of causality. Hume suggested that the reason we come to believe that causes bring about certain necessary effects relates to unreflective habit, to our becoming *accustomed* to recurring phenomena. We see clouds, and then we see the rain follow, over and over again, and so we come to believe that clouds cause rain. The only basis of the belief is habit or expectation. This, in particular, Kant could not accept. The causal laws established by the natural sciences were more than merely human habits or subjective expectations. Philosophers should be able to say more about the interaction between human cognitive faculties, the world observed, and the truths hoped for. If they could do so, they could go beyond Hume's unsatisfying suggestions. They might also be able to salvage (from a less dogmatic perspective) the rationalist's interest in reason—the capacity of the human mind to find certain abstract concepts within itself—and the age-old engagement with important metaphysical questions.

◇ A New Theory of Knowledge and the Structure of Rational Thought

Kant wanted to criticize previous philosophers, but then also to build up a more effective vision of how rational beings synthesize information from experience, interact with such information, and form stable ideas about it. How could he accomplish this?

First, Kant claimed that we need to recognize a special way in which humans make and verify truth claims. We need to describe properly the types of judgments that humans make. Others had not explained this adequately, and it hindered their views. To put it in Kant's terms, we need to recognize that humans make various judgments, including "synthetic a priori judgments."

What do those technical terms mean? It turns out that much hangs on the answer because Kant claims that if he can demonstrate the necessity of synthetic a priori judgments, that should establish the possibility of a new approach to key philosophical issues and allow him to avoid the dilemmas of rationalists and empiricists.

A judgment is an operation of thought whereby we connect a subject and a predicate, and where the predicate qualifies the subject. For example, "roses are red" is a judgment, where "roses" is the subject and "are red" is the predicate, which tells us something about the subject. "Synthetic" judgments are related to empirical observations. If someone tells you that "Some swans are black," you demand evidence to support it. The statement does not offer you secure knowledge until it is backed up by empirical findings. Has anyone ever seen black swans? The statement can be accepted as true only if we have supporting information after the fact (or "a posteriori," as opposed to "a priori," prior to experience). And if we traveled to Australia, we could observe black swans.

We also recognize "analytic" judgments, or judgments verified without empirical observations. Take the statement "a triangle has three sides." We grasp the truth of this judgment a priori, without relying on empirical evidence. When we think of a triangle, we presuppose information about the sides. In other words, the idea of a triangle already *includes* the idea of three sides. All we need to do is analyze the subject ("a triangle"), and we can see that the judgment is true. The same goes for the statement "a body is extended." The predicate does not add anything to the subject. Rather, we already presuppose that a body necessarily has the character of extension. In synthetic judgments, in contrast, the predicate adds something new to the subject. Analyzing the idea of a rose does not tell us that it is red. What Kant wants to say is that many philosophers identify these first two types of judgment, but they miss the fact that there is a third type. They recognize synthetic judgments, which are a posteriori, and analytic judgments, which are a priori. But they miss the "synthetic a priori" type. And the mistake, according to

Kant, explains many philosophers' inability to account for important truths and their mischaracterizations of the structure of thinking.

Kant believed that we made synthetic a priori judgments frequently. For example, take a mathematical statement like $7 + 5 = 12$. We believe this is known without the need for further verification. It is known a priori. However, such a statement is not analytic. The number twelve cannot be derived from what we know about the numbers seven and five alone. Something must be done actively by the mind, to achieve the synthesis of the concepts "seven," "five," and "plus." In physics, we may believe that the proposition "in all changes in the material world the quantity of matter remains unchanged" is based on a priori knowledge because we make this judgment independently of our experience of change. However, it must be simultaneously synthetic, not analytic, because the idea of permanence is not readily discovered in the concept of matter. Other statements associated with metaphysics, and dealing with questions about God, the cosmos, or human freedom, exhibit the same quality. A statement like "humans are free to choose" seems to be synthetic because the idea of being free seems to add new knowledge to the subject "humans." Yet, simultaneously, the statement is necessary in advance of experience (a priori) because to wonder if the statement is true is to assume that we can decide what answer is correct. Asking a question implies that the answer is not already determined. Moreover, our choices and decisions every day convince us without a doubt that we are free. Therefore synthetic a priori statements do exist. They show that some claims are necessary, universally true, and at the same time informative about the world, according to Kant.

Having said this much, Kant needed to show how recognition of synthetic a priori judgment led to a new way to view the mind's organizing structures, as well as the way the mind could establish truth claims. A new critical philosophy should revamp the way we understand knowledge acquisition and the structure of cognitive faculties, especially the role of human reason. The discovery of synthetic a priori judgments led Kant to propose a new theory of the way the mind works.

The structure of rational thinking is complex and active. While what we expect to verify about our observations generally requires reference to sensory experiences (as empiricists would have it), we also find that at various levels of thinking there are a priori notions brought to bear on the way we receive representations formed through the senses (a recognition that shows some debts to rationalism). So, for Kant the mind organizes the raw data of sensations in various ways *before* the data become conscious. Not only is the mind never passive, but it brings certain presuppositions to the world it observes. This point, in turn, helps explain synthetic a priori judgments. The unconscious organization allows us to make judgments that are necessary, universal, and about the world as we experience it. This does not mean that every observation is marred by radically subjective bias. In fact, these basic judgments are not subjective at all, because the mind is structured in the *same way* for all of us and because we share the same a priori intuitions or concepts.

Overall, this is Kant's dramatic proposal: that philosophers can and should study the *mind* in order to understand features of the *world*. Kant called it a "Copernican revolution" in philosophy. Copernicus displaced the stationary earth and put the sun at the center of the solar system, with the earth revolving around it. Similarly, Kant reversed the relation of the mind and the world. Instead of believing that the world is central and the mind depends on it, he suggested that the mind is central and the world we experience depends on the structure of the human mind. Thus, to understand the world, we must study the mind.

But now what can we say about the structure of the mind in general? What exactly can we say every human mind grasps a priori? First and fundamentally, all grasp the notions of space and time. Empiricists would object to this right away. They would say that we never grasp these ideas in advance of experience, or a priori. We observe them. We understand space by noticing that one object is next to another. We observe and grasp time by observing how events succeed or precede one another. Kant says, "not quite." By observing particular spaces, we do not come to understand how things are situated in one all-containing, wider spatial system. Moreover, we do not have the ability to think of or observe objects *not* in space. Any physical object we think of *must* take up space. Therefore, our concept of space is not derived from experience; rather, it helps create experience. It makes human experience possible. As for time, the infinity of time extends beyond any particular temporal experience we have. We cannot grasp it by observing the relation between discrete events. Kant says, "Time and space, taken together, are the pure forms of all sensible intuition, and so are what make synthetic a priori propositions possible." Space and time are lenses through which we filter *all* of our particular sense perceptions. From the outset, the mind works on and with experience.

Beyond the intuitions of space and time, Kant believes we bring other abstract categories of thought or concepts to observations. These provide further conditions for structuring what we observe. That is, experience is not only filtered through our sense of space and time, but judged by what Kant calls "categories of understanding." They include concepts of quantity (or our understanding of amounts and one or many), quality (which focuses on whether a judgment is positive or negative), relation (which primarily means cause and effect), and modality (which allows us to think of something as possible or impossible). We cannot think about the world or make observations without bringing these categories of understanding to bear on experience.

One additional set of a priori ideas and structures of the mind has to be taken into account. For Kant, these come from the faculty of *reason*. Reason is the faculty with which humans try to create their final, coherent synthesis of experience by coordinating the relations between the categories of understanding previously discussed. Reason is a highly ambitious faculty, attempting to grasp conditions beyond sense experience to unify all of experience. In attempting to do its work, reason starts from its own a priori ideas, too.

The ideas of reason, for Kant, include a unified notion of the self, of the cosmos, and belief in God. All are necessary, Kant claims, in order to have a coherent grasp of the world. For example, in order to have any knowledge, we must presuppose a self that knows and that unifies the various operations of the mind. But we do not observe anything we can call a self. As Hume had said, we can observe a thought or a feeling but never a self. Nevertheless, every person's experience is organized around a unified perspective, what we call "my position, not yours," "my memories, not yours," or "my pleasures and pains, not yours." Reason alone provides this highly abstract projection. The same holds for the regulative idea of a world. Reason tries to create a synthesis from many events, forming a concept of the world in general or the world as a whole. Finally, while we may not have "the slightest ground to assume in the absolute manner the object of this idea," reason requires that we operate *as if* one supreme being existed as the source and cause of all.

Kant's original contribution was to show how the complex faculties of the mind may operate and how *interaction* occurs between the world observed and the a priori intuitions of space and time, categories of the understanding, and the ideas of reason. This interdependence that Kant explored so thoroughly helped to answer distinct questions about the nature of knowledge and how humans acquire it. It also immediately raised a key concern. How could Kant claim that he had surpassed his predecessors? Didn't this talk of the categories of the understanding, and of reason doing so much work before testing ideas through experience, only demonstrate that Kant was a rationalist at heart?

Kant did recognize that his talk of abstract categories of the understanding, for example, could be misconstrued. Whatever some may think about the effort to demonstrate such categories or the a priori rules associated with them, he did want to be clear that the categories have to be *applied* in experience. A priori categories are simply the beginning of how we come to acquire knowledge. They do not actually tell us anything until there is empirical material to work on, Kant claimed. We have to translate a bare abstraction into a world of experience. The raw data of sensation, or "percepts," are chaotic without the structure imposed by the mind. But the structures are meaningless without some content to work on. As Kant said, "percepts without concepts are blind, but concepts without percepts are empty." Kant offered various arguments to fill out a characterization of the mind that avoided recreating the same problems arising from the dramatic distance between subject and object that plagued the rationalists.

What about the ideas of reason? These were said to help arrange and set limits on the categories of our understanding. But reason also operates at a very great distance from the events in the physical world. Kant admitted as much but argued that any metaphysical claims derived from his ideas were quite cautiously constructed. The faculty of reason establishes *limits*. Like categories of the understanding, reason's a priori ideas do not lead to anything substantive. For example, the idea of the unified self is "a bare consciousness which accompanies all concepts." It is a regulative ideal and prior to experience, but nothing substantial is determined by the Cartesian "I think." The same holds for the regulative concept of the world. "The cosmological ideas are nothing but simply regulative principles," says Kant. We need the ideas of reason, but since they do not correspond to any object in experience, they cannot support elaborate systems such as those the rationalists constructed. They are necessary for experience to occur, but they are not part of experience. We have to call them regulative ideas only and remain satisfied with a degree of rational faith where such ideas are concerned.

This is what allows Kant to say that the metaphysicians who claim not only that God is a regulative idea, but is proven through reason alone, remain arrogant or foolish. Rationalists mistakenly insisted that reason gave them "objects absolutely" instead of "objects in the idea." This is where speculative metaphysics went wrong and made dogmatic assertions. Kant agrees, again, with empiricists who claimed that we cannot know reality in itself, beyond experience. But Kant moves beyond empiricism by claiming that the subject matter of metaphysics is important. It's true that there can be no *science* of metaphysics. But the philosopher can think about metaphysical questions seriously and discover truths about all of reality as humans experience it.

In sum, Kant distinguished between the world as it appears to all humans and the world as it really is. Philosophy can establish objective knowledge of the world of appearances, of the "phenomenal world," as he called it. But philosophers should not go further. They must not expect to prove, scientifically, knowledge of the realm beyond sense experience, or what Kant called the "noumenal realm." They may wish to know the independent reality, or "things in themselves," something they have often reached for. But not even reason, which responds to our felt need for a synthesis of experience at higher levels of explanation, can give us more than a limited ability to understand reality and discover the necessary conditions of knowledge. Philosophers and the project of philosophy can be sustained, but they must remain chastened.

ᴖ Ethics and Practical Reason

In the wake of his first *Critique*, Kant turned to other concerns, particularly ethics. Such concerns broadened the impact of his ideas and reinforced how his views about human reason had practical as well as theoretical import.

Like many born in the eighteenth century, Kant was moved by what we have come to call "Enlightenment" ideas. Although perhaps less engaged with politics than some of his continental colleagues, Kant eventually associated his observations about a priori knowledge and metaphysics with other practical considerations about ethics, historical progress, and law. In his short essay "What Is Enlightenment?" Kant opens with the passionate plea to think for yourself. Like so many of his time, he championed the idea that each individual is a responsible, rational being, capable of governing himself or herself in matters of moral duty. Moreover, these claims were important in the context of Kant's initial efforts to establish a thoroughly modern theory of knowledge. Kant believed that the observable world is determined by natural laws. However, human minds share a certain structure that stands apart from, even as it helps organize and make meaningful, this world of phenomena. So too, when it comes to practical ethical conduct, humans possess a free will that has the capacity to give itself moral guidance and stand apart from the egotistical, self-interested impulses of everyday life. Humans might not always choose to act in accord with the rational rules that define moral duty, as Kant puts it. But we possess such a moral capacity, and it is bound up with our practical capacity to reason, which remains distinct from the continuous influence of slavish desires and passions. (Later romantics, and even utilitarians such as Bentham, might claim otherwise.)

In several related texts (including the *Groundwork of the Metaphysics of Morals* and the *Critique of Practical Reason*), Kant ventured into a more thorough explanation of the formal features of practical reason. Practical reason, unlike theoretical reason, focuses attention on discovering how we *ought* to behave and how we should assess our life plans. In presenting his arguments, Kant first tried to convince his readers that any proper assessment of right conduct could never be based on the *consequences* of an action. Morality is a matter of *intention*, not consequences of actions. We judge people by what they try to do, not by the actual results of their actions. For example, suppose a young person begins to experiment with drugs. His teacher wants to guide him back to a better path, so she gives him tickets to a play, hoping he will pursue his interest in theater. But suppose the student sells the tickets to buy more drugs. Most people would say the teacher was admirable and did a good thing, even though the actual consequences of her action were negative. Now consider another case. Suppose one of the student's friends gives him money to buy drugs, hoping the student will become as dependent as the friend is. But the student uses the money to go to the play instead. Did the friend do the right thing? Of course not. His intention was to get the student hooked on drugs, and therefore his action was wrong. The fact that the action led to a good educational outcome is irrelevant to the morality of the case. The decisive factor in morality is intention.

Kant believed that our natural thinking about right and wrong indicated that morality was a matter of trying to do what was right. It was a matter of doing our duty as opposed to following our inclinations. But what was our duty? Kant argued that all rational creatures, as they try to make certain scientific observations, not only share structures of thinking and interacting with their world, as discussed earlier; they also, as free creatures, share a capacity to check their behavior against an a priori idea of practical reason—a universal principle Kant called the "categorical imperative." Fully formulated, such a practical principle or imperative is expressed as follows: "act only on that maxim whereby you can at the same time will that it should become a universal law." In other words, our moral duties are those actions that we can wish that everyone performed. This imperative was not a principle that simply told us what to do, Kant said. Like the a priori ideas from the first *Critique*, it remained formal. It provided a limit, a simple but effective check on behavior.

For example, a person might be tempted to tell a lie. Can one will that everyone tell lies whenever they are tempted? No, because if the principle "Tell lies" became a universal law, then no one would trust anyone's statements and all communication would break down. If you knew that people lied as often as they told the truth, you would never trust them. Even lying itself would be useless. Communication depends on the common assumption that what people say is true. Thus Kant's test of moral duty is "universalizability," or the question "What if everyone did that?"

Many saw this view of duty given by a rule of practical reason as too mysterious and not proven. But just as he had tried to salvage metaphysical claims in the first critique, Kant demanded that we at least project the possibility of acting as self-legislating moral beings. He had earlier distinguished between the world as it appears to the human mind and the world as it really is. The same distinction applies to the self. We appear to ourselves to be selfish, driven by emotions, and committed to personal happiness above all. But our ability to do our duties, out of pure respect for a universal law, shows that a different kind of self lies beneath the appearances. We may not be able to prove scientifically the imperative of practical reason, but humans, while subject to natural necessity or causality as part of the phenomenal realm, must think of themselves *as if* they are free to do right. As part of the noumenal realm, they are capable of imagining themselves not simply determined by the world of sense experience and natural laws, but as rational beings capable of acting freely and able to fashion their own rules about how they ought to behave.

For all these quarrels, Kant remained within the mainstream of eighteenth-century philosophical trends. Indeed, many nineteenth-century, anti-Enlightenment writers criticized Kant for his devotion to the outlook of his time. Mid-eighteenth-century thinkers from countries such as France and England had placed significant emphasis on the discoveries of natural science. The *philosophes* of the French Enlightenment had championed human reason in decision making in opposition to what they saw as stifling traditions of church and state. Reason should clear away what habit and tradition may have presumed "natural," they said. And many such thinkers were optimistic about the present as well as the future, not simply after this life but here on earth. Kant embraced elements of these ideas in his own way. He remained committed to providing a foundation for scientific truth claims and supporting the autonomous use of reason in assessing good conduct. In later work, he explored how legal obligations could never be imposed by force or the commands of God but must be held as a subset of chosen moral obligations. Kant even adopted aspects of Rousseau's attempt to ground political authority on a contractual arrangement willed by the people. He admired mixed constitutions and supported aspects of the French Revolution.

While apparently supportive of Christianity, Kant wrote on religion, again late in life, suggesting that a properly religious attitude could be cultivated by purity of heart in adopting and vigorously pursuing a priori moral duties commanded by reason. Moral practice must ultimately lead to belief in God and the projection of an afterlife. While certainly not as radical as some of his predecessors (the French *philosophes* wrote at one point that "reason is to the *philosophes* what grace is to the Christian"), such ideas did prove provocative to Prussian authorities of the time, who declared Kant's writings subversive and demanded that he refrain from making further comments on religion. Kant consented, with some protest, but he weighed in on this and other controversial areas of interest, and he did so with a level of originality and perhaps daring that, at least within his own context, unsettled orthodox authorities of significance.

We have emphasized Kant's relationship to the eighteenth century. For nineteenth-century German thinkers, Kant's wide-ranging, systematic work proved a considerable force as well. Even where thinkers like Hegel rejected elements of Kant's work, such conflicts often reinforced Kant's importance to the conversation of philosophy. There were neo-Kantians on the Continent who remained supportive and British academics who by the end of the nineteenth century had their own distinct interpretations of Kant as well. One significant testament to Kant's continued influence in the twentieth century can be seen in recent works by John Rawls. Rawls has spent several decades making Kant's ethics, especially his commitment to autonomy, more widely accessible. He has emphasized the implications of Kant's idea for social contract doctrines and has shown how they may help legitimate public principles of justice for Western liberal democracies today. In the wake of Rawls' popular *A Theory of Justice*, interest in Kant and his potential to contribute to moral and political theory continues to grow.

∾ CHRONOLOGY

1724   birth of Immanuel Kant in Königsberg, Prussia

1740   enrolls in the University of Königsberg

1746   begins working as a private tutor, continued for nine years

1755   appointed lecturer at the university, very popular, publishes *A General History of Nature and a Theory of the Heavens*

1762   Rousseau's *Social Contract*

1770   promoted to professor at the university, publishes *On the Form and Principles of the Sensible and the Intelligible World*

1781   *The Critique of Pure Reason*

1783   *Prolegomena to Any Future Metaphysic*

1788   *Critique of Practical Reason*

1789   French Revolution begins in Paris

1790   *Critique of Judgment*

1793   *Religion within the Limits of Pure Reason*, forbidden by the Prussian government to write anything else on religion

1795   *On Perpetual Peace*

1797   *Foundations of the Metaphysics of Morals*

1804   dies in Königsberg

∿ SUGGESTED READINGS

Bencivenga, E. *Kant's Copernican Revolution*. New York: Oxford University Press, 1987.

Ewing, A.C. *A Short Commentary on Kant's Critique of Pure Reason*. Chicago: University of Chicago Press, 1987 (1938).

Kemp Smith, N. *A Commentary to Kant's "Critique of Pure Reason."* Second Edition. Atlantic Highlands, NJ: Humanities Press, 1992 (1923).

Kitcher, P., ed. *Kant's Critique of Pure Reason: Critical Essays*. Lanham, MD: Rowman and Littlefield, 1998.

Korner, S. *Kant*. Baltimore: Penguin, 1955.

Stevenson, L. *The Metaphysics of Experience*. New York: Oxford University Press, 1982.

Weldon, T.D. *Kant's Critique of Pure Reason*. Second Edition. New York: Oxford University Press, 1958.

CHAPTER 11

Marx
Philosophy as Changing
the World

Ernie Alleva

~ Preview

"The philosophers have only interpreted the world in various ways; the point, however, is to change it." Marx believes that philosophy must be connected with action. Otherwise, it is merely pompous wordplay. Not only should beliefs lead to practice, but practice does in fact lead to beliefs. People's actions and daily activities strongly influence their thinking and values. One's understanding and philosophy do not occur in a vacuum. Instead, they are conditioned by one's work, one's source of income, one's friends, one's prospects for the future, the government one obeys, and all aspects of social life. Philosophers have tried to live in a kind of Platonic heaven, but Marx wants to bring them out of the clouds and down to earth. Marx shows how societies

changed through history and how, as a result, philosophies and consciousness changed. The task facing philosophers today is to understand capitalism, since the system of money and finding work shapes virtually every aspect of our consciousness. And to understand capitalism objectively, we must escape from its influence; we must change it. (The Editor)

∾ Introduction

In an oft-quoted passage from Theses on Feuerbach, Marx tells us, "The philosophers have only *interpreted* the world, in various ways; the point, however, is to *change* it."[1] Marx is clearly a philosopher who has changed the world, largely by means of his interpretation of the world. Although it is difficult to gauge the influence of an individual's ideas on the world at large, it is not implausible to claim that the popular influence of Marx's thought, correctly understood or not, surpasses that of any philosopher in the Western tradition. Since Marx's time, numerous political movements and parties have identified themselves as "Marxist," and for much of the past century, a substantial portion of humanity has lived under regimes claiming to follow Marx's views. But Marx himself would be quick to note that popularity or claimed allegiance in the world at large (and perhaps even among philosophers) may have little to do with the truth or intellectual significance of a thinker's ideas. And with respect to some of those in his own day who were taken to be Marxists, Marx is reported to have said, "What is certain is that I am not a Marxist."[2]

Karl Marx was born to a middle-class family on May 5, 1818, in the German city of Trier. His parents were Jewish, but the family converted to Christianity when he was a child. Marx's father was a successful lawyer, and Marx initially studied law at the universities of Bonn and Berlin, but he eventually turned to the study of philosophy, obtaining his doctorate in 1841. Given the conservative political climate at the time and his radical views, an academic career was not a serious option for Marx. Instead, he went on to work in radical journalism and became increasingly involved in the working-class movement. In 1843 he married his childhood sweetheart, Jenny von Westphalen, with whom he had six children and with whom he lived until her death in 1881. Marx met Friedrich Engels, widely viewed as the co-founder of Marxist thought, in Paris in 1844. They became close friends and were intellectual and political colleagues for the remainder of Marx's life. Marx's early political activities resulted in numerous legal problems, and he was expelled from both Prussia and France. He lived in various places in Europe until settling in London in 1849, where he lived in exile until the end of his life. Marx was a prolific writer, producing a substantial corpus of journalistic and more theoretical or scholarly work, a good deal of the latter unpublished in his lifetime. But his writing brought him little money. Much of his adult life was spent in poverty and ill health, and he often depended on Engels and other friends for financial support. In addition to his extensive research and writing, Marx devoted considerable time and effort to working-class causes and played key leadership roles in the International Working Men's Association and other organizations. He died in London on March 13, 1883.

✍ Marx and Philosophy

Marx has an uneasy relationship to philosophy, and his status as a philosopher is a matter of dispute. He was trained as a philosopher and wrote a doctoral dissertation in philosophy, and much of his early writing, characterized by himself and others as "philosophical," consisted of analysis and criticism of his philosophical predecessors and contemporaries, including Hegel, Feuerbach, and many others. However, much of what Marx says about philosophy and his fellow philosophers is highly critical, if not hostile. He sometimes characterizes philosophy, along with religion, morality, and law, as "ideology," not a term of praise coming from Marx's pen. And a good case can be made for the view that Marx himself took his later thought as going beyond or outside philosophy as he understood it. He sometimes describes his own approach to certain questions as "scientific" and contrasts it with philosophical approaches. And within intellectual life today, much of his work is regarded as a contribution to areas of social science, such as economics, sociology, and history, rather than to philosophy proper.

However, I think that none of this precludes viewing Marx as engaging in philosophy and taking him seriously as a philosopher. Philosophers are a contentious lot, and they are frequently critical of their fellow philosophers.[3] And one thinker's philosophy is another's science or religion. Precisely what counts as philosophy and what is properly contrasted with it, whether it be science, art, religion, myth, or commonsense belief, has always been and continues to be a matter of considerable philosophical disagreement. And one might claim that adopting a "scientific" approach to certain questions is itself to take a philosophical position about how they should be understood and addressed. Marx wouldn't be the first (or last) philosopher to have claimed to have gone beyond philosophy and to have come up with something different or better, something "scientific," and there are numerous figures in the history of philosophy who are today viewed as having made contributions to the social and natural sciences as well as doing philosophy, for example, Aristotle, Hobbes, Descartes, Leibniz, Hume, Smith, Mill, and James, among others. I won't here try to resolve scholarly disputes about either the nature of philosophy or precisely how to situate Marx within or in relation to philosophy, since this goes well beyond the scope of this essay. Instead, I shall examine some of his core concerns and ideas that I believe are philosophical by most traditional standards and that have been of enduring interest to philosophical readers and critics of Marx.[4]

The primary focus of Marx's thought is the human world. Although philosophers often take something more—the whole of existence, the universe, being, whatever exists, human and nonhuman—as their ultimate object of inquiry, Marx has relatively little to say about the nonhuman world. However, he does embrace what can be described as a broad ontological "naturalism" or "materialism," where there is no room for supernatural or nonmaterial entities, where humans are understood as wholly situated within and as part of the natural world. But he, like many other philosophical naturalists or materialists, leaves systematic inquiry and understanding concerning the nonhuman aspects of the world to the physicists, chemists, biologists, and other natural scientists. With respect to the human world, Marx's concerns are largely matters of social and political inquiry: questions regarding human nature, human freedom, human history, the development and organization of societies; the evaluation and criticism of human relationships and institutions; and of alternative ways of thinking about all of this. In the sections that follow, I explore some of Marx's ideas regarding these and related issues. But first, by way of introduction, I shall discuss some of Marx's views about philosophy.

Perhaps a good place to start is the preceding quote from Theses on Feuerbach: "The philosophers have only *interpreted* the world, in various ways; the point, however, is to *change* it."[5] What exactly is wrong with philosophers interpreting the world or, more precisely, *only* interpreting the world? And what is Marx proposing? Is he saying that philosophers shouldn't philosophize at all, that they shouldn't try to interpret or understand the world, but instead that they should turn to changing the world?

Given Marx's support for and active involvement in causes aiming at radical social change, it is tempting to understand him as expressing an impatience with theoretical inquiry and proposing an anti-intellectual call to action, something like: "Enough with all of this abstract theory and intellectual hairsplitting. Let's get on with the more pressing task of making a better world: To the barricades!" But I think that this view is too quick and not quite right. No doubt, Marx did engage in various kinds of radical political activity in order to bring about what he thought would be a better world, and he thought that his fellow philosophers should join him in this. However, given the broader context of this quote, his other writings, and the fact that so much of his own life was focused on interpreting the world, on intense study and writing, I think that it is clear that Marx is not claiming that there are no significant intellectual tasks worth doing with respect to interpreting the world. Instead, I think that he is saying that, given the traditional philosophical aims of correctly understanding the world (as well as overcoming various problems related to mistaken understandings of the world, such as certain forms of human suffering and unhappiness, in particular, forms of alienation), there are limits to what can be achieved through philosophical reflection and criticism alone. Why does Marx think this? He thinks that certain mistaken or illusory views about the world are ultimately rooted in the social world itself, in how people live and work and how this contributes to their understanding of the world, and that the only hope for getting certain things about the world right is to change the world and bring about conditions in which social life does not foster mistaken beliefs about the world. In order to avoid a false or distorted understanding of the world and to achieve a correct understanding, humans will have to change the world, that is, create a world that does not systematically generate and sustain erroneous views about the world.

Perhaps put another way, Marx thinks that philosophers have their heads in the clouds. They raise abstract problems or questions about reality, knowledge, consciousness, and so on and come up with abstract solutions or answers to them through philosophical reflection, argument, and theory. They produce interpretations of the world, philosophical theories, that are a priori or highly speculative and that view philosophy as an independent branch of knowledge, above the fray of ordinary social life. But they fail to see the ways in which human thinking in general and their own thinking in particular are themselves products of social and historical conditions; they fail to see certain connections between philosophical problems and theories and other more mundane and practical aspects of human life. And as a result, they think that certain philosophical problems can be solved by reflection and criticism alone, by coming up with a correct interpretation of the world. But, if Marx is right, philosophers have been looking in the wrong place for the sources of and solutions to certain problems. Such problems don't arise from bad theorizing or a lack of reflection or rationality on the part of philosophers, or at least not from these alone. They arise from features of social life itself, and an adequate understanding of the world will require that social life itself be changed.

These are provocative claims, and one might raise numerous questions about them. Do they apply to philosophy in general? Do they apply to all philosophers and philosophical problems or only to certain ones? Is Marx correct in his analysis and criticism of philosophy? Does he adequately support his claims? Are there reasons for thinking he is mistaken? These are important issues that can't be explored here. Rather, I shall note that Marx's claims about philosophy are embedded in a broader understanding of the human world, his "materialist" conception of history and society, to which I now turn.

∿ The Materialist Conception of History

Central to Marx's thought is a theory of history that provides an interpretation of human societies and an account of their historical change and development. His views about history were in part an attempt to understand in a systematic way the profound social, economic, political, and intellectual changes taking place in the modern world. Among these changes were the transition from feudalism to capitalism, the Industrial Revolution, the American and French revolutions, European colonial domination of substantial portions of the world, the Scientific Revolution, and the Enlightenment. In addition, much of Marx's thinking about history was a critical response to the outlook of the influential German philosopher Hegel, who provided an "idealistic" understanding of human society and history.

On Hegel's view, the various forms of human thought and culture found in distinct historical civilizations are aspects of the development of the "world spirit," a grand person or agent, a God-like entity, that is the ultimate reality. Human history is the world spirit becoming increasingly self-conscious, becoming aware of itself as a being whose essence is to be free and who gradually realizes that essence through the course of history. Thus, human history is not a haphazard or meaningless series of events. Instead, it involves a kind of progress over time, and Hegel explains this progress in terms of the activity of the world spirit. The different forms of religious, political, artistic, and intellectual life in successive periods of human history reveal stages in the world spirit as it achieves a more adequate understanding of itself and becomes progressively more free. For Hegel, self-awareness in all spirit or mind requires activity in a reality it takes to be outside, or other than, itself. One becomes self-aware by perceiving and reflecting on what one does in that external reality. Thus, the world spirit becomes aware of itself by recognizing its expression in something that it views as not itself, the material or natural world in which human history takes place. And when fully self-aware, it understands that the natural world is in fact not distinct or separate from itself, but is an aspect of itself that it creates, a projection of itself that it needs for achieving self-awareness and for realizing its freedom. Although the development of the world spirit takes place through the activity of human individuals and cultures, this process is not something that people understand as they play their part in this development. It is only at the end of this long process that they are in a position to make sense of all of this and have an adequate understanding of their role in it.

Marx agrees with Hegel that history is not a haphazard sequence of events and that there is sense to be made of historical change in terms of a kind of progress. However, he criticizes Hegel's and other idealistic approaches to understanding history that take the development of spirit, whether of a grand world spirit or of human consciousness and self-understanding, as the basic moving force in history. Instead, he proposes a "materialistic" account that focuses on the ways in which people produce their livelihood and how these influence other aspects of social and cultural life.

> In direct contrast to German philosophy, which descends from heaven to earth, here we ascend from earth to heaven. That is to say, we do not set out from what men say, imagine, conceive nor from men as narrated, thought of, imagined, conceived, in order to arrive at men in the flesh. We set out from real, active men, and on the basis of their real life-process we demonstrate the development of the ideological reflexes and echoes of this life-process. . . . Morality, religion, metaphysics and all the rest of ideology and their corresponding forms of consciousness no longer seem independent. They have no history of development. Rather, men who develop their material production and their material relationships alter their thinking and the products of their thinking along with their real existence. Consciousness does not determine life, but life determines consciousness.[6]

This alternative approach to understanding history is explored by Marx in various writings, but there is no better summary than the sketch Marx provides in the Preface to his *A Contribution to the Critique of Political Economy*.

> In the social production of their life, men enter into definite relations that are indispensable and independent of their will, relations of production which correspond to a definite stage of development of their material productive forces. The sum total of these relations of production constitutes the economic structure of society, the real foundation, on which rises a legal and political superstructure and to which correspond definite forms of social consciousness. The mode of production of material life conditions the social, political and intellectual life process in general. It is not the consciousness of men that determines their being, but, on the contrary, their social being that determines their consciousness. At a certain stage of their development, the material productive forces of society come in conflict with the existing relations of production, or—what is but a legal expression for the same thing—with the property relations within which they have been at work hitherto. From forms of development of the productive forces these relations turn into their fetters. Then begins an epoch of social revolution. With the change of the economic foundation the entire immense superstructure is more or less rapidly transformed. In considering such transformations a distinction should always be made between the material transformation of the economic conditions of production, which can be determined with the precision of natural science, and the legal, political, religious, aesthetic or philosophic—in short, ideological forms in which men become conscious of this conflict and fight it out. Just as our opinion of an individual is not based on what he thinks of himself, so can we not judge of such a period of transformation by its own consciousness; on the contrary, this consciousness must be explained from the contradictions of material life, from the existing conflict between the social productive forces and the relations of production.[7]

Here Marx presents a three-tiered framework for classifying features of economic and social life that are essential to his materialist account of society and historical change: (1) "productive forces" employed in the process of production: labor power (human capacities, knowledge and skills, etc.) and means of production (raw materials and instruments of production, such as tools, machines, etc.); (2) "relations of production": social roles or relationships between people regarding the effective control of productive forces used in the process of production (e.g., owning a tool or a factory, being a slaveholder or a slave, being a lord or a serf, being an employer or an employee, etc.), which together form the economic structure of society; and (3) a legal and political "superstructure" and forms of social consciousness.

Despite obvious differences, all societies have the features this framework picks out, and given this framework, Marx explains fundamental historical change in terms of the relationship between the forces and relations of production. He believes there is a long-term tendency for the productive forces to grow in productive power, and what drives historical change is this tendency humans have to develop their productive capacities, their abilities to transform and control nature, in order to satisfy human needs and wants. At a given stage of the development of the productive forces, different relations of production can have different influences on the use and growth of the productive forces. Not all ways of controlling and organizing production are equally good with respect to making effective use of particular skills, technology, raw materials, and so on. Some will do a better job and some a worse job, and over time relations of production will be adopted and endure to the extent that they facilitate the use and growth of productive forces. When existing relations of production come in conflict with the growth of the productive forces and no longer foster such growth but restrict or prevent it, they will eventually be replaced by new ones that provide for further development of the productive forces. When this occurs, there is a revolutionary change in the organization of society.

There is a similar connection between the relations of production and the features in the third category above, the legal and political superstructure and forms of social consciousness that prevail in society. Forms of legal and political organization and beliefs and attitudes systematized in widely held ideological outlooks do not function independently of the existing relations of production in a society, and on their own they do not account for historical change and development. Instead, they are tethered to the existing relations of production. Whether they are adopted and persist or change over time depends on how well they help maintain and legitimate those relations. And when there are fundamental changes in the relations of production, there will be corresponding changes in the legal and political framework and in social consciousness.

In summary, for Marx, historical development is ultimately rooted in the tendency humans have to develop their productive powers. Fundamental changes in various aspects of economic and social life are tied to the growth of human productive capacities. In an overly simplified statement of this conception, Marx says, "The handmill gives you society with the feudal lord; the steam-mill, society with the industrial capitalist."[8]

To avoid possible confusion, it is worth noting that there are at least two distinct kinds of "materialism" to which Marx is committed. One is a kind of ontological or metaphysical thesis: the materialism or naturalism mentioned previously regarding what kinds of entities do and do not exist, that is, the view that everything is part of the material or natural world and that there are no nonmaterial, nonnatural, or supernatural entities, such as God, angels, or Cartesian souls. The other is a social scientific thesis: the historical materialism discussed here concerning the relationships between certain aspects of human life and society, such as between ways of organizing economic life and political relationships or forms of social consciousness. Although Marx embraces both kinds of materialism, the two involve distinct claims that are in principle separable. One could be an ontological materialist and reject the view that "life determines consciousness" (perhaps the beliefs and attitudes about social life that prevail in a society have a life of their own and are largely independent of the way people organize production). And one could accept the view that ways of organizing productive life determine consciousness but reject the claim that all entities are material entities (perhaps a nonmaterial God exists or perhaps humans have Cartesian souls).

What should one make of Marx's materialist view of history? Critics have raised numerous conceptual and empirical questions about it. Is it philosophy, social science, or perhaps a bit of both? How, if at all, can it be evaluated? Can it be confirmed or disconfirmed by empirical evidence? Is Marx right about how particular aspects of human activity and social organization interact and change over time?

Some critics argue that there is no way in principle to confirm or disconfirm Marx's claims. For example, they argue that the distinction Marx makes between the relations of production and the legal and political superstructure cannot be conceptually separated or adequately differentiated, or they claim that the relationships that Marx posits between them are insufficiently clear or precise to be confirmed or disconfirmed. Others think such claims can in principle be confirmed or disconfirmed but think that the evidence is not decisive one way or the other, while still others argue that there is clear evidence against Marx's claims. Some critics challenge the claim that there is a general tendency of the productive forces to grow over time and instead suggest that the tendency in fact exists only in certain times and places. Others argue that the dependencies that Marx claims between various aspects of social life, where certain material or economic features are the independent or driving factors, are not supported by the available evidence. And in some cases, critics have defended one or another "idealist" or antimaterialist understanding of historical development, where factors such as religious belief or the law are claimed to be independent explanatory factors.

∿ Capitalism and Alienation

Marx proposed an account of human history and society that applies to the organization and development of human societies generally, and he studied and wrote a good deal about precapitalist societies. But his primary aim was to understand and evaluate the workings of capitalist society.

What is capitalism for Marx? As a way of organizing economic life, capitalism might be characterized in various ways, but for Marx it involves at least the following features: (1) private property in the means of production, where private individuals own the means of production and are free to use them to make a profit; (2) labor power is a commodity, where individual producers own their own labor power, the capacity to labor,[9] and are free to exchange it with employers for a wage in a labor market; and (3) commodity production, where production is for exchange in the market rather for direct consumption by producers. Although forms of each of these have existed to varying degrees within certain precapitalist societies, such as some feudal and slave-owning societies, these features are not central features of economic life in such societies. Instead, most production is organized and controlled in other ways, for example, where means of production are communally owned, where individuals are not owners of their labor power and are not free to sell it on a labor market, and where what is produced is for direct use or consumption rather than for exchange in the market.

What does Marx think is wrong with capitalism? Central to Marx's criticism of capitalism is an account of the worker within the labor process under capitalism. In early writings unpublished in Marx's lifetime, the *Economic and Philosophical Manuscripts of 1844*, Marx gives an account of alienated or estranged labor involving several interrelated features: the worker's alienation from the product of labor, from the activity of labor, from the worker's "species being," and from other human beings.

The Worker's Alienation from the Product of Labor

In the labor process the product of labor, what the worker produces, is an external realization or "objectification" of the worker's activity; labor is congealed in external objects as the worker transforms and appropriates the material world according to the worker's purposes and plans. Under certain conditions, this can involve satisfying self-expression and self-fulfillment for the worker: the worker identifies with the product; it is seen and valued as an expression of the worker and is a source of self-worth and dignity for the worker. But Marx argues that under capitalist conditions of production this objectification of labor in the product of labor involves a separation between worker and product, a "loss of reality" for the worker, where the product is not under the control of the worker. Rather than belonging to or being an expression of the worker, it confronts the worker as something independent and hostile, at odds with the worker's freedom and well-being.

> The worker puts his life into the object; but now his life no longer belongs to him but to the object . . . the worker becomes a slave of his object . . . the more the worker produces, the less he has to consume; the more value he creates, the more valueless, the more unworthy he becomes; the better formed his product, the more deformed becomes the worker; the more civilized his object, the more barbarous becomes the worker. . . .[10]

The Worker's Alienation from the Activity of Labor

Not only is the worker alienated from the product of labor, the worker is also alienated from the labor process, the activity of laboring itself. The worker's own activity is not under the control of the worker and is valued by the worker only instrumentally, that is, as a means of subsistence and not as something intrinsically meaningful or worthwhile; in itself, labor is unpleasant and unsatisfying, something to be avoided rather than valued.

> . . . labour is external to the worker . . . he does not affirm himself but denies himself, does not feel content but unhappy, does not develop freely his physical and mental energy but mortifies his body and ruins his mind. The worker therefore only feels himself outside his work, and in his work feels outside himself. He is at home when he is not working, and when he is working he is not at home. His labour is therefore not voluntary, but coerced; it is *forced labour*. It is therefore not the satisfaction of a need; it is merely a *means* to satisfy needs external to it. Its alien character emerges clearly in the fact that as soon as no physical compulsion exists, labour is shunned like the plague. External labour . . . is labour of self-sacrifice, of mortification . . . the external character of labour for the worker appears in the fact that it is not his own, but someone else's, that it does not belong to him, that in it he belongs, not to himself, but to another. . . .[11]

The Alienation of the Worker from the Worker's Species Being

"Species being," perhaps the most difficult aspect of Marx's account of alienation to understand, is also a key to understanding the other features of alienation he describes. It is because the worker has a particular nature or "species character" as a human being that work under the conditions Marx describes is alienating.[12] Being a species being involves the capacity to produce in a way in which one is conscious of oneself, of one's activity, of the product of one's labor as one's product, and of oneself and other humans as beings having this nature. In essence, it is a capacity for a kind of self-awareness or self-consciousness, and because of this capacity, humans are able to reflect on and make choices regarding what and how they produce. And, thus, they are able to act freely. They are not limited to one kind of productive activity or purpose. Instead, they can produce "universally," in an indefinite number of ways and for purposes beyond satisfying basic biological needs.

> Man is a species being, not only because in practice and in theory he adopts the species as his object . . . but also because he treats himself as the actual, living species; because he treats himself as a *universal* and therefore free being. . . . The whole character of the species—its species character—is contained in the character of its life-activity; and free, conscious activity is man's species character.[13]

For Marx, humans realize and express their nature as species beings through their productive activity.

> It is just in the working-up of the objective world, therefore, that man first really proves himself to be a *species being*. This production is his active species life. Through and because of this production, nature appears as *his* work and his reality. The object of labour is, therefore, *the objectification of man's species life:* for he duplicates himself not only, as in consciousness, intellectually, but also actively, in reality, and therefore he contemplates himself in a world that he created.[14]

But under capitalism, work is not an adequate fulfillment or expression of the worker's nature as a species being. People work merely in order to survive, rather than because work is satisfying or worthwhile in itself.

> . . . labour, *life-activity, productive life* itself appears to man merely as a *means* of satisfying a need—the need to maintain the physical existence. . . . Life itself appears only as a *means* to life. . . . In tearing away from man the object of his production, therefore, estranged labour tears from him his *species life,* his real species objectivity . . . in degrading spontaneous activity, free activity, to a means, estranged labour makes man's species life a means to his physical existence.[15]

The Alienation of Humans from One Another

Finally, Marx claims that individuals are alienated from each other within working life.

> What applies to a man's relation to his work, to the product of his labour and to himself, also holds of a man's relation to the other man, and to the other man's labour and object of labour . . . one man is estranged from another, as each of

them is from man's essential nature . . . the estrangement of man, and in fact every relationship in which man stands to himself, is first realized and expressed in the relationship in which man stands to other men. . . .[16]

Marx's analysis and criticism of alienation is not limited to the domain of work. In various places he discusses alienation in relation to other aspects of social life, such as religion, the family, and the state. But given Marx's materialist account of social life, the forms of alienation that exist within these other spheres are not viewed as being autonomous or independent of the alienation within working life. Instead, they are ultimately rooted in the economic organization of capitalist society.

Marx's account of alienation includes both what might be characterized as "subjective" and "objective" features. Alienation involves certain kinds of subjective or psychological states: particular beliefs and attitudes, certain feelings of unhappiness or suffering, or negative attitudes toward work. It also involves certain objective conditions and relationships concerning what a worker is able or unable to do, whether the worker is free or coerced in relation to work, and what the worker does or doesn't do in the context of work. It's not always clear from Marx's discussion precisely how he views the role of each of these in characterizing alienation and which, if either, is more important in understanding alienation. Are both defining or central features of alienation? Can one be an alienated worker but not feel unhappy or dissatisfied in relation to work? And can one be a nonalienated worker but be unhappy or dissatisfied at work nonetheless? Ultimately, I think that for Marx the core of alienation is an objective condition: a kind of unfreedom, an inability to control one's activity. By their nature, humans have certain capacities that enable them to be free, to be self-determining, to control and direct their own activity. But under certain conditions they cannot develop and effectively exercise these capacities. Instead, they are subject to economic forces that are products of their own activity, but that they are unable to control and direct. Thus, alienation consists in a condition where something that is an essential aspect of oneself, one's own productive capacity, is a hostile and alien force that one is unable to control.

I have focused on Marx's discussion of alienation here. This is not the whole of what he has to say about capitalism, and some of the issues he explores in these early writings are not adequately explained or developed. Much of his later work is an attempt to develop his ideas more fully and to address in greater detail a range of basic questions regarding capitalism: What is it? How does it work? How is it different from other ways of organizing social and economic life? How has it developed? What are its long-term tendencies? He explores these and related questions, often in connection with technical issues in economic theory and methodology and extended historical analysis, in *Grundrisse, A Contribution to the Critique of Political Economy, Capital,* and other later writings.

Despite Marx's criticisms of the conditions of the worker under capitalism, it is important to note that he also thinks that capitalism, unlike previous forms of society, creates material conditions needed for overcoming alienation. Capitalism creates an unprecedented level of productive capacity that makes material abundance possible for the first time in human history, and he thought that without such abundance alienation could not be eliminated. Humans cannot adequately develop and exercise their capacity for freedom at a subsistence level of existence. Thus, capitalism is an essential step in the achievement of human freedom. However, despite capitalism's impressive historical achievements in developing human productive capacity, Marx thought that there were limits to such development under capitalist relations of production and that in the long run capitalism would not endure. He argued that there were long-term economic tendencies under capitalism that would eventually hinder rather than promote the growth of productive capacity and, thus, would make it increasingly unattractive as a way of organizing economic life. He thought that the result would be a revolutionary transformation in which capitalism would be overthrown by workers who "have nothing to lose but their chains" and who "have a world to win."[17] In Volume I of *Capital* Marx provides a dramatic description of what he thought would be the eventual outcome of the long process of capitalist development.

> Along with the constantly diminishing number of magnates of capital, who usurp and monopolize all advantages of this process of transformation, grows the mass of misery, oppression, slavery, degradation, exploitation; but with this too grows the revolt of the working-class, a class always increasing in numbers, and disciplined, united, organized by the very mechanism of the process of capitalist production itself. The monopoly of capital becomes a fetter upon the mode of production, which has sprung up and flourished along with, and under it. Centralisation of the means of production and socialization of labor at last reach a point where they become incompatible with their capitalist integument. This integument is burst asunder. The knell of capitalist private property sounds. The expropriators are expropriated.[18]

∼ Communism

Given his diagnosis of alienation under capitalism, what is Marx's vision of a society without alienation? What would a future organization of society that overcomes alienation involve?

One might think that alienation could be overcome by certain kinds of economic reforms under capitalism. If a core component of alienation concerns the impoverishment of the worker, perhaps better wages for workers will solve the problem. However, Marx is clear that he thinks that such reforms won't work.

> A *forcing-up of wages* . . . would therefore be nothing but *better payment for the slave* and would not conquer either for the worker or for labour their human status and dignity. . . .[19]

On Marx's view, alienated labor is inseparable from the wage system and private property that characterize capitalism. So, even if improved wages were a real possibility under capitalism, which Marx doubts, and even if wages were equalized for all,[20] workers would only be better-paid "slaves," that is, they would still be alienated. What would be required to eliminate alienated labor and to achieve for workers "their human status and dignity"? Marx thought that something radically different was needed, a setup without the wage system and private property, where the workers themselves controlled their productive activity. This radical alternative was communism.

What exactly is communism for Marx? What would a communist society be like? How would economic and social life be organized? Although his life was dedicated to bringing about communism, Marx never provided a detailed account of communist society. His comments on the topic are relatively brief and not fully worked out, and certain important issues are not addressed. Despite these difficulties, what positive account of communist society does Marx provide?

In Volume I of *Capital*, Marx provides one description:

> . . . a community of free individuals, carrying on their work with the means of production in common, in which the labour-power of all the different individuals is consciously applied as the combined labour-power of the community.[21]

Under communism there will be no class divisions and no exploitation of workers by the owners of capital. Private property in the means of production is replaced by common ownership, and the market exchange of labor and the products of labor is replaced by the collective control of labor and the products of labor by the community of producers in accord with a consciously adopted plan for production and distribution. The alienation of the workers under capitalism, their lack of control over their own labor and the products of their labor, is eliminated and replaced by activity that exercises and expresses their essential human capacities for self-directed production.

In the *Critique of the Gotha Program*, Marx describes a two-stage development of communist society involving an initial transitional stage and a later "higher" stage, where the principles governing the distribution of the means of consumption are different in each. In the first stage, after deductions for certain common funds,[22] individual producers receive back from society means of consumption proportional to the labor each supplies, and thus there will be inequalities in consumption based on differences in the labor supplied: ". . . one man is superior to another physically and mentally and so supplies more labour in the same time, or can labour for a longer time."[23] The reason for these inequalities is that during this transitional stage

> [w]hat we have to deal with here is communist society, not as it has *developed* on its own foundation, but, on the contrary, just as it *emerges* from capitalist society; which is thus in every respect, economically, morally, and intellectually, still stamped with the birth marks of the old society from whose womb it emerges . . . these defects are inevitable in the first phase of communist society as it has just emerged after prolonged pangs from capitalist society. Right can never be higher than the economic structure of society and its cultural development conditioned thereby.[24]

People don't change overnight. Thus, in the early stage of communism, the distribution of consumption goods among workers will follow the same principle that prevails under capitalism, where labor is paid in proportion to the labor supplied. However, as communist society develops "on its own foundation," as humans develop under communism, labor and human motivation regarding labor will be gradually transformed, and means of consumption will come to be distributed according to a different principle.

> In a higher phase of communist society, after the enslaving subordination of the individual to the division of labour, and therewith also the antithesis between mental and physical labour, has vanished; after labour has become not only a means of life but life's prime want; after the productive forces have also increased with the all-round development of the individual, and all the springs of cooperative wealth flow abundantly—only then can the narrow horizon of bourgeois right be crossed in its entirety and society inscribe on its banner: From each according to his ability, to each according to his needs![25]

In the above quote and in the *German Ideology,* another aspect of communism that Marx highlights and contrasts with previous forms of society concerns the division of labor.

> . . . the division of labour offers us the first example of how . . . man's own deed becomes an alien power opposed to him, which enslaves him instead of being controlled by him. For as soon as the distribution of labour comes into being, each man has a particular, exclusive sphere of activity, which is forced upon him and from which he cannot escape. He is a hunter, a fisherman, a shepherd, or a critical critic, and must remain so if he does not want to lose his means of livelihood; while in communist society where nobody has one exclusive sphere of activity but each can become accomplished in any branch he wishes, society reg-

ulates the general production and thus makes it possible for me to do one thing today and another tomorrow, to hunt in the morning, fish in the afternoon, rear cattle in the evening, criticise after dinner, just as I have a mind, without ever becoming hunter, fisherman, shepherd or critic.[26]

In addition to transforming the control and organization of production and distribution, Marx portrays communist society as eventually eliminating institutions of law, the state, the family, and religion, all of which involve forms of human alienation and oppression for Marx. Given Marx's materialist understanding of society, once the various material factors that give rise to and sustain these institutions are transformed under communism, there will be no need for the persistence of these institutions, which are based on and facilitate the capitalist organization of society. Instead, forms of nonalienating and non-exploitative human association will be created, and certain needs and wants generated by previous forms of social life will be replaced by new needs and wants that develop under communism.

Aside from these relatively broad strokes, we are not given much more detail by Marx regarding how all of this will come about, or about precisely what new forms of social life will develop under communism. Probably one reason for this lack of attention to the details of communist society is that Marx thought that such things can't be figured out in advance by someone living under capitalism. Instead, these are things to be worked out by people living under significantly different conditions and facing very different problems and alternatives. He was highly critical of what he viewed as "utopian" attempts to articulate an ideal state to which reality was supposed to adjust, and he often criticized fellow communist and socialist thinkers for being utopian in this regard. He thought their views involved assumptions about individuals and institutions that were unrealistic and far removed from anything that exists or is likely to exist. In contrast, he thought communist society would have to be based on and develop from existing individuals and institutions rather than idealized or imagined ones. Precisely how all of this would work out in practice could not be anticipated by someone in Marx's position, thus his self-described "confining myself merely to the critical analysis of the actual facts, instead of writing recipes . . . for the cook-shops of the future."[27]

Understandably, some critics of Marx take this lack of detail regarding communist society as a serious shortcoming in his work. If people are to aspire to and work for a communist future, it is not unreasonable to ask about how things are likely to work or indeed whether they will work at all. A related criticism is that, despite his aim of being realistic or "scientific" in his assumptions, Marx too falls into utopian speculation about the organization of society under communism. The empirically viable or nonutopian alternatives to the capitalism that Marx criticizes, whether versions of capitalism, socialism, mixed economies, or something else, may be quite different from the communist future that Marx sketches. There may be significant conflicts or trade-offs that cannot be avoided in any workable economic setup, for example, between high levels of economic output and satisfying work or a clean environment.

～ Morality and Ideology

What role does morality or moral philosophy play in Marx's thought? It is difficult not to read Marx as a moral critic of capitalism. Whatever else Marx is doing by way of philosophical or empirical (historical, sociological, and economic) analysis, criticism, and explanation, his account of alienation and exploitation under capitalism surely seems to include a moral condemnation of capitalism. Throughout his writings Marx discusses capitalism in morally charged language, in terms ordinarily used to express moral outrage and harsh moral judgment. Working conditions under capitalism involve "torture," "degradation," and "brutality" for the worker,[28] and exploitation of the worker by the capitalist is characterized as "theft."[29] Thus, the language and tone of much of what Marx says concerning capitalism seem to presuppose or involve various moral commitments and judgments on his part. And if communism isn't morally preferable to capitalism, in what sense is communism supposed to be desirable? And why should Marx or anyone else work to bring it about? However, once one considers certain other things Marx says (and doesn't say) about morality, his stance may not be so clear.

Marx produced no explicit or systematic moral philosophy addressing normative issues of moral right and wrong, virtue and vice, duty, justice, rights, the human good, and so on, analogous to, say, Aristotle's *Nicomachean Ethics,* Kant's *Grounding for the Metaphysics of Morals,* Hegel's *Philosophy of Right,* or Mill's *Utilitarianism.* His comments on morality and moral concerns are scattered throughout various writings, and much of what he has to say consists of critical evaluation of the views of others rather than an explication or defense of his own views. Marx's views regarding morality are a topic of much interpretive controversy. And some interpreters claim that what Marx says regarding moral concerns is paradoxical, inconsistent, or inadequate.

Much of what Marx says about morality, moral philosophy, and related issues of rights and justice is harshly critical with respect to both particular moral outlooks and morality in general. Within his materialist understanding of society, Marx often characterizes morality, along with law and religion, as ideology. Like the rest of ideology, morality is neither autonomous nor fixed but arises from and changes in relation to the material conditions of society. It involves mistaken or illusory views regarding human beings and society and has no claim to truth, objectivity, or universality. It serves class interests, masking alienation and exploitation and legitimating oppressive institutions and social relationships. Given this view of morality, how, if at all, can Marx engage in moral criticism and evaluation? Can he appeal to a moral outlook that is nonideological, that doesn't rest on illusion or deception, and that doesn't serve sectarian interests? Do his views leave room for a positive conception of morality that avoids the shortcomings of other forms of morality? And if there is such a conception, what precisely is it?

Some of Marx's comments seem to reject all appeals to morality, to moral values and ideals, and to considerations of justice, rights, or fairness.

> The communists do not preach morality at all. . . . They do not put to people the moral demand: love one another, do not be egoists, etc.[30]

> Communism is for us not a *state of affairs* which is to be established, an *ideal* to which reality [will] have to adjust itself. We call communism the real movement which abolishes the present state of things.[31]

> I have dealt more at length with . . . "equal right" and "fair distribution" . . . in order to show what a crime it is to attempt, on the one hand, to force on our Party again, as dogmas, ideas which in a certain period had some meaning but have now become obsolete verbal rubbish, while again perverting, on the other, the realistic outlook, which it cost so much effort to instill into the Party but which has now taken root in it, by means of ideological nonsense about right and other trash so common among the democrats and French Socialists.[32]

Given all of this, where does Marx stand regarding morality? There are a variety of alternative interpretations.

Probably the most common interpretation holds that what Marx says about morality doesn't preclude his appealing to a nonideological morality as a basis for criticizing capitalism and endorsing communism. Just as Marx thinks there can be correct scientific understandings of history and society that are not ideologically distorted, there can also be moral views like this that can serve as a legitimate basis for moral evaluation and criticism of social arrangements. On this view, his negative views on morality concern morality as it has usually been understood and practiced rather than morality per se. Marx's main concerns are to criticize and avoid both conservative moral outlooks that endorse the oppressive status quo and utopian outlooks that have no chance of being realized in practice. However, even among interpreters of Marx who agree about this much, there is still considerable disagreement about how to work out the details of a plausible positive moral outlook consistent with the bulk of Marx's thought. Thus, there are numerous proposals for reconstructing Marx's moral views, including, but not limited to, ones that interpret his views as variations on one or another traditional approach to moral philosophy, including versions of Aristotelianism, Kantianism, and utilitarianism, among others.

Yet other interpretations attribute different kinds of "antimorality" or "beyond morality" views to Marx. One version, perhaps the least plausible, takes Marx's thought to be wholly descriptive or scientific, with no moral or nonmoral normative component. On this view, Marx is only engaged in descriptive or positive social science, providing descriptions, analyses, and explanations regarding capitalist and other societies, that tell us about how they develop; how they are organized and operate; how they depend on and generate particular beliefs, attitudes, and behavior, what tendencies they have regarding future change and development; and so on. But if this view is correct, one needs to explain how Marx's many seemingly normative comments are to be understood.

A perhaps more plausible antimorality interpretation holds that while Marx eschews appeals to morality, he is nonetheless committed to certain *nonmoral* normative values or ideals, such as human freedom, self-realization, or community, and these can be employed in criticizing capitalism and supporting communism. At least one difficulty with this view is distinguishing moral from nonmoral values or ideals in a satisfactory way. Given that various moral outlooks take freedom, self-realization, and community to be core moral values or ideals, what does the proposed distinction between moral and nonmoral values or ideals amount to?

However one proposes to resolve these tensions in Marx's thought, what Marx takes to be the shortcomings of capitalism and the advantages of communism are reasonably clear and uncontroversial among Marx scholars. But exactly how, if at all, to understand all of this within a coherent moral framework that Marx might accept remains unclear.

∿ Concluding Remarks

> *For them that must obey authority*
> *That they do not respect in any degree*
> *Who despise their jobs, their destinies*
> *Speak jealously of them that are free*
> *Cultivate their flowers to be*
> *Nothing more than something*
> *They invest in*
> > Bob Dylan, *It's All Right Ma*
> > *(I'm Only Bleeding)*[33]

Marx's thought presents many challenges for the introductory as well as the advanced student. Interpreting and assessing his work can be difficult and frustrating. He wrote an enormous amount, and many of his ideas underwent change and revision over time. Some of his works were left unfinished, and some of his ideas are obscure, insufficiently developed, or in tension with one another. He provided no overview or summary statement of what he took to be his core ideas or contributions (and certainly nothing analogous to *Marx for Beginners* or *Marx in 90 Minutes*), and on many issues the background knowledge needed to engage Marx on his own ground is overwhelming. His writing can be long-winded, repetitive, and polemical (being generous to his opponents is not one of Marx's virtues). And, if all of this were not enough, one might well wonder about the contemporary significance or relevance of his work, given the persistence of capitalism since Marx's day and the recent collapse of Marx-inspired communist regimes in the Soviet Union and Eastern Europe. Hasn't he been shown to be mistaken or obsolete? Why bother with Marx? I shall close with a few thoughts that might help motivate grappling with Marx and that might help explain some of the enduring interest and appeal regarding his work, whatever its difficulties and shortcomings.

Despite the many changes in the world since Marx's time, the capitalist framework that Marx analyzed and criticized is, in broad outline, still very much with us. (In fact, in many parts of the world, it is really just taking hold.) Many of the problems that Marx addressed regarding alienating work, social and economic inequality, and economic instability are live concerns for many living under capitalism today. Although working conditions and the standard of living for the vast majority of people in capitalist societies are much better today than in Marx's day, many people in those societies confront jobs they dislike, have little control over their lives at work, and view the economic future with ongoing uncertainty and anxiety.

More than any other philosopher in the modern Western tradition, Marx speaks to these concerns. He forces us to take a hard and critical look at life under capitalism and to take alternative possibilities seriously. For those who think that a substantially different and better way of life can be achieved in practice, coming to grips with the inadequacies of Marx's thought about these matters should be an essential, and perhaps sobering, step in examining and evaluating alternatives to capitalism. For those who think that, all things considered, capitalism is about the best humans can do, engaging Marx's criticism and commentary should be no less valuable in clarifying and honestly weighing the burdens and benefits of capitalism. And for everyone who thinks about these matters, Marx's reminders about how, despite their best efforts, humans repeatedly embrace ideas and outlooks that provide mystified and distorted understandings of their social world should provide grounds for pause when it comes to thinking that we have all of this figured out.[34]

∾ NOTES

1. K. Marx, *Theses on Feuerbach,* in R. Tucker, ed., *The Marx-Engels Reader,* Second Edition (New York: W.W. Norton, 1978), 145.

2.   F. Engels in a letter to E. Bernstein, quoted in G. Haupt, "Marx and Marxism," in E. Hobsbawm, ed., *The History of Marxism, Vol. I: Marxism in Marx's Day* (Bloomington: Indiana University Press, 1982), 276.

3.   My colleague, Murray Kiteley, has proposed that the term "quarrel" be used to refer to a collection of philosophers (analogous, say, to a gaggle of geese or a flock of sheep).

4.   Marx co-authored several works with Engels, and after Marx's death Engels edited and published many of Marx's writings and wrote a number of works developing what he took to be their shared views. But there is scholarly controversy about the relation between Engels' work and the ideas of Marx. I shall sidestep such controversy here and only discuss works written by Marx or by Marx and Engels jointly.

5.   K. Marx, *Theses on Feuerbach,* 145.

6.   K. Marx and F. Engels, *The German Ideology,* in Tucker, ed., *The Marx-Engels Reader,* 149–150, 154–155.

7.   K. Marx, *A Contribution to the Critique of Political Economy,* in Tucker, ed., *The Marx-Engels Reader,* 4–5.

8.   K. Marx, *The Poverty of Philosophy* (New York: International Pubs., 1963), 109.

9.   In Marx's account of the employment relationship under capitalism, strictly speaking the worker sells labor power, the capacity to labor, to an employer for a given period of time in exchange for a wage, rather than labor, that is, the activity of producing.

10.   K. Marx, *Economic and Philosophical Manuscripts of 1844,* in Tucker, ed., *The Marx-Engels Reader,* 72–73.

11.   Ibid., 74.

12.   For Marx, "species character" refers to the essential character or nature of a species, that is, what makes it the species that it is, whatever the species. Thus, each species has its own distinct species character. Species being is the species character of humans.

13.   K. Marx, *Economic and Philosophical Manuscripts of 1844,* in Tucker, ed., *The Marx-Engels Reader,* 75–76.

14.   Ibid., 76.

15.   Ibid., 75–77.

16.   Ibid., 77.

17.   K. Marx and F. Engels, *Manifesto of the Communist Party,* in Tucker, ed., *The Marx-Engels Reader,* 500.

18.   K. Marx, *Capital,* Volume I, in Tucker, ed., *The Marx-Engels Reader,* 438.

19.   K. Marx, *Economic and Philosophic Manuscripts of 1844,* 80.

20.   "Indeed, even the *equality of wages* demanded by Proudhon only transforms the relationship of the present-day worker to his labour into the

relationship of all men to labour. Society is then conceived as an abstract capitalist." K. Marx, *Economic and Philosophic Manuscripts of 1844*, 80.

21. K. Marx, *Capital*, Volume I, 326.
22. To cover costs for depreciation, investment, insurance, and administration, for the common satisfaction of certain needs, such as education and health services, and for the support of those unable to work.
23. K. Marx, *Critique of the Gotha Program*, in Tucker, ed., *The Marx-Engels Reader*, 530.
24. Ibid., 529, 531.
25. Ibid., 531.
26. K. Marx and F. Engels, *The German Ideology*, 160.
27. K. Marx, *Capital*, Volume I (Harmondsworth: Penguin Books, 1976), 99.
28. Ibid., 381.
29. K. Marx, *Grundrisse* (New York: Random House, 1973), 705.
30. K. Marx and F. Engels, *The German Ideology* (Moscow: Progress Pubs., 1964), 267.
31. Ibid., 47.
32. K. Marx, *Critique of the Gotha Program*, 531.
33. *Bob Dylan Song Book* (New York: M. Witmark & Sons, 1965).
34. I thank Lisa Leizman and Phil Washburn for helpful comments and suggestions on drafts of this essay.

∾ CHRONOLOGY

1815   Congress of Vienna creates a balance of power in Europe, restores monarchs overthrown in the aftermath of the French Revolution and during the Napoleonic wars

1818   birth of Karl Marx in Trier, Northern Germany

1830   Manchester in England has one hundred thirty cotton mills, up from fifty in 1800

1832   G.W.F. Hegel publishes *The Philosophy of History*

1841   receives Ph.D. from University of Berlin

1842   becomes editor of liberal newspaper, *Rheinische Zeitung*, after being denied university appointments by the Prussian government for his political views; British government finds that the average life span for the urban working class is seventeen, compared with thirty-eight for people in rural areas

1843   newspaper closed by the government, Marx emigrates to Paris, meets Friedrich Engels

1844   writes on economics and political philosophy, later published as *Economic and Philosophic Manuscripts*

1845   after being expelled from France, Marx and Engels move to Brussels, where Marx writes *The German Ideology*

1846   works with The Communist League, an association of emigré German workers

1848   publishes *The Communist Manifesto;* revolutions break out in several European countries, Marx returns to Paris

1849   after the failure of the revolutions, Marx moves to London; lives in poverty, begins his "long, sleepless night of exile"

1850   forty-seven cities in Europe surpass one hundred thousand inhabitants, up from twenty-two in 1800

1859   publishes *The Critique of Political Economy*

1864   helps organize the International Workingman's Association

1867   publishes Volume 1 of *Capital*

1871   defeat of France in Franco-Prussian War, Paris Commune established; Marx defends radicals in *The Civil War in France*

1883   dies in London

1884   Engels publishes *Origin of the Family, Private Property, and the State*

⌣ SUGGESTED READINGS

One-Volume Selections of Works by Marx

Elster, J., ed. *Karl Marx: A Reader*. New York: Cambridge University Press, 1986.

McLellan, D., ed. *Karl Marx: Selected Writings*. Second Edition. New York: Oxford University Press, 2000.

Tucker, R., ed. *The Marx-Engels Reader*. Second Edition. New York: W.W. Norton, 1978.

Wood, A., ed. *Marx: Selections*. New York: Macmillan, 1988.

Biographical Works

Berlin, I. *Karl Marx*. Fourth Edition. New York: Oxford University Press, 1978.

McLellan, D. *Karl Marx: His Life and Thought*. New York: Harper & Row, 1973.

Introductory Works

Elster, J. *An Introduction to Karl Marx*. New York: Cambridge University Press, 1986.

Schmitt, R. *Introduction to Marx and Engels*. Second Edition. Bolder, CO: Westview Press, 1997.

Singer, P. *Marx*. New York: Oxford University Press, 1980.

Suchting, W.A. *Marx: An Introduction*. New York: New York University Press, 1983.

More Advanced Works

Arnold, N.S. *Marx's Radical Critique of Capitalist Society*. New York: Oxford University Press, 1990.

Brudney, D. *Marx's Attempt to Leave Philosophy*. Cambridge, MA: Harvard University Press, 1998.

Buchanan, A. *Marx and Justice*. Totowa, NJ: Rowman and Littlefield, 1982.

Carver, T. ed. *The Cambridge Companion to Marx*. New York: Cambridge University Press, 1991.

Cohen, G.A. *History, Labour, and Freedom: Themes from Marx*. New York: Oxford University Press, 1988.

Cohen, G.A. *Karl Marx's Theory of History*. Expanded Edition. Princeton, NJ: Princeton University Press, 2000.

Cohen, M., T. Nagel, and T. Scanlon. *Marx, Justice, and History*. Princeton, NJ: Princeton University Press, 1980.

Elster, J. *Making Sense of Marx*. New York: Cambridge University Press, 1985.

Little, D. *The Scientific Marx*. Minneapolis: University of Minnesota Press, 1986.

Lukes, S. *Marxism and Morality*. New York: Oxford University Press, 1987.

Miller, R. *Analyzing Marx*. Princeton, NJ: Princeton University Press, 1984.

Peffer, R.G. *Marxism, Morality, and Social Justice*. Princeton, NJ: Princeton University Press, 1990.

Plamenatz, J. *Karl Marx's Philosophy of Man*. New York: Oxford University Press, 1975.

Torrance, J. *Karl Marx's Theory of Ideas*. New York: Cambridge University Press, 1995.

Wood, A. *Karl Marx*. London: Routledge & Kegan Paul, 1981.

CHAPTER 12

Mill
Philosophy as Experiment

Maria Antonini

~ Preview

For Mill, philosophy is an adventure. To be a philosopher is to keep an open mind about any ideas or actions and to evaluate them by their consequences, not by preconceived notions. It is to ask "What if . . . ?" Mill conceives of philosophy as an attempt to apply the experimental attitude of the natural sciences to other areas, particularly social and moral questions. For example, in judging an action as right or wrong, we should consider the outcome of the action. If it makes more people happy than alternative actions, then it is morally right. In social policy, Mill says that societies should give individuals complete freedom to do or say whatever they want, so long as they do not harm others. Encouraging diversity and experimentation will produce the best society for all. Should men and women be equal? The only way to answer the question is to ask what would happen if we tried it. Philosophy is the continual struggle to clear away prejudice, rigidity, fear, arrogance, and other limiting attitudes so that we can try new things and learn from experience. (The Editor)

∿ Introduction

In 1831 the twenty-two-year-old Charles Darwin left England to begin a five-year voyage around the world. He encountered virtually every kind of organism, most habitats, and many types of human society. It was a remarkable postgraduate education. His experiences later culminated in *The Origin of Species* (1859), which changed the way people think about the living world and our place in it.

After his momentous voyage of discovery, Darwin settled down into the life of a country gentleman. Perhaps he is typical of the "eminent Victorians" about whom so much has been written. (Queen Victoria ruled England from 1837 to 1901.) In some ways he seemed rather conventional, proper, even timid; but in other ways, he was the most intrepid adventurer and radical revolutionary. In the world of ideas, he not only challenged accepted religious views, he upset many of the comfortable assumptions that had guided Western civilization for centuries. And not only in ideas. He was willing to go to the Pacific Islands, South America, Tierra del Fuego, and other places to see for himself. His personal manner and his careful scientific method may make some people forget how daring and courageous he was.

John Stuart Mill was another eminent Victorian who was similar to Darwin in some ways. In most externals, his life conformed to the expectations of the English middle class. He worked as a bureaucrat in a large corporation for most of his life. But in his writings and his philosophy, he sailed out into uncharted waters, and he encouraged others to make their own voyages. He fearlessly attacked the establishment, although he used facts, evidence, and reason as his weapons. The guiding thread in Mill's thought was the experimental attitude. He believed that the only way to discover the truth—and indeed, the only way to live one's life—was to make an attempt. Whatever one thinks, one should have the courage to try it and then see what the consequences are.

The experimental attitude means several things. He shared with the sixteenth-century French essayist Michel de Montaigne a contempt for "arguments by authority," in other words, the belief that such and such is true because a renowned thinker has said it is. Mill, like Montaigne, stressed learning from observation and experience as the truest route to knowledge. If a label is needed, Mill's particular vision of philosophy combined aspects of philosophical materialism, empiricism, and naturalism. As a philosophical materialist and empiricist, he rejected the idea that the world of consciousness and intuition, separated from knowledge that is accessible to the senses, is more real than the physical world. He was, therefore, charting a different path from the rationalism of Descartes and Kant, on the one hand, and from his more intuitionist and nature mystical contemporaries, the New England Transcendentalists Emerson and Thoreau, on the other. He said:

> The notion that truths external to the mind may be known by intuition or consciousness, independently of observation and experience is, I am persuaded, in these times, the great intellectual support of false doctrines and bad institutions. . . . There never was such an instrument [intuitionism] devised for consecrating all deep-seated prejudices.[1]

Mill continued the tradition of British empiricism by rejecting all claims to kinds of knowledge that cannot be tested by experience or experiment.

Rationalists wanted to find the truth once and for all, but Mill (like Darwin) recognized that people and societies change. He made no secret of his distrust of intellectual elites at Cambridge and Oxford, whom he viewed as thinking they had a monopoly on philosophical truths. He preferred to blend the principles of natural science and the social sciences to devise what he saw as a more reasonable and measurable ethical system, more subject to discussion, analysis, and fine-tuning as circumstances shifted. Right and wrong do not depend on eternal truths, but on the actual consequences of our actions for human happiness. For him, societies will change as they make sense of sociological and psychological knowledge, branches of knowledge that were only then beginning to take shape as recognizable fields of study in a modern sense. Mill saw persons as rational beings who were engaged in inferring or "figuring out" the general laws of moral behavior as they went through the experiences of their lives.

The experimental attitude applies to personal and social development as well as the search for the truth and moral goodness. Mill (like Socrates before him) believed it was crucial for each individual to take a self-propelled journey, similar to a Native American vision quest, to discover what he or she believes. Without this, there is always the danger that people will act more as sponges absorbing cultural influences around them than as dynamic, free, and autonomous beings. The spirit of his age, as he perceived it, was one of rapid, creative progress—in industrial growth and in social organization—and he exuberantly wished to facilitate his country's move in this direction. Accordingly, Mill is recognized as a leading founder (along with his English predecessors John Milton and John Locke) of the political theory of liberalism. To the extent that he would afford almost total protection of free speech and press (unless the expression caused actual harm to others), he is also associated with the libertarian tradition. His ideas had a great impact on the emerging body of First Amendment constitutional law in the United States.

In promoting the experimental attitude, Mill argued that all people's experiences are equally important. He distinguished himself as, arguably, the first male philosopher in the Western tradition to consistently stress the importance to the whole human enterprise of not denying the same rights of liberty to women that had traditionally and culturally been reserved for men. We see Mill's particular approach to philosophy very clearly in his essay *On the Subjection of Women* (1869). Here he demonstrated that just because women were customarily regarded as subordinate in his culture did not mean that they were by nature subordinate or inferior. He pointed out the logical fallacy of arguing that what is merely a custom or a social arrangement is really natural or, to his more theistic readers, willed by God. Rather than accept tradition without question, it would be more reasonable to allow women to try the same things as men and see what they can do.

The philosophical school of naturalism influenced Mill to look to nature and other living beings as a guide to truth about humanity. He believed that we all try to seek pleasure and avoid pain, and this observation should be useful in planning our social lives and institutions. Naturalism also posits that there is no absolute standard of right and wrong that transcends the individuals who think up these standards; there is no purpose or telos or transcendent plan for the universe. Mill was a humanist in the sense that he believed members of societies can create good lives for themselves by being open-minded, recognizing what people actually want, and using trial and error to make progress.

∾ Mill's Life

No one had more influence on John Stuart Mill's early intellectual development than his father, James Mill, who was a close friend of the thoroughly materialist English thinker Jeremy Bentham. John Stuart Mill was born in 1806, and his educational background was anything but typical. The senior Mill, following the Lockean dictum that the young mind is a *tabula rasa* (blank slate) and, as part of an attempt to test the limits of how malleable the human mind can be when presented with a comprehensive education, taught the young John at home. At age three, John was learning ancient Greek and Latin and, by the age of seven, was well on the way to mastering a classical European education. His father's principle, in line with Bentham's, was that moral education was not dependent on religious instruction but was contingent on the development of reason.

At age eight, John began teaching the younger children geometry and algebra, as well as history, his favorite subject. At twelve he took up Aristotle's logic, in Greek, and made a thorough study of economics. (One of Mill's most important works was *A System of Logic* [1843], in which he tried to expand Aristotle's system and codify the logic of the social sciences.) He spent his fourteenth year in France, studying biology, chemistry, and math, as well as French society. While Mill mastered more subjects than most people, his father did not expect him simply to accumulate information. "One of the great objects of education," James Mill said, "should be to generate a constant and anxious concern about evidence." He taught John to think for himself, look for reasons, and question authorities.

When he was seventeen, John joined his father at India House, the headquarters of the East India Company, which administered British interests in India. He spent his entire career there. But three years later, he experienced what he later called an emotional crisis. On the outside, nothing changed, but on the inside, he says he felt that his life was empty and flat.

> I put the question distinctly to myself. 'Suppose that all your objects in life were realized, that all the changes in institutions and opinions which you are looking forward to, could be completely effected at this very instant; would this be a great joy and happiness to you?' and an irrepressible self-consciousness distinctly answered 'No'![2]

His intellectual development had been extraordinary, but his father had neglected his emotional development. In his early twenties Mill had to teach himself about beauty and squalor, joy and grief, spontaneity, empathy, and love. He learned to enjoy the romantic poets Wordsworth and Coleridge. And he met and fell in love with Harriet Taylor. Unfortunately, she was already married, although unhappily. She and Mill became companions and incurred the disapproval of London society as a result. After Mrs. Taylor's husband died in 1848, she and Mill were married three years later.

Mill formed his mature positions in part by reacting against some of the dominant traditions in European thought. In his rejection of intuition as a suitable basis for truth-gathering, Mill put distance between himself and the American Transcendentalists mentioned earlier. Led by the Bostonian Ralph Waldo Emerson, this school of thought suggested that Nature is synonymous with God and that the human task is to understand our nature, both individually and collectively. By so doing, we gain insight into the Divine. In an address made to the graduating class of Harvard Divinity School on July 15, 1838, Emerson said:

> The intuition of the moral sentiment is an insight of the perfection of the laws of the soul. These laws execute themselves. They are out of time, out of space, and not subject to circumstance.[3]

For Mill, this was the kind of statement that he found, along with other examples of pantheistic mysticism, to have a "ghostly grasp of reality"; in other words, they were vague and empirically untestable, in his view.

Mill followed Bentham in criticizing the Enlightenment tradition of natural rights, including Thomas Jefferson's postulation of "inalienable rights" to life, liberty, and the pursuit of happiness. According to Bentham, it is difficult to understand what people mean when they say that governments often suppress and deny rights and, at the same time, that rights are inalienable. If they are inalienable, how can governments take them away? Perhaps Jefferson meant that governments *ought* to respect rights and never violate them. But Bentham says that doesn't make sense either. Governments must take away some people's rights to liberty (they imprison criminals), property (they collect taxes), and even life (they kill some people to protect others). The whole idea of rights is simply a swamp of confusion. Bentham called it nonsense. And talk of "natural" rights is "nonsense on stilts."[4] Mill agreed, and offered an influential alternative theory of governments and individuals in his own works.

A third area where Mill criticized conventional thinking was views of human nature. The nineteenth century saw advances in zoological and anthropological studies, most significantly Darwin's *On the Origins of Species,* that cast doubt on earlier Aristotelian and Thomistic beliefs. Aristotle had argued for a sharp line of demarcation between humans and nonhumans based on radically different functions or abilities. Thomas Aquinas had defended Church dogma limiting the possession of souls to humans alone and not "lower" animals.[5] These ideas had come to seem like "phantoms" to modern observers of nature and animals, such as Darwin, Bentham, and Mill. Bentham wrote in his *Introduction to the Principles of Morals and Legislation:*

> The day may come when the rest of the animal creation may acquire those rights which never could have been withholden from them but by the hand of tyranny. The French have already discovered that blackness of the skin is no reason why a human being should be abandoned without redress to the caprice of a tormentor. It may one day come to be recognized that the number of the legs, the villosity of the skin, . . . are reasons equally insufficient for abandoning a sensitive being to the same fate. . . . The question is not, Can they reason? Nor Can they talk? But, Can they suffer?[6]

Mill followed his early mentor's line of reasoning against the self-serving use of other creatures when he wrote, "But was there ever any domination which did not appear natural to those who possessed it?"[7]

Mill was a radical philosopher in the sense that he always tried to uncover the roots of received opinions and beliefs. (The word "radical" is derived from the Latin word *radix,* which means root.) Bentham had been an intellectual force to reckon with in a Europe that was experiencing accelerating industrial change and a move away from traditional religious loyalties. Mill was not an atheist in the strict sense of the word. While doubting that a deity or an afterlife could ever be proven, along with the eighteenth-century Deists who had come before him, he appeared optimistically to believe that some intelligent Force or Power reigned in the universe, while stopping short of expressing belief in a Creator per se. He said that the appropriate attitude toward religious ideas was hope, not belief.

Mill did not try to disown the particular demons that possessed him. He was a man who saw far and dared to speak of the internal contradictions and hypocrisies of the British Empire, a regime that had amassed enough power by the end of the nineteenth century to subjugate three-quarters of the earth's peoples. The British took pride in their recognition of the importance of political liberty, since their own Glorious Revolution of 1688 had elevated Parliament over an absolute hereditary monarchy and its presumption of the "divine right of kings." Mill's vision of liberty would come to include wider political and social liberties and a fight against entrenched habit and tradition that dictated the "terms of order."

He spoke out against a university system aligned with the Church of England, which ostensibly espoused the tenets of Christian egalitarianism while practicing an elitism that favored the sons of the landed gentry in pursuing admission to Oxford and Cambridge. Sons of common laborers (and daughters of any parentage, for that matter) were rarely allowed to enter the bastions of privilege.

Over the course of a long public career, Mill demonstrated his interest in social questions of the day—writing for influential progressive journals like *The Westminster Review,* administering the offices of the East India Company, and lecturing at major universities. In 1865 he was elected to Parliament, representing Westminster. His positions were often controversial and came under frequent attack by conservatives. His commitment to women's liberty and equality, particularly the right to vote, most likely was responsible for the loss of his seat in Parliament after a single term.

In spite of his commitment to reason and experiment, Mill had his share of prejudices. It is true that he opposed English laws directed against Irish independence, yet it is also undeniable that his interest in promoting national self-determination did not extend to those subjected to British rule in India. His father's and his own administrative positions in the British East India Company made it difficult for him to see how he ignored his own principles in the case of India. His assessment of the "Indian question" was that Hinduism, or the little he knew of it, and which he blithely dismissed as not much more than a system of ancient superstitions, had rendered the Indian people "childlike," unable to rule themselves without the more "enlightened" Western (British) leaders.

∿ Utilitarianism

The main influence on Mill was his father, and the main influence on his father was Jeremy Bentham. To understand Mill's conception of philosophy, we need to take a step back and look at Bentham's ideas. Bentham was born in 1748, and Mill's father was one of his most active supporters in the early 1800s. Bentham was a strong proponent of a school of thought called "utilitarianism." (His influence as a utilitarian has been second only to Mill's own.) The label "utilitarian" comes from the word "utility," but Bentham gave the word "utility" a special meaning. In his *Introduction to the Principles of Morals and Legislation* he said:

> Nature has placed mankind under the governance of two sovereign masters, *pain* and *pleasure*. It is for them alone to point out what we ought to do, as well as to determine what we shall do. On the one hand, the standard of right and wrong, on the other the chain of causes and effects, are fastened to their throne.[8]

In this passage Bentham makes two claims. The first is a thesis about psychology. Everyone always tries to obtain some pleasure, such as eating, sleeping, flirting, being praised by others, or feeling good about giving money to a charity, or tries to avoid some pain, such as being hungry, being afraid, being embarrassed, or feeling guilty. Feeling pleasure and avoiding pain are the only things people value, according to Bentham, and are the basic motivations of all our actions. By "utility" Bentham meant the amount of pleasure an action brings (or the pain it avoids). If a person must choose between finishing an interesting book or making dinner, the person is weighing the utilities of the two actions. And he or she will choose the action that appears to have greater utility.

The second claim Bentham makes in the passage is that *right and wrong* depend on utility, too. Pleasure and pain alone tell us what we ought to do. In other words, the standard of morality is the amount of pleasure or pain (utility) an action produces. If making dinner leads to more pleasure than finishing the book, then making dinner is the morally right thing to do. Of course, Bentham meant "in the long run." Eating ice cream every night for dinner may be pleasurable in the short term, but in the long term it will produce more pain than pleasure (pain in the form of obesity, vitamin deficiency, bad teeth, and so on). We all want to maximize our pleasure and happiness, but sometimes we don't understand the best way to do that.

Bentham also meant "for all parties concerned." One person's happiness is no more and no less valuable, objectively, than another's. Every person's happiness is equally valuable, Bentham said. If I want to amuse myself by firing my gun in random directions, but the result is that another person is wounded or killed, then my action is wrong. Not because I violated a religious rule against killing, or my conscience tells me it is wrong, or anything mystical. My action is wrong because the other person's suffering outweighs my pleasure. Utilitarians summed up their theory by saying that the goal of morality is to produce "the greatest amount of happiness for the greatest number of people."

But a problem arises. If the laws of psychology tell us that people always pursue pleasure, and if the morally right thing to do is to pursue pleasure, then how can people ever do what is wrong, according to Bentham? Must Bentham conclude that everyone always does the right thing? One answer to this problem is that people do not take the time to think through the consequences of their actions. The psychological law is that people always do what they think will produce the most pleasure, but sometimes they are mistaken. Or sometimes people let a small, immediate pleasure outweigh a large, distant pleasure. They watch TV instead of beginning their research for a report that is due in a month. Sometimes we just aren't rational or intelligent, and that makes us behave in immoral ways.

But a second answer is that societies sometimes reward wrong actions. Social institutions are arranged in ways that sometimes make it more profitable to be dishonest than to be honest. Society sometimes promotes greed rather than compassion. Thus Bentham believed that the way to improve people's moral character was to give them a good education so that they could think rationally about the consequences of their actions. But it is also necessary to reform society, change the system of rewards and punishments, so that it pays to be morally good and does not pay to be evil. Bentham was particularly interested in crime, punishment, and prison reform.

Mill accepted most of Bentham's ideas about morality. In 1863 he wrote *Utilitarianism,* in which he modified and defended Bentham's theory. Many people had objected to Bentham's idea that everyone always pursues pleasure. Given a choice between listening to a lecture and eating a big meal, many people would attend the lecture. That shows that some people value knowledge more than pleasure, critics said. But Mill believed Bentham was right. We should simply recognize different types of pleasure: mental and physical. Mill said mental pleasures are actually more valuable than physical pleasures. "Better a Socrates dissatisfied than a pig satisfied," he said. The pleasures of thinking and knowledge are so great that it makes sense to give up a greater quantity of physical pleasures for the sake of a smaller quantity of mental pleasure.

Other critics said that the principle of utility would lead to injustice. Suppose a wild mob is convinced that a young immigrant has committed a terrible crime. They surround the police station where the immigrant has taken refuge. The police are greatly outnumbered, and the mob is about to explode. If the police captain is a utilitarian, he will ask himself, "how can I produce the greatest happiness for the greatest number of people or produce the least suffering for the fewest people?" If he tries to protect the immigrant, the mob will turn violent, many people will be hurt or killed, stores burned, and the suffering will be intense, widespread, and long-lasting. If he hands over the suspect to the mob, the young man will be killed. To a utilitarian, critics say, the choice is clear. The lives and fortunes of many outweigh the life of one. The police captain should hand over the immigrant. But obviously that would be unjust. The suspect deserves a trial. Our sense of justice and fairness will not allow us to sacrifice one person to increase the pleasure or reduce the anger of many. This shows that the utilitarian theory of morality is mistaken, according to critics.

Mill agreed that it would be wrong to sacrifice one for the pleasure of many, but he said that the principle of utility can explain why it would be wrong. Over the centuries, all societies have learned the value of justice and have seen the consequences of injustice. All societies have adopted laws and rules for administering justice, including rules for investigating crimes to determine guilt and innocence. Why are these rules valuable? Mill asked. Because in the long run they lead to greater happiness for more people than not having the rules or allowing kings to have arbitrary power. So in the case of the immigrant, while it may *seem* that ignoring the rule of law and satisfying the mob would reduce suffering, in reality it would not. In the long run, ignoring the rule of law and undermining people's faith in the system of justice would lead to more crime, rebellion, anarchy, and suffering for more people than respecting the rule of law. The hypothetical case is no objection to the principle of utility.

Mill's utilitarian theory of morality exemplifies his experimental attitude because it makes consequences the standard of right and wrong. Is turning over the immigrant right or wrong? Ask yourself what would happen if you did it. If it would lead to a greater amount of happiness than any alternative action, for all concerned, then it is right; but if not, then it is wrong. Utilitarianism is the experimental attitude applied to morality.

⌒ Mill and Liberty

Mill was a utilitarian, but after his crisis of 1826, he decided that he should combine the utilitarians' focus on the common good with an equally strong commitment to the individual's search for self-realization, autonomy, and beauty in his or her own life. In fact, many feel that these two aims are not reconcilable, but Mill himself did not see this as a paradox at all. Just as Plato had believed that there is a relationship between virtue and intelligence, Mill believed that the search for individuality does not preclude a strong sense of social duty, and that the more fulfilled our lives as individuals are, the more we will be inclined toward a concern for the welfare of others. This belief, with its critics today on both the Left and the Right, still defines liberal political theory.

The largest portion of Mill's philosophical legacy is contained in his brief classic *On Liberty* (1859). The critical idea he developed in this work was that the best society (the one that achieves the greatest happiness for the greatest number) can emerge only if individuals are free to express their opinions, particularly those ideas of a political or civic nature.[9] Ideas different from or even abhorrent to some people or even to the majority of people still deserve governmental protection.

This freedom is crucial to the development of autonomous individuals and to the progressive development of society at large. However, it must be pointed out that Mill recognized that in certain contexts expressing an opinion may have harmful effects on others. Unanimous consent is hardly ever achieved on how to apply this deceptively simple decision rule in actual dilemmas that arise. It is the consequences of speech, not the speech itself—for example, incitement of a riot—that prompted Mill to set limits on speech at all. But is speech ever evil in itself? Mill answered in the negative, even though the speaker may legitimately be held liable for and prosecuted for actions stemming from his or her speech on the part of others.[10] He stated:

> The object of this Essay is to assert one very simple principle as entitled to govern absolutely the dealings of society with the individual in the way of compulsion and control, whether the means used by physical force in the form of legal penalties, or the moral coercion of public opinion. That principle is, that the sole end for which mankind are warranted, individually or collectively, in interfering with the liberty of any of their number is self-protection. In the part which merely concerns himself, his independence is, of right, absolute. Over himself, over his own body and mind, the individual is sovereign.[11]

Mill is saying that people should be free to say or do anything they want, so long as they don't hurt others. In matters of belief, thought, opinion, and ideas, one's independence should be "absolute."

To us in the twenty-first century, Mill's book may seem unnecessary. Of course, people should be free, we might say, and people are free. The government does not censor the press any more, at least in developed countries. But Mill's point is that government is no longer the threat to liberty. Our neighbors are. In modern societies with rapid, easy communications and all-pervasive media, public opinion becomes an almost irresistible force. "Image is everything," people say. Society has acquired innumerable means of influencing people's perceptions, feelings, and desires. Being laughed at and ostracized is a much more effective way of making people conform than threatening to lock them in jail.

> When society is itself the tyrant—society collectively over the separate individuals who compose it—its means of tyranny are not restricted to the acts which it may do by the hands of its political functionaries . . . it practices a social tyranny more formidable than many kinds of political oppression. . . . Protection, therefore, against the tyranny of the magistrate is not enough, there needs protection also against the tyranny of the prevailing opinion and feeling; against the tendency of society to impose, by other means than civil penalties, its own ideas and practices as rules of conduct, on those who dissent from them; to fetter the development, and, if possible, prevent the formation, of any individuality not in harmony with its ways.[12]

Mill called this new threat to liberty "the tyranny of the majority," and his essay was an attempt to overthrow it.

Why this almost total grant of protected liberty for individuals? In the end, Mill believed that the closest approximation to truth is attained only when thoughts expressed in this "marketplace of ideas" are free to flourish. He supported his belief with three main reasons. First, we can never be absolutely sure that we are right about anything. It is always possible that we could be mistaken. Previously unheard-of or bizarre ideas may be correct, so we should allow people to express them. Second, some ideas, false in their totality, may still contain elements of truth or partial truths that could, in the future, lead thinkers and explorers in a new direction of inquiry if these ideas are not suppressed. Third, we don't really understand what we believe until we know *why* we believe it. And the best way to understand why we believe something is to discuss the issue with someone who holds a different belief. Therefore, neo-Nazis should be free to express their opinions, not because they may be right, but in order for us to understand fully why they are wrong.

> If all mankind minus one were of one opinion, and only one person were of the contrary opinion, mankind would be no more justified in silencing that one person, than he, if he had the power, would be justified in silencing mankind . . . the peculiar evil of silencing the expression of an opinion is, that it is robbing the human race; posterity as well as the existing generation; those who dissent from the opinion, still more than those who hold it. If the opinion is right, they are deprived of the opportunity of exchanging error for truth; if wrong, they lose what is almost as great a benefit, the clearer perception and livelier impression of truth, produced by its collision with error.[13]

We develop our own insights by listening to the thoughts and experiences of others, evaluating this shared experience for ourselves through our own lens or filter, and then engaging in further discussion with others. If the communication of such experience is suppressed, the overall quest for knowledge and experience is thwarted.

We can see by this that Mill was supremely optimistic about the power of a liberal education. Along with John Locke before him, Mill believed that we are born as "blank slates" with no innate ethical propensities, contrary to what Plato and other philosophers had believed. Mill saw that our ideas are shaped by learning and nurture, not by hereditary influences or experiences gained in past existences. It was through education that he believed we would come to know more clearly what we believe by knowing how and why we think the way we do. In order to know what we think with conviction, we must know and be able to respond to opposing arguments, what he refers to as "antagonist modes of thought,"[14] thereby coming to know why we reject these contrary arguments. The goal will be a recognition of the multifaceted nature of "truth" and the value of a diversity of opinions.

In order to ensure that all talents in the society would be utilized, Mill supported compulsory education. But he did not believe that the government, which compelled parents to provide an education, should also be the one to provide it. Being suspicious of state-run programs, he nevertheless called for the state to provide financial assistance to parents who required it. It is risky to speculate on what Mill might say if he were alive today, but he might be sympathetic to those who favor public money (vouchers) for private schools. However, he was also strongly opposed to elitism, or special treatment for a few. He rejected Plato's privileged education for his Guardian class and Bentham's social engineering by the wisest. So he might favor more equal educational opportunities, in public schools under government regulation, for all children.

The test of which ethical rules would survive over time would be those that survived reflective discussion and not those followed merely because they have been the habit, convention, or tradition for a very long time. Examples of this might be challenges made to practices relating to numerous aspects of social organization or the habitual eating of animals simply because to do so is a very old custom.

We see the revulsion Mill had for the way that custom has exerted a stranglehold on thinking. He recognized that it is culture, not nature, that has often determined how societies have functioned, and that these cultural ways of living should be subjected to scrutiny in the name of reducing as much suffering as possible in the world or at least making things a bit less unjust.[15]

It is in the final "Applications" section of Mill's *On Liberty* that we see most clearly the dynamism of his work and the proof that his questing, somewhat tentative approach in Victorian England is still fresh and evolving in our own time. We are still struggling with some of the same issues he considered. For example, Mill discussed the religious freedom of Mormons in the United States to practice polygamy as more important than both how far this principle deviates from American society's norms and how much he himself was repulsed by "harems," which he saw as a form of exploitation of women, even slavery, under patriarchal principles in the name of theology. While we have outlawed polygamy in the United States, we still hear debates about what should be allowed under the heading of religious freedom and what should be banned.

In a later discussion of commerce and free trade, he agreed with the right of sellers to sell and buyers (at least, if they are of legal age) to buy alcoholic beverages while supporting the government's right to hold accountable drinkers of these beverages who hurt others while under the influence. Mill's principle was that people should not be free to harm others, but they should be free to do what the majority thinks is harmful to themselves. According to Mill, if an action is a "self-regarding error," one that has no consequences for others, then there should be neither governmental interference nor restriction on it. Nor should social pressure coerce people. He would restrict only "other-regarding errors," that is, actions that harm others. Does taking drugs harm others? If a person on drugs steals a car or assaults someone, then he or she has harmed others. But that is not the issue. Everyone agrees that stealing and assault should be punished. Does taking drugs by itself harm anyone other than the user? If the answer is no, then Mill would say people should be free to buy and take drugs of any kind. He also says that people freely enter into obligatory relations with others. If a man fails to support his wife and children because of his dependence on alcohol, he can be punished, according to Mill.

Further along in Mill's discussion of these civil liberties, he differentiated between printing critical opinions of controversial public figures in newspapers (which he supported) and holding protest meetings outside the person's home, with the possibility of inciting a riot (which he did not support).[16] He questioned the wisdom of governments ever aligning themselves with either the current temperance (prohibition of alcohol) movement or movements that called for the mandatory closing of shops on Sunday at the request of some of the Christian clergy.

What other contemporary issues might Mill take an interest in? Legislation is currently pending in some U.S. states to ban the use of handheld cellular phones while driving. At issue here is the way these telephones pose a potential risk of distraction, affecting other drivers. The findings and methodologies of social science are being employed to research the wisdom of this ban, an approach that Mill, writing at an earlier stage of the industrial and technological revolution in England, had advocated. These are all examples of debates that are within the purview of Mill's definition of philosophy.

Consider the debate in American legislatures over the pros and cons of requiring cigarette manufacturers to include photographs of diseased lungs on its packaging (as the Canadian government, at this writing, has already decreed)—a graphic reminder of the risks of smoking. It is impossible to know with certainty whether Mill would view this requirement as a merely annoying intrusiveness of government or as a wise and balanced communication between a government and its citizens. But he had written of his dislike for what he called a "nanny society" in which adults are baby-sat, if you will, by their government. We have no sure way of knowing what decision Mill might make on the heated public debates over restrictions on handgun sales or on the legalization of marijuana or other currently regulated substances. He does write, though:

> The modern conviction, the fruit of a thousand years of experience, is that things in which the individual is the person directly interested, never go right but as they are left to his own discretion; and that any regulation of them by authority, except to protect the rights of others, is sure to be mischievous.[17]

The implication in this final chapter of his *On Liberty* is that if harsh penalties are imposed for activities deemed illicit by a majority of the population (e.g., gambling in his day), this interference hinders individuals from making conscientious and deliberate decisions of their own. To indulge or not, while fearful of government penalty, does not constitute a freely determined choice. One who is compelled by force or merely by the desire to avoid criminal sanctions can hardly be considered autonomous.

Completely free expression and discussion are necessary for finding the truth and therefore are more likely to produce the greatest amount of happiness. Mill also devoted one chapter of *On Liberty* to the related topic of individuality. He said conformity in action and behavior is just as regrettable as conformity in belief. In fact, they are interrelated. The best society will encourage people to develop all their potential talents; they should explore, imagine, and experiment with ways of life without feeling the cold breath of social disapproval. He wrote:

> . . . as it is useful that while mankind are imperfect there should be different opinions, so it is that there should be different experiments of living, that free scope should be given to varieties of character, short of injury to others.[18]

People can't know for sure what is best for them until they try different things. And a society that tolerates many different styles, habits, and preferences will give people a greater range of possibilities to consider, and thus a better chance of finding the most satisfying way of life for themselves.

Mill matched his zeal for protecting the rights of adults to be let alone and to have privacy with his zeal to protect children from social ills. The Victorian child was viewed as a small version of an adult, and a significant proportion of the children of the laboring poor did not see daylight as they worked in dank factories from the age of seven. Mill went to great lengths in his writings and in his parliamentary speeches to argue for recognition of childhood as a time when special solicitousness was warranted.

∾ The Subjection of Women

The civil and social conditions of women in Victorian England and elsewhere were never far from Mill's mind. In his essay *On the Subjection of Women* (1869) he announced:

> The object of this Essay is to explain as clearly as I am able, the grounds of an opinion which I have held from the very earliest period when I had formed any opinion at all on social or political matters, and which, instead of being weakened or modified, has been constantly growing stronger by the progress of reflection and the experience of life: that the principle which regulates the existing social relations between the two sexes—the legal subordination of one sex to the other—is wrong in itself, and now one of the chief hindrances to human improvement; and that it ought to be replaced by a principle of perfect equality, admitting no power or privilege on the one side, nor disability on the other.[19]

Mill's language is measured and moderate, but his ideas are daring. He believed in "perfect equality" between men and women.

It was this view that had prompted Mill to make the dramatic gesture to disavow publicly the rights of property that English law granted him upon his marriage to Harriet Taylor and to pen this detailed essay. English "laws of couverture" pertaining to marriage in Mill's day granted sole legal title to the husband of any economic assets the wife brought to the marriage, whether inherited or earned during the marriage, and further granted him sole legal custody of any children of the union. Wives were rendered legal nonentities, and their interests were subsumed under their husband's name.

Above and beyond his criticism of these deficiencies in English law (incidentally, the state of U.S. law was not substantially different),[20] Mill was engrossed in exposing what he saw as a sadly high incidence of loveless and merely conventional marriages among the bourgeois or middle classes of Victorian English society. This situation he attributed to the strong pull of convention and class pressures, the economic dependence of women without access to higher education, and the forces of inertia and religious sanction to maintain such unions under almost any circumstances. To fashion more independence for women, he continued to argue for "an unfettered experiment" in seeing what women are capable of accomplishing outside the restricted realm of the hearth and home. Mill applauded the benefits he believed would accrue in unleashing their talents, thereby creating greater happiness for women and for their male companions—all admittedly a very radical proposal in his milieu.

> I consider it presumptuous in anyone to pretend to decide what women are or are not, can or cannot be, by natural constitution. They have always hitherto been kept, as far as regards spontaneous development, in so unnatural a state, that their nature cannot but have been greatly distorted and disguised; and no one can safely pronounce that if women's nature were left to choose its direction as freely as men's, and if no artificial bent were attempted to be given to it except that required by the conditions of human society, and given to both sexes alike, there would be any material difference, or perhaps any difference at all, in the character and capacities which would unfold themselves.[21]

Here is another example of appealing to what is "natural" when we have not observed nature. We cannot observe men and women in a natural state, because people have been socialized. Women especially have always been restricted and trained to accept a narrow domestic role. The only way to know what women are capable of is to give them the same freedom that men enjoy.

Mill in this essay went so far as to throw down the gauntlet, issuing a challenge to his fellow Englishmen. He wittily said (to paraphrase): To those of you who are blocking the doors to women's admission to higher education and the professions: if you are so convinced that women are by nature incapable of succeeding, then you have nothing to fear. If you are right about this, women will not survive the competition and you will be vindicated. But your credibility is called into question if you insist on erecting barriers against such "incompetent creatures doomed to fail." Here Mill was using irony, suggesting that it is fruitless to speak definitively about women's fitness and suitability for any task if they are not allowed to try. He wrote:

> I believe that their [women's] disabilities elsewhere are only clung to in order to maintain their subordination in domestic life, because the generality of the male sex cannot yet tolerate the idea of living with an equal.[22]

Mill's vision of the possibility of marriage being a "friendship between equals" was inseparable from his vision of the larger society's benefit from an increase of happier households. A clear example of how Mill combined this concern for the individual with a utilitarian concern for the whole society occurs in this passage from the essay:

> The family is a school of despotism in which the virtues of despotism, but also its vices, are largely nourished. The family, justly constituted, would be the real school of freedom. . . . What is needed is that, it should be a school of sympathy in equality, of living together in love, without power on one side or obedience on the other this it ought to be between the parents.[23]

These words are consistent with arguments he made in Parliament. There he spoke out in criticism of the dismissive way in which the law treated violence within the family. It is clear from this that he did not believe in protecting domestic privacy at the expense of harm to some members of the family, a good example of how he saw his "harm principle" applied in an actual scenario. Implicit in Mill's philosophy was the exposure of the lie of domination, in all its guises, posing as legitimate authority. He stated:

> People are not aware how entirely, in former ages, the law of superior strength was the rule of life; how publicly and openly it was avowed . . . how very recent a day it is that the affairs of society in general have been pretended to be regulated according to any moral law.[24]

Do we only pretend to regulate society by a moral law? Mill abhorred domestic abuse and wife beating as one more form of tyranny, in this case based on brute force. We must all question at one time or another how much has really changed since the days in ancient Greece, brought to life in Plato's *Republic*, in which Thrasymachus cynically taunts Glaucon with the line "Is not Justice merely the interest of the stronger?"

Mill was a thinker who saw a strong connection between poverty, early marriage, and large families. At age sixteen he was arrested for distributing birth control information in impoverished neighborhoods of London. Public opinion viewed such ideas as obscene, immoral, and irreligious, while Mill reiterated that he focused on the likely consequences of a lack of birth control—probable starvation and misery. Later in life, as a Member of Parliament from Westminster in London, he sponsored legislation that would make it impossible to obtain a marriage license unless a man could prove his financial ability to support a wife and children.[25] This position he took was problematic, to say the least, fraught with ideological controversy. For him, it was a move designed to lessen the burgeoning poverty in nineteenth-century England, made ever more extreme by the uprooted conditions of rural folk fleeing to the cities during the Industrial Revolution.[26]

Mill's goal was to build a society composed of intelligent, well-informed, self-determined individuals. Such individuals in turn, he believed, would be more likely to desire and promote the welfare of others, being more capable of seeing how all of nature's creatures seek their own preservation. Mill's way of using philosophy held out the promise of one day including all sentient creatures (those beings who feel and can suffer), not just the human creatures, among those who are entitled to moral consideration of their value as individuals. Mill's insistence on valuing the wisdom gained through observing nature (rather than following the fallible dogmas of this or that theological figure as to who may or may not have a "soul") might be refreshing for some ecologically minded modern persons who revere nature and who are alienated from hierarchical moralities that seem to include the illusion that we are living on a single-species planet.

In conclusion, what Mill saw as necessary for advancing knowledge and wisdom as we move through time was a removal of religious or metaphysical illusions that stifle an open-ended search for new insights and experiments with new possibilities. He believed that only thinkers who had given up baseless illusions could contribute meaningfully to this search. If this was what "the modern" was shaping up to mean, then Mill was standing on the cusp of modernity. But it is doubtful that persons of a contemplative nature, albeit living in this exceedingly secular modern world, would be willing to cast off all vestiges of "the things of the spirit" that sustain them. It may be difficult to find many persons who could satisfy Mill's requirement of having no "religious or metaphysical illusions." And even if we could find such a team of reformers, might it not be that their resemblance to the majority would be so weak that they would not be welcomed to make decisions for the rest?

∾ NOTES

1. J.S. Mill. "Autobiography," Book I, 233–234. In *The Collected Works of John Stuart Mill*. Robson and Stillinger, eds.
2. Ibid., Book I, 137–138.
3. Ralph Waldo Emerson, quoted by Unitarian minister Frank Hall in Minuteman Newspapers, Westport, CT, July 26, 2001.

4. See D.H. Monro, "Bentham, Jeremy," in Paul Edwards, ed., *The Encyclopedia of Philosophy,* vol. 1 (New York: Macmillan, 1967), 284.

5. It may be of interest that Pythagoras was the first ancient Greek to speak of the existence of souls and to state that these souls were possessed by all animals. (The root of "animal" is *anima*—the ensouled one.) It was with the Judeo-Christian and Islamic traditions that the idea of souls was reserved for human animals—perhaps partly to put distance between the emerging Western religious traditions and the idea of "transmigration of souls" or "reincarnation" endemic to Eastern religious traditions. See *The Heretic's Feast: A History of Vegetarianism* (Hanover, NH: University Press of New England, 1996), by Colin Spencer, for a historical overview of how notions, usually negative and false, about animals were incorporated into ethical doctrines of religious traditions and how individuals who defied those notions were persecuted.

6. Jeremy Bentham, *An Introduction to the Principles of Morals and Legislation,* Chapter 17. In *John Stuart Mill and Jeremy Bentham: Utilitarianism and Other Essays.* Cranston, ed.

7. J.S. Mill, "On the Subjection of Women," 141. In *Mill*. Ryan, ed.

8. Jeremy Bentham, *An Introduction to the Principles of Morals and Legislation,* Chapter 1. In *John Stuart Mill and Jeremy Bentham: Utilitarianism and Other Essays.* Cranston, ed.

9. John Milton and Thomas Jefferson had both believed in the necessity of free discussion for the maintenance of good government.

10. American courts and lawmakers have grappled for decades with these issues, ranging from limitations on World War I protest expressions to homemade bomb recipes in *The Anarchist's Cookbook* of the Vietnam War era to current television shows that may have the effect of provoking young viewers to imitate dangerous stunts. In truth, it is not completely clear how Mill might view contemporary questions of liability for actions committed by others who read printed matter. Contemporary observers are familiar with the impact of books like *The Turner Diaries,* with their far-right racialist and xenophobic theories, on budding neo-Nazis and Aryan supremacists. Mill, though, seems to oppose all prior restraint on printed publications while taking a more cautious approach toward the spoken word.

11. J.S. Mill. "On Liberty," 48. In *Mill*. Ryan, ed.

12. Ibid., 44.

13. Ibid., 53.

14. J.S. Mill. *Early Draft of John Stuart Mill's Autobiography.* Stillinger, Jack, ed. (Ann Arbor, MI: Books on Demand) Book X, 122.

15. It would take later philosophers working in the utilitarian tradition, notably Professor Peter Singer with his classic texts *Animal Liberation*

(1975) and *Writings on an Ethical Life* (2000), to show how utilitarian ethical principles similarly compel us to take notice of the appalling cruelty visited upon nonhuman creatures at slaughterhouses, animal "shelters," and research laboratories. It is in these settings that one may hear the echoes of Thrasymachus' reply to Glaucon in Plato's *Republic* that it really does look as if "justice is the interest of the stronger." We see here the evolution of an idea—ethical vegetarianism and preserving, not taking, life—that had its genesis in the "modernist" philosophy of utilitarianism.

16. In this case corn dealers, whose insistence on charging high tariffs even in times of famine and crop failure in Ireland amounted to complicity in murder, in the eyes of many critics.

17. J.S. Mill, "On the Subjection of Women," 146. In *Mill*. Ryan, ed.

18. J.S. Mill, "On Liberty," 84. In *Mill*. Ryan, ed.

19. J.S. Mill, "On the Subjection of Women," 133. In *Mill*. Ryan, ed.

20. In the middle of the nineteenth century, American women could not vote, could not hold elective office, and could not serve as jurors. (They were judged by men.) If they were married, their husbands had the legal right to any inheritance they might receive and any wages they might earn. Women were excluded from almost all institutions of higher learning, and most lucrative employment, and so, if unmarried, were forced to live with their fathers or brothers. In cases of divorce, women had few rights and usually lost custody of their children. See Miriam Schneir, ed., *Feminism in Our Time* (New York: Vintage Books, 1992), x.

21. J.S. Mill. "On the Subjection of Women," 178. In *Mill*. Ryan, ed.

22. Ibid., 172.

23. Ibid., 168.

24. Ibid., 138–139.

25. A similar piece of legislation, advanced by the Wisconsin state legislature in the 1970s, would have denied marriage licenses to spouses who had failed to meet child support and/or alimony payments from previous marriages. It did not survive strict judicial scrutiny on the grounds of "interference with a fundamental right to marry and procreate," as the law now stands under Supreme Court precedent.

26. We see that Mill's economic thought (as opposed to his views on speech and expression) more closely parallels that of his utilitarian predecessors in that it aims to protect the masses more than the individual entrepreneur. The younger Mill was concerned with classic Lockean-derived protection of liberty of contract for individuals; the older Mill, influenced by his wife Harriet Taylor, no doubt, had come to admire the thought of non-Marxian socialists, particularly the French theorists Fourier and Saint-Simon.

∼ CHRONOLOGY

∼ SUGGESTED READINGS

Cranston, M., ed. *John Stuart Mill and Jeremy Bentham: Utilitarianism and Other Essays.* New York: Penguin Press, 1987.

LeFebure, M. *Thomas Hardy's World: The Life, Times, and Works of the Great Novelist and Poet.* London: Carleton Books, 1997.

Mazlish, B. *James and John Stuart Mill: Father and Son in the Nineteenth Century.* New York: Basic Books, 1973.

Morley, J. "Nineteenth Century Essays." In *Classics of British Historical Literature* Series. Peter Stansky, series editor. Chicago: University of Chicago Press, 1970.

Okin, S.M. "John Stuart Mill, Liberal Feminist" in her *Women in Western Political Thought.* Princeton: Princeton University Press, 1979.

Robson, J., and J. Stillinger, eds. *The Collected Works of John Stuart Mill.* Volume 1. Toronto: University of Toronto Press, 1981.

Ryan, A., ed. *Mill.* New York: W.W. Norton, 1997.

Singer, P. *Animal Liberation.* New York: Random House, 1975.

———— *Writings on an Ethical Life.* New York: Ecco Press, 2000.

Thomas, W. *Mill.* New York: Oxford University Press, 1984.

CHAPTER 13

Nietzsche
Philosophy as Creating Values

Betty Weitz

⟶ Preview

*Centuries of faith have come to an end in Western civilization. "God is dead,"
Nietzsche tells us. Without divine purpose in the universe, there is no human
purpose. Without a divine legislator, there is no law or moral standard. We are
alone and morally destitute in an indifferent universe.*

*Yet, like a phoenix rising from its ashes, humanity has the power to rein-
vent itself. We must create new values. We must assume the role of shapers of
our own destinies.*

*Hope lies in our creative power. Humankind is the supernal artist. Will
we rise above the status quo or, like automatons, accept a dead present and an
empty future?*

*Each of us has a mandate, to discharge our powers and surpass our own
best expectations. Nietzsche exhorts us to "reach for a dancing star." He tells*

us to live everyday as if we were to repeat it for eternity for only from that per-
spective can we live authentic lives.

⮑ Introduction

Who is Nietzsche, and why is there so much discussion of his philosophy in our own time? Friedrich Nietzsche, a German philosopher, died in 1900, at the beginning of the twentieth century. What can he possibly have to say to us now, we of a different culture who are living at the dawn of a new millennium?

The aim of philosophy is to search for wisdom. As one face of wisdom, Nietzsche asks what it means to live at this point in the history of Western civilization. What is our place in the grand scheme of things—or, from Nietzsche's viewpoint, is there any grand scheme at all? Nietzsche finds himself living at a time in Western history where faith in a deity no longer prevails. Furthermore, the idea of history as narrative, an unfolding story of the progressive development of humankind toward some grand culmination, is no longer credible. Neither divine purpose nor a necessary evolution of human nature will determine the future of human affairs. What human nature turns out to be, he tells us, will be determined by our own choices. Our destiny lies in our own hands.

Where there is no divine order to the universe, the foundation for values and ethics comes into question. How are we to establish moral rules if there is no universal system against which to measure them? How are we to make moral choices, and how are we to live purposeful lives in our modern age? What are the key elements that can make life meaningful in our contemporary world?

Philosophy has always questioned what the "good life" is. Is the "good life" necessarily a happy one? And what do we mean by "happy"? Is a happy life purely a hedonistic one of material satisfactions and pleasure? Nietzsche calls that kind of life one of the "voluptuary" and warns youth against its empty promise and lack of fulfillment. A fulfilled life, for Nietzsche, is a very demanding one. Nietzsche's everyday life was certainly not cheerful; it appears miserable and lonely. He appears as a solitary figure. We might bear in mind the aphorism of Edward Gibbon (eighteenth century English historian): "Conversation enriches the understanding, but solitude is the school of genius."[1] His work appeared to fill his life. The Nietzsche we know is through his work; it is Nietzsche the philosopher. In his work, he expresses the anguish of existence but also its joy. Nietzsche is as much poet as philosopher; he sings his hosannas to the glory that he believes could be humankind.

For Nietzsche, a good life is one in which the individual is always reaching beyond his or her seeming limits. He calls for a life of intense rigor in the continual pursuit of self-transcendence. The emanation of such a life force is what he means by the "will to power." In such vitality, he tells us, rests the nature and the future of the human species. Such a demanding life, for Nietzsche, is the only truly human option. Whether Nietzsche lived the good life depends on whether we define a life as he does and whether we accept his view of the uncertainty and disequilibrium of human existence.

It is well known that Nietzsche's life was a difficult one. He suffered emotionally as well as physically from an assortment of debilitating afflictions. He worked long hours enduring crippling migraines, and was plagued by insomnia and a severe gastric disorder. Is that the Nietzsche whose life we must consider? Or is the real Nietzsche the voice in his works that exhorts us to "reach for a dancing star," abandoned as we are in a meaningless universe?

He was the son and grandson of Lutheran pastors. His father died when he was four years old. He was born near Leipzig, in Röcken, Germany, in October 1844. He elected classical and theological studies initially, later turning to classical philology when he attended the universities first of Bonn and later of Leipzig. A brilliant student, he was appointed in 1869 to a position as professor of classical philology at Basel University in Switzerland at the tender age of twenty-four. After only ten years, in 1879, he retired from his professorship. He had been suffering ill health since his mandatory military service in 1867, when he incurred a chest injury while trying to mount a restive horse. The injury was possibly exacerbated in 1870, when he was serving as a medical orderly in the Franco-Prussian War. The University of Basel granted him a small pension. He traveled, living in boarding houses mainly in France, Italy, and Switzerland. It was during this period that he worked tirelessly, developing his philosophy and writing most of his great works. Some say he worked long hours even when suffering excruciating pain. He appears to us throughout his works as a driven man.

Nietzsche never married, and the woman he was most ardent about, Lou Andreas-Salomé, chose the philosopher Paul Reé in his stead. She was a student of philosophy and theology whom Nietzsche met when he was thirty-seven and she was twenty-one. She became a writer, an associate of Freud, and wrote a book on Nietzsche. Walter Kaufmann, in his introduction to his translation of a selection of Nietzsche's works, tells us: "He thought . . . he had . . . found a companion and intellectual heir . . . who might fashion his many stimulating suggestions into a great philosophy." Kaufmann goes on to say that she was "unquestionably of extraordinary intellectual and artistic endowment" and that "he never found another human being to whom he could expound his inmost ideas."[2] Nietzsche misinterpreted her interest in him. Even before that time in Geneva, in 1876, he proposed to a Dutch woman, Mathilde Trampedach, a piano student. She turned him down. Much has been made of Nietzsche's misogyny, his animosity toward women. Yet, his advice on marriage calls for two equals who come together as independent persons in their own right rather than from need. He tells us to seek a "companion" in his sense of the word. His own choices seem to bear that out. Both of these women, with whom he desired to spend his life, had extraordinary capacities and talents of their own. Throughout his productive years he lived alone, whether by choice or not. We will never know whether being alone enhanced or impeded his creative power. It does not appear that he deliberately sacrificed his personal life for his work. He could simply have been unlucky or inept in personal relations.

Toward the end of his life, in 1889, when Nietzsche was in Turin, he witnessed a coachman beating a horse. He enclosed the horse's neck with his arms, embracing it, some think to protect it. He suffered a seizure and fell to the ground. He was helped to return to his lodging. After that event, when he wrote letters to his friends, they became concerned about his sanity. One concerned friend, Franz Overbeck, went to Turin and escorted Nietzsche to Basel, where he was hospitalized. After a brief stay, he was taken to Jena, Germany, where he was committed to an asylum. In March 1890, he was released to his mother, who escorted him to her home in Naumberg, where she cared for him until her death in 1897. After the death of his mother, his sister, Elisabeth Förster, took him to Weimar, along with his manuscripts, to a house she had rented for that purpose, separate from her own dwelling. He was never to recover his sanity. While the books he had written up to that time were published during the years of his insanity, it was doubtful that he even knew it; he stayed in a condition of physical and mental impairment until his death in 1900. Elisabeth Förster used her authority over his estate after his death to exploit his unpublished notes and to publish them according to her own distorted interpretation for political purposes of her own. She and her husband were committed proto-fascists. The terrible irony is that Nietzsche excoriated the "idol" of the state, the totalitarian idol, and was opposed to the very anti-Semitism that she and her husband espoused. Scholars today distinguish Nietzsche's true philosophy from the bogus ideas later promulgated by Elisabeth Förster.

There has been much speculation about his illness. Some have attributed it to syphilis contracted as a young man or during his service as a hospital orderly in the Franco-Prussian War, while others wonder if his mental decline was caused by the same brain disorder that caused his father's death. Still others think it may have been caused by the medications he took for his various physical ailments. No one knows for certain what caused his insanity and early demise. Some believe his madness was precipitated by his confrontation with nihilism or his daring to "go under," to penetrate deep within his own psyche where he believed the fount of the creative spirit resides, but where, he as well as Freud and others tell us, we repress our worst fears and nightmares.

∾ Nietzsche and Nihilism

Philosophy questions the nature of existence. Within that comprehensive inquiry, Nietzsche addresses the issue of human existence: he asks what a human life really means, how one should live it, and, even more specifically, how one should live in our contemporary world.

"God is dead," is Nietzsche's well-known declaration. This idea of the absence of God resonates throughout contemporary Western culture and is expressed in our everyday popular culture. The nihilism that Nietzsche encountered in the nineteenth century is the same nihilism that informs and shapes the tenor of our own time.

What do we mean by "nihilism"? Nihilism is the human condition Nietzsche confronts in Western civilization in this period of its history. It is the consequence of the fading from the culture of a divine presence and the consequent loss of meaning. Without a creator, humankind is of little significance, for no longer are we made in the image of God, central to creation, for whom all else was created. Without a God, there is no divine purpose to the universe and, consequently, no human purpose. Without a lawgiver there is no law and, therefore, no basis for truth or for moral values. The moral structure of the universe is gone. And gone is the assured eternal dimension of the world and of the human spirit.

With the loss of God comes a blinding freedom. Abandoned and alone, we are thrown into a universe of chance. Given this bleak view, Nietzsche proposes that we embrace the freedom and take up the challenge to find meaning and purpose in a godless universe.

Humanism and the Death of God

> . . . the madman forced his way into several churches and there struck up his *requiem aeternum deo*. Led out and called to account, he is said to have replied nothing but: "What after all are these churches now if they are not the tombs and sepulchers of God?"[3]

Nietzsche declares, "God is dead,"[4] in *Thus Spoke Zarathustra*. Zarathustra, his prophet and the voice of Nietzsche, does not issue the decree, nor is he trumpeting the news with joy and elation, as may first appear to be the case. Nietzsche draws the necessary conclusion from the prevailing culture: belief in a divine entity no longer prevails. Faith is gone, or "the candles in the churches are out," as one twentieth-century poet and playwright so eloquently states it.[5]

Atheism would appear to be a strange position for Nietzsche, the son and grandson of Lutheran pastors. Yet, we might consider that his profound concern about the loss of God, and the moral questions it raises, reveal a deep religious consciousness, but in the larger sense of "religious." Perhaps it takes just such a religious consciousness to be aware of the enormity of the cataclysm that was overtaking Western civilization. He sees humanity in relation to an empty universe and confronts the questions that issue from the human situation at this point in its history.

Rather than a joyful announcement, Zarathustra's bold assertion is just the denouement in the drama of Western civilization; it is the expression of the rising tide in philosophy, art, music, literature, in all emanations of the culture, of the end of traditional religion. While the death knell for Western religion is sounded definitively by the voice of Nietzsche's prophet, Zarathustra, the specter of the loss of divinity has emerged gradually in the West following the advent of the Scientific Revolution of the seventeenth century and the Enlightenment of the eighteenth. Both movements, fruits of the Renaissance, celebrated the ascendancy of human reason as the central and most powerful instrument for understanding and ordering the world.

Humanism, the resurgence of the primacy of human powers in the Renaissance, is usually thought of as a positive phenomenon; it has, however, another dimension. It is with the ascendancy of human powers as central and defining that the dislodging of the deistic presence occurs. An anthropocentric cosmology eclipses the deistic one. This "Copernican revolution" replaces God at the center of the cosmos with human reason. No longer willing to be vulnerable to the vagaries of the natural world, humanity will attempt to order nature according to its own design. But, at the same time, we must bear the loss of that transcendent entity from whom purpose and a grander picture emanates.

What are the consequences of this revolution in cosmology in Western civilization? Nietzsche makes us aware that with the loss of deity our lexicon of values is lost, too. The decrees and commandments that invested the universe with moral structure are gone by the end of the nineteenth century, along with the declared phantasm of their author. He is telling us that with this crisis in Western civilization we can no longer assume definitive truths and laws by which we ought to abide. He perceives humankind as alone and morally destitute in a silent and indifferent universe.

In *Irrational Man,* William Barrett, a twentieth-century American philosopher, quotes Nietzsche: "Do we not now wander through an endless Nothingness." Then Barrett tells us: ". . . the passage in which Nietzsche first speaks of the death of God is one of the most heart-rending things he ever wrote. The man who has seen the death of God, significantly enough, is a madman, and he cries out his vision to the unheeding populace in the market place. . . . Here we are no longer dealing with the abstractions of logical argument, but with the fate that has overtaken mankind."[6] Barrett makes the point that Nietzsche's is a *lived* atheism; it is not an academic debate. Nietzsche's anguish is our own, and it is palpable: "Do we not feel the breath of empty space? Has it not become colder? Is not night continually closing in on us?"[7]

Nietzsche's vision informs the French philosopher Sartre's[8] twentieth-century atheist existentialism. Sartre tells us that we are "forlorn." By that he simply means that we fully accept that God does not exist, and we face the consequences of that recognition. Now there is no meaning to our actions other than that with which we choose to endow them.[9] There is no way to validate or invalidate choices. The choice is self-justifying; the chooser declares it so by selection. This is the source of what Sartre calls "anguish." It is the agony of decision, free-floating, with no way of justifying it even after we have taken the action. Furthermore, in deciding, one posits the choice as a value for all humankind. The responsibility weighs heavily upon the doer, who must shoulder it alone and realize that the choices she or he makes shape the world and fashion the nature of humankind.

In a godless universe, human existence is absurd. The conclusions drawn from this idea are clearly evidenced in the twentieth-century absurdist writer Samuel Beckett. His play *Waiting for Godot* is the well-known expression of the ridiculous and tragic figure that Western humanity cuts in the modern age; it depicts the tragedy of the vacuousness of human experience in the twentieth century. Nihilism in Beckett's play is the central vibrating presence. The question the play poses is: Waiting for what?

According to Nietzsche, there is a crisis in Western civilization that calls for extraordinary measures. He sees us as stranded in a random universe without defining purpose or direction. Yet, Nietzsche believed that as potential creators, if we have the courage, we can create meaning in a meaningless world and shape the future of humankind. The task of humanity is to invent its own destiny. Nietzsche is pessimistic that we will carry out this task. As heir to Nietzsche, Sartre tells us: "Man is the future of man."[10] Sartre does not mean that we will necessarily choose wisely. He simply means that we will be whatever we make of ourselves for better or for worse.

∼ Nietzsche's Concepts

The Will to Power

The central idea that informs all of Nietzsche's work is the will to power. What is this power? It sounds ominous until you understand what Nietzsche means by this key phrase. Wrestle with your demons, your fears—fear of others, fear of failure, fear of death—conquer your inertia, your sloth, surmount the desire for the comfort of blind conformity. He wishes us self-loathing as the sign of our struggle.

The ultimate aim, for Nietzsche, is power over the self as a liberating principle freeing the spirit from the obstacles in its path toward its continuous realization. In this struggle with ourselves and with circumstances, Nietzsche wishes us lives of torment and suffering. He believes such is the mark of the struggle to go beyond our seeming capacity and to effect the act of creation that entails continual self-transcendence.

He cites Socrates, not the conqueror, as a paradigm of such power. Socrates in meeting the disapprobation of the powerful in his society, even when facing death, adhered to his principles. Socrates is a prime example of self-knowledge and self-mastery. Regardless of circumstances, Socrates maintained his essential identity. In Plato's portrayal of Socrates in the *Phaedo*, Socrates, upon his deathbed, admonished his pupils to take care of them*selves*. What he means is that they should take care of their *souls,* to work to strengthen and maintain their integrity. This steadfastness of spirit is what typifies power for Nietzsche. He believed that Socrates empowers others by his actions in his time as well as our own. (Although Nietzsche did not agree with all of Socrates' philosophy, he admired this aspect of his thought.)

The will to power is the discharge of a natural vitality that is the expression of a fundamental life force. Expressed positively, it is the drive that creates human culture, the ability to create issues from authentic individuality that can be stunted by societal influences. One expression of the will to power is to live authentically and to exercise individuality in all types of human endeavor. Nietzsche challenges us to sustain our originality in spite of social pressure to conform to false and mundane values.

A social issue emerges in Nietzsche's thought that stresses the survival of individuality in the modern age. As the individual became more collectivized in the historical development of mass society and the rise of nation-states, a more uniform populace appeared to loom as the faceless future of humankind. The Industrial Revolution and mass production took their toll upon individual expression. With the rise of nation-states, Germany was unified toward the end of the nineteenth century, and Nietzsche perceived that nationality was becoming the basis of identity, especially in the new Germany. His concern was most evident when he inveighs against the new "idol" of the state in *Zarathustra*. He opposed the surge of German nationalism that was particularly vehement in his time. For Nietzsche, to adopt nationality as self-definition is to hide behind the mask of one more false idol in order to evade the fearful responsibility inherent in absolute freedom.

The exercise of will, for Nietzsche, is an act of creation against a senseless void. He sees us as nothing more than sheer will; a vortex carving meaning out of a senseless flux.

The idea of will as the primary driving force behind all living things was originated by Arthur Schopenhauer (1821–1881). For Schopenhauer, the basis of all life is the blind will to exist. Nietzsche was influenced by Schopenhauer, and the blind will to exist turns into a purposeful drive in Nietzsche's philosophy, a conscious striving for ceaseless transcendence.

Ressentiment

Ressentiment, the major concept in Nietzsche's *Toward a Genealogy of Morals*, can be seen as the antithesis of his idea of the will to power. There is no equivalent word in German for what can be rendered in English as "resentment," and so Nietzsche coined the term *ressentiment* from the French.[11] Who is resentful of what? According to Nietzsche, Christian doctrine is an expression of the "slave's" resentment toward the "master." "Envy" is a synonym one might use for what Nietzsche means by *ressentiment*. From Nietzsche's perspective, there is resentment or envy of the master's power, strength, self-affirmation, egoism, success.

While Nietzsche is harking back to the ancient Greek period when slavery was part of the political structure, he is not advocating slavery. Nietzsche's classification of master/slave morality in the *Genealogy* is a device for characterizing certain psychological attitudes. The same individual can, at one time, act as the master, exhibiting strength and resolution, and, at another time, act as the slave, expressing resentment or envy toward another's success. We are all capable of both attitudes. Autonomy is the key issue, and this means that we should be the authors of our own actions. In the slave mode, we are not acting but reacting. The impetus of our behavior is not our own but comes from outside. Circumstance or the behavior of another evokes the response. Resentment or envy in reaction to the success of another is ignoble, for Nietzsche, and does not do justice to our own capabilities. It calls for lessening the other's success instead of intensifying our efforts to increase our own. The other's success should spur us on to higher accomplishment.

Resentment or envy creates the values of good and evil. "It is the *ressentiment* of those who are denied the real reaction, that of the deed," says Nietzsche. Whereas "noble morality" issues from the self and looks to the self for the origin of the deed as an act of self-affirmation, "slave morality" concentrates on the other and "says No to what comes from outside, to what is different, to what is not oneself." Slave morality defines itself by the negative. "No, is its creative deed," says Nietzsche.

As a system of revenge against the strong, he tells us, Christianity celebrates humility, subservient behavior, and condemns the proud, autonomous individual. It calls for the fall of the high and the mighty. It is the slave mode of the human personality expressing itself. In his view, Christian ideals are an inversion of the ancient Greek value of the assertion of strong personality. Christian values eclipsed the Greek ideal of human excellence *(arête)*. He is speaking about two opposing moral ideals for humankind: the heroic code of the ancients versus the ideal of humility for Christianity. (We should keep in mind that the Christian ideals that Nietzsche condemns occur in many different religions.)

And so Nietzsche tells us that Christian values go against the best human attributes or health of the species: they sanctify as holy that which enervates the human spirit. Instead of encouraging vigor and self-assertion, such religious dogma condemns them as defiance against the will of God and mandates resignation, the acceptance of suffering, as human destiny. Nietzsche makes the point that to treat this life and this world as merely the prologue to life after death in a better world, an afterworld, is to be life-denying. It is the attempt to evade the uncertainty of our existence.

In what seems like a tall order, Nietzsche believes we can choose to love our enemies. His model is the Greek one of respecting one's adversary in battle rather than the Christian ideal of forgiving of one's enemy. He calls for an honest assessment and appreciation of our enemies so that we may accord them a high level of respect as a "bridge to love"; this is the sign of our own nobility. He does not want us to dwell upon the "vermin" of the injustices we suffer; that preoccupation can destroy us. And to always see the enemy as an "other," the "evil" one, is never healthy or edifying. The problem with Christianity, Nietzsche says, is that it poses the non-Christian as an infidel, the evil one who must be vanquished as a not acceptable other. To posit evil as the opposite of good is to define oneself as good only in relation to an other who is evil. Self-affirmation should originate in the self not as a result of constructing a false other to serve that purpose.[12] Something is *bad* rather than *evil* in Nietzsche's scheme only as a pale contrast to an original act; the original creative act is infused with life and passion, while its contrast is a pale imitation.

Nietzsche tells us that whereas the ancients assumed an active stance and celebrated this world, *carpe diem* ("seize the day"), the Christian ethic reverses the early Greek values and embraces a morality of passivity that denies this world and the true potentiality of the human spirit. From Nietzsche's standpoint, the subjugation of human will to divine will is at the heart of Christian doctrine. Instead of asserting human will and striving for self-transcendence, we are taught to doubt ourselves. Self-abnegation in the face of divine will is our salvation, according to this theology, as Nietzsche perceives institutional Christianity. The human image presented by Christianity is one of helplessness and dependency upon the love and compassion of a godhead.

Gravity is the enemy, according to Nietzsche. Not to take oneself, one's "accidents and misdeeds," and even one's enemies too seriously is the sign of what we would characterize as a mature nature and what Nietzsche calls a "noble" nature. Noble values, according to Nietzsche, focus on the life-affirming deed and consider the negative only after that fact.

As we have seen, Nietzsche is most certainly opposed to the traditional Judeo-Christian ethic we usually take for granted in Western civilization.

The Übermensch *and* Amor Fati

Can one reasonably say that any ethic emerges in Nietzsche's thought? The opposite of the will to create, which is how Nietzsche defines what is good, is destruction. As one examines his concepts of the will to power and *ressenti-*

ment, it is reasonable to conclude that what we would call evil is, for Nietzsche, a diminishing of human potentiality. Whether it is the extreme of taking a life (see "On the Pale Criminal" in *Zarathustra*) or the more ordinary and everyday surrender to death of the spirit, we are contributing to what he would view as the antithesis of the human project. For that project, he uses the term *Übermensch* to signify the reaching beyond our present circumstances to ever-receding horizons of possibilities. The *Übermensch* is essentially the aim of the will to power. Some commentators interpret the concept of the *Übermensch* as a future human type. However, it is reasonable to say that it is neither a destination nor a resting place; it is the *act* of never-ending self-transcendence of the species.

This act calls for the continuous exercise of our regenerative power. As a positive value, it is life-enhancing and is at the opposite pole from the destructive impulse. In condemning destructive acts toward others, Nietzsche sees them not only as harming another but also as self-diminishing. This view is apparent in "On the Pitying" in *Zarathustra*.

> And if a friend does you evil, then say: "I forgive you what you did to me; but that you have done it to yourself—how could I forgive that?" Thus speaks all great love: it overcomes even forgiveness and pity.[13]

Concern for the other is revealed here. While there is a strong solitary element in Nietzsche's philosophy, there is a social aspect as well.

With his concept of the *Übermensch,* Nietzsche expresses his positive value of the power to reinvent ourselves, which he believes resides in human freedom. Our task is not simply a solitary endeaver, although it can appear that way. Individual effort engenders social consequences. Fashioning individual destinies means shaping the future of humankind as we create a new culture.

Nietzsche's concept *amor fati*—to love one's "fate"—is his celebration of life just as it is; he tells us to love the inherent struggle and not to wish it to be different. He urges us to embrace this life in all its fearful aspects and complexity—in opposition to that part of the Christian ethic that calls for resignation and denial of this world in favor of a longing for the next.

Yet, Nietzsche realizes that there are no signposts to guide us on our journey. He recognizes that his quest is a dangerous one. He informs us that there are depths to the human spirit as capable of massive destruction as of creation.

Dionysus

In *Thus Spoke Zarathustra* Nietzsche writes:

> I say unto you: one must still have chaos in oneself to be able to give birth to a dancing star. I say unto you: you still have chaos within yourselves.[14]

For Nietzsche, there is a dark element in human nature; unbridled, it expresses hatred, jealousy, and envy and produces "fights of annihilation." Yet, he tells us, it is this Dionysian power that fuels the highest human efforts that culminate in the highest achievement. Dionysus is the expression of our own wild nature, of the dark passions within from which emanate the highest forms of art and the foulest deeds of humankind. Dionysus is the source of all creativity.

Nietzsche's thesis in his first work, *The Birth of Tragedy Out of the Spirit of Music,* is that the synthesis of two principles, the Apollonian and the Dionysian, was necessary to give birth to the height of Greek culture, as represented by Greek tragedy. The god Apollo, the Apollonian principle, represents harmony wrought by rationality as it shapes a work of art. Dionysus, on the other hand, represents a seething ecstasy, a relentless striving, a rapture that can carry one to excess. This expression is seen most readily in music. While Dionysus is dangerous—he knows no bounds—Apollo represents restraint and moderation. These two forces in conflict, the Apollonian and the Dionysian, were necessary to give rise to Greek civilization.[15] "Only the Apollonian power of the Greeks was able . . . to harness the Dionysian flood, and to use it creatively,"[16] Kaufman comments on Nietzsche's *Birth of Tragedy.* We might view Apollo as our rational aspect, the conceptual knowledge or craftsmanship that gives a work its form. Dionysus can be viewed as the unconscious issuing forth from which artists draw their creative powers and original visions.

The Apollonian principle can be seen in the measured harmony and balance that give Greek architecture its noted quality and exquisite beauty. Dionysus, the god of the vine, is represented in the frenzy of the festivals of music and dance held by the Greeks in his name. Nietzsche's point is that Greek tragedy emerged from music and dance. First came music and dance, the expression of Dionysian ecstasy; but then it took Apollo, the rational element, to give form to this expression, and so Greek tragedy was born. Both aspects, of course, are human characteristics and are necessary for the complete individual and for the work of art.[17] As we have noted, in his later works Nietzsche will emphasize the role of Dionysus, even though he incorporates both elements as necessary for his awakened individual. Better to recognize and incorporate the "devil" within, to harness those powers, Nietzsche tells us, than to deny their existence. For Dionysus can be a dangerous god who can be destructive as well as creative in his expression as an element of human nature. In *The Birth of Tragedy* and in *Homer's Contest,* Nietzsche tells us that the great achievement of the Greeks was that they initially turned this dark, destructive force into the fount of their great civilization.

Many are the beneficiaries of the legacy of Nietzsche's incisive powers of observation, among them Freud. In *Civilization and Its Discontents,* Freud issues a warning to take seriously the savage nature of this primal dynamic, which he calls *thanatos,* the death drive inherent in human nature; it may prove to be the end of us all. "Sublimation" is the term Freud emphasizes to express the harnessing of this great power that is creative of all human culture. He questions whether it will always be channeled in the constructive mode and warns that, when thwarted, the irrational erupts into violence; he offers the pessimistic view that *thanatos* may well prevail over its constructive counterpart. Writing this work at the end of the third decade of the twentieth century, with the specter of Hitler rising in Europe, Freud presents the possibility of an apocalyptic vision of the future of civilization, and expresses some doubt about the survival of humankind. Sublimation, the fact that we harness that power for the purpose of the creation of civilization, is his only hope for our survival. For proof of the existence of this savage component of human nature, Freud simply points to the evidence of human history. It is the *irrational* element in humankind that engenders both violence and the work of art.

Irrationalism[18]

"It was intelligence," Kierkegaard says, writing of his task and himself in his Journals—"it was intelligence and nothing else that had to be opposed."[19]

In *Irrational Man*, William Barrett quotes Kierkegaard (Danish philosopher, 1813–1855) and then goes on to say that Kierkegaard, a man of genius, had an immense intelligence and that he does not disparage but reveres it. At the same time, however, Barrett tells us, "at a certain moment in history this intelligence had to be opposed, and opposed with all the power and resources of a man with brilliant intelligence."[20]

The term "intelligence" as it is used here is equated with reason. The modern age of science would develop, and by the eighteenth century doubt would emerge about certain kinds of human knowledge. Subsequently, scientific inquiry would call for empirical facts, hard facts, observable data. Only they would be considered true knowledge. Scientific man is the rational creature.

Reason reigned supreme in the Enlightenment of the eighteenth century. It promised to illuminate the secrets of the universe, bring social justice, and ameliorate human misery. Progress in science would yield a better world. It was a time of promise. But according to Søren Kierkegaard[21] and Nietzsche, something had been lost. Truth was not merely a rational calculation; such truth is, perhaps, only the tip of the iceberg. Not that they disparage the use of reason—it is the severing of reason from a larger consciousness that they oppose. What were being lost were the deeper instincts of the human animal. These philosophers call to a deeper intelligence, that which informs art.

Nietzsche and Kierkegaard, each in his own way, oppose the tyranny of reason. For Kierkegaard, faith dwells in opposition to the *lone* demands of pure reason. For Nietzsche, the source of reality lies deep in the primal drives of the human spirit. Such philosophers cast doubt on the idea of the Enlightenment, that the new scientific man will manage nature, tame its wildness, dissolve the mystery.

And so Kierkegaard embraces a Christian God at a time when Western civilization is retreating from a religious culture and turning toward a rational world view. He is going against the tide. In a certain sense Kierkegaard, firmly rooted in a profound and personal religious center, and Nietzsche, godless, are brothers in an age of modern skepticism and reliance on reason alone.[22] Nietzsche, in a godless age, turns to the early Greeks and embraces a pagan god, Dionysus. Dionysus is his guide to the unconscious and primal, to the instincts and passions. Nietzsche will explore the inner world, the dark recesses where the wellspring of the creative spirit resides. Both thinkers stand firm against the tide of cool rationalism and the belief in a humanistic ordering or manipulation of the universe enveloping Western civilization in their own century and in the century to come. Both look to the passionate center of the individual. For one, Kierkegaard, it is the religious center; for the other, Nietzsche, it is a godless dimension. They call attention to the nonrational element, the irrational, in human nature.

Both philosophers acknowledge the nihilism of their time and its challenge to the future. In addition, the modern age has wrought mass society. Kierkegaard harks back to the origin of Christianity before its institutionalization by the Church. Religious experience lies, for Kierkegaard, in the most private domain of the individual spirit. And for Nietzsche, only the herd animal succumbs without questioning to the "wisdom" of the collectivity that may simply express the fashion of the day. Both speak for the private domain, which appears to be retreating before a mass society.

Reason alone has not worked. It has not fulfilled the promise of the Enlightenment. The Enlightenment, with the ascendancy of human reason, was to be the panacea that would solve all problems of human suffering; justice would abound, and human misery would dissolve before the power of the exercise of human reason. In the heady elixir of scientific inquiry, with the Scientific Revolution starting in the seventeenth century and the political revolutions in the eighteenth—the fruition of Renaissance humanism—belief was strong that human reason is the gateway to truth. The universe would unveil its mysteries, and the nature of the physical world and of human existence would be revealed.

Such optimism did not recognize the constant of the savage and mean-spirited element in human nature. That Dostoevsky (1821–1881) understood. In *Notes from Underground,* he mocks the premise of the Enlightenment and its "Crystal Palaces,"[23] both actual and metaphorical, and the supposed progress of science in changing the human condition. According to Dostoevsky, never will such superficial inquiry pierce the darkness of the human soul, revealed in all its petty splendor through the character of his narrator in *Notes*. His point is that our nature remains the same, and it isn't a pretty sight. The hope of the Enlightenment is a false one for Dostoevsky.

Nietzsche, in a world without God, seeks to penetrate the mystery of human existence beyond the limits of rational calculation. The human quest, for Nietzsche, is a search for meaning in a seemingly meaningless universe. What meaning he finds will be in the sheer will to exist, but not merely to exist as a stone exists. What does it mean to be human or, in Nietzsche's terms, to be beyond the stasis of what he calls "the last man"? The ultimate human essence is the artist—the "creator." The last man is insufficient; he or she is the herd animal, acculturated, tamed, empty of spirit, plodding and unthinking. The heart of being human is becoming. There is no stasis; all is will.

By limiting inquiry to the narrow province of reason we have lost our center, according to both Kierkegaard and Nietzsche. For Nietzsche, power to create issues forth not from sheer rationality but from the force of our passions that must be exercised if we are to live according to his idea of what it means to be human.

Nietzsche, an atheist, is still possessed by a god, but it is the god Dionysus, the god of the passions, as Barrett tells us.[24] Kierkegaard, a Christian, calls on us to embrace the mystery with a leap of faith; such faith is agonizing; there is no proof of this *holy* moment. It entails the agony of Abraham when he takes his beloved son Isaac to the ritual site and reaches for the knife to slit his throat. Danger lies in both directives.

～ Perspectivism and Truth

In contemporary thought, there is a movement called "postmodernism." Many postmodernists see Nietzsche as the progenitor of their view of truth: that truth is nothing more than perspective. From this point of view, there can be many "truths." The perspective from which you are looking determines what you perceive as truth. The culture from which you come, the time in which you live, the language you speak—such are the contingencies that contribute to your signification of what is true. The postmodernist claims that we are each situated in a time and a place and bear the cultural and historical biases of that situation; beliefs are products of a largely cultural framework of time, place, and language.

From the postmodernist view, there is no fundamental structure in itself to discover; all is invention, how we configure it, including science. There are "facts," but we arrange them in different ways. There is no bedrock of truth. Moral systems prevail that have different sources of origin, usually cultural. There is no one underlying basis for moral rules. That means that there is no one system of morality, whether it is the edicts handed down by a God, such as the Ten Commandments, or a rational system of ethics such as that devised by the German eighteenth-century philosopher Immanuel Kant. In addition, there is no universal human nature. Each of us is acculturated by language, different belief systems, habits, and modes of thought that cause us to perceive and shape the "world" in a certain way. Does that necessarily mean that all systems of truth and morality have equal value? That they do is the position of "relativism."

Relativism claims that since there is no metaphysical origin of truth or morality—no eye of God—against which to measure particular systems, there is no way to claim that some beliefs are more true or that certain systems of morality are better than others. The latter position is called "moral relativism." Some claim that there is a difference between "perspectivism" and relativism: that for perspectivism there is not necessarily an equality of value for different systems. Moral systems or ideas can have different values. For example, some moral systems may work better than others; they may yield better consequences, such as to enhance human life. Some truths may have more credible evidence, appear more plausible, or work better within a given theory.

Regardless of the claims of the distinction between perspectivism and relativism by some postmodernists, one might suppose that perspectivism does seem to foster relativism, since what one individual considers evidence another may not, and what system of belief one values as good others may view differently. From the perspectival position, one could challenge the basis of priority of one system of values or the truth of one idea over another. Furthermore, many have pointed out that the proposition "It is true that there is no truth" is self-refuting.

False Idols: Philosophize with a Hammer

Is there a truth for Nietzsche? Nietzsche excoriates false idols of customary belief systems. We cling to such idols from habit and in order to hide from the truth of our naked existence and the uncertainty of the human situation. The truth, for Nietzsche, also includes the exercise of a vital human power, the will to create a world of culture and values. We, at our best, are the expressions of the will to power that can forge a positive future and create new values.

The world or reality, according to Nietzsche, is our construction, and we must face and realize that it is the philosopher's task to continue reconstructing it.

> The belief which holds that the world, which *ought* to be, *is* real, is a belief of the unproductive, of those who will not create a world as it ought to be. They imagine that it is there, and they seek ways and means to attain it.[25]

One does not discover the way the world is, for Nietzsche; we invent it. Any meaning we find is imposed on a formless nothing. Truth is formed from possibilities. Philosophers are the "legislators" who create values. Values do not come from some higher source or metaphysical realm but are of human invention.

> Genuine philosophers, however, are commanders and legislators: they say, *"thus it shall be!"* They first determine the Whither and For What of man, and in so doing have at their disposal the preliminary labor of all philosophical laborers, all who have overcome the past. With a creative hand they reach for the future, and all that is and has been becomes a means for them, an instrument, a hammer. Their "knowing" is *creating*, their creating is a legislation, their will to truth is—*Will to Power.*[26]

The "hammers" of philosophy are the tools for destruction and creation. These tools philosophers must use ruthlessly to test old values and beliefs for their soundness and viability and to clear the ground for the construction of new ones. That is why, in *Twilight of the Idols,* he tells us that one must philosophize with a hammer used like a "tuning fork," not simply to destroy old idols but to sound them out, and to hammer and chisel new ones. It is a dangerous enterprise, for we are creating new values in a void with no standard against which to measure them. The truth for Nietzsche is that this is the human condition. We have no choice but to be the creators of values. We have always been the creators of values. Values work for a while as truths, but when they lose their viability, we must discard them and create new ones. Not to recognize this human state of affairs is to hide one's head in the sand and to follow along blindly adhering to long dead belief systems that no longer enhance the human project. What is true for Nietzsche is that there is this inherent possibility of a life force, the will to power, capable of exercising a legislative capacity. Will we necessarily exercise it? We may or may not, depending upon the nature of our culture and of philosophy in our own time. There is a truth for Nietzsche: it is that humankind must exert the will that gives form and meaning to an otherwise meaningless existence.

Is there a human nature for Nietzsche? He sees the human animal as one of unlimited power with inherent possibilities that are creative both of self and of world. For Nietzsche, the aim of our species should be the *Übermensch.* That is a difficult concept often misconstrued. Some say he means a future *type* that the human species chooses to fashion through sheer will. But Nietzsche always stresses the endlessness of the quest, that it is a *continuing* process, one that has no end state. The opposite of that striving, simple acculturation, following one's contemporary culture, produces only what Nietzsche derisively calls "the last man," a passive, plodding creature who blindly and unthinkingly treads customary paths. The truly human future calls for *legislators* who "with a creative hand . . . reach for the future."

In *Beyond Good and Evil,* published in 1886, Nietzsche does seem to take human will to its furthest ascendancy by giving it a central and exclusive place in the cosmos. We must remember that Nietzsche is a voluntarist, and will does seem to take primacy and appear as the alpha and omega of his theory, especially in his later thought. The view of Nietzsche presented by postmodernism emphasizes this dimension of Nietzsche.[27]

Nietzsche's Immorality

Nietzsche rejects not only the Judeo-Christian ethic but also a logical system of morality propounded by Immanuel Kant in the eighteenth century. Kant claimed a rational basis for his system; namely, that it is grounded in human reason alone rather than derived from any divine source. Nietzsche says that what he purports to be an ethical system devised from reason is really no more than the reiteration of what Kant learned to believe as a Christian.

Nietzsche condemns traditional values unthinkably heeded from fear or habit. He says that the Ten Commandments were viable at one time as the invention of a people who were overcoming *their* past values. According to Nietzsche, the new "tablets" were an expression of that ancient people's genius in transcending their own dead past and reinventing themselves. Now, he tells us, we must move on, since those tablets no longer work for us.

Nietzsche calls such systems a "herd" morality; he believes they call for blind adherence to an ethic we do not really believe or examine. Nietzsche exhorts us not to settle for the ordinary or the customary, but to critically examine ideas and values, which through repetition and conformist adherence have led to mindless actions issuing from dead values. Yet, Nietzsche has a pessimistic view of how many will exercise the necessary courage and vigor. He sees the herd instinct prevailing in human behavior.

His rhetoric, extreme at times in order to wake us from our slumber, is what leads to misunderstanding. But what does Nietzsche offer us in the way of direction toward new values? The sheer exercise of will appears to offer no basis. Some say he has eliminated all values. But as Kaufmann has pointed out, "Nietzsche himself was a fanatical seeker after truth and recognized no virtue above intellectual integrity."[28]

Yet, one could argue that in the absence of traditional values, derived from the commandments of God or any humanly devised rational system of ethics, Nietzsche offers no ground, no objective basis, for asserting one value over another. One can no longer assert right or wrong actions from the source of human or eternal law. This is the well-recognized Nietzschean predicament. We are heir to this problem in contemporary ethics. Nietzsche, however, did not initiate this problem—it occurred earlier. The crucial issue of the ground for truth in the absence of God first emerges with the skepticism of the empiricist David Hume in the eighteenth century.[29]

Nietzsche's ethic is a difficult one. It is easily misunderstood. He does not propose an immorality or even amorality, as some people read him.

Nietzsche emphasizes that we are responsible for our actions. Liberty is not license for him. Those historical figures he admired most were, in his view, paragons of the dictum "know thyself" and were "masters of their passions," as Kaufmann tells us. He is desperately seeking a new morality and the exercise of our critical faculties in searching for one. With the end of the supernatural, the dichotomy of good and evil no longer prevails. We have the source of both reason and passion within us, and it is the successful combining of these two elements of the human psyche that will resurrect us into the new being—one who is beyond the dichotomy. That is what he means when he says that we are "beyond good and evil"; it is the debasement of the passions as the source of what institutional religion calls evil that he opposes.

Toward the end of his life, in his later works, he does increasingly emphasize the passions as represented by the Greek god Dionysus. He rails against those who resist the inevitable truth of their human situation, that they must reinvent themselves. He is in search of an ethics, one for our age. He seems to assume that there is the possibility of an intuitive proclivity in humankind toward life enhancement.

∽ *Thus Spoke Zarathustra*

Prologue

Nietzsche wrote *Thus Spoke Zarathustra* in the years 1883 to 1885. It is a series of "Speeches," as Nietzsche terms them, or parables written in metaphorical language. They are at the same time poetry and philosophy. Deeply personal, yet universal, they lead us to the subterranean depths of our own consciousness.

Zarathustra, the voice of Nietzsche, is the central character and narrator. He knows much about us; Nietzsche is the master psychologist. Zarathustra goes "up the mountain" alone and then descends to the world of ordinary people. His cup is full, overflowing; he must "empty" it once again. He attempts to share his vision with the populace. Blinded by cultural conditioning, they do not heed him. They accept without query their automatic lives.

The act of the visionary or the artist occurs in solitude. The painter paints alone, the writer writes alone, one "climbs the mountain" alone. When "the cup is full," one wishes to share, and the artist or the sage offers it to others. Zarathustra says, "Behold, I am weary of my wisdom, like a bee that has gathered too much honey; I need hands outstretched to receive it."[30]

While the search is solitary, the "descent," or act of sharing, is Nietzsche's social aspect. However, as in Plato's allegory of the cave, the one who ascends to witness reality is jeered, mocked, called mad, considered a pariah, and even, at times, put to death. A resistant society responded in this way to Jesus and Socrates. Challenged and terrified by the visionary, who issues the call to rise above the comfort of the status quo, the populace turns against him. The one who "climbs the mountain" in solitude to rekindle his or her "ashes" into fire, and then descends to share the bounty with others, can be spurned or, even worse, can suffer a lethal fate.

On the Three Metamorphoses

> In the loneliest desert, however, the second metamorphosis occurs; here the spirit becomes a lion who will conquer his freedom and be master in his own desert.[31]

Always the image of solitude, the mountain or the desert, prevails as a metaphor for the "place" where the creative act occurs. Nietzsche tells us in his Speech *On the Three Metamorphoses:* First, be a camel; endure the burden of learning the traditional knowledge of your discipline, the accumulated work of your predecessors. Second, be the defiant lion; rebel against the traditional tenets of the discipline. Third, be a child. The third stage is the act of creation. Artists see the world anew, and perceive and create an original vision, their own.

To rise above the "human," as Nietzsche understands it, is to create new worlds in art, science, or any human endeavor. In the history of art, as in science, the artist presents a new vision but draws on the resources of former artists. And so the history of art, science, all aspects of human culture continues to evolve. One must learn, rebel, and originate to "give birth to a dancing star," says Nietzsche.

The Tree on the Mountainside

> The more he aspires to the height and light, the more strongly do his roots strive earthward, downward, into the dark, the deep—into evil.[32]

The Tree on the Mountainside is Nietzsche's advice to the young. The tree is his metaphor for the youth. He understands the youth's dismay in asserting his freedom. What is the authentic choice? Some adolescents choose a destructive path in their quest for freedom. The possibilities are there, and the youth encounters them in his striving "upward" in his search for autonomy. The more he strives upward to reach the "height" and the "light," the deeper into the earth he penetrates, into the subterranean region of his own primal drives, where the power of Dionysus is fiercest. It is dangerous terrain.

Yet Nietzsche calls on us to explore the depths, even though we are entering a dangerous region. Dionysus has the propensity for mayhem, but the god of intoxication and frenzy is also the god of rapture and music. Only there, at the seat of the passions, is the power to originate. Barrett comments on Nietzsche's own disintegration and madness in his later years:

> He who would make the descent into the lower regions runs the risk of succumbing to what the primitive calls "the perils of the soul"—the unknown Titans that lie within, below the surface of our selves. To ascend again from the darkness of Avernus is, as the Latin poet tells us, the difficult thing, and he who would make the descent had better secure his lines of communication with the surface.[33]

The more the youth reaches for his freedom, the deeper his roots descend "earthward" into subterranean depths. Nevertheless, Nietzsche tells him, he must extend his reach and not cast away his "love and hope." He warns him not to give up his true passion, not to live for "brief pleasures." He cites the difference between the lovers of life and "voluptuaries"—those who surrender their true passion, those "who [have] lost their highest hope," then opt for "brief pleasures and barely cast their goals beyond the day." They are the ones who tell themselves that "spirit too is lust." As a result, "the wings of their spirit broke; and now their spirit crawls about and soils what it gnaws. Once they thought of becoming heroes: now they are voluptuaries."[34] Nietzsche ends with this exhortation: "Hold holy your highest hope!"

"Holy" is a powerful word, and Nietzsche does not use it lightly. It puts human striving in a special category. For Nietzsche, a human life is beyond mere choice, as Sartre later defines it. A human life, for Nietzsche, is a continuing apotheosis against a negative ground with no end state.

In an indifferent universe, we are "thrown" into a world of chance, a world that is not ordered in any particular way. The essential task Nietzsche sets for humankind is to be the supernal artist.

According to Nietzsche, a nihilistic universe changes the face of humanity forever. No longer formed in that divine image, we must, as our own progenitors, create a new humanity. "The book thus opens with the symbols of rebirth and resurrection, and this in fact is the real theme of *Zarathustra:* How is man to be reborn, like the phoenix, from his own ashes?" *Zarathustra* has been called a book of resurrection.[35]

✍ Eternal Recurrence

Most of us do not account for our lives until our deathbed. There we perceive, for the first time, what our lives really mean. Nietzsche affords us the deathbed view while we are still in the midst of our lives.

While Nietzsche posits a scientific explanation for his theory of eternal recurrence, that is not where its impact lies. Nietzsche's metaphysical claim is: given that matter is finite and time is infinite, the same configurations can be repeated eternally so that our planet, when it disintegrates, continues as energy or quanta of the universe and can form again, repeating its configuration end-lessly. Other configurations can recur again and again as well, even after inter-vals of vast spans of time, so that one lives the identical life repeatedly.

But the existential weight Nietzsche gives the idea of eternal return has far greater significance than any metaphysical claim. Imagine making life decisions from the point of view of Nietzsche's hypothetical: If I had to relive this same life over and over again in all its detail for eternity, how would I choose to live? If we assume his hypothetical—as if it were the first time we have ever lived—at the moment of making crucial decisions, it awakens us to the significance of life choices. It gives pause for thought *at the moment* we make choices of voca-tion, of relationships, and when considering chances taken and not taken.

Nietzsche asks if there is a single moment that you would celebrate to repeat. Eternal recurrence poses the painful question: Has there ever been a moment in your life when you would have welcomed this idea and uttered, "never have I heard anything more divine," or does the thought of repeating your life countless times only bring forth the cosmic shudder?

With eternal recurrence, Nietzsche reveals a perspective that allows for a true reckoning about the authenticity of one's life, a view usually reserved for the deathbed. In one case it can be life-affirming, in another, devastating, the "most abysmal thought." His rendition of this long-standing idea of eternal return offers both an injunction and an imperative.[36]

∾ Epilogue: The Cosmic Mystery

It would be a mistake to suppose that with his "announcement" of the death of God Nietzsche had ended the inquiry. The "death of God" for Nietzsche meant the end of the limited deistic concept prevailing in Western tradition. He was pursuing the inquiry that is at the heart of philosophy. It is the question that speaks to the mystery of existence. Physicists are still asking the funda-mental questions and exploring the origins of the universe. As Dennis Overbye, the deputy science editor of the *New York Times*, said in a recent article on Einstein:

> To Einstein, God was a code word for the mystery and grandeur of the universe, a wellspring of awe, a reminder that there was something at the core of existence that all his equations could only graze. . . .[37]

∾ NOTES

1.   Quoted by Sylvia Nasar in *A Beautiful Mind* (New York: Simon and Schuster, 1998), 58.
2.   Walter Kaufmann, *The Portable Nietzsche* (New York: Viking Press, 1954), 12.

3. Nietzsche, *The Gay Science,* trans. Walter Kaufmann (New York: Vintage Books, 1974), 182.
4. *The Portable Nietzsche,* trans. Walter Kaufmann (New York: Viking Press, 1954), 124. Nietzsche has made this statement before *Zarathustra,* most notably in Section 125, as well as in Section 108 of *The Gay Science,* which was published in 1882 just prior to *Zarathustra.* Parts One and Two of *Zarathustra* were published separately in 1883.
5. Archibald MacLeish, *J.B.* (Boston: Houghton Mifflin, 1958), 153.
6. William Barrett, *Irrational Man* (New York: Doubleday-Anchor Books, 1958), 165.
7. Ibid.
8. Jean-Paul Sartre (1905–1980), French existentialist philosopher and writer.
9. Sartre, *Existentialism and Human Emotions,* 21.
10. Ibid., 23.
11. Why go to the French language rather than another? Kaufmann explains this choice in the following way: "Nietzsche's emergence from the influence of Wagner, who extolled everything Germanic and excoriated the French, was marked by an attitude more Francophile than of any other major German writer—at least since Leibniz (1646–1716), who preferred to write in French. Nietzsche saw himself as the heir of the French *moralistes.* . . ." Walter Kaufmann, ed., Preface, *Toward a Genealogy of Morals* (New York: Vintage Books, 1969), 5.
12. Nietzsche, *Toward a Genealogy of Morals,* 10.
13. "Thus Spoke Zarathustra," *The Portable Nietzsche,* 202.
14. Ibid., 129.
15. See Walter Kaufmann, *Nietzsche* (Princeton: Princeton University Press, 1974), 128.
16. Ibid.
17. Ibid., 128.
18. I am especially indebted in this section to William Barrett's insightful commentary on Nietzsche and Kierkegaard in *Irrational Man.*
19. Barrett, *Irrational Man,* 133.
20. Ibid.
21. Nineteenth-century Danish existentialist philosopher (1813–1855).
22. Ibid.
23. The Crystal Palace covered almost nineteen acres and housed "The Exposition of Industry of All Nations" in London in 1851, where new inventions were among the exhibits. It symbolized the progress of technology and its promise for the future. That idea extends beyond the

progress of technology to belief in social progress and the rationality of humankind as the instrument to end wars and discord. This idea offered the promise of a better future for humankind, namely, that through social and political reform and revolution, utopian societies would come into being and change the nature of human relations.

24. Barrett, *Irrational Man*, 159.

25. Nietzsche, *Unpublished Notes,* cited by Arthur C. Danto, *Nietzsche as Philosopher*, 228.

26. Nietzsche, *Beyond Good and Evil,* 211, cited by Danto in *Nietzsche as Philosopher*.

27. A philosophy that proposes that the basis of all reality, all of nature and the cosmos, is sheer will. The German philosopher Arthur Schopenhauer is the foremost voluntarist.

28. Kaufmann, *Nietzsche,* 16.

29. David Hume (1711–1776), Scottish philosopher, the foremost empiricist, casts doubt on knowledge founded on a priori truths, truths not based on experience. Metaphysical truths such as the existence of God or causality are thus suspect. Scientific method as the sole route to truth is the outcome of his philosophy of skepticism.

30. Nietzsche, *Thus Spoke Zarathustra, The Portable Nietzsche,* 122–123. Nietzsche's prophet is warned by the saint of the danger of sharing his new wisdom with the populace at large. In the Prologue of this work, Zarathustra has just descended from the mountain.

> "No stranger to me is this wanderer: many years ago he passed this way, Zarathustra he was called, but he has changed. At that time you carried your ashes to the mountains; *would you now carry your fire into the valleys? Do you not fear to be punished as an arsonist? . . .*" [italics mine]. Zarathustra has changed, Zarathustra has become a child, and Zarathustra is an awakened one; what do you now want among the sleepers? . . .
> Zarathustra answered: "I love man."
> "Why," asked the saint, "did I go into the forest and the desert? Was it not because I loved man all-too-much? . . . *Love of man would kill me*" [italics mine].
> Zarathustra answered: "Did I speak of love? I bring men a gift." . . .
> "Give them nothing!" said the saint. . . . And if you want to give them something, give no more than alms, and let them beg for that!"
> "No," answered Zarathustra, "I given no alms. For that I am not poor enough." . . .
> "Then see to it that they accept your treasures. *They are suspicious of hermits and do not believe that we come with gifts. Our steps sound too lonely through the streets,*" [italics mine].

31. Ibid., "On the Three Metamorphoses," 138.

32. Ibid., 154.

33. William Barrett, *Irrational Man*, 160.

34. Nietzsche, "On the Tree on the Mountainside," *The Portable Nietzsche*, 156.

35. Barrett, *Irrational Man*, 168.

36. Nietzsche, *The Gay Science, The Portable Nietzsche*, 101.

37. Dennis Overbye, "Did God Have a Choice: The Universe Is Knowable Up to a Point," *New York Times Magazine*, April 19, 1999, 180.

~ CHRONOLOGY

1818	Arthur Schopenhauer's *The World as Will and Representation*
1843	Søren Kierkegaard's *Either/Or*
1844	birth of Friedrich Nietzsche in Röcken, eastern Germany, son and grandson of Protestant ministers
1859	publication of Darwin's *Origin of Species*
1869	after studying at Bonn and Leipzig, Nietzsche is appointed professor of philology at the University of Basel at age twenty-four, the youngest person ever to win such a position
1870	served as a medical orderly in the Prussian army
1872	*The Birth of Tragedy*
1874	Richard Wagner, friend of Nietzsche, completes *The Ring of the Nibelungs*
1879	Nietzsche resigns his teaching post because of his poor health
1883	parts 1 and 2 of *Thus Spoke Zarathustra*
1886	*Beyond Good and Evil*
1887	*The Genealogy of Morals*
1889	collapses in Turin, committed to an asylum
1890–1900	cared for by his mother and his sister
1900	dies in Weimar

~ SUGGESTED READINGS

Barrett, W. *Irrational Man*. New York: Doubleday, 1958.

———. *What Is Existentialism?* New York: Grove Press, 1964.

Danto, A.C. *Nietzsche as Philosopher*. New York: Macmillan, 1965.

Dostoevsky, F. *Notes from Underground* and *The Gambler*. Translated by Jane Kentish. New York: Oxford University Press, 1991.

Heidegger, M. *Being and Time*. Translated by John Macquarrie and Edward Robinson. New York: Harper & Row, 1962.

————. *Nietzsche.* 2 vols. Translated by David Farrell Krell. San Francisco: HarperCollins, 1991.

Kaufmann, Walter. *Existentialism from Dostoevsky to Sartre.* New York: Meridian Books, 1956.

————. *Nietzsche.* Princeton: Princeton University Press, 1974.

————. Translated by and gen. ed. *Basic Writings of Nietzsche.* New York: Random House, Modern Library Giant, 1968.

————. Translated by and gen. ed. *The Portable Nietzsche.* New York: Viking Press, 1954.

Magnus, B. and K.M. Higgins, gen. eds. *The Birth of Tragedy* and *The Case of Wagner.* Translated by Walter Kaufmann. New York: Vintage Books, 1967.

————*The Cambridge Companion to Nietzsche.* Cambridge: Cambridge University Press 1996.

Nietzsche, F. *Beyond Good and Evil.* Translated by Walter Kaufmann. New York: Vintage Books, 1989.

————. *The Gay Science.* Translated by Walter Kaufmann. New York: Vintage Books, 1974.

————. *On the Genealogy of Morals and Ecce Homo.* Translated by Walter Kaufmann. New York: Viking, 1967.

Rorty, R. *Objectivity, Relativism, and Truth.* New York: Cambridge University Press, 1991.

Sartre, J.-P. *Existentialism and Human Emotions.* Translated by Bernard Frechtman and Hazel Barnes. New York: Philosophical Library, 1957.

————. *Saint Genet: Actor and Martyr.* Translated by Bernard Frechtman. New York: Mentor, 1963.

CHAPTER 14

James
Philosophy as Practice

Gail E. Linsenbard

∿ Preview

Is there an American philosophy? William James is the best-known American philosopher and one of the creators of a philosophical outlook called "pragmatism." James believes philosophy begins and ends with human experience. Philosophers should examine all kinds of experiences and ask what they mean and how they fit in with other experiences. Other philosophers had emphasized experience, but James includes a much wider range. He carefully and willingly studies emotions, moods, habits, and even unusual experiences he himself didn't have, such as religious conversion and psychic encounters. All are part of human experience. Philosophy not only grows out of experience, it must have some practical application to experience. James says philosophy may be interesting for its own sake, but its true value lies in its power to make us better people. In fact, he says, the truth of a belief depends on its conse-

quences. Beliefs and actions must be tested by their outcomes, pragmatists say. Wisdom consists of being open to the widest possible range of experiences and being able to reconcile apparent conflicts. (The Editor)

∿ Introduction

> All I can tell you is the thought that with me outlasts all others, and onto which, like a rock, I find myself washed up when the waves of doubt are weltering over all the rest of the world; and that is the thought of my having a will, and of my belonging to a brotherhood of men possessed of a capacity for pleasure and pains of different kinds. . . . And if we have to give up all hope of seeing into the purposes of God, or to give up theoretically the idea of final causes . . . , we can, by our will, make the enjoyment of our brothers stand us in the stead of a final cause. . . .
>
> *(Letters, I:147–148)*[1]

It is difficult to find in the history of ideas a philosopher who expresses more sympathy, sentiment, and humanity than William James. James wanted philosophy to be "brought home" to living, experiencing human beings who live in a world that is often dangerous and uncertain. Any adequate philosophy, he insisted, should endeavor to be accessible and genuinely felt by as many people as possible. In all of James' philosophical writings, the idea of philosophy as a way of living is repeatedly emphasized; he was deeply committed to the view that the value of philosophy lies in the real, felt, and practical difference it can make in the actual lives of human beings. In emphasizing the value of philosophy as practice, James was a public philosopher who addressed himself much more to ordinary people than to specialists or other philosophers.

James repudiated those scientific and philosophical views that claimed to have special access to "Truth" or "Reality," and he regarded with suspicion and rancor attempts by philosophers and scientists to remove themselves and their theories from the concrete, lived experiences of persons. He had little patience for academic debates about the origin of the universe or how we know for certain that we are not dreaming. Science and philosophy, he held, are not closed systems severed from the ordinary experiences of persons; scientific theories and philosophical claims, as human constructions, are fallible and must thus be regarded as provisional. James held that the pretension of science to offer definitive or "final" results is itself unscientific, and he claimed that all truths, including those of science and philosophy, must lend themselves to revision and modification in the face of changing facts and compelling evidence. He loathed all forms of dogmatism as pernicious and futile attempts to close an open universe. Hence James held that the philosopher's task is to investigate, probe, question, classify, wonder about, and, no less, celebrate a vastly open and richly textured world. James' own success in this is evident in his lifelong commitment to philosophy as both a theoretical and a practical pursuit. James practiced philosophy as much as he wrote about it. Not only was he a teacher of philosophy, he was also a public lecturer who spoke on various philosophical topics throughout his career.

In his many lectures and writings, James argues repeatedly that, rather than offer fixed, final answers or solutions to difficult questions and problems, philosophy should attempt to assume the more useful task of helping people to feel more at home in the midst of their sensed, or felt, homelessness. "Particular philosophies," he said, "are the expressions of man's intimate character,"[2] and all philosophies, he observed, share a concern to express our most deeply felt needs, even though many seem to have lost their vision along the way: "We crave alike to feel more truly at home with (the universe), and to contribute our mite to its amelioration."[3] It is clear, then, that for James, philosophy is necessarily and inextricably linked with human concerns and interests.

Notwithstanding the notable influences on his thought, James was a profoundly creative and original philosopher. As a psychologist and philosopher, his lifelong pursuit was to describe and understand mental processes and their relation to the world. Early on, he adopted a "pragmatic attitude" that sought the meaning and truth of our beliefs and concepts in their felt effects or consequences. But it would be wrong to suppose that James was a crude consequentialist, finding meaning *only* in the results or ends of our actions and intentions. Pragmatism, the doctrine for which he is famous, states quite rightly that anything we regard as meaningful, good, or true must be meaningful, good, or true *for someone, somewhere, and in some practically discernible* way.

In conceiving of philosophy as practice, James was always mindful of finding ways to improve the lives of others. He despised complacency as much as he hated social injustice and cruelty. His intellectual curiosity was coupled with a deep moral sense, and he resolved early on to live a moral life and to convince others why morality mattered. For James, the need to relieve suffering or remedy injustice was as much a part of human experience as gravity or digestion and should be acknowledged in any realistic philosophy. He fought hard for the tolerance of difference and celebrated the particularity and multiplicity of persons. James was in fact both a philosopher and a cultural critic who, although immersed in the academic world, criticized scientism and academic professionalism as elitist, arrogant, and false. In fact, James was painfully aware of his own privileged and elite position in society. As the grandson of one of America's wealthiest businessmen, he worried that his vision of humanity could not authentically represent those whose lives were most deeply impoverished. James' concern about the experiences of others only underscores his intellectual honesty, deep sense of humanity, large sensitivity, and fellow feeling.

Throughout his life, James eloquently and passionately defended the individual against what he took to be a tendency in science and philosophy to reduce or ignore human experiences. One might say, then, that James' principal philosophical interest was to understand and sympathize with all people's lived experiences, trials, and tribulations. On his view, philosophy should function in a way that brings together what different people have to offer, and that helps individuals survive and flourish in a contingent world with real possibilities and real dangers.

~ James' Life and Career

William James was born in 1842 in New York. His mother, Mary Robertson Walsh James, was an intelligent, witty, and caring woman. Her even temper and emotional stability provided the James family with a needed and invaluable sense of balance; she was, as it were, the "rock" of the household to whom all family members turned for emotional support. James' father, Henry Sr., was an opinionated and temperamental man whose deep religious feeling and keen intelligence exercised a permanent influence on William. Precocious and willful, young William idolized his father and sought his approval and praise at every turn, which were not always forthcoming.

The elder James was a philosopher in his own right, often seriously engaged in metaphysical and theological problems of the day. But his religious sentiment was neither dogmatic nor orthodox; he was principally concerned with spiritual reform and progress. In fact, he was deeply attracted to the Transcendentalism of Emerson and Thoreau, and enthusiastically passed their teachings on to his children as the "new Gospel" of reform. Emerson was among the various guests received in the James household, where lively conversation and spirited debate occurred on a regular basis.

The oldest of five children, William was a loving brother who frequently offered counsel to his younger siblings. He was especially close to his younger brother, Henry James, the novelist, and his younger sister, Alice James, the diarist. The children's father believed that a truly proper education should take place on both sides of the Atlantic. This experience gave William an extraordinarily cosmopolitan upbringing; in addition to being taught at the family dinner table, from 1855 to 1866 James studied in schools in England, France, Germany, and Switzerland. He soon developed a deep appreciation for European culture and letters that would later inspire multiple trips abroad. In addition to his native English, James would soon command fluency in both French and German. While studying in Paris, James made frequent visits to the Louvre and developed a strong interest in painting. In 1860 he went to Newport to study painting formally, but soon abandoned it at his father's insistence that painting was a frivolous and irresponsible pursuit; in fact, James himself felt that he could never become more than a mediocre artist.

In 1861 James decided to redirect his keen intelligence and fertile imagination to the field of science and enrolled in the Lawrence Scientific School at Harvard to study chemistry and, later, comparative anatomy and physiology. While at the Lawrence School, James became intrigued with the evolutionary naturalism of Darwin, whose insights he would soon apply to his own work on mental processes and relations. Although because of his poor health James did not enlist in the Union Army when the Civil War broke out, his younger brothers did. He was therefore strongly engaged in the conflict. In 1864 James entered Harvard Medical School, although without the intention of ever practicing medicine. He interrupted his medical studies in 1865 to join an expedition to Brazil with the famous scientist Louis Agassiz. But he contracted a viral infection similar to smallpox and suffered from debilitating eye problems that would disturb him for the rest of his life. During this journey, James became increasingly preoccupied with philosophical questions and problems that led him to believe he was more adapted to the speculative, reflective life.

James, like his father, fought depression for much of his life, and he also suffered from a nervous disorder that contributed to his fragile sense of physical and psychological well-being. In 1869, the year he received his medical degree from Harvard, James' depression became quite acute, and a year later culminated in a full-blown and lengthy emotional breakdown, at which time he experienced profound melancholy, loneliness, and utter impotence. During his collapse, James found himself in the midst of an intellectual crisis that convinced him that a "philosophical cast of mind" was indispensable in offering him a purpose in life and a reason for being. Philosophy, he firmly believed, could become for him a gospel of hope and a way of salvation.

James' emotional and intellectual crisis is important philosophically because it involved him in a mental conflict between the scientific and religious world views, both of which he found deeply compelling. He wondered how he could harmonize the demands of science, which viewed the world and its entities in a mechanistic, deterministic way, with the demands of religion, which viewed God as the creator of the world and allowed for free will. It was at this critical time that James encountered the French philosopher Charles Renouvier (1815–1903), whose ideas persuaded him that he was intellectually justified in believing in free will. Following his study of Renouvier, James announced that his first act of free will would simply be to believe in free will. Despite Darwin's undeniable impact and the pervasive sway of science, James held steadfastly to the view that our fate is not decided by biological or physical science; the view that the universe is composed of nothing but matter in motion governed by deterministic laws was deeply repugnant to him. James' encounter with Renouvier proved to be a profound turning point in his career because he was now committed more than ever before to the study of philosophy as a way of changing himself and the world. James thus fully embraced philosophy as a result of his desire to overcome the felt opposition between science, which denied free will, and his more religious, humanistic inclinations, which allowed it. Early on, then, James nurtured a deeply humanistic interest, which supported his commitment to both philosophical and religious problems.

In 1872 James became an instructor of comparative anatomy and physiology at Harvard, where he remained until his retirement in 1907. Although he maintained an interest in physiology throughout his life, he became increasingly fascinated with psychology and philosophy. At Harvard he wrote his enormously influential textbook *The Principles of Psychology* (1890) and established the first psychology laboratory in the United States. Thus, he was one of the founders of the discipline as an independent science. He was also interested in psychopathology and parapsychology; both, he thought, deserved serious study in their own right. In 1884 he organized the Society for Psychic Research in Boston and remained a loyal member until his death.

In 1878 James married Alice Gibbens, an intelligent, strong, and devoted woman who greatly appreciated James' sympathy and sincere humanity. James' marriage to Alice marked an important turning point in what had for him been an emotionally tumultuous and unstable life. He said that marriage offered him a calm and repose that he had never before known. James' marriage, coupled with his firmly established reputation at Harvard, allowed him finally to emerge from a period of uncertainty and instability; notwithstanding frequent bouts of depression and physical malaise, he felt that he could at long last truly enjoy his life.

Although James was often restless and irritable, he was able to establish strong, lasting friendships and was loved and admired by many people. His earliest friendships at Cambridge were with Chauncey Wright, Oliver Wendell Holmes, Jr., and the brilliant philosopher and mathematician Charles Sanders Peirce, to whom James dedicated his influential essay "The Will to Believe" (1896). In the early 1870s Peirce, Wright, and James organized the Metaphysical Club (ironically named to suggest their skeptical attitude toward metaphysics as it was then conceived) for philosophical discussion and analysis. In addition to many strong collegial friendships, James established close working relationships with his graduate students, who deeply appreciated his invaluable mentorship. Among James' most gifted students were Gertrude Stein and W.E.B. Dubois.

In 1907 James retired from teaching but continued to write and lecture widely. During his retirement James developed a keen interest in mysticism, and engaged once again in psychical research, but this time with an emphasis on unorthodox, "superstitious" extrascientific investigation. He was especially interested in the experience of what he called "mystical over-beliefs," those beliefs for which we have no empirical warrant. After suffering for some time from heart disease, James died at home in 1910. Alice James noted in her diary that her husband "had worn himself out."

∿ James' Psychology

James' philosophy is inextricably linked with his psychology; the two interests influence each other. In fact, he regarded philosophical inquiry as psychologically "healthy" and "fit." He investigated the motives that lead people to philosophize, and in 1879 reported (in "The Sentiment of Rationality") that people have two kinds of motives: theoretical or logical and practical or emotional. Philosophers seek a coherent world view not only from pure intellectual curiosity, but also out of an emotional need to feel secure and competent. Both kinds of motives give people standards by which to judge beliefs. James thought philosophers should ground their theories more directly on the facts of everyday experience, and thus psychology becomes a starting point for philosophy.

The subject matter of psychology is mental life or mental events—perceptions, thoughts, memories, desires, emotions, decisions, actions, habits—and the proper method of studying mental events is to observe them in oneself. When you face a choice and make a decision, what actually happens? What images go through your mind, what feelings, what changes in you between indecision and decision? Observing one's own mind is called "introspection," and James believed such observations were just as important as other scientists' observations of stars or animals or electricity. In fact, at Harvard, James experimented with various drugs to observe their effect on his own consciousness.

Using the introspective method, James described what he called the "stream of consciousness." Even though we use the words "thought," "feeling," "choice," and so on, consciousness is not made up of discrete pieces, or atoms, as earlier philosophers had assumed. It is more like a stream; each instant has a focus, perhaps, but it is strongly colored by memories of the past and anticipations of the future. James challenged the traditional emphasis on seeing and thinking as keys to the mind. We actually spend more time doing and making, trying and reacting, than sitting and thinking. According to James, the primary function of the mind is to enable us to reach our goals and solve practical problems, not to contemplate objects.

Strongly influenced by the evolutionary theory of Darwin, he vividly described the adaptive and selective function of the mind. He held that all of our feelings and emotions—including religious ones—are purposive because they assist us in surviving and discovering what the world is really like. If we assume, as evolutionary theory does, that each part of reality has a particular function that is good *for something*, then it is up to us to discover what that something is. The human mind, like a bat's wing or a giraffe's neck, is an evolved adaptation to features of the environment, and by studying the mind we can better understand the world that shaped it. In this sense, James held that the world itself must reflect our truest experiences, and by "truest" he meant those we have come to trust most because they have served us well in the past.

James believed philosophers can draw conclusions about the nature of reality from observing the mind in action, that is, from direct experience. He claimed that consciousness was correlated with—but not reduced to—certain brain processes. While brain states do indeed give rise to mental states, our mental life is *no less real;* our mental life, he observes, arising as it does out of physical states, can directly alter the physical world. In fact, he held that consciousness could not be reduced to either immaterial substance or matter. But he also argued that consciousness is not an entity or a faculty of the brain. James understood the mind-body problem as a problem about the nature and function of consciousness and its relation to the body and brain. Arguing against a dualistic account of the person, he held that, fundamentally, we are metaphysically complex organisms and the subjects of multiple and varied experiences. Our concepts of physical objects (such as chairs or brains) and mental entities (such as thoughts or feelings) are both constructed from the more fundamental experiences of the stream of consciousness. He claimed, then, that while thoughts most certainly do exist, they do not exist in the manner of material or immaterial substance.

ᴄ⁄ **Free Will and Morality**

One of James' most basic convictions was that experience is our only source of information about reality. But experience for James is more than visual perception or quantitative science. If an experience is a common human experience, then it is just as reliable evidence about the world as any other experience. Championing freedom against the deterministic claims of science, James insisted that the will is itself effective in the world and that we experience it as such.

To defend his view, he wrote "The Dilemma of Determinism" (1884). Determinists believe that everything that happens is completely caused by prior events. Whatever happens had to happen, they say, and could not have occurred differently. Thus, our belief in future possibilities and free will is illusory. The history of the universe up to the present time has strictly determined the future, although we don't know what it will be. But it is also a fact, James points out, that we feel regrets, for example, about one man murdering another. We feel that things should have been different. Determinists say that such feelings are mistaken. The murder was the result of innumerable prior circumstances and was therefore necessary. But now determinists face a dilemma, because they also claim that the feeling of regret is caused and necessary. Our feeling of regret tells us that the murder was wrong and unacceptable, not a necessary strand in the fabric of the world. Insofar as regret is explained and logical, the murder is wrong and bad. But insofar as the murder is explained and logical, the *regret* is wrong and bad. The world, as determinists picture it, is "fatally unreasonable" and "absurd," at war with itself, according to James. "It must be a place of which either sin or error forms a necessary part," he says. It is more rational to reject determinism, accept real possibilities in the future, and picture the world as open.

James was committed to finding beliefs that could support a meaningful life. He claimed that in order for our moral life to be meaningful, the belief in human freedom was necessary. He insisted quite straightforwardly that his metaphysics adapt to his ethics. In "The Dilemma of Determinism" he says:

> If a certain formula for expressing the nature of the world violates my moral demand, I shall feel as free to throw it overboard, or at least to doubt it, as if it disappointed my demand for uniformity of sequence, for example; the one demand being, so far as I can see, quite as subjective and emotional as the other is.[4]

Strictly speaking, he held that disparate "causes" and "effects" are really fictions reflective of the prevailing tendency in science and philosophy to overintellectualize human experience. James asks, "What difference would it make if we believe that the will is free rather than determined?" He replies that believing in free will makes all the difference since, without it, our undeniable experience of ourselves as responsible would be completely undermined and the moral life would be impossible. James not only makes the point, as Kant previously did, that in order to act morally it is necessary to act under the idea of freedom, but he also claims that freedom is itself a fact of human experience. Liberty and freedom, then, are at the center of his moral philosophy; an act has no ethical quality unless it is chosen from among several other possibilities—unless we could have done other than what we did. James maintained, then, that our very capacity to make moral judgments itself implies that determinism is false and freedom is real.

James, intent on rescuing free will from the clutches of scientific determinism, argued that our identity is not immutably fixed or static; it is *created* by us on the basis of our experiences and encounters with the world. Thus, James argues for a Promethean self that is always self-making; choices and actions not only reflect the world as it is experienced, but also create value and, hence, change in the world: our choices and actions, he held, have real, concrete consequences in the world.

Equally important to James' moral view are human ideals, most notably the ideals of freedom, equality, and unity. James criticizes the Platonic separation of the Good from the world of experience and claims that ideals are made real through the efforts of our will. To act morally, for James, is to achieve a synthesis among multiple and diverse moral ideals, and the philosopher's task is to show how this may be best accomplished:

> So far as the world resists reduction to the form of unity, so far as ethical propositions seem unstable, so far does the philosopher fail of his ideal. The subject matter of his study is the ideals he finds existing in the world; the purpose which guides him is this ideal of his own, of getting them into a certain form.[5]

In other words, he held that to live morally, we ought to seek to respect an individual's end as our own and satisfy as many ends as we can. He was especially sensitive to the plight of those who had been excluded from society because they lacked the intellectual and material resources to participate fully. James thought that the most urgent question philosophy could ask is "How can we build genuine cooperation and consensus that will allow the world to become more truly human?" His preoccupation with this question led him in his lecture "On a Certain Blindness in Human Beings" (1897) to offer an argument for respecting differences. Because humans tend to be self-absorbed in pursuing their own affairs, he observed, we are afflicted by a shortsightedness or blindness to the needs and feelings of others. Before we can acquire genuine respect for differences, we must first earnestly confront our own shortcoming of selfishness as a human fact and then try to move beyond it.

In his lecture "The Moral Philosopher and the Moral Life" (1897), James rejects as falsely reductive the view that we ultimately desire and seek pleasure and insists that our moral lives are enormously complex and intricate. He defends humanistic ideals as our most important moral judgments, and argues that human choice is wholly compatible with the authority of objective moral values that we collectively sustain as a community whose fundamental interests converge.

Thus James' moral philosophy is committed to the importance of believing in and serving moral ideals. He earnestly believed that through political and social reform the moral ideals of humanism could take root and grow. The moral philosopher, he noted, should passionately commit herself to the happiness of humankind as an "outlasting cause." Our lives become significant when we take felt risks, face known obstacles, and commit ourselves to real causes that will have a life beyond ours:

> The most characteristically and peculiarly moral judgments that a man is ever called on to make are in unprecedented cases and lonely emergencies, where no popular maxims can avail, and the hidden oracle alone can speak; and it speaks often in favor of conduct quite unusual, and suicidal as far as gaining popular approbation goes.[6]

One difficulty that arises in James' moral philosophy is his insistence that all human ideals and perceptions of reality must be, as it were, taken in and validated. Some critics have argued that his moral philosophy is especially in trouble because it seems to embrace a strong form of relativism in allowing a voice to even the most undesirable ideals. It seems certain, however, that James does not in fact endorse moral relativism, even though he might sometimes speak as though he did. If we refer back to the quotation in the Introduction, we may appreciate that James wishes to emphasize the fact that we live in a human world with human problems: we must count on each other if we are to live in a more or less humane world. But this manifestly does not mean that anything goes. James is simply reminding us that the only court of appeal in terms of action is a human one, and that together we forge values for or against ourselves: "Whether a God exists or no God exists...we form at any rate an ethical republic here below."[7]

⟿ Religion

We have seen that James struggled to allow his natural confidence and conviction to master his equally natural skepticism and doubt. It is therefore not surprising that he could make room for what he called the "religious hypothesis" in his philosophy. In his most seminal works on religion, "The Will to Believe" and *The Varieties of Religious Experience,* James forcefully argues for our *right* to believe in God and the immortality of the soul despite the fact that we have insufficient evidence to ground such beliefs. In "The Will to Believe" he claimed that, where rational grounds are absent, we are nonetheless justified in believing on the basis of our passions, which are also reasonable: "Our passional nature not only lawfully may, but must, decide an option between propositions, whenever it is a genuine option that cannot by its nature be decided on intellectual grounds."[8]

In this area James was greatly influenced by Kant, who had earlier stated the importance of showing the limits of science in order to make room for faith. Religion, said James, is a vital human resource because of its ability to satisfy human needs, comfort human hearts, and offer hopeful expectations in a world that is often fraught with uncertainty, despair, and anguish. Religious experience and faith, he held, are "life-answering," and hence, given his Darwinian perspective, our "most important function." Certainly James thought that the pragmatic value of religious faith was readily apparent; the convincing evidence for religious truth, he held, was its practical and healthy effects on people (with some avoidable exceptions). Religion was thus deemed by James to offer the kind of option for people that he described as "live," "forced," and "momentous."

While James himself did not experience the presence of God, he felt justified in accepting the testimony of others concerning God's presence in their experiences. The testimony of others, he thought, was of singular importance because it demonstrated "that we can experience union with *something* larger than ourselves and in that union find our greatest peace."[9] James vigorously defended the "God hypothesis," then, as not merely needful but legitimate. We have seen that James' philosophy favors a view of persons that embraces all possible experiences. He was especially interested in the ethical and religious experiences of the "whole man," and argued in *The Varieties of Religious Experience* that religious experiences are neither mysterious nor unanalyzable. He described conversion, mystical experiences, neurotic religiosity, and other religious phenomena in the same perceptive, open-minded way that he had described aspects of consciousness in *The Principles of Psychology*.

James avoided the theological problem of how to reconcile the existence of evil in the world with an infinitely good and merciful God by holding that "the only God worthy of the name *must* be finite." In claiming that God is finite, he declared that God must be acquitted of responsibility for failing to intervene to prevent evil: "when we cease to admire or approve what the definition of a deity implies," as many of us are inclined to do when God ceases to intervene in the face of suffering or evil, "we end by deeming that deity incredible."[10] A finite deity, James claims, is compatible with religious experience and, moreover, *needs* our cooperation in reducing suffering and fighting against evil in the world. According to James, then, we are neither doomed to hell fire nor saved in heaven; our "salvation" is strictly contingent on the cooperative enterprise we have with God to create a more just world. For James, religious belief supplants our moral will and encourages us to actively and collaboratively fight against injustice, cruelty, and oppression.

Not surprisingly, James found institutional forms of Christian worship disagreeable and artificial. As "secondhand" interpretations, orthodox religious services were far removed from the direct experiences of persons. The Bible, he said, is a human book, and is not an authoritative source of truth superseding human observations and feelings. While James himself had no dogmatic or institutional allegiance, he is probably one of the most spiritually aware philosophers the world has ever known. He certainly felt a deep spiritual presence and faith in his own life and was eager to share his feelings and views about his experiences with others. James maintained that "the best things are the most eternal things," and he thought that we would be better off if we believed them to be true. Religious belief, then, is "cashed out" in terms of its satisfactory consequences for persons and for the universe; we may actually "save" the universe and ourselves, he said, if we only believe that it is possible and worthy of our efforts.

James held that there are many gospels of faith, and no single one may be privileged as the "true" one. What is more, he said, the varieties of religious experience include mystical and supernatural experiences no less than more orthodox expressions. James himself was especially interested in mysticism and, indeed, regarded his own views about it as one room among others in the open hotel of humanity.

❧ Pragmatism

From the beginning of his career, James employed certain concepts and principles, which he gradually organized into a philosophical position he called "pragmatism." It is important to note that James conceived of pragmatism as an extension of British empiricism. In an 1898 public address on "Philosophical Conceptions and Practical Results," James identifies pragmatism with the empirical method of Locke, Berkeley, and Hume. He also credits his friend and colleague, Peirce, as the first to actually formulate the principle of pragmatism, despite the fact that Peirce strenuously disagreed with James' characterization of it as a theory of truth.[11]

What is pragmatism, according to James? First and foremost, he says, it is a philosophical method for testing and confirming ideas. He tells us that pragmatism is "a method for settling metaphysical disputes that might otherwise be interminable," and that it does not stand for any special results" but seeks to accommodate all approaches to truth that will acknowledge the "tangled, muddy" reality of "concrete, personal experience."[12] In *Pragmatism*, James distinguishes between tender-minded and tough-minded approaches in the philosophical quest for truth. Tender-minded thinkers are inclined to be rationalist, intellectualist, idealistic, firmly wedded to principles, religious, defenders of freewill, and dogmatic. Tough-minded thinkers tend to be lovers of fact, committed to pluralism, and skeptical of religion and free will. James proposes pragmatism as a method that can synthesize tough and tender-minded approaches in philosophy. But *how* does he think it can do this? As a philosophical method, pragmatism interprets concepts and theories in terms of their consequences, or what James sometimes refers to as their "cash-value." The pragmatist wants to know what *practical difference* it would make if this world view be the true one:

> What difference would it practically make to anyone if this notion rather than that notion were true? If no practical difference can be traced, then the alternatives mean practically the same thing and all dispute is idle.[13]

Here James is saying that if we can find no discernible difference between two possible statements, concepts, or theories, then we may conclude that there *is* no difference and that the dispute is merely verbal. As a method, then, pragmatism relies on the actual, real difference between competing views or theories; it attempts to ascertain what exactly would be at stake if we were to give up one theory in favor of the other.

James held that pragmatism is more than a method for settling philosophical disputes; it is also a theory of meaning and truth:

> The truth of an idea is not a stagnant property inherent in it. Truth *happens* to
> an idea. It *becomes* true, is *made* true by events. Its verity is, in fact, an event, a
> process: the process, namely, of its verifying itself, its *verification*. Its validity is
> the process of *validation*.[14]

"True," James held, names "whatever proves itself to be good in the way of
belief."[15] As a theory of meaning and truth, pragmatism asserts that our ideas
must be capable of being applied to a practical situation in order for them to
be true, meaningful, or instrumental. For example, some scientists wonder if
the universe will expand forever or if, millions of years in the future, it will collapse again into a single point. James asks what difference it would make in
anyone's life to accept one of these theories or the other. If it would make no
difference at all, then the issue isn't simply unimportant; it is meaningless.
James criticized some philosophical ideas of his day (about "the Absolute") on
the grounds that they were meaningless, because the philosophers could not
point to any real effect of believing the theory or not believing it. But James
was careful to add that one must consider what difference it would make to
anyone, not just oneself. Meaning and truth ultimately depend on the community's experience, not only a single individual's experience.

James' view of pragmatism as a theory of truth was enormously controversial. The suggestion that truth "happens" to an idea, which James maintained, or that our ideas "become true" insofar as they "agree" with reality was,
according to James' critics, either seriously dubious or completely false. James'
colleagues, including especially Peirce and Josiah Royce, as well as the two leading British philosophers, G.E. Moore and Bertrand Russell, were harshly critical
of his homespun account of truth as having "cash-value," being "profitable,"
"expedient," and "instrumental." Following heated exchanges at Harvard and
elsewhere, James' colleague F.C.S. Schiller sympathetically noted, "Then for the
first time did I realize the enormous capacity of the philosophic mind for mis-
construing James."[16] For his part, James vigorously defended his pragmatic conception of truth as one that resonates most with our experience:

> An idea that will carry us prosperously forth from any one part of our experi-
> ence to any other part, linking things satisfactorily, working securely, simplify-
> ing, saving labor, is true for just so much, true in so far forth, true
> *instrumentally*.[17]

Upholding his commitment to the primacy of experience, James boldly asserts
that unless an idea, concept, or theory can be translated into what is experienced, it is meaningless. A theory, idea, or world view is true insofar as it is
instrumental to us and "pays off" now and in the future.

James' conception of truth did not in fact break with more orthodox conceptions. In maintaining that truth is rightly ascribed to propositions in language, not to things, James was in good philosophical company. He eagerly endorsed, for example, the correspondence theory of truth, which sees truth as a property of beliefs or judgments that correspond with reality. That is, the proposition "Snow is white" is true if it corresponds with, or accurately represents, a fact in the world. James did, however, break from traditional views in speaking about truth as that which "works," is "profitable," "instrumental," "expedient," "useful," has "cash-value," or "satisfies" in seeking a "resting place" for our ideas. Ideas, according to him, "become true" or "are made true by events." They are said to be true insofar as they are capable of corroboration, verification, and assimilation. James claimed that the process of *determining* correspondence is the essential factor in truth, not the bare correspondence itself. Mere correspondence by itself, independent of human investigations, is an empty abstraction. James does not conceive of truth as being a fixed or static property; rather than elevate truth to some otherworldly, wholly rational status, he insisted that true ideas are simply those that we can verify and confirm in experience; true ideas "work" for us and help us to get along well in the world.

As a theory of truth, James notes that pragmatism is compatible with the way people actually go about developing ideas and beliefs. His view of truth is in this sense naturalistic; truth is a function or habit that exists in beliefs themselves and that leads to satisfactory results. Truth, he held, is best determined by its usefulness in solving real problems. James offers a vivid example to illustrate his meaning: Suppose you are lost in the woods and approach two divergent paths. At the end of one path is a cabin with lights on inside, and at the end of the other there is only darkness and uncertainty. Which path should you take? Given your interest in survival and comfort, you should obviously take the path that leads to the well-lit cabin. This example is simple but to the point; it illustrates how the pragmatic method helps us to choose between two or more possibilities by evaluating the practical consequences of our proposed actions. Thus, true ideas for James are prompted by our interest in survival:

> The importance to human life of having true beliefs about matters of fact is a thing too notorious. We live in a world of realities that can be infinitely useful or infinitely harmful. Ideas that tell us which of them to expect count as true ideas in all this primary sphere of verification, and the pursuit of such ideas is a primary human duty.[18]

In *Pragmatism* James tells us that a large stock of our truths remain provisional and await more complete verification. He notes that less verified truths "form the overwhelmingly large number of truths we live by," and in this sense "truth lives for the most part on a credit system." In order for truth to "work," he says, it must cause the least disturbance to our previously held truths; it must not upset our general stock of beliefs. Moreover, newly acquired truths must not upset our commonsense, shared experience. In this sense, James holds, truth works to the extent that it enables us to synthesize or reconcile our previous beliefs, our new experiences, and other people's experiences. Thus, future truths prove to be both corrective and accommodating. We constantly make adjustments in our set of beliefs.

James emphasized that pragmatism is a way of thinking and learning, not a doctrine. The pragmatic method

> lies in the midst of our theories, like a corridor in a hotel. Innumerable chambers open out of it. In one you may find a man writing an atheistic volume; in the next someone on his knees praying for faith and strength; in a third a chemist investigating a body's properties. In a fourth a system of metaphysics is being shown. But they all own the corridor, and all must pass through it if they want a practicable way of getting into or out of their respective rooms.[19]

Indeed, James finds pragmatism so utterly congenial that he confidently notes, "Every sane and sound tendency in life can be brought under it."[20]

∼ Radical Empiricism and Pluralism

Radical empiricism represents James' belief that experience is ultimately what counts in understanding the world and its inhabitants. What makes James' empiricism "radical" is his willingness to extend it to metaphysics—to the nature of existence and reality. In "The Will to Believe," James notes that radical empiricism is a position that never takes conclusions concerning matters of fact as final; it regards all conclusions as working hypotheses that may very well be modified in the future in light of changing discoveries. James' doctrine of radical empiricism vigorously challenged the old rationalist philosophies of Plato, Kant, and Hegel, as well as the idealism of his contemporaries, Josiah Royce and F.H. Bradley, all of whom argued for a "higher" reality or an "Absolute Being," accessible only to thought rather than perception. James desperately wanted to reorient philosophy from its traditional supposed authority as the arbiter of "Truth" and "Reality." There is no "Truth" out there waiting to be discovered, he said; there is no mysterious kind of Being behind the experienced world.

In *Some Problems of Philosophy*, James contrasts radical empiricism with rationalism. Rationalists, he says, "are men of principles, empiricists the men of facts." While rationalist philosophers move from the whole to its parts (or from universal truth to particular facts), deduce facts from principles, and claim final truth on behalf of their system of deduced conclusions, empiricist philosophers begin with particular experienced facts, move from parts to wholes, and explain principles as inductions from facts. Moreover, the empiricist never claims to have discovered final Truth or Reality. James thus insists that only those matters of fact that are drawn from experience should be debated by philosophers; any subject that falls outside of experience also falls outside the province of philosophy: "the only material we have at our disposal for making a picture of the whole world is supplied by the various portions of the world of which we have already had experience."[21] Thus, for James, human experience must be the necessary starting point of any respectable philosophy.

As a radical empiricist, James attempts to bring philosophy home to the ordinary lives of human beings and distances it from all prevailing ideologies that mistrust the senses. He repudiates the rationalist assumption that reality is fixed and complete, and champions the more modest view that reality is in-the-making in the same way that history is in-the-making. The universe, he says, "is still pursuing its adventures; no one can claim to have the final say concerning what is really real and what is truly true because we are still discovering, learning, and correcting previous views in light of new evidence."[22] James holds that the universe is relentlessly open, loose, unfinished, and receptive to human experiment, trial and error.

It is no wonder that James' conception of philosophy scandalized his more thoroughly dogmatic philosophical colleagues at Harvard and abroad. He himself welcomed disagreement and remarked that their views are but a few among many. Indeed, one thing that distinguishes James as a philosopher is his willingness to think and write on the margins of the mainstream and to embrace a whole set of uncertified possibilities in a world of constant, rapid change. Thus we see that, for James, the empiricist's approach to truth and reality is tentative, modest, careful, respectful of facts and experience, and always open to modification. Since human beings are fallible creatures, they must be willing to hypothesize, test, verify, and modify the claims they make on the basis of their experiences. In essence, then, the philosophical disputations that are really meaningful, in James' view, are those that take the datum of experience, rather than concepts, as fundamental.

Another important feature of James' empiricism is his insistence on the reality of relations. He tells us, for example, that radical empiricism maintains that relations are no less real than the terms united by them. Everything that is experienced, he claims, may be allowed to be real, and a *causal relation* is as real as the events it relates. Here James differs from the empiricism of David Hume, who argued that the mind is unable to perceive causal connections between two disparate events or terms. Since James maintains that relations are themselves real, he does not privilege either the mind or the body as the ultimate principle of reality and thereby renders the classical mind-body problem otiose. What exist ultimately are only pure experiences: they may be interpreted as part of the stream of thought or as physical objects, depending on which interpretation works. Thus radical empiricism asserts the reality of many things, including the relations between things. This notion of "manyness" brings us to James' idea of pluralism.

In *A Pluralistic Universe,* James defines and justifies pluralism and its relation to radical empiricism. He observes that the universe is teeming with variety and fullness, and that we have only begun to appreciate its hidden secrets. James' rejection of abstract, absolute truth fits well with his view that the universe is multifaceted, richly textured, and full of novelty. He held that "reality, life, experience, concreteness, immediacy, use what word you will, exceeds our logic, overflows and surrounds it."[23] James insists that the world resists conformity to an absolute ideal or to logic, with its rigid demands for clarity and cogency. The world, he said, is not logical; it is wholly unpredictable and "untidy." For example, one of the fundamental starting points of Aristotelian logic is the principle that a meaningful statement is either true or false, but not both. ("A or not A.") But sometimes the statement "It is raining" is both true and false. "It's not exactly rain," one wants to say, "but not exactly not-rain, either; it's in between." All too often, the rules of logic just do not apply to our messy reality. James once commented that "technicality spells for me the death of philosophy," a remark that certainly suggests his distaste for mathematics and logic as proper avenues for approaching philosophy.

Just as radical empiricism insists that the lived experiences of individuals have many fringes because they are multiple and varied, so pluralism affirms that the world itself has many tangled fringes. Since there is no universal Mind or Idea under which human experience is neatly gathered and organized, James' world view allows for the existence of real contingency, ambiguity, and chance (what he calls "tychism"). The world, he said, is a scene of perpetual transition and animation; the unity we perceive is often the result of our own efforts to establish connections out of the multiplicity of our experiences. Unity, then, is not immediately given; it is postulated and verified by us. According to James, what is characteristic of our experience is the intermingling and overlapping of one thing with another. While radical empiricism affirms the priority and reality of concrete experiences and relations between experiences, pluralism affirms that the world is full of multiplicity, contingency, variety, novelty, and chance.

In "The Will to Believe" James tells us that "There is but one unconditional commandment, which is that we should seek incessantly, with fear and trembling, so to vote and to act as to bring about the very largest total universe of good which we can see."[24] Here, James' pluralism is evident in our moral lives. Just as there are multiple perspectives and experiences, there are, he held, multiple goods and evils in the world. We ought, to the best of our ability, to promote the former and prevent the latter. In fact, James argued, the promotion of goodness in the world constitutes the psychologically healthy attitude. Since there are multiple perspectives, our own view concerning the good is necessarily limited. It is thus in our interest to listen to other voices with respect to the good so that our own grasp of truth and reality may be enlarged and, hopefully, enhanced.

Toward the end of his life, James extended both his methodological empiricism and his pluralism to larger metaphysical questions concerning religion and the nature of the self and the world: "We are indeed internal parts of God and not external creations, on any possible reading of the panpsychic system."[25] And "Every bit of us at every moment is part and parcel of a wider self . . . it quivers along various radii like the wind-rose on a compass, and the actual in it is continuously one with possibles not yet in our present sight."[26] And finally, "This world may in the last resort, be a block-universe; but on the other hand, it may be a universe only struggling along, not rounded in and closed. Reality may exist distributively, just as it sensibly seems to, after all."[27] The idea of each of us being part of God and of a wider self in an open universe underscores James' belief that the task of the philosopher is to help us to pursue the social, moral, and spiritual ideals of inclusiveness, harmony, and compassion so that we might inhabit a more loving world.

∿ Concluding Remarks

We have seen that James regards pragmatism as a preferred method because it confronts real problems in the world and challenges traditional philosophy's ahistorical, essentialist tendencies that often ignore or deny our actual experiences. To be sure, James' conception of philosophy directly challenges what he regards as philosophy's tendency to remain insular, complacent, and removed from the real problems and injustices people face in the world. In offering pragmatism as a philosophical method and theory of truth and meaning, James hoped to make the world more philosophical, and hence better equipped to solve problems and ameliorate suffering.

We have also seen how James' pragmatism easily embraces a moral philosophy that is immediately tied to a problem-solving practice and a commitment to humanistic ideals. On his view, it is axiomatic that we have urgent moral responsibilities to those who suffer from the cruelties of economic and social injustice. The fact of human suffering, he observed, provides us with incontrovertible proof that there is something seriously "wrong with the world." James believed that a philosophy that removes itself from the business and sufferings of the world is no philosophy at all. Indeed, in our world of ubiquitous social, political, and economic injustice, there is much work to be done. One of the most important task of philosophy, then, is to guide us toward achieving more inclusive ideals that respect multiple points of view and enlarge our sense of humanity.

What makes William James a remarkable philosopher is his genuine and sustained commitment to concrete humanistic ideals. In fact, James himself preferred the word "humanistic" to describe his own philosophical outlook. However, "pragmatism" soon became the widely accepted term that characterized his views. By "humanism" James meant to signify a philosophy that acknowledges the distinctive human element in creating truth, meaning, and value in the world. All that is thought and done for better or for worse, he observed, leaves a human mark:

> To an unascertainable extent our truths are man-made products. Human motives sharpen all our questions, human satisfaction lurk in all our answers, all our formulas have a human twist.[28]

Here James emphasizes his view that truths are human creations and are based on human goals. The human element is utterly pervasive and can only be ignored at great peril to ourselves and to the universe. We have seen that James was a man of combined intellectual and emotional genius who also suffered deep personal anguish and was sometimes thrown into despair. He had great disdain for those conceptions of philosophy that were abstract and removed from the daily concerns of real people. Philosophy for James was a mode of living and a practice; it must, at the very least, demand an account of human experiences and hardships so that alternative ways of life might be conceived that will allow more people to live well. In this regard, James' commitment to bring the value of philosophy as a practice and way of life home to ordinary people is unparalleled in the history of ideas.

∾ NOTES

1. Henry James, ed., *The Letters of William James,* 2 vols. (Boston: Atlantic Monthly Press, 1920).
2. Frederick H. Burkhardt, Fredson Bowers, and Ignas K. Skrupskelis, eds., *The Works of William James,* vol. 4: *A Pluralistic Universe* (Cambridge, MA: Harvard University Press, 1975–1988), 14.
3. Ibid., 11.
4. "The Dilemma of Determinism" in G.H. Bird, ed., *William James: Selected Writings* (London: Everyman, 1995), 272.
5. "The Will to Believe" in Burkhardt et al., vol. 6, 141–142.
6. William James, *The Principles of Psychology,* vol. 2 (New York: Dover, 1950), 672.
7. "The Will to Believe" in Burkhardt et al., vol. 6, 198.

8. Ibid., 200.
9. *The Varieties of Religious Experience* in Burkhardt et al., vol. 13, 413.
10. Ibid., 264–265.
11. Peirce was in fact so furious that James had misunderstood him that he renamed his form of pragmatism "pragmaticism," a term so ugly, he said, that it would not be stolen by bandits.
12. William James, *Pragmatism, and Four Essays from The Meaning of Truth* (Cleveland: Meridian Books, 1963), 17.
13. Ibid., 42.
14. Ibid., 133.
15. Ibid., 42.
16. F.C.S. Schiller, *Must Philosophers Disagree?* (London: Macmillan, 1934), 97.
17. *Pragmatism*, 49.
18. Ibid., 134.
19. Ibid., 32.
20. Ralph Barton Perry, *The Thought and Character of William James* (Nashville: Vanderbilt University Press, 1996), 299.
21. *A Pluralistic Universe* in Burkhardt et al., vol. 4, 9.
22. *Pragmatism*, 123.
23. *A Pluralistic Universe* in Burkhardt et al., vol. 4, 96.
24. "The Will to Believe" in Burkhardt et al., vol. 6, 158.
25. *A Pluralistic Universe* in Burkhardt, et al., vol. 4, 143.
26. Ibid., 131.
27. Ibid., 148.
28. *Pragmatism*, 159.

CHRONOLOGY

1842 born in New York City
1855 begins attending schools in England, France, Germany, and Switzerland
1860 studies painting for one year in Newport ("There is nothing on earth more deplorable than a bad artist.")
1861 enrolls at Harvard, studies chemistry, biology, and anatomy
1865 accompanies scientific expedition to Brazil, contracts smallpox, eye infection
1867 goes to Germany for his health and to study physiology
1869 awarded medical degree from Harvard Medical School

1870   falls into an emotional crisis, studies Renouvier on free will ("My first act of free will shall be to believe in free will.")

1873   begins teaching anatomy at Harvard, later teaches psychology and philosophy

1875   establishes first psychology laboratory in the United States, experiments with drugs to observe their effects on his own consciousness

1878   marries Alice Gibbens ("I have found in marriage a calm and repose I never knew before.")

1879   "The Sentiment of Rationality"

1884   "The Dilemma of Determinism"; organizes the Society for Psychic Research in Boston

1890   publishes *The Principles of Psychology* to wide acclaim

1892   visits twelve-year-old Helen Keller in Boston, accompanied by graduate student W.E.B. Du Bois

1894   writes favorable review of Sigmund Freud and Josef Breuer's first paper on hysteria

1896   "The Will to Believe"

1899   joins the Anti-Imperialist League, protests the Spanish-American War, opposes American policy in the Philippines

1902   delivers the Gifford lectures, published as *Varieties of Religious Experience*

1904   "Does Consciousness Exist?" and "A World of Pure Experience"

1906   delivers lecture "The Moral Equivalent of War" at Berkeley (published in 1910), observes reactions to the San Francisco earthquake

1907   *Pragmatism*

1909   *A Pluralistic Universe*

1910   dies August 26 at vacation home in New Hampshire

∼ SUGGESTED READINGS

Barzun, J. *A Stroll with William James*. New York: Harper & Row, 1983.

Bird, G. *William James*. London: Routledge & Kegan Paul, 1986.

Brennan, B.P. *William James*. New Haven, CT: College and University Press, 1968.

Catkin, G. *William James: Public Philosopher*. Baltimore: Johns Hopkins University Press, 1970.

Lamberth, D.C. *William James and the Metaphysics of Experience*. Cambridge: Cambridge University Press, 1999.

O'Connell, R.J. *William James on the Courage to Believe.* Second Edition. New York: Fordham University Press, 1997.

Putnam, H. *Pragmatism: An Open Question.* Oxford: Blackwell, 1995.

Putnam, R.A., ed. *The Cambridge Companion to William James.* Cambridge: Cambridge University Press, 1997.

Reck, A.J. *Introduction to William James.* Bloomington: Indiana University Press, 1967.

Roth, J.K. *Freedom and the Moral Life: The Ethics of William James.* Philadelphia: Westminster Press, 1969.

Thayer, H.S. *Meaning and Action: A Critical History of Pragmatism.* Indianapolis: Bobbs-Merrill, 1968.

CHAPTER 15

Wittgenstein

Philosophy as Investigating Language

John J. Ross

∿ Preview

Wittgenstein says that the purpose of philosophy is to show the limits of language. In the past, philosophers had focused on the physical world, society, history, consciousness, and other things, but Wittgenstein says that the key to unraveling philosophical questions is analyzing language. In the simplest cases, sentences picture facts. For example, in the sentence "Fred threw the ball," the words refer to the elements of the situation (Fred, ball, throwing), and the arrangement of the words mirrors the arrangement of the elements. But sentences such as "God resides in heaven" or "Justice is the highest virtue" do not picture any observable facts, so they are meaningless, Wittgenstein says. But are they unimportant? Wittgenstein can only give indirect hints about such topics, since he must use language itself. Philosophers should examine the manifold ways we actually use words and families of words. They should study "language games" and show how philosophical puzzles arise when we break the rules without realizing it or try to make words perform jobs they are not suited to perform. (The Editor)

∿ Introduction

It would be hard to overestimate Ludwig Wittgenstein's impact on twentieth-century philosophy. He is credited with being a major influence on two schools of thought: Logical Positivism and Linguistic Analysis. Wittgenstein also made important contributions to the studies of mathematics, logic, psychology, and even engineering. He was noted for his talents as a musician, sculptor, and architect. Many of his contemporaries held him in very high esteem—sometimes even awe. When Wittgenstein returned to teaching at Cambridge in 1929 after a fifteen-year absence, he was first met by the distinguished economist John Maynard Keynes. Keynes recorded the event in a note to his wife: "Well God has arrived. I met him on the 5:15 train." In 1939 Wittgenstein applied for the position of professor of philosophy that was recently opened by G.E. Moore's retirement. The philosopher C.D. Broad remarked, "To refuse the chair to Wittgenstein would be like refusing Einstein a chair of physics."

Although commentators often break Wittgenstein's thought into two distinct periods—"early" and "late"—I think his concept of philosophy changed little, if at all, over the years. In his two main works, *Tractatus Logico-Philosophicus* and *Philosophical Investigations,* Wittgenstein holds that the aim of the philosopher is to come to grips with the limits of language. In the preface to the *Tractatus,* first published in German in 1921, Wittgenstein wrote, "what can be said at all can be said clearly, and what we cannot talk about we must pass over in silence." In the *Investigations,* published posthumously in 1953, he wrote, "Philosophy is a battle against the bewitchment of our intelligence by the means of language." For Wittgenstein, the problems of philosophy, such as skepticism, solipsism, and relativism, have their origins in the workings of language, and therein lies their solution. The philosopher tries to show how language actually functions, with the goal of unraveling the convoluted tangle of philosophical threads and providing clarity of thought. Wittgenstein's method attempts to answer philosophical problems, not by proposing a better theory but by removing the confusion that generated the question in the first place.

This method may not seem like traditional philosophy since all of the grand philosophical themes appear to be missing, such as investigations into the existence of God, theories of knowledge, metaphysics, and so on. In a certain sense, all of these ideas *are* discussed by Wittgenstein, but in a striking new way. Wittgenstein's approach to these traditional topics of philosophy was so novel that it has often been misunderstood. It has been thought that Wittgenstein was an atheist or a logical positivist who wanted to get rid of these aspects of our thinking. But I don't think this is the case. I would like to show in this essay that Wittgenstein believed that these ideas represent an extremely important aspect of human life that we have been approaching in a very confused way. For Wittgenstein, it is most important for the philosopher to clarify our language surrounding these issues, for only then can truth begin to emerge. However, Wittgenstein wants to show that this truth cannot be expressed in the way that we assume it can. Of all these ideas, I would like to focus on Wittgenstein's treatment of ethics, since this was so pivotal to his thought.

Although Wittgenstein spent the majority of his working life in England and is most often associated with Anglo-American Analytic Philosophy, he was born and educated in Vienna. Many writers have pointed out that Wittgenstein's philosophical searching, particularly his understanding of the nature of ethics, was greatly influenced by the intellectual arena in Vienna at the turn of the twentieth century. Also, I think it will become evident that Wittgenstein's philosophical works were the culmination of an intensely personal search.

∼ Cultural Influences

In 1889, during the waning days of the Hapsburg Empire, Ludwig Wittgenstein was born into one of Austria's, if not Europe's, wealthiest families. Ludwig's father, Karl, was a self-made multimillionaire. His family was of Jewish origin but had converted to Protestantism in his grandfather's time, probably because of the pervasive Austrian anti-Semitism. Ludwig's mother was Roman Catholic, and Ludwig was a baptized—though eventually non-practicing—Catholic. The magnificent Wittgenstein home in Vienna was a cultural mecca. Many of the great musicians and artists of the day, such as the composer Brahms, benefited from the family's extensive patronage of the arts.

Culturally and intellectually, the Vienna of Wittgenstein's time was nearly unrivaled in Europe. Over the years it had attracted the likes of Mozart, Beethoven, and Brahms, and was home to Schubert, Mahler, and Strauss. In the sciences, Vienna gave us Mach, who had a great influence on Einstein; Boltzmann, the father of statistical mechanics; and, of course, Freud. The list of geniuses is indeed long and impressive, but there was also a darker side to Viennese life. Some of Vienna's most prominent intellectuals, including the aforementioned Boltzmann, committed suicide. Vienna also gave us Hitler.

Vienna during this time was a city of paradox. On the surface, it was a city of magnificent architecture and grand boulevards dotted with cafes and shops offering the finest in luxuries. Strauss waltzes filled the air. A growing, wealthy middle class, enjoying the benefits of a booming economy, built lavish homes, spent excessively, and patronized the arts to signify their wealth and taste.

But for many, particularly a group of young intellectuals, Viennese culture was all pretense and façade. The middle class's infatuation with art was an attempt to reclaim a bygone era—the glory days of the Austrian Empire. Clearly, wealth alone does not confer nobility, but it does allow one to acquire its trappings. For these young intellectuals, the middle class was interested in art as mere decoration and ornament. The meaning of the art—its depth, particularly any moral significance—escaped them entirely. Since they wanted the art to reflect the past, any innovation was not allowed.

These young Viennese thinkers brought the darker side of life in Vienna into focus, revealing their society as morally bankrupt. Business was most important to the middle class, and it could be quite Machiavellian. Ruthless yet successful, the Viennese businessman enjoyed a decadent, hedonistic lifestyle, yet outwardly insisted on a strict Christian moral code and a fastidious adherence to the manners of Old World European civilization. This patriarchal society developed a repressive educational system in which students were indoctrinated into a rigid Christian value system that the adult population professed but did not practice. Marriage and family life could be quite harsh. A man felt that his marriage was good if the match advanced his business interests; love was not important. The concerns of women were not considered, and they were not expected to have a life outside the home. Children were expected to succeed on their fathers' terms, and failure was not tolerated. As far as the society at large was concerned, there was little compassion for the poor, unfortunate, or unsuccessful. Various political groups openly practiced racism and anti-Semitism. As one might expect, suicide was nearly epidemic, particularly among the young and talented (including three of Wittgenstein's brothers). It is small wonder that Freud's practice was so successful in such an environment (even though it was more or less officially disdained).

Among the Viennese intellectuals who critiqued and tried to alter this state of affairs were Arnold Schonberg in music, Adolf Loos in architecture, and, perhaps most importantly, the journalist and social critic Karl Kraus. Kraus' newspaper *Die Fackel (The Torch)* was a lightning rod for the criticism of the superficiality and what he and many others saw as the moral degeneracy of Viennese society.

A thorough examination of these thinkers would be beyond the scope of this chapter. For our purposes, we can say that they shared the view that many of their contemporaries in the arts had been alienated from the arts along with the middle class, for whom art was mere decoration. Art had become all form and lacked content. Even in architecture, function, logical simplicity, and clarity of design had become lost in layers of clutter that was supposed to be beautiful but was actually useless and without purpose. For the architect Adolf Loos, ornament was literally a crime—a fraudulent substitute for quality in materials and craftsmanship. In general, these thinkers held that art should reject ornamentation and style, and that the artist of every discipline should strive for purity. Above all, the purpose of art should be moral and should reveal the character of the artist, meaning that only a person of integrity could create true art. For Kraus, nowhere was this more evident than in language. Kraus was fond of saying, "I cannot get myself to accept that a whole sentence can ever come from half a man."[1] Language—and any medium of communication could be seen as a language—revealed the person, and there was no distinction between ethics and aesthetics. The artist who simply manipulated a medium for money, style, or conformity to a particular school was not a person of integrity and therefore was usually the subject of a scathing polemic in *Die Fackel*. Without this personal and moral dimension, no artistic endeavor was worthy of the name. The Krausians extolled the virtues of authors such as Kierkegaard and Tolstoy, whose intensely personal moral dilemmas became the subject of their works and whose lives reflected simplicity and lack of pretense. These ideas were to have a profound effect on the young Wittgenstein.

∾ *Tractatus*

In 1908 Wittgenstein went to England and registered as a research student in engineering specializing in aeronautics at the University of Manchester. At some point he became interested in logic and the foundations of mathematics. His intense interest in this subject apparently coincided with reading Bertrand Russell's *Principles of Mathematics*, which was published in 1903. After reading Russell's work, Wittgenstein sought out the brilliant and original German logician Gottlob Frege. Wittgenstein was excited by his meetings with Frege, but apparently Frege was more puzzled by Wittgenstein than anything else. He advised Wittgenstein to go to Cambridge and study with Russell, which Wittgenstein did.

At the turn of the twentieth century, Russell and his colleague G.E. Moore started a philosophical revolution at Cambridge that came to be known as "Analytic Philosophy." In a strong reaction to the philosophy of the period, which was dominated by German Idealism, Russell and Moore's approach to philosophical problems called for a logical analysis of the concepts that philosophers use. By using this approach, coupled with a realist and eventually empiricist theory of knowledge, Russell and Moore intended to rid philosophy of what they saw as the convoluted excesses of Idealist metaphysics. In much the same way, the Logical Positivists, such as Moritz Schlick and Rudolph Carnap, turned to logical analysis and empiricism in order to purge scientific discourse of metaphysical speculation. The positivists proposed a theory of meaningfulness. They said that if a word refers to something one might be able to perceive (see, hear, touch, taste, smell), then it is meaningful. But if it doesn't, then it is meaningless. Since words like "God," "soul," "virtue," "human rights," "beauty," and others do not refer to entities or qualities people can perceive, they are all meaningless and should be discarded as metaphysical rubbish. As we shall see, Wittgenstein agreed with the positivists in some ways but not in others.

Wittgenstein began attending Russell's lectures in 1911. At first, Russell did not know what to make of this intense young man who would discuss logic and mathematics incessantly, to the point of following Russell back to his rooms and sometimes continuing the discussion long into the night. But soon Wittgenstein absorbed all that Russell could teach on logic, and Russell began to think of Wittgenstein first as a protégé and then as a colleague. However, Russell may have misjudged Wittgenstein's passion for philosophy, though he certainly witnessed it. He relates one late-night philosophy discussion during which Wittgenstein nervously and silently paced the floor. "Are you thinking about logic or your sins?" asked Russell. "Both" replied Wittgenstein. I don't think Russell appreciated the depth of that remark, but I believe Wittgenstein was absolutely serious. Indeed, for Wittgenstein, as a true Krausian, philosophy, which Wittgenstein now clearly saw as wrapped up in logic, must be a strict discipline that is intensely personal and requires a moral commitment.

By the outbreak of World War I in the summer of 1914, Wittgenstein was already at work on the *Tractatus*. Although he was the son of a wealthy aristocrat and could have avoided active military service, Wittgenstein enlisted in the Austrian army. Apparently Wittgenstein worked on the *Tractatus* continuously throughout the war, carrying the manuscript with him in his knapsack when he was finally transferred to the front after repeated requests. At the end of the war, Wittgenstein had no success in getting the book published. Thanks to the intervention of Russell, the book was published in an English translation with a German parallel text in 1922. Wittgenstein believed he had solved the problems of philosophy once and for all, so he promptly gave it up and settled into a career as a grade school teacher. He was not to return to university academic life until 1929.

What I do here is give a basic overview of the main ideas of the *Tractatus* as they relate to Wittgenstein's conception of philosophy. Wittgenstein's idea in the *Tractatus*, as stated in the preface to the work, is to mark off the limits of language.

> The whole sense of the book might be summed up in the following words: what can be said at all can be said clearly, and what we cannot talk about we must pass over in silence. Thus the aim of the book is to draw a limit to thought, or rather—not to thought, but to the expression of thoughts: for in order to draw a limit to thought, we should have to find both sides of the limit thinkable (i.e.,

we should have to be able to think what cannot be thought). It will therefore only be in language that the limit can be drawn, and what lies on the other side of the limit will simply be nonsense.[2]

What this has to do with ethics may not be immediately obvious. But if we think back to Wittgenstein's Viennese influences, the connection becomes clearer. The culture's focus on ornament and decoration in the arts and language obscured or disguised a morally bankrupt society. The truth demands clarity of expression, and a moral life demands the truth.

In a letter to a potential publisher of the *Tractatus* Wittgenstein states:

> The book's point is an ethical one. I once meant to include in the preface a sentence which is not in fact there now, but which I will write out for you here, because it will perhaps be a key to the work for you. What I meant to write, then, was this: My work consists of two parts: the one presented here plus all that I have not written. And it is precisely this second part that is the important one. My book draws limits to the sphere of the ethical from the inside as it were, and I am convinced that this is the only rigorous way of drawing those limits. For now I would recommend you to read the preface and the conclusion because they contain the most direct expression of the point of the book.[3]

We have already mentioned the preface. Examining the "conclusion" is a little difficult since no section is clearly marked as the conclusion. If Wittgenstein is referring to the last remark of the *Tractatus*—"7. What we cannot speak about we must pass over in silence"—then, well, I think we should back up a bit and look at the last few remarks of the book.

6.52   We feel that even when all possible scientific questions have been answered, the problems of life remain completely untouched. Of course there are then no questions left, and this is itself the answer.

6.522   There are, indeed things that cannot be put into words. They make themselves manifest. They are what is mystical.

6.53   The correct method in philosophy would really be the following: to say nothing except what can be said, i.e., the propositions of natural science—i.e., something that has nothing to do with philosophy—and then, whenever someone else wanted to say something metaphysical, to demonstrate to him that he had failed to give a meaning to certain signs in his propositions. Although this would not be satisfying to the other person—he would not have the feeling that we were teaching him philosophy—this method would be the only strictly correct one.

I believe this last remark best sums up Wittgenstein's overall approach to philosophy. If we put these ideas together with those in the preface, a picture of Wittgenstein's main point begins to emerge. There are limits to what language can express, and these limits are part of the essence of language. What language can express is restricted to empirical propositions—the propositions of science. Through an examination of the workings of language these limits manifest themselves, and once we see these limits to language we realize that the major problems of life remain untouched. The propositions of philosophy about the existence of God or the soul, the nature of reality, the Good, and so on attempt to speak about what lies beyond the limits of language, limits that can be shown. Using the method outlined in the *Tractatus,* we dissolve the problems we encounter regarding these ideas. Ultimately we must pass over these ideas in silence.

Three ideas are fundamental to Wittgenstein's analysis of language in the *Tractatus.* Of prime importance is symbolic logic, or Russell and Whitehead's "propositional calculus." Symbolic logic attempts to translate our arguments into symbolic form, thus allowing them to be analyzed and tested for validity with mathematical precision. In the *Tractatus,* Wittgenstein makes a number of important contributions to the development of symbolic logic. The second important idea is sometimes called "logical atomism"—also of Russellian extraction. Finally, we will examine the "picture theory" of the proposition—apparently Wittgenstein's original contribution.

Let us begin with logical atomism. The idea of logical atomism appears in the *Tractatus* as an attempt to show how words acquire meaning by naming what Wittgenstein calls "objects" or what are sometimes more descriptively referred to as "logical atoms." Thus an object for Wittgenstein is not one of the ordinary large-scale objects of our experience—tables, rocks, houses, cars, or the like. Rather, the things of our ordinary experience are composites. As composites, they may be analyzed or broken down into their ultimate components—logical atoms—which are so called because they can't be broken down any further. We use the term "logical atom" here so that we can distinguish what Wittgenstein is doing from what a scientist is referring to by "atom." These are two similar concepts, but they should not be confused. An atom for the physicist might be seen as a fundamental building block of nature. But a logical atom or object is closer to a component of a theory of knowledge than it is to physical theory. What Wittgenstein has in mind was probably inspired by Russell's sense-data theory of perception. In this theory, derived from John Locke, a perception such as "snowball" is seen as being composed of several distinct and irreducible elements given to us through our senses. In this case, we might say that the elements or data are the distinct sense experiences such as round, hard, cold, and white. The perception snowball is a construct of these distinct experiences. For Russell, these distinct experiential components of the perception snowball are his logical atoms. In some texts he refers to these atoms as "particulars." The *Tractatus* and *Investigations* call Russell's idea "individuals." (*Tractatus Logico-Philosophicus* 5.553, *Philosophical Investigations* # 46).

Wittgenstein states that his objects are similar to Russell's individuals. The world, as we mentioned, is composite and so can be broken down into its ultimate constituent components—or objects. Thus, reality is ultimately composed of objects. Whether object here means more than sense data and possibly refers to a metaphysical constituent of reality is an interesting and open question.

Wittgenstein's analysis of meaning in the *Tractatus* revolves around the naming relation a word has to an object. A word is meaningful if it names an object—or something that can be broken down into its constituent objects. If not, then it has no actual referent and must be considered nonsense. Meaningful propositions are built out of meaningful words or names. A proposition is meaningful or has sense not simply because of reference but because it "pictures" or models reality or a "state of affairs," as Wittgenstein puts it. That is, the relationship between the names in a proposition that has sense correctly corresponds to or mirrors at least a possible relationship between objects in reality. Thus, a meaningful proposition correctly expresses a fact or the possibility of a fact. Another way of looking at this would be to note that an essential feature of the sense of a proposition is that it may be true or false. What accounts for this feature is the structure of the proposition that enables it to picture reality, that is, possible or actual states of affairs or facts. Thus, the proposition "says" something about the world, and its sense is "shown" in its structure—an idea that will become clearer momentarily, when we discuss Wittgenstein's picture theory of the proposition. The proposition displays its sense. To explain or try to understand the sense of a proposition through language is pointless since this would require a further proposition, and then we would have to explain that proposition. To try to understand the sense of a proposition this way would require an infinite number of propositions, which would get us nowhere. This distinction between showing and saying is central to the *Tractatus*.

The story goes that the picture theory came to Wittgenstein when he witnessed a model being used to explain a traffic accident in a courtroom. The model conveyed what happened in the accident because there was a one-to-one correspondence between the components of the model and their relationship to each other and to what had actually happened in the accident. Propositions, Wittgenstein thought, work in the same manner. Looking at the simple proposition, "Fred throws the ball," we realize we might draw a simple picture that would in fact say the same thing—like something you would see in a children's book that teaches reading. If you set up the picture from left to right—Fred, his arm pointing to the right, the ball traveling to the right—and then labeled the picture in that order, the proposition and the picture would be, practically speaking, indistinguishable. The constituent members of the proposition stand in the same relation to each other as do the constituent objects in the actual activity. In this way, propositions represent reality and so convey meaning. We can see that since the words "God," "the soul," "the Good," and so on do not name objects in the above sense, for Wittgenstein there can be no meaningful propositions about them. For example, since the word "God" signifies something spiritual, it does not name an atomic element of reality or even a composite of such elements or objects. The proposition "The snowball hits the tree" can be broken down into simple objects of our experience—things we can point to. While we can imagine something in connection with the proposition "God resides in heaven," there is nothing in the proposition to which we can actually point. This lack renders the proposition meaningless; however, as we shall see, this does not mean that such ideas are unimportant.

The simplest possible propositions, those that cannot be broken down any further, are what Wittgenstein calls "elementary propositions." For ease of understanding, we can think of elementary propositions as connected using Russell and Whitehead's symbolic logic. What Wittgenstein says on the topic of logic is complex and often original—he made many improvements on Russell's original idea—but to develop these ideas fully would take us beyond the scope of this essay. The gist of the idea is that elementary propositions are connected using logical connectors or operators such as "and," "or," and "if–then." So we would have propositions like "Fred threw the ball and hit the batter," "Fred will throw or Fred will catch," "If Fred throws wildly then he will hit the batter," and so on. Theoretically, at least, any number of propositions may be connected in this manner. Clearly, "and," "or," and the like do not name objects or components of reality and are not meaningful through reference. There is nothing in our experience to which we could point that could correspond to "and" or "if–then." These logical connectors are merely useful in connecting propositions. Propositions have sense because they picture at least a possible state of affairs. If we think of the above propositions—"Fred will throw or Fred will catch," and so on—in a purely formal way (that is, as "A or B," and "If A then B"), then we can see that propositions of logic do not picture states of affairs. Since propositions of logic do not picture states of affairs, they do not have sense—they do not say anything about the world. But again, this does not make logic unimportant. Logic shows its meaning or usefulness because it is a necessary device for connecting propositions.

Thus, propositions about the world are meaningful through their application as pictures of reality. These propositions are connected logically. Logic itself says nothing about reality, and logical propositions are not meaningful in the way propositions about the world are meaningful. Logic for Wittgenstein is more like a set of mathematical equations. It is merely the scaffolding on which we hang our propositions.

From the preceding we can, it is hoped, see something of the grand scheme of the *Tractatus*. Propositions are meaningful if the arrangement of names that make up the proposition correctly represents an arrangement of objects. Propositions can be meaningfully connected only through the correct application of logic. Outside of this there is only nonsense. Thus, the sentences of, say, metaphysics or theology, since they are neither pictures of reality nor combinations of such pictures, must be considered nonsense.

The relationship of the above to ethics may not be immediately obvious. It may be very difficult to see that the "point of the book is an ethical one." One difficulty is that all this sounds very much like the ideas of the Logical Positivists and Analytic philosophers, whose aims were to rid discourse of metaphysical terms. Of course, there are similarities here. But there is also a crucial difference. Wittgenstein does not want to limit metaphysical or ethical discourse because these ideas are not necessary, but rather because these ideas are vitally important.

We should look at a few more of the closing remarks of the *Tractatus:*

6.41   The sense of the world must lie outside the world.

6.421   It is clear that ethics cannot be put into words. Ethics is transcendental.

6.43   If the good or bad exercise of the will does alter the world, it can only alter the limits of the world, not the facts—not what can be expressed by means of language.

6.432   *How* things are in the world is a matter of complete indifference to what is higher. God does not reveal himself in the world.

Careful attention should be paid to these remarks. If what is beyond our propositions has no meaning or importance, why should Wittgenstein waste any time on them? Why would he call attention to the fact that the sense of the world is beyond the world if there is nothing there? Why talk about the good or bad exercise of the will if morality just doesn't matter? He says that God does not reveal himself in the world, not that there is no such thing or that God should be completely ignored. Clearly, he is trying to say that these things are important, yet they are or should be inexpressible.

Again, I think Wittgenstein's intention here becomes clearer if we remember the intellectual concerns of the Vienna of Wittgenstein's youth. There the pretense and façade of Christian values hid an almost complete lack of scruples. Art, indeed language itself, which supported this pretense, was mere ornamentation that failed to further or in fact prevented the attainment of any moral depth. Clearly, ethics must involve the relationship of the self to the world. Once this clutter is removed, the self or character of the person in all its simplicity is laid bare and must be confronted. One is here reminded of the Socratic message "Know thyself." The picture may not be a pretty one, but now it is the responsibility of the individual to achieve his or her own integrity or authenticity. This authenticity is not supplied by the externals of a bankrupt (or any) culture; it must come from within. The *Tractatus* represents Wittgenstein's attempt to restore pristine clarity to language and thus remove the clutter from our philosophizing and writing about ethics. What can be said can be said clearly; the rest we must pass over in silence. Our traditional philosophizing on these topics only clouds what is so important by adding layers of nonsense that can never penetrate these profound mysteries. Unlike traditional philosophy, ethics is not a matter of demonstrating or proving anything. It is an intensely personal search. I think Wittgenstein might agree that one must be ethical, not just talk about it. The ethical sphere is not reached through talk; the ethical makes itself manifest. Ethics must be shown and not said.

In other words, ethics lies outside what can be said meaningfully. It is nonsense, but clearly important nonsense. If we see the unsayability of ethics, I think we can see why Wittgenstein held St. Augustine—particularly the *Confessions*—in such high regard. In that work, Augustine wrestles with the central problems of faith on an intellectual level and ends up in almost complete despair, since he still finds himself unable to commit totally to an ethical life. It is a mystical experience that is almost totally inexpressible that leads to his conversion and to a whole new world for Augustine, although externally nothing has changed.

Thus, Wittgenstein believed that with the *Tractatus* he had shown the limits of language, and therefore of philosophy. In 1920 he moved on to more practical activities. He took a position as an elementary school teacher in an Austrian village. But his new career wasn't entirely satisfying, and in 1929 he returned to Cambridge to teach philosophy. Chief among the reasons for his return to Cambridge seems to have been that Wittgenstein came to realize that the *Tractatus* was in need of some revision.

◌ *Philosophical Investigations*

Wittgenstein's 'later' philosophy was transmitted initially through his lectures, and although he discouraged note taking in his classes, some notes eventually did circulate. Wittgenstein also prepared two sets of typewritten notes that became known as the *Blue Book* and the *Brown Book*. He distributed these to select students and sent a copy of the *Blue Book* to Russell. The reaction in all quarters was generally puzzlement since this new work, besides being difficult to understand, appeared to be a radical departure from the *Tractatus*. Russell claimed he could make nothing of it at all. In addition, Wittgenstein made voluminous notes on a variety of philosophical topics. Some of these notes are quite polished, and Wittgenstein intended to work some of these notes into a book to be published during his lifetime. Much of this later material has been published, though it is difficult to say which, if any, Wittgenstein would have thought to be in publishable form. Most scholars agree that *Philosophical Investigations*, which is taken from these notes, is probably close to something Wittgenstein would have published.

Although the meaning of *Philosophical Investigations* is controversial, Wittgenstein clearly still sees language as the source of our philosophical problems, and being clear about how language actually works is the means to the solution or, rather, dissolution of our philosophical problems. The chief difference between the early and late work is one of method, which many scholars see as a shift from ideal to ordinary language philosophy. Wittgenstein came to see that the meaning of our ordinary language was not the result of the rigid structure of logical atomism he had envisioned in the *Tractatus;* rather, the meaning of our ordinary language is found in the way the words and sentences are actually used within that language. Language has its own rules or grammar that can be uncovered by analysis. Wittgenstein calls the system of rules and circumstances that delineates the use of a word and therefore shows its meaning a "language game." His analysis in the *Investigations* largely consists of comparing the use of a word in a language game that represented the "philosophical" use of the word with how the word is actually used in the language game that is its original home. The result shows how the philosophical use is misplaced. Thus, the meaning of a word is derived from its original context, and trying to use it outside of that context is trying to get the word to do a job it was not designed to do, resulting in nonsense. Wittgenstein often compares a word to a tool. A tool has its proper use (or meaning) in a specific context, but outside that context it generally will have an unintended result. A hammer is great at driving a nail, but trying to use it to adjust your carburetor will probably result in disaster. So Wittgenstein in the later work is still showing the limits of language, but by looking at language as it stands, not by positing an ideal linguistic structure that must be uncovered. If looked at correctly, language is capable of conveying meaning as it is.

There are many famous examples from the *Investigations* of Wittgenstein's procedure. One such example is Wittgenstein's discussion of "understanding."[4] Just what our ability to understand is or says about the nature of human beings has long been the object of philosophical speculation. Wittgenstein's main concern is to examine the source of our confusions about the nature of the understanding and, ultimately, to dissolve these confusions. Philosophers, for Wittgenstein, ought not to advance or defend any theories, psychological or otherwise, regarding our ability to understand. Rather, the job of the philosopher is to clear up the various misconceptions about understanding by returning the word "understanding" to the original language game that is its proper home.

This last point is often the source of a great deal of difficulty when reading Wittgenstein, especially the *Investigations*. So we should spend a little time elaborating on the task of the philosopher. In the *Tractatus,* as we noted earlier, for Wittgenstein the propositions of philosophy or logic are not empirical propositions. The propositions of logic are merely tautologies or equations that say nothing about the world. The correct philosophical method shows how propositions of philosophy fail because they try to cross the boundaries of language. This approach may seem very unsatisfactory because philosophers have been advancing theses since the time of Thales, and philosophers have come to think of their discipline as akin to science in that if a thesis is judged to be wrong then it should be refuted, and a better thesis should take its place. But for Wittgenstein, a philosopher is not like a scientist who performs dissections or uncovers fossils. The tools of a philosopher have always and only been logic, language, and meaning. Once we see this limitation, we must realize that a philosopher must be restricted to the arena bounded by logic and language. Language and meaning are enormously complex but can be understood through logical analysis, which is not an empirical or fact-finding procedure. As we noted above, logic, in the *Tractatus*, is a system of equations, and so a conclusion in logic is not proven the way a scientific theory is proven, that is, by uncovering facts. If it is true that $a = b$ and $b = c$, then I can say that it is true or proven that $a = c$. But this truth or proof relies only on symbols and in the meaning of "=," not on any fact about the natural world. For Wittgenstein in the *Tractatus*, meaningful propositions are founded on logic, and this delineates what can be said. The job of the philosopher consists in appealing to logic to show these boundaries, and so he or she is not advancing theories that are proved or disproved by facts. The philosopher is only engaging in logical analysis.

Of course, it could be objected that Wittgenstein is not entirely consistent in the *Tractatus*. Logical atomism and the so-called picture theory of propositions are very much like traditional philosophical theories. This tendency to theorize on the nature of language is very likely one of the flaws Wittgenstein found in the *Tractatus* that he tried to correct in the *Investigations*. Thus, in the *Investigations*, Wittgenstein reworks and expands this theme. As we noted above, the chief difference between the early and later work is that Wittgenstein came to realize that clarity of meaning is not derived by uncovering the underlying perfect logical structure of language. Rather, language has its own perfectly good system of rules or grammar that shows how a word is used and so shows the meaning of that word. But the main idea is still the same as it was in the *Tractatus*. Through analysis of grammar or the internal logic of language we show the limits of language—again, not by uncovering any facts about the natural world. Philosophy is not about proving or disproving theses; it is about showing how certain philosophical uses of a word cause confusion and how, through a correct understanding of the logic or grammar of language, this confusion may be dissipated.

Wittgenstein notes that we often think that, for example, "understanding," or any word, derives its meaning by referring to a particular object. This idea, which was at the heart of the *Tractatus*, Wittgenstein now sees as the source of a great deal of confusion, for it causes us to seek the object that is the referent of the word "understanding," thinking that this object, once found, will explain what understanding is. However, if we look at the various uses of "understanding," no such object readily presents itself. Wittgenstein examines several circumstances in which we would say that someone "understands." For example, we try to teach someone to continue the series of even numbers. At some point the student may say something like

"Now I understand!" and then continues the series on his or her own. We may then agree that our student understands. Notice that this is a perfectly meaningful use of "understand," yet there was no specific object or thing that we could point to that would automatically correspond to the word. If we still insist that there must be a specific referent for the word, then we may think that "understanding" must refer to some mental or psychological process that is for the present hidden and certainly mysterious, but that will reveal itself under philosophical scrutiny. But Wittgenstein sees this as the source of much misguided philosophy—that is, the advancing of various meaningless theses to explain just what this strange process must be. If we give up the idea that "understanding" must refer to an object in order to be meaningful, then this rash philosophical inquiry into this strange mental process will come to an end. When the word is returned to its original language game, it ceases to look so mysterious.

In addition to "understanding," Wittgenstein discusses a number of concepts that would be associated with philosophy of mind. Many writers have pointed out that Wittgenstein in the *Investigations* was dealing with many paradoxes that can arise from modern thought, particularly from Cartesianism and empiricism. For example, Descartes begins his analysis in the *Meditations* by shutting out all sensation and examining his ideas through introspection. He then finds that all of his ideas may be doubted, even those that are very simple, such as where he is or who he is. After all, Descartes argues, although he remembers these things clearly, it is certainly possible that his memory is deceiving him. He could even imagine that there is an all-powerful evil genius who is somehow constantly deceiving him about everything, an idea that leads to absolute skepticism. However, all this doubt does lead him to one absolutely certain proposition—the famous *Cogito ergo sum*—"I think, therefore I am." Even if someone is uncertain of everything, it is clear that only an existing thing can doubt. Absolute doubt or skepticism is wrong because it leads to at least one certain statement: the one who doubts must exist.

But Descartes' problems are far from over. Descartes may have defeated absolute skepticism, but there is a price. A thinker may be certain of his or her existence and the existence of his or her ideas, but whether there is anything in reality corresponding to those ideas can still be doubted. One still might be deceived about what philosophers call the "reality of the external world." Descartes tries to get around this doubt by appealing to the existence of God. If God exists and is all good, then he wouldn't allow me to be deceived about what I clearly and distinctly perceive to be true. However, Descartes' proof for the existence of God seemed far from convincing to many thinkers, and many objected that this reliance on God was contrary to both the spirit of Descartes' writings and that of the Enlightenment, which wanted to ground truths in science, not theology. But without the existence of God, the end result of Descartes' thought as it stands must be skepticism.

Worse yet, many thinkers point out that not only is the existence of an external world in doubt, but also there is no reason to conclude that anything but the original thinker exists. There is no way to demonstrate the existence of other minds. This position, known as "solipsism," is contrary to our experience, but if you fundamentally doubt your experience, the conclusion seems inescapable.

Further, the mind here seems like a very strange thing. For Descartes, bodies take up space and are extended, but ideas do not take up space and are unextended—they have no size, shape, or weight. (The idea of ten pounds does not weigh ten pounds; the idea of ten feet is not ten feet long.) Thus, the mind is not of the same "stuff" as the body; but just what "mind stuff" is or how this stuff is connected to the body Descartes couldn't explain to everyone's satisfaction. This question has perplexed philosophers ever since and is often referred to as the "mind-body problem."

Empiricism represented an alternative viewpoint on these problems. Although there are many versions of Empiricism, most empiricists advocated what is often called a "sense-data" theory of ideas. Empiricists start with the assumption that there is an external world. According to empiricists, our ideas are based on sense impressions derived from our experience of that world. These sense impressions, sometimes called "sense data," include color, texture, and taste. As we noted above, for a sense-data theorist such as Russell, my idea of a snowball is directly linked to my sense experience of a snowball—round, hard, cold, white, and so on. The idea here is that our ideas must be necessarily connected with an external world, and this connection seems to get around the problem of skepticism. But a theory of knowledge that equates ideas with sensations is not without skeptical problems of its own. Aren't sensations internal or private? Don't they happen within the knower? After all, there are no sense impressions outside a perceiver. If this is true, then how do I know that my sense experience is the same as that of anyone else? Maybe my sensations are unique to me, and if that is so, how can I be sure that there is anything beyond my sense experience? I am back in the same old muddle of skepticism and even solipsism.

Wittgenstein attacks this problem not by proposing a more successful theory, but by showing that the basic ideas that are the source of the problem arise from a misinterpretation of language and the way language operates. Although Wittgenstein treats these ideas in various places in the *Investigations,* one famous discussion centers on the idea of a private language.

The "private language argument" follows a discussion on the way words refer to sensation. We should note here that calling Wittgenstein's treatment of a question an argument could be misleading. As with the previous discussion of "understanding," it would be more correct to say that Wittgenstein uncovers many of the previously overlooked assumptions in a picture of how language operates in a particular case. Once all these assumptions are brought to the surface and followed to their conclusions, we often see that the picture self-destructs. The expressions involved do not or cannot actually do what we thought they could.

Wittgenstein saw that the puzzle over how words refer to ideas and sensations was at the heart of the problems generated by Cartesianism and Empiricism. If we return to Descartes and his *Meditations,* we remember that he begins by shutting out all sensations and focusing only on his ideas. He seems to be able to examine his ideas the way that we would examine an ordinary object, except through an interior examination with what we might call his "mind's eye." At first glance there seems to be nothing wrong with this description. We have often had the experience of mulling over ideas or thoughts while forgetting about the outside world—as in daydreaming. The difficulty arises when we start treating this description philosophically, as perhaps the description of some inner psychological mechanism—as if, say, the "mind's eye" were the name of a part of the mind in the way that the eye is a part of the body. Instead of simply using an ordinary expression for thinking, we think we are referring to something that can be examined almost as if we were doing psychology. This picture, if we think it refers to something real, can make it seem as if our ideas are open to examination (by the mind's eye) in the same way as objects on a table. But the "objects" of the mind are somehow, in this model, private. After all, no one else can look into my mind; no one can know its contents unless I tell them. Thus, it seems as if the language of my ideas refers to something private, and so when I am talking about my ideas, these words "mean" or refer to my private inner experience. But using this model for the language of our mental life is at the root of skepticism and solipsism. We have created an inner world to which only the knower has access. Since my words refer to something within me, then only I can be certain of their correct meaning. When I say I have a certain experience or feeling such as "love" or "pain," and since I can't directly compare my inner experience to someone else's, then how can I ever know whether someone else has the same feeling that I have? Even if we take something simple like the perception of color, we see that with this model, since my perceptions are internal and my color words refer to this inner experience, then it is perfectly possible that everyone sees something different than I do when I say, for example, "I see a red balloon." On this model, I can never make what is important to me—my thoughts, feelings, and experiences—truly known to anyone else. I am cut off and alone.

Wittgenstein dissolves the assumptions leading to this solipsistic conclusion by showing that it derives from the Tractarian idea of language. As we saw in the discussion of "understanding," this is the idea that words have meaning only as names or by referring to things. By using a number of examples and language games, Wittgenstein shows that this Tractarian model would make our thoughts and experiences meaningless or irrelevant. A well-known illustration that Wittgenstein uses to make this point is that of the beetle in the box.

Suppose everyone had a box with something in it: we call it a "beetle." No one can look into anyone else's box, and everyone says he knows what a beetle is only by looking at *his* beetle.—Here it would be quite possible for everyone to have something quite different in his box. One might even imagine such a thing constantly changing.—But suppose the word "beetle" had a use in these people's language?—If so it would not be used as the name of a thing. The thing in the box has no place in the language-game at all; not even as a *something*: for the box might even be empty.—No, one can "divide through" by the thing in the box; it cancels out, whatever it is.

That is to say: if we construe the grammar of the expression of sensation on the model of "object and designation" the object drops out of consideration as irrelevant.[5]

So, if we think that our words for thoughts are meaningful because they have a private referent, we misconstrue the way we speak about our experiences. In fact, to interpret our subjective experiences using this Tractarian model actually ends up making what we are talking about irrelevant. If the meaning of our words for our experiences was actually based on the model of "object and designation," then our words would be quite meaningless and this is clearly not the case. If you tell a doctor that you are in pain, it is possible that he or she might not believe you, but I'm sure the doctor would know what you mean. Our words cannot have a private definition or meaning. A language so constructed would not be a language at all. We, of course, may keep our thoughts private, but the meaning of our words must be public. We must think in a language, and a language, to be a language, must include the possibility of communicating. Thus, we cannot be logically cut off from the community of language users, and this necessary connection circumvents the problem of solipsism. If I can describe or talk about my experiences, then they cannot be understood only by me—they can be shared.

Many of the problems stemming from Cartesianism can be dissolved once we let go of the notion that when I talk about the mind I am entering a world of unique or privileged access. In a sense, our language will not permit us to give this picture any meaning. It is fine as a metaphor, but we should not confuse this with a pathway to a science of the mind.

Clearly, the problems stemming from Empiricism have the same source and will benefit from a similar analysis. If we think our words are meaningful because they refer to sensations or sense data, we end up in the same "privacy" muddle. The word "red" does not only name or get its meaning from my personal experience of red. If it did, as we saw above, the word would be meaningless.

One of the puzzling things about the relationship of the *Tractatus* to the *Investigations* is the lack of any extended discussion of ethics. Many reasons have been suggested for this lack. That Wittgenstein no longer had any interest in ethics is unlikely since his biographers and students tell us that he was still passionately concerned with the topic. Some commentators have suggested that his silence on ethics in the *Investigations* corrects a defect in the *Tractatus*. In that earlier work, he counts ethics among those things that we cannot talk about, yet he manages to have quite a lot to say on the topic. The silence of the *Investigations*, then, if he still held the same opinion on ethics, would be more consistent. If, however, we are to treat the language game with ethics as we would any other language game, it is strange that he did not treat it. I tend to think Wittgenstein is discussing ethics in the *Investigations*, but, again, in a novel way that often escapes notice. If we return to the earlier idea that ethics is about the relationship of the self to the world, then we can see from the above that the Cartesian and empiricist paradigms cannot give true knowledge of either. As we saw in the *Tractatus*, the ethical must make itself manifest—it must be shown. Rather than fostering a true understanding and manifestation of the self, the Cartesian and empiricist approaches offer us only roadblocks and detours. Again, I think Wittgenstein is showing that these pictures actually present us with layers of nonsense that must be cleared away before the self and the world can truly emerge. Clearly, the theme of the *Tractatus* remains: our problems are the result of encountering the boundaries of language. I think Wittgenstein would still say that much of what really matters lies on the other side of this boundary and that "What we cannot speak about we must pass over in silence."

∿ NOTES

1. Paul Engelmann, *Letters from Ludwig Wittgenstein* (New York: Horizon Press, 1968), 123.
2. Ludwig Wittgenstein, *Tractatus Logico-Philosophicus*, translated by D.F. Pears and B.F. McGuinness (London: Routledge, 1961), 3.
3. Allan Janik and Stephen Toulmin, *Wittgenstein's Vienna* (New York: Simon & Schuster, 1973), 192.
4. Ludwig Wittgenstein, *Philosophical Investigations*, translated by G.E.M. Anscombe (New York: Macmillan, 1968), 138–155.
5. Wittgenstein, *Philosophical Investigations*, 293.

∿ CHRONOLOGY

1889	born to a wealthy family in Vienna, educated at home up to age fourteen
1900	*The Interpretation of Dreams*, by Sigmund Freud
1905	Einstein publishes his first paper on relativity
1907	Picasso shows his "Les Demoiselles d'Avignon," develops cubism in painting

1908   Wittgenstein goes to England to study engineering

1912   becomes interested in the foundations of mathematics, goes to Cambridge to study with Bertrand Russell

1913   moves to a village in Norway for solitude; Stravinsky's ballet music, "Rite of Spring," causes a riot in Paris

1914   Archduke Ferdinand, heir to the throne of Austria-Hungary, assassinated, First World War begins; Wittgenstein volunteers for the Austrian army, begins working on the *Tractatus*

1916   wins several decorations for bravery with an artillery regiment on the Russian front, promoted to officer rank

1918   captured and imprisoned in Italy, continues to work on *Tractatus*

1919   after the war, gives away a very large fortune

1920   gives up philosophy, becomes an elementary school teacher in the Austrian Alps

1921   *Tractatus Logico-Philosophicus* published in German, with an English translation in 1922

1925   works as a gardener in a monastery, designs his sister's house in Vienna, attends some meetings of the Vienna Circle, a philosophical discussion group

1929   returns to Cambridge to teach philosophy

1942   during Second World War, works as a porter in a hospital

1947   retires from teaching, moves to a cottage on the coast of Ireland

1949   *The Concept of Mind* by Gilbert Ryle, influenced by Wittgenstein

1951   dies of cancer in Cambridge

1953   *Philosophical Investigations* published

1962   *How to Do Things with Words* by J.L. Austin, an example of ordinary language philosophy

∾ SUGGESTED READINGS

Barrett, C. *Wittgenstein on Ethics and Religious Belief*. Oxford: Basil Blackwell, 1991.

Edwards, J.C. *Ethics without Philosophy: Wittgenstein and the Moral Life*. Tampa: University Presses of Florida, 1982.

Fann, K.T. *Wittgenstein's Conception of Philosophy*. Oxford: Basil Blackwell, 1969.

Grayling, A.C. *Wittgenstein*. New York: Oxford University Press, 1988.

Janik, A., and S. Toulmin. *Wittgenstein's Vienna*. New York: Simon & Schuster, 1973.

Kenny, A. *The Legacy of Wittgenstein*. Oxford: Basil Blackwell, 1984.

Malcolm, N. *Ludwig Wittgenstein: A Memoir*. New York: Oxford University Press, 1958.

Schulte, J. *Wittgenstein: An Introduction*. Translated by William H. Brenner and John F. Holley. Albany: State University of New York Press, 1992.

Sluga, H., and D.G. Stern, eds. *The Cambridge Companion to Wittgenstein*. Cambridge: Cambridge University Press, 1996.

CHAPTER 16

Beauvoir

Philosophy as Freedom

Gail E. Linsenbard

 Preview

Simone de Beauvoir helped to create two of the most important movements of the twentieth century: existentialism and feminism. The common thread in all her interests is freedom. For Beauvoir, philosophy is the devotion to freedom. But freedom is extremely complicated. We are hindered by natural and social aspects of our situation. Paradoxically, we try to deny our freedom and become objects with fixed, simple defining properties. Such a life is hypocritical, unrealistic, and dishonest, Beauvoir says. Moreover, it is an impossible pursuit because, as persons, we must exist rather than simply be. That means we must exercise our freedom in action; we are not free not to be free. Women in particular have been threatened, deceived, and denied their freedom. Freedom, then, involves all the traditional philosophical issues, and more: identity, consciousness, moral values, society, commitment, and every aspect of human existence in the most intricate relations. Philosophy is the never-ending effort to face the fact of our freedom and to avoid dishonesty concerning not only our own freedom and possibilities, but the freedom and possibilities of others as well. (The Editor)

～ Introduction

In the year Simone de Beauvoir was born, 1908, the prospects for women were incredibly dim. In addition to being denied the right to vote and hold property in their own name, women were disenfranchised in multiple other ways. Most institutions of higher learning would not admit them, maintaining the prevailing view that women's proper place was in the home caring for their husbands and children. It is striking how strenuously both men and women maintained the view that women were simply less intelligent and capable than men, thereby making it easier to justify their inferior status in society. By contesting the social constructions of women, Beauvoir demonstrated that society maintains its views about women not because it has to, but because it chooses to. In challenging society's views of women, Beauvoir helped both men and women to transcend the political, social, and economic barriers that had prevented women from becoming fully human.

Beauvoir believed that philosophy could be expressed in multiple genres. Her central philosophical interest was to reveal the importance of human freedom and responsibility through literature, plays, autobiography, and critical essays, as well as through more formal philosophical works. Beauvoir was not, however, merely content to write abstract treatises; her life history is a testimony to her sustained commitment to actively fight oppression and promote human freedom. Writing philosophy became for her a way of acting responsibly in the world and challenging the moral and political status quo. The act of writing, she held, must always be committed to bringing about a more just world. The philosophical ideas Beauvoir so passionately expressed reflect her own life's trajectory; there simply is no distance between the philosopher and the person. Indeed, Beauvoir believed, as did Socrates, that the good life is the morally defensible life; showing us how to live such a life is the proper role of the philosopher.

To be sure, Beauvoir sincerely believed that her own efforts would help bring about a more just society. And in fact, the world is a different place as a result of Beauvoir's contributions. The values she inscribed in the world through her choices and commitments are certainly present today: Because of her influence, for example, the subordination of women, at least in Western nations, is no longer easily justified as natural or necessary.

⌒ A Sketch of Beauvoir's Life

Simone de Beauvoir was born in Paris in 1908. Beauvoir and her younger sister, Helene, were given a strict Catholic upbringing and education. Their mother, who was devoutly Catholic and overprotective, sought to inculcate in her daughters a similar religious devotion and a firm sense of duty. Beauvoir's father was an atheist and amateur theater actor who long considered himself among the chosen elite of the Parisian aristocracy. In truth, however, his bungled business adventures kept the family financially unstable and insecure. He was ultimately unable to join the ranks of the upper bourgeois society to which he thought himself naturally entitled; this was for him a constant disappointment.

Beauvoir's father was very impressed with young Simone's intellectual curiosity and ability. During Beauvoir's formative years, he encouraged her to excel in her studies and assisted her in reading and writing exercises. In fact, Beauvoir was indeed a gifted child, learning to read at the age of three. Although Beauvoir's father believed that she and her sister should have a proper education, he was conservative in his views and held that their appropriate role in society as women was to become housewives and mothers. But since the family lacked a fortune, and was thus unable to provide their daughters with dowries, it became clear that Simone and Helene would have to take up a profession. This suited Simone just fine. In fact, her family's misfortune turned out to be her good luck, since she could now devote herself almost entirely to intellectual pursuits and fulfill her dream of becoming a writer. Beauvoir wisely used her family's unfortunate financial situation to her full advantage.

Beauvoir's early formal education took place at a Catholic girls' school, where, in 1924, she received her baccalaureate. She subsequently registered at the Institut Catholique in Paris to earn a degree in mathematics and then at the Sainte-Marie in Neuilly to earn undergraduate degrees in literature, Latin, Greek, and philosophy. Under the tutelage of her philosophy teacher, she was encouraged to go on to prepare for the *agregation* in philosophy (a very prestigious higher teaching degree), whereupon she would be eligible to teach at the *lycees* (high schools) throughout France. For Beauvoir, however, this also signaled the beginning of a university career. In 1928 and 1929 she remained in Paris and attended courses in philosophy at the Sorbonne and lectures at the prestigious, elite Ecole Normale Superieure. She wrote her dissertation on the seventeenth-century German rationalist philosopher Gottfried Leibniz, and in 1929 graduated from the Sorbonne with a degree in philosophy.

Without having the advantage of special upper secondary school preparation for the *agregation*, and without actually having been a student at the Ecole Normale Superieure, Beauvoir took second place in the enormously competitive exam for the *agregation* in philosophy—an incredible achievement. First place went to a registered *normalien* named Jean-Paul Sartre, who, it should be noted, had previously failed his first examination. Beauvoir had actually met Sartre some months earlier because she was invited to join his study group in preparation for the philosophy exam. Evidently, it was known that her knowledge of Leibniz was extensive, and Sartre and his friends needed tutoring. This encounter would mark the beginning of a rich lifelong relationship. Sartre and Beauvoir never married or had children together, although later in their lives they each adopted adult daughters.

Beauvoir's close personal and intellectual relationship with Sartre lasted for over fifty years. Throughout this time they never lived together, but they saw each other every day if they resided in the same city, often working together or sharing a meal. Each shared, discussed, critiqued, and commented on the ideas of the other, and neither ever sent a manuscript to a publisher until the other was completely satisfied with it. To be sure, theirs was a unique relationship of sustained intellectual reciprocity and mutual respect.

As we have seen, Beauvoir eluded early on the imposition of a proper "feminine" role as her natural destiny. The only destiny she would claim for herself would be one that was freely chosen by her rather than one that was prescribed for her because she was a woman. Beauvoir fulfilled her chosen destiny through literary and philosophical expression that forcefully confronted the political, social, and economic injustices of her time and promoted freedom as a fundamental human value. One of the most tragic injustices, she thought, was society's treatment of women. In her most well-known book, *The Second Sex,* she seeks an explanation for the long-standing subjection and oppression of women, and argues that the subjection of women has been sustained through human choices.

Beauvoir's literary and philosophical acumen and her sharp analytical mind were coupled with an intense desire to share her thoughts, feelings, ideas, and indeed her concrete life experiences with others. She was passionately committed to writing and published a variety of works including philosophical essays, historical and sociological treatises, novels, dramas, autobiography, newspaper articles and interviews, and correspondence. When in 1943 Beauvoir published in occupied Paris her first novel, *She Came to Stay,* she had finally become the writer she had hoped to become.

Beauvoir was immediately and passionately engaged in a world whose values she repeatedly contested. Adamant about women's reproductive freedom, she founded the French pro-choice group *Choisir* and signed an abortion rights petition in which more than three hundred well-known women declared that they had had abortions, which were still illegal in France. She also joined the French Resistance during the German occupation and spoke out against French colonialism, supporting the war for Algerian independence and working to end French and United States involvement in Indochina. In 1945 Beauvoir and Sartre founded the influential leftist journal *Les Temps*

Modernes, which was dedicated to democratic socialism and to the idea that responsible literature must be politically committed. This journal is still active today. Although Beauvoir and Sartre were both influenced by Marxism, they never joined the Communist Party. Following the war, which both claimed had been their true political awakening, they aligned themselves with socialism and democratic socialist movements in France, remaining henceforth politically and socially active throughout their lives. Beauvoir's observation in *The Second Sex* concerning the emancipation of women underscores her commitment to socialism: "It is not to be supposed, however, that the mere combination of the right to vote and a job constitutes a complete emancipation: working, today, is not freedom. It is only in a socialist world that woman in acquiring the one secures the other."[1]

Among the books Beauvoir published and wrote just after the war was her first moral essay, *Pyrrhus et Cineas* (1944), wherein she explained the importance of the concept of situation to human freedom. In 1944 she began writing the novel *Tous les hommes sont mortels (All Men Are Mortal)* and the play *Les Bouches inutiles (Who Shall Die),* which reveals the moral dilemmas people must grapple with while their city is occupied. In 1945 Beauvoir published what has come to be known as the novel of the Resistance, *Le Sang des autres (The Blood of Others).* Set during the German occupation, it addresses the difficult moral decisions that members of the French Resistance had to make. It is clear that the war years had a dramatic impact on Beauvoir's life and philosophy. The harsh realities of war, and especially the unimaginable horrors of the Nazis and the collaboration of many of the French people during the occupation, significantly changed Beauvoir's outlook. She could no longer justify her pacifism or idealism, which, during the 1930s, were defended by her as necessary despite the growth of fascism.

⚭ Beauvoir and Existentialism

Beauvoir's conception of philosophy is inextricably linked to her belief in the importance of responsible action in the world. In fact, according to her, philosophy and action cannot be divorced from one another. Philosophy, she says, must concern itself with responsible commitment and engagement in the world. If we wish to justify our lives in a meaningful way, we will not merely content ourselves with contemplating abstract ideas; we will strive to practice our ideals and actively address the injustices of our time. Indeed, we have seen that Beauvoir wrote not only formal philosophy but also several novels. Perhaps she thought that philosophical ideas were best communicated in the genre of fiction, or, alternatively, that she could best describe philosophical problems and moral dilemmas by creating imaginary characters whose lives reflected the real-life struggles of existing people. In any case, Beauvoir practiced what she preached; the act of writing was for her a way of transforming her concept of philosophy into action.

Beauvoir and Jean-Paul Sartre are probably best known as the leading French existentialists during the postwar period (this in spite of the fact that they both rejected the label; another French philosopher, Gabriel Marcel, first classified them as existentialists at a colloquium in 1945). Existentialism is better understood as a distinct philosophical movement rather than a formal school of thought. It is not a comprehensive or systematic philosophy, but rather an endeavor to describe the reality of human existence in the world. As a response to the cultural crisis in the West brought on by the aftermath of World War II, existentialism sought to make sense out of the increasingly common problems of human estrangement, anxiety, and despair. One could certainly argue that these same problems confront us today, despite our efforts to cover them up.

Most fundamentally, then, existentialism is preoccupied with the *problem* of human existence; its central concern is to treat human existence *as such* as a legitimate philosophical inquiry. But why, one might ask, is human existence conceived of as a problem? Traditional philosophical approaches, the existentialists held, have attempted to cover up or reject the importance of human existence as such. Adopting the phenomenological method of Edmund Husserl, whereby fundamental human experiences are described as purely as possible, existentialists attempt to reveal and disclose what it means to exist as an experiencing human being. Existentialists are thus less preoccupied with what we might call traditional philosophical questions concerning problems of perception, knowledge, truth, and reality. This is not to say that they do not comment on problems of perception, knowledge, truth, and reality—they often do—but when they do, their goal is not so much to offer grand theories or solutions to these problems as it is to describe, from a human and hence a necessarily limited point of view, just how these problems matter to us.

It is interesting to note that existentialism has its roots in Classical Greek philosophy. Beginning with the presocratics and extending to the dialogues of Plato, the formal philosophy of Aristotle, and the philosophy of the Stoics, the central themes of existentialism can be readily identified. Questions concerning what it means to exist as a human being, how we should understand the world in which we live, and how we should conduct ourselves in relation to others are specifically existential questions that have their origin in early Greek thought.

In addition to their ties with Classical Greek philosophy, the existentialists were also influenced by some of the leading nineteenth- and early twentieth-century philosophers. Among the more prominent nineteenth-century figures who influenced the existentialists were Hegel, Kierkegaard, Nietzsche, Marx, and Engels. The most significant twentieth-century thinkers who influenced them were the German philosophers Husserl and Heidegger. Beauvoir especially appreciated Kierkegaard's insistence that philosophy concern itself first and foremost with the subjective, concretely existing individual. Although Beauvoir was greatly influenced by Hegel, as a committed existentialist she still found agreement with Kierkegaard's critique of Hegelian rationalism (the idea that we can know the world objectively) and idealism (the idea that our thinking coincides with reality). Against the so-called System, wherein Hegel claims that "objective Spirit" or "Reason" moves through human beings, cultures, societies, and nature, Kierkegaard posited the irreducible importance of the concretely existing human being, whose own subjective existence is desperately in need of our attention. Both Kierkegaard and Beauvoir, for example, speak about human despair and anxiety—about how we have lost our way and, in a tragic sense, also ourselves. But Beauvoir soon parts company with Kierkegaard on the issue of God's importance to human life. Kierkegaard held that one's "leap of faith" in God and one's relationship to God were the most important events in human life. As an atheist, Beauvoir was not interested in the issue of our relationship to God. She remained throughout her life a philosopher who was passionately committed to finding ways to promote freedom as a value—a task, she insisted, that was necessarily human and, hence, this-worldly. She writes:

> A God can pardon, efface, and compensate. But if God does not exist, man's faults are inexpiable. If it is claimed that, whatever the case may be, this earthly stake has no importance, this is precisely because one invokes that inhuman objectivity which we declined at the start. One can not start by saying that our earthly destiny has or has not importance, for it depends upon us to give it importance. It is up to man to make it important to be a man, and he alone can feel his success or failure.[2]

Existentialism was also a response to certain social and political questions that emerged in war-torn France. We have already hinted at how the German invasion and occupation of France helped Beauvoir to see that the moral problem was a distinctively human problem. Following the war, and much to the surprise of Sartre and Beauvoir, existentialism soon became a fashionable doctrine and spread far and wide across diverse intellectual and literary circles. The label "existentialism" was applied so widely and carelessly that Sartre later complained that in the process it had either lost its original meaning or had become so completely distorted that it no longer stood for anything at all. Because its meaning has become so stretched, existentialism is often seriously misunderstood and unfairly criticized.

Existentialism holds that (1) persons are free to determine their own lives and (2) persons are responsible for the choices they make. Both Beauvoir and Sartre declare that "existence precedes essence," by which they mean that persons exist first, or are born into the world, and then later define themselves. Sartre offers an example of a paper cutter to explicate his precise meaning. A paper cutter, he says, is an object that has been made by a manufacturer or inventor who already had a conception of it in mind. The inventor decides upon the mode of production, the production materials, the design, and the purpose of the paper cutter. She then produces the paper cutter according to her chosen method of production, and during this process the paper cutter's essence is determined (i.e., what it essentially is and how it shall be used). Hence, the paper cutter's essence precedes its existence; the idea or concept of the paper cutter precedes the paper cutter's actual appearance in the world. It is in this sense, Sartre notes, that the *essence* of the paper cutter is determined. But with respect to human reality, things are quite different; for human reality, he says, existence precedes our essence. We are born into the world quite independently of any preordained plan, concept, or format; there is no genetic, biological, or psychological blueprint to which we adapt or conform. In effect, there is no distinctively human nature. Now surely this is not to say that Sartre and Beauvoir deny that we have discoverable genes, physiology, and hormones that are significant in understanding our physical constitution. Nor do they deny that we have certain motivational dispositions, emotions, and desires that are significant in understanding our psychological constitution. They do grant that we have physical and psychological qualities, but they claim that none of these qualities, independently or collectively, constitute us. And we are certainly not, they claim, made "in the image of God"; we make ourselves in our *own* image. Hence our essence is created by us, not for us.

Existentialists do not mean to suggest that we are in any way radically free, acting, as it were, independently of anything or anyone else. We must remember that for existentialists our freedom is always *situated,* which is to say that we are free with respect to the particular world in which we and others exist. To be sure, we are born into a particular world—or society—with given limitations, obstacles, and constraints. How we respond to these limitations, obstacles, and constraints is of the utmost importance because our efforts will invariably inscribe values into the world that affect others. Since we live in what Beauvoir and Sartre call a "peopled world," our projects will either diminish or promote the freedom of others; this is why Beauvoir and Sartre claim that freedom and responsibility are correlative and interdependent.

∽ Beauvoir's "Ethics of Ambiguity"

From the start, Beauvoir's philosophical interests focused on concrete ethical issues. Her philosophy may be said to be humanistic because it deals with distinctively human problems and concerns, and confers ultimate value on existing human persons and relationships. From her first published novel, *She Came to Stay* (1943), to her award-winning political novel, *The Mandarins* (1954), and including her memoirs and documentary studies, one sees Beauvoir returning again and again to themes that raise moral concerns about political commitment and intersubjective relations. To be sure, Beauvoir's questions concerning how we should act and toward what good are perhaps the most important questions that philosophy can ask. In addition to her early moral essay, *Pyrrhus et Cineas* (1944), Beauvoir wrote another work on ethics, *The Ethics of Ambiguity* (1948). In this work she attempts to reveal the moral implications of existentialism and defend the existentialist commitment to human freedom and responsibility.

Beauvoir begins her study by stating that all previous attempts to formulate an ethics have failed to capture what she regards as a critical issue for ethics, namely, the fundamental ambiguity of human existence. What does this mean? Contrary to other moral theories, Beauvoir's humanistic ethics does not offer an objective basis or standard for adjudicating between right and wrong action. She does not, for example, defend as the source of values the Platonic Form of the Good, the Aristotelian Golden Mean, the Christian God reflected in acts of Christian Love, the Kantian Categorical Imperative, or the Utilitarian calculus of Ends or Consequences of actions. Beauvoir claims that all of these attempts to describe our moral life fail because they hide or ignore the fundamental ambiguity of human existence.

By "ambiguity" Beauvoir means to suggest that there is a paradoxical feature of human existence. She explains that human existence is ambiguous precisely because it must constantly seek for itself reasons or justifications for its existence without *ever* being able to succeed in actually justifying itself once and for all. "Thrown into the world" (an expression Beauvoir borrows from Heidegger), we must freely create our own purpose or reason for being, and yet the fact that we are free precludes the possibility of ever being able to completely justify our existence. We may, Beauvoir says, attempt to justify our existence through the ongoing process of making and remaking ourselves throughout our lives. To be sure, this attempt to "found ourselves" is never in vain because it is only through our own efforts and projects that our lives become meaningful to ourselves and to others. Our existence is ambiguous, then, because it is always in question; we can attempt to justify ourselves only to the extent that we engage or commit ourselves through action, and this process of engagement must continue until we die. Beauvoir tells us that "Existence asserts itself as an absolute which must seek its justification within itself and not suppress itself, even though it may be lost in preserving itself. To attain his truth, man must not attempt to dispel the ambiguity of his being but, on the contrary, accept the task of realizing it."[3] Our ambiguity, then, is precisely the tension between our freedom and our ceaseless effort to attempt to justify our existence; it is the fact of never being able to justify ourselves finally because we are free.

We have seen that Beauvoir is committed to the view that persons are always free in a particular situation. Since we are free to choose ourselves, there are no other values that precede the ones that each person chooses for herself or himself. This is why Beauvoir rejects the proposed standards of the various ethical theorists previously mentioned. To accept these or other standards or criteria removes the possibility of freely choosing values for oneself. On Beauvoir's account, since there are no preordained values or laws, then there must be another source of values, and that source, she argues, is human reality itself. It is in this sense that human beings are themselves the foundation of values. Hence our lives are inescapably shot through with moral questions; since moral decisions are also human decisions, the ambiguity of ethics is the ambiguity of human existence. And again, our situation is ambiguous precisely because, while there is nothing outside of us to which we can appeal as a source of justification for our actions, we must nonetheless *be our own* justification for our existence throughout our lives. In this sense, Beauvoir claims that our freedom is both our beginning and end; it is the foundation of the very possibility of creating values at all. Freedom, then, is not some abstract quality attached to us; it is what we are. According to Beauvoir, our choices will be judged to be authentic and moral if they take freedom as a fundamental value. It is in this sense, she observes, that "To wish to be moral and to wish to be free are a single decision."[4]

Because we are free, we are constantly going beyond a given state of affairs, or transcending ourselves. Our life, which Beauvoir and Sartre refer to as our "Project," is characterized by a constant reaching out toward a future and a tearing away from the established or "given" world through the human activities of questioning and negating (e.g., saying "No" to values we find unjust or hurtful to others). Thus Beauvoir insists that only human reality can call the world and its values into question and, in so doing, alter the present configuration of the world. This "going beyond" through projecting possibilities in our future is exactly our freedom. For Beauvoir, then, philosophy is understood as uncovering our humanity and bringing values into being—as disclosing and unveiling values in the world.

Beauvoir's philosophy asks us to become aware of the important sense in which we create or invent value in the world. Indeed, in an important sense, we *make* the world what it is. Since we live in a world that is inhabited by other people, the choices we make invariably affect others. This last point is crucial: Beauvoir claims that since we live in a peopled world, our bond with others is *ontological;* that is, the fact that we are necessarily bonded with others is fundamental to what it means to exist as a human being. Here again, we see the importance of action in Beauvoir's conception of philosophy: what we do and fail to do for ourselves and for others is her central preoccupation.

On her view, morality is our response to our ambiguous human situation: we must always choose ourselves and thereby inscribe value in the world, becoming a sort of foundation for ourselves while never ceasing in the process of choosing and, hence, making and remaking the only human world in which we live. The world has the particular configuration it does because of the human choices that have been made; human choices have created value and have willed the world to be one way rather than another. This bringing-into-being of the world by conferring value on it through human choices is precisely why Beauvoir's ethics is distinctively humanistic. If values were ready-made and given to us antecedently, we would not be free to invent them.

If we are to live authentically and morally, we must recognize and affirm freedom in ourselves and in others. And we must, moreover, take freedom as a fundamental value and as the end of our actions. To adhere to any other external moral absolute or objective standard as the source of human agency, without admitting that *it* is also chosen, is to deny our fundamental ambiguity and adopt an attitude of dishonesty, or an attitude of what Sartre and Beauvoir call *mauvais foi* (bad faith).

∽ Beauvoir's Feminist Philosophy as a Philosophy of Freedom

In *The Second Sex* Beauvoir examines the origins of women's oppression and draws on a wide range of disciplines to support her arguments including anthropology, biology, psychology, political and social sciences, history, physiology, and philosophy. In noting the multiple influences on her analysis of woman, as well as the trajectory of her own study, she writes:

> In our attempt to discover woman we shall not reject certain contributions of biology, of psychoanalysis, and of historical materialism; but we shall hold that the body, the sexual life, and the resources of technology exist concretely for man only in so far as he grasps them in the total perspective of his existence. The value of muscular strength, of the phallus, of the tool can be defined only in a world of values; it is determined by the basic project through which the existent seeks transcendence.[5]

Here Beauvoir is saying that human choices and values will determine what meaning our body, our sexual life, and our technology will have for us. She does not reject the contribution of the biological sciences, psychology, or the economic incentives of industry and production. But on her view, none of these factors, alone or collectively, can decide the meaning of human existence. Since existence precedes essence, we are not determined by our genes, our "drives," or the material forces of production. So, while Beauvoir allows the data of biology and the insights of Freud and Marx into her philosophical equation, she insists that none of these influences by themselves constitute human existence. Beauvoir consistently maintains that we are defined only through our free projects and acts: "It is human existence which makes values spring up in the world on the basis of which it will be able to judge the enterprise in which it will be engaged."[6]

In *The Second Sex* Beauvoir traces the origins of human existence and the development of consciousness back to two important sources: (1) the Hegelian notion of the struggle for recognition and (2) the Marxian idea of productive activity.[7] Following Hegel, she claims that all human beings desire to set themselves up as separate, individual, and concrete subjects in relation to a collectivity of which they are a part. Each desires to assert and affirm a self, and each seeks the recognition of the other. But woman, Beauvoir maintains, has in fact never been permitted to participate in the process of recognition. While man has historically affirmed himself as self-conscious in his struggle for recognition (through battles and wars, for example), woman's role has been fundamentally different. It is in woman's exclusion from the struggle for recognition that she has experienced herself as absolute "Other":

> The warrior put his life in jeopardy to elevate the prestige of the horde, the clan to which he belonged. And in this he proved dramatically that life is not the supreme value for man, but on the contrary that it should be made to serve ends more important than itself. The worst curse that was laid upon woman was that she should be excluded from these warlike forays. For it is not in giving life but in risking life that man is raised above the animal; that is why superiority has been accorded in humanity not to the sex that brings forth but to that which kills.[8]

Here we see that while man sees himself as a participatory subject and a human being, he sees woman as "the sex" and as an object that will serve him and his sexual needs. Beauvoir further argues that since throughout history man has always held power over woman, he has been able to assert himself easily as an absolute and essential subject, relegating woman to the status of "inessential Other." She observes that man has in fact always been the defining Subject because he has always assumed a privileged status in relation to woman. Hence, while woman is "defined and differentiated by man in reference to man," man conceives of himself only in reference to other men; man is the Subject and the Absolute; woman is the Other.[9]

Beauvoir argues that in setting up woman as Other, men have falsely imputed to her an essential nature. She notes that the various ideologies about women have been forged by patriarchal society in order to keep them in a subordinate position and to justify their oppression. In this way, she argues, women have been mystified by men, and this mystification has extended to women's own concept of themselves. Yet, we have seen that Beauvoir insists that woman does not (and cannot) have a predetermined essence since, from the first, she is free to create for herself whatever essence she chooses. Hence, Beauvoir claims, the ideologies, images, and constructions of women are only myths that attempt to falsely set up the "eternal feminine" against the contingent and concrete existence of actual women.

Beauvoir also follows the insights of Hegel in tracing the origin of oppression to the process of recognition. She states that class division, war, conflict, and human opposition have occurred throughout human history and must be understood in terms of a more fundamental hostility:

> These phenomena would be incomprehensible if in fact human reality were simply a *Mitsein* [Being with] based on solidarity and friendliness. Things become clear, on the contrary, if following Hegel, we find in consciousness itself a fundamental hostility towards every other consciousness; the subject poses himself only in setting himself up against another—he sets himself up as the essential, and constitutes the other as the inessential, the object.[10]

Here Beauvoir describes the phenomenon of human division and conflict. On her view, human beings do not at first experience themselves as allies; they regard others as a threat to their freedom. According to Beauvoir, the moral challenge is to overcome these hostilities and forge bonds of cooperation with others that will help create a more just society.

With Marx, Beauvoir stresses the importance of productive activity to human development; however, unlike recent feminists, she does not critique Marx's views from a feminist perspective. Marx claims that human productive activity, whereby individuals produce some kind of object—for example a tool, a book, or a bridge—creates history and allows individuals to transcend their mere animal nature and transform the environment. According to Marx and Beauvoir, the production of goods is different from the production of children. Beauvoir agrees with Marx that being pregnant, giving birth, suckling infants, and raising children tie women to their animal functions and prevent them from participating with men in the creation of culture and society. She writes that "giving birth and suckling are not activities, they are natural functions; no project is involved; and that is why woman found in them no reason for a lofty affirmation of her existence—she submitted passively to her biological fate."[11]

Beauvoir's uncritical endorsement of Marx's view of women's role in the creation of society has been criticized by recent feminist philosophers. They have forcefully argued that far from being a perceived weakness, woman's reproductive capacity is in fact the source of both her strength and her unique contribution to society. Woman's maternal experience, they argue, place her in a unique position to forge different kinds of values that are indispensable to human life, for example, the values of human solidarity, care, reciprocity, compassion, and love. Since these maternal values have been attacked and derogated by men as "weak" and "womanly," it must be shown that, far from thwarting human life, they are the very source of our humanity.

Beauvoir makes two points in response to this feminist view, referred to as the "ethics of care." First, it must be noted that although women are able to give birth and become mothers, it does not follow that this natural capacity will lead to the creation of a more caring society. After all, Beauvoir would surely say, there are bad mothers—mothers who abuse, abandon, and even kill their children. Beauvoir's second point is that insofar as women's existence is defined in terms of their reproductive function, they remain enslaved to the species and effectively cut off from the conscious (Hegel), productive activity (Marx) that men enjoy. The result of women's productivity has historically been to bear and rear children, and in this, Beauvoir maintains, they cannot fully realize their possibilities. Since men's existence has not been tied to reproduction and the perpetuation of the species, they have been able to transform themselves through their creative conquest of nature and the environment. With respect to the contribution men make, Beauvoir tells us that "in serving the species, the human male also remodels the face of the earth, he creates new instruments, he invents, he shapes the future."[12] Because of men's biological privilege in relation to their role in the reproduction of the species, that is, because they do not become pregnant, go through labor, give birth, breastfeed infants, and—for the most part—take care of and nurture children, they have been able to participate in society in a much more diverse and complete way than women. According to Beauvoir, as long as women remain enslaved to their reproductive function and role—which, she insists, is also a choice—they will remain outside the struggle for recognition and, in a certain sense, outside history. Since women have historically never set themselves up collectively as subjects, as men have, and since they have never made men the Others, men have never felt threatened by women or feared that they would be objectified by them. The World, History, Society, and Culture have, in the main, been the unchallenged domain of men.

We have seen that for Beauvoir, woman has been relegated to maternal existence on the basis of her biological function. As a result, the existence of woman has not been seen as culturally or historically progressive. In reproducing life, woman has failed to transcend it; she has remained outside both the Hegelian struggle for recognition and the Marxian mode of productive activity. Man, on the other hand, has transcended not only his own animal nature, but woman as well: in his conquest of nature, he has successfully subjugated woman and made her Other:

> Woman has ovaries, a uterus; these peculiarities imprison her in her subjectivity, circumscribe her within the limits of her own nature. It is often said that she thinks with her glands. Man superbly ignores the fact that his anatomy also includes glands, such as the testicles, and that they secrete hormones. He thinks of his body as a direct and normal connection with the world, which he believes he apprehends objectively, whereas he regards the body of woman as a hindrance, a prison, weighed down by everything peculiar to it. "The female is a female by virtue of a certain lack of qualities," said Aristotle; "we should regard

the female nature as afflicted with a natural defectiveness." And St. Thomas for his part pronounced woman to be an "imperfect man," an "incidental" being. This is symbolized in Genesis where Eve is depicted as made from what Bossuet called a "supernumerary bone" of Adam.[13]

In *The Second Sex,* Beauvoir devotes an entire chapter to the data of biology. She challenges traditional sexist assumptions and notes that the importance of biology to the history of women is due to the significance that the body has to our relation to the world: "For, the body, being the instrument of our grasp upon the world, the world is bound to seem a very different thing when apprehended in one manner or another." But she then argues that biological facts "are one of the keys to the understanding of woman . . . I deny that they establish for her a fixed and inevitable destiny. They are insufficient for setting up a hierarchy of the sexes; they fail to explain why woman is the Other; they do not condemn her to remain in this subordinate role forever."[14] Here Beauvoir states clearly that the biological differences between the sexes are not determinative in the human world. Although she grants that the "division of the sexes is a biological fact and not an event in human history,"[15] on her view the biological differences between men and women are not decisive. Unlike nonhuman animals, whose biology acts on them like a brute and inexorable force, it is *we* who have decided what meaning our biology has and will have for us. It is a contingent, not an absolute, fact that human society has deemed women to be inferior on the basis of their reproductive capacity; human society has *decided* that women are to be defined, valued, and understood primarily in terms of their biological role in the perpetuation of the species: "Our task is to discover how the nature of woman has been affected throughout the course of history; we are concerned to find out what humanity has made of the human female."[16] Here again we see that Beauvoir's conception of philosophy emphasizes the importance of human freedom in relation to the subordinate situation of women in society.

According to Beauvoir our situation encompasses our physical, historical, socioeconomic, and relational condition. The body, she notes, is also a situation: "if the body is not a thing, it is a situation . . . it is the instrument of our grasp upon the world, a limiting factor for our projects."[17] Here Beauvoir suggests that women's comparative physical weakness and their role in the reproductive process have restricted their grasp on the world and limited their projects. The significance placed on the biological differences between men and women, and especially the importance attached to women's unique role in the reproduction of life, were, according to Beauvoir, original obstacles to women's full and equal participation in society. It is not surprising, then, that she goes on to argue that women must liberate themselves by taking control of their reproductive activity and by determining the possibilities of their own existence.

Beauvoir is careful to point out that the role of woman as Other characterizes the general situation of women as a *class.* Throughout history men have defined, dominated, transcended, oppressed, and subjugated the class of women. Women know and experience themselves as Other in relation to men; their desires, wants, needs, passions, and reason-for-being have been inextricably tied to the desires, wants, needs, passions, and reason-for-being of men. Women, then, have not been self-defining or independent; their being-for-others has, for the most part, been a being-for-man. Men, says Beauvoir, have been the rulers of the world, and in this capacity they have "described the world from their point of view which they have confused with absolute truth."[18] Man, she notes, generally regards himself as "Man," "Culture," or "Society," while woman is conceived of as "Nature," "Body," "the Sex," or "Immanence." This point of view has been the dominant one and, despite notable gains in women's rights, it still remains deeply entrenched in the political, economic, social, and cultural structure of our lives.

Beauvoir is suspicious of abstract rights since they have not secured for women a rightful and just place in the world:

> this world, which has always belonged to the men, is still in their hands; the institutions and the values of the patriarchal civilization still survive in large part. Abstract rights are far from being completely granted everywhere to women. . . . And abstract rights, as I have just been saying, have never sufficed to assure woman a definite hold on the world: true equality between the two sexes does not exist even today.[19]

Beauvoir claims that historically men have always viewed women as objects, and to the extent that women have allowed or even encouraged this way of being, they have been in a certain sense, complicit in their oppression. But she acknowledges that, on the whole, women are born into a situation that compels them to adopt a position of inferiority since they themselves do not freely choose it. Importantly, though, the fact that women are born into a society that denies them equal opportunities in education and employment does not mean that they are inferior by nature, since for Beauvoir, there is no fixed human nature.

We can see, then, that Beauvoir's existentialist commitments reach deeply into her feminist philosophy. Women have historically been and are now inferior to men because of the human choices that have been made and continue to be made by others. Since woman's role as Other has been historically created and socially maintained, Beauvoir acknowledges that women will find it difficult to emancipate themselves and forge different kinds of values. But the future remains open, she says, and it will be up to both women and men to assume an attitude of authenticity with respect to the present and future situation of woman. It will be up to all persons to work toward liberating woman fully and completely in every sphere of her social, economic, and political existence.

One might wonder how Beauvoir can consistently maintain that we can be both free and oppressed. That is, how can she claim that women are both free and determined (insofar as they are oppressed by men)? This apparent inconsistency is resolved if we appreciate the paradoxical character of freedom. Beauvoir maintains that as a free person, I reach out toward a future of possibilities, but my very reaching out necessarily meets resistance in the world. To be sure, we live in a world that offers resistance, and such resistance is a contingent fact of our existence. But far from eliminating freedom, resistance paradoxically is a necessary condition for it. In this regard, Beauvoir writes that "The resistance of the thing sustains the action of man as air sustains the flight of the dove; and by projecting himself through it man accepts its being an obstacle; he assumes the risk of a setback in which he does not see a denial of his freedom."[20] Now, in addition to our experiencing "natural" resistance or force in the world (gravity, for example), there is also resistance that is not natural, and this is precisely what Beauvoir calls "oppression." She states that when our freedom "falls uselessly back upon itself it is because it is cut off from its goals" and that this "is what defines a situation of oppression. Such a situation is never natural: man is never oppressed by things; in any case, unless he is a naive child who hits stones or a mad prince who orders the sea to be thrashed, he does not rebel against things, but only against other men."[21] Thus, Beauvoir notes that "one does not submit to a war or an occupation as he does to an earthquake: he must take sides for or against, and the foreign wills thereby become allied or hostile. It is this interdependence which explains why oppression is possible and why it is hateful."[22]

There is thus a unique sense in which only *freedom* can oppress another *freedom*. Both Beauvoir and Sartre have said that what is especially pernicious about oppression, is that it "steals" the other's freedom from her. As an oppressor, I can act on the one I am intending to oppress *only if she is at first free* (I cannot oppress things). Indeed, Beauvoir claims, this is what defines the situation of oppression. Thus, while limitations and obstacles pose real threats to our possibilities (what Beauvoir refers to as our "practical freedom"), they can never eliminate what Sartre and Beauvoir refer to as our "ontological freedom," which is our being as human persons. Our ontological freedom ceases to be only when we cease to be—in death. Beauvoir's image of the dove in flight helps to explain the paradox of freedom: In providing resistance, the air sustains the dove's flight and is necessary to its ability to fly. Similarly, resistance sustains human action and is necessary to our ability to overcome adversity; our freedom must act on or against *something*.

Beauvoir would say, then, that while men have by and large decided the role and meaning woman will assume in society and have thus made woman Other, they have not in fact determined woman once and for all. After all, their conception and understanding of woman is only a partial one, and one that Beauvoir has shown to be sexist, oppressive, and false. It will be up to both women and men to attempt to remove the layers of mystification and forge a new conception of woman that more accurately and justly reflects her true humanity.

It would appear, then, that Beauvoir's analysis of the oppression of women is logically and conceptually consistent with her claim that women are free. While it remains a contingent fact that women have been and continue to be oppressed by men, women are nevertheless free to respond to and act against their oppressors in various ways. In fact, Beauvoir maintains that even under the most oppressive conditions, women remain ontologically free; otherwise, it would be impossible to oppress them in the first place.

There are times when Beauvoir suggests, implies, or states clearly that oppression is wrong, hateful, and unjust. But how is she able to justify these claims? That is, if Beauvoir rejects any external source of justification by which we can judge our actions to be right or wrong, isn't it inconsistent for *her* to issue what are clearly moral judgments? If, as she claims, all values are indeed freely chosen, created, or invented, then how do we (and how does *she*) adjudicate between two or more conflicting values? What—in her view—is wrong with someone freely oppressing another person? For Beauvoir there are no objectively existing values; values exist in consequence of human choices, not independently of them. Each of us, she says, lives in a "peopled world"; we cannot escape the fact that our lives are connected to the lives of others. So what we do, she insists, inescapably affects the lives of others and what others do inescapably affects us—for better or worse. Will we forge bonds of cooperation or conflict? Ultimately it is up to us. Beauvoir's conception of philosophy places freedom at the front and center and urges us to recognize honestly that we *need* each other in order to live genuinely human lives.

We have seen that Beauvoir rejects all forms of essentialism, the view that there is an essence or "nature" that determines what human beings are. She also rejects reductionism, the view that human beings can be reduced to or ultimately explained in terms of some salient given fact—for example, their genes or biology. In rejecting both essentialism and reductionism, Beauvoir also criticizes the idea that masculinity and femininity are biological givens ("one is not born, but rather becomes, a woman," she says). Beauvoir places great importance on human creativity and invention. We have already noted how, in her view, our lives are always socially and historically mediated; that is, in addition to our biology, we are duly influenced by the particular historical and social setting in which we find ourselves. But since Beauvoir insists that nothing decides or determines us in advance, *we can always make more out of what has already been made of us.* So how women respond to the fact that others have attempted to make them Other will make all the difference.

∿ Concluding Remarks

At the beginning of the twenty-first century, Beauvoir's philosophy resonates most strongly with the feminist movement and, in particular, with the struggle to recognize and extend legal and political rights to women everywhere. Her pioneering study of the oppression of women in *The Second Sex* is recognized throughout the world as perhaps the most influential and important work that has inspired feminist theory and practice in its multiple formulations.[23] Remarkably, Beauvoir's sustained interest in the oppression of women occurred during a time when there was no organized women's movement, and when women in France and throughout the world were expected to fulfill what was deemed their natural role as mothers, caretakers, and housewives.

Beauvoir's philosophy is a philosophy of freedom, action, and responsibility. As an existentialist, she was strongly committed to promoting human freedom as a fundamental moral value. As a towering intellectual and literary figure in her native France and worldwide, and as a major figure in the history of women's emancipation, it is no surprise that Beauvoir's death on April 14, 1986, commanded international attention. A short epitaph written in a newspaper headline on the day following her death read: "Women, you owe her everything." And indeed we do.

∾ NOTES

1. Simone de Beauvoir, *The Second Sex*, edited and translated by H.M. Parshley (London: Jonathan Cape, 1968; original edition, 1953), 55.
2. Simone de Beauvoir, *The Ethics of Ambiguity*, translated by Bernard Frechtman (Secaucus, NJ: Citadel Press, 1948; original edition, 1948), 16.
3. Ibid., 13.
4. Ibid., 24.
5. *The Second Sex*, 55.
6. *The Ethics of Ambiguity*, 15.
7. I am following the insight of the Beauvoir scholar and commentator Eva Lundgren-Gothlin in her book *Sex & Existence: Simone de Beauvoir's 'The Second Sex,'* translated from the Swedish by Linda Schenck (Hanover, NH: Wesleyan University Press-University Press of New England, 1996).
8. *The Second Sex*, xv–xvi.
9. Ibid., 16.
10. Ibid., 17.
11. Ibid., 88.
12. Ibid., 89.
13. Ibid., 33.
14. Ibid., 60.
15. Ibid., 19.
16. Ibid., 33.
17. Ibid., 61.

18. Ibid., 162.
19. Ibid., 153.
20. *The Ethics of Ambiguity,* 81.
21. Ibid.
22. Ibid., 82.
23. For example, liberal, socialist, radical, and eco-feminists. Of interest, the Beauvoir scholar Margaret Simons has persuasively argued that Beauvoir's work is most closely connected to radical feminism, and that her work has crucial implications for both socialist and radical black theorizing on racial oppression.

CHRONOLOGY

1908	birth of Simone de Beauvoir
1929	graduates from the Sorbonne with a degree in philosophy
1931	begins teaching at women's colleges in France
1940	France falls to German invaders, Paris occupied
1943	Beauvoir publishes her first novel, *She Came to Stay*
1945	war ends in Europe, Beauvoir and Sartre found their journal *Les Temps Modernes*
1947	*The Ethics of Ambiguity*
1949	*The Second Sex*
1954	*Les Mandarins,* novel about French intellectuals
1958	*Memoirs of a Dutiful Daughter,* first of several autobiographical works
1962	protests French involvement in Algeria, receives death threats
1970	*Coming of Age,* critical of the treatment of the elderly
1980	death of Sartre
1986	death of Beauvoir

SUGGESTED READINGS

Bergoffen, D.B. *The Philosophy of Simone de Beauvoir: Gendered Phenomenologies, Erotic Generosities.* Albany: State University of New York Press, 1997.

Cooper, D.E. *Existentialism: A Reconstruction.* Second Edition. Oxford: Basil Blackwell, 1999.

Fullbrook, E., and K. Fullbrook. *Simone de Beauvoir: A Critical Introduction.* Cambridge: Polity Press, 1998.

Mahon, J. *Existentialism, Feminism, and Simone de Beauvoir*. London: Macmillan, 1997.

Pilardi, J. *Simone de Beauvoir Writing the Self: Philosophy Becomes Autobiography*. Westport, CT: Greenwood Press, 1999.

Scholz, S.J. *On de Beauvoir*. Belmont, CA: Wadsworth, 2000.

Vintges, K. *Philosophy as Passion: The Thinking of Simone de Beauvoir*. Bloomington: Indiana University Press, 1992.

APPENDIX 1
Internet Resources

∼ Chapter 1. Confucius

Analects
http://classics.mit.edu/Confucius/analects.html

∼ Chapter 2. Presocratics and Socrates

Thales Fragments
http://www.forthnet.gr/presocratics/thaln.htm
Parmenides
http://home.ican.net/~arandall/Parmenides/
"The Apology of Socrates"
http://classics.mit.edu/Plato/apology.html
"Crito"
http://www.bartleby.com/2/1/2.html

∼ Chapter 3. Plato

The Republic
   http://classics.mit.edu/Plato/republic.html
"Symposium"
   http://classics.mit.edu/Plato/symposium.html

∼ Chapter 4. Aristotle

Selected Works
   http://www.knuten.liu.se/~bjoch509/philosophers/ari.html

∼ Chapter 5. Marcus Aurelius

Meditations
   http://classics.mit.edu/Antoninus/meditations.html

∼ Chapter 6. St. Thomas Aquinas

Summa Theologica
   http://www.newadvent.org/summa/

∼ Chapter 7. Descartes

Discourse on Method
   http://www.utm.edu/research/iep/text/descart/des-meth.htm
Meditations
   http://www.utm.edu/research/iep/text/descart/des-med.htm

∼ Chapter 8. Locke

Essay Concerning Human Understanding
   http://www.ilt.columbia.edu/Projects/digitexts/locke/understanding//
   title.html
Second Treatise of Government
   http://etext.library.adelaide.edu.au/1/181s/

✑ Chapter 9. Hume

Treatise of Human Nature
   http://socserv2.mcmaster.ca/~econ/ugcm/3ll3/hume/treat.html
Enquiry Concerning Human Understanding
   http://www.bartleby.com/37/3/
Dialogues Concerning Natural Religion
   http://www.utm.edu/research/hume/wri/dialogue/d-edint.htm

✑ Chapter 10. Kant

Prolegomena to Any Future Metaphysics
   http://www.utm.edu/research/iep/text/kant/prolegom/prolegom.htm
Fundamental Principles of the Metaphysic of Morals
   http://www.knuten.liu.se/~bjoch509/works/kant/princ_morals.txt
Critique of Pure Reason
   http://www.knuten.liu.se/~bjoch509/works/kant/cr_pure_reason.txt

✑ Chapter 11. Marx

The Communist Manifesto
   http://csf.colorado.edu/psn/marx/Archive/1848-CM/cm.html
Economic and Philosophic Manuscripts
   http://www.marxists.org/archive/marx/works/1844/manuscripts/
   preface.htm

✑ Chapter 12. Mill

Utilitarianism
   http://www.library.adelaide.edu.au/etext/m/m645u/
On Liberty
   http://www.bartleby.com/130/
The Subjection of Women
   http://www.library.adelaide.edu.au/etext/m/m645s/

∾ Chapter 13. Nietzsche

The Genealogy of Morals
  http://www.geocities.com/thenietzschechannel/onthe.htm
Twilight of the Idols
  http://www.cwu.edu/~millerj/nietzsche/twilight.html

∾ Chapter 14. James

"The Will to Believe"
  http://www.utm.edu/research/iep/text/james/will/will.htm
Varieties of Religious Experience
  http://etext.lib.virginia.edu/toc/modeng/public/JamVari.html
Pragmatism
  http://paradigm.soci.brocku.ca/~lward/James/James1_toc.html

∾ Chapter 15. Wittgenstein

Tractatus Logico-Philosophicus
  http://www.kfs.org/~jonathan/witt/tlph.html

∾ Chapter 16. Beauvoir

The Second Sex
  http://www.marxists.org/reference/subject/philosophy/works/fr/
  2ndsex.htm

APPENDIX **2**
Time Line

Many dates are approximate.

THE ANCIENT WORLD

3000 BCE	origin of civilization: irrigation, writing, use of metals
2680	the Great Pyramid of Egypt
1027–256	Classical Age of China
750	Homer, *Iliad, Odyssey*
600	Thales
551–479	**Confucius**
520	Pythagoras
500	Heraclitus
480–430	Golden Age of Athens
469–399	**Socrates**
431–404	Peloponnesian War between Athens and Sparta
427–347	**Plato**
384–322	**Aristotle**

323	death of Alexander the Great
341–270	Epicurus, founder of Epicureanism
335–262	Zeno of Citium, founder of Stoicism
218–201	Second Punic War between Rome and Carthage
102–44	Julius Caesar
64 AD	Rome burns, Emperor Nero blames the Christians
121–180	**Marcus Aurelius**
325	Emperor Constantine convenes council at Nicaea, solidifies influence of Christianity in the empire
354–430	St. Augustine
455	vandals sack city of Rome

THE MIDDLE AGES

525	St. Benedict writes his monastic rule
732	battle of Tours, Charles Martel repels Muslim invasion of Europe
800	Charlemagne unites much of Europe, crowned Holy Roman Emperor
1033–1109	St. Anselm of Canterbury
1095	first crusade launched by Catholic Church to recapture the Holy Land from Muslims
1163	cathedral of Notre Dame in Paris begun
1225–1274	**St. Thomas Aquinas**
1320	*The Divine Comedy,* Dante (1265–1321)
1348	the Black Death devastates Europe
1337–1453	the Hundred Years War between France and England weakens the nobility

RENAISSANCE AND REFORMATION

1455	Johann Gutenburg invents printing with movable type, prints the Bible
1498	Leonardo da Vinci paints "The Last Supper"
1499	Vasco da Gama establishes sea trade route between Europe and India
1513	*The Prince,* Machiavelli (1469–1527)
1517	Luther challenges the Catholic Church, splits Europe

1534	Henry VIII creates the Church of England
1533–1592	Michel de Montaigne
1572	St. Bartholomew's Day massacre of Protestants in France

THE SEVENTEENTH CENTURY

1564–1616	William Shakespeare
1605	*Don Quixote,* Miguel de Cervantes (1547–1616)
1628	*On the Movement of the Heart and Blood in Animals,* William Harvey (1578–1657)
1632	*Dialogue concerning the Two Chief World Systems,* Galileo Galilei (1564–1642)
1641	***Meditations,* René Descartes (1596–1650)**
1642–1648	English Civil War undermines royal power, King Charles I beheaded (1649)
1651	*Leviathan,* Thomas Hobbes (1588–1679)
1661	Louis XIV, the Sun King, takes power in France, promotes political absolutism
1687	*Mathematical Principles of Natural Philosophy,* Isaac Newton (1642–1727)
1690	***Essay Concerning Human Understanding, Second Treatise of Government,* John Locke (1632–1704)**

THE EIGHTEENTH CENTURY (THE ENLIGHTENMENT)

1726	*Gulliver's Travels,* Jonathan Swift (1667–1745)
1739	***A Treatise of Human Nature,* David Hume (1711–1776)**
1749	"The Art of the Fugue" by Johann Sebastian Bach
1751	Diderot begins publishing the *Encyclopedia* in Paris
1756–1763	the Seven Years War weakens France, extends British sea power
1759	*Candide,* Voltaire (1694–1778)
1762	*The Social Contract,* Jean-Jacques Rousseau (1712–1778)
1769	James Watt invents the steam engine
1776	*The Wealth of Nations,* Adam Smith (1723–1790)
1781	***Critique of Pure Reason,* Immanuel Kant (1724–1804)**
1789	the French Revolution shatters France, terrifies everyone, introduces modern political ideas

THE NINETEENTH CENTURY

1802	Beethoven's Third ("Heroic") Symphony
1804	Napoleon crowns himself emperor of France
1808	*Faust*, Johann von Goethe (1749–1832)
1815	the Congress of Vienna creates a balance of power among European states
1828	election of Andrew Jackson as president of the United States, popular participation in government
1832	Reform Bill in England extends the voting franchise
1848	***The Communist Manifesto,* Karl Marx (1818–1883)**, unsuccessful revolutions throughout Europe
1859	***On Liberty,* John Stuart Mill (1806–1873)**; *The Origin of Species*, Charles Darwin (1809–1882)
1861–1865	American Civil War, abolition of slavery
1870	Franco-Prussian War establishes Germany under Bismarck as a major power
1874	Richard Wagner completes his opera cycle, *The Ring of the Nibelungs*
1879	Edison invents the electric light
1886	***Beyond Good and Evil,* Friedrich Nietzsche (1844–1900)**
1898	Spanish-American War, United States takes over Philippines, gains international power

THE TWENTIETH CENTURY

1900	*Interpretation of Dreams*, Sigmund Freud (1856–1939)
1905	Einstein's first paper on relativity
1907	***Pragmatism,* William James (1842–1910)**
1909	Henry Ford uses the assembly line to manufacture the Model T
1914	First World War begins
1917	revolution breaks out in Russia, leads to civil war, Lenin's victory
1921	***Tractatus Logico-Philosophicus,* Ludwig Wittgenstein (1889–1951)**
1922	James Joyce's *Ulysses* banned in the United States
1929	stock market crash in New York begins the Great Depression

1933	Hitler takes power in Germany
1940–1945	Second World War
1946	ENIAC, first electronic computer
1948	India wins independence from Great Britain
1953	***The Second Sex,*** **Simone de Beauvoir (1908–1986)**
1961	East Germany builds Berlin Wall
1969	astronauts reach the surface of the moon
1978	birth of the first test-tube baby

Index